Not Just Victims

THE ASIAN AMERICAN EXPERIENCE

Series Editor
Roger Daniels, University of Cincinnati

*A list of books in the series appears at
the end of this book.*

Not Just Victims

Conversations with Cambodian
Community Leaders in the United States

Edited and with an Introduction by
SUCHENG CHAN

Interviews by Audrey U. Kim

University of Illinois Press
Urbana and Chicago

Library of Congress Cataloging-in-Publication Data
Not just victims : conversations with Cambodian community leaders
in the United States / edited and with an introduction by
Sucheng Chan ; interviews by Audrey U. Kim.
    p.   cm. — (The Asian American experience)
Includes bibliographical references (p.   ) and index.
ISBN 0-252-02799-x (cloth : alk. paper)
ISBN 0-252-07101-8 (paper : alk. paper)
1. Cambodian Americans—Social conditions—Case studies.
2. Cambodian Americans—Psychology—Case studies.
3. Cambodian Americans—Interviews.
4. Refugees—United States—Interviews.
5. Cambodia—History—1975–1979—Anecdotes.
6. Political atrocities—Cambodia—History—20th century—Anecdotes.
I. Chan, Sucheng. II. Kim, Audrey U. III. Series.
E184.K45+   2003
973'.049593—dc21   2002007574

Contents

Foreword
Roger Daniels

ONE OF THE MOST important contemporary problems in Asian American historiography is the fact that the lion's share of the literature deals with its two charter groups, Chinese and Japanese immigrants and their descendants, even though members of those two groups have constituted only a minority of the Asian American population since sometime in the 1970s. No historian has done more toward redressing this imbalance than Sucheng Chan, emeritus professor of Asian American studies at the University of California, Santa Barbara. After her first book, a stunning monograph about Chinese in California's agriculture, she has become the most versatile and prolific practitioner of Asian American history. She has published general surveys of Asian Americans in both California and the nation, edited and written a long introduction to a memoir by a pioneer Korean immigrant woman, edited two anthologies of previously unpublished essays, edited a series of Asian American books by others, and published a number of articles and essays on Asian American history, Asian American studies, and gender.

In a pioneering volume, *Hmong Means Free: Life in Laos and America* (1994), which is a kind of predecessor to the present work, she inspired and supervised a group of her Hmong students to interview their family members, edited the results, and provided a long introduction. The result, it seems to me, remains the best single work on the Hmong in America.

In the present work she turns her attention to Cambodian Americans. For most of that minority of Americans who have any clear notions about Cambodia, their awareness began with Sydney H. Schanberg's Pulitzer Prize–winning stories in the *New York Times* in 1975 about the communist takeover there and some of the horrific events that followed. For many, that awareness pretty well ends there or with such representations of Cambodian history as the film *The Killing Fields* and with a consciousness that large numbers of Cambodians, like other Southeast Asians, survived the horror and came to America as refugees. Chan explicates these events and the fallout from them in her detailed introduction, which is a model capsule history of Cambodia and its calamities.

But her purpose in arranging for, editing, and publishing these interviews is not just to retell the Cambodian horror story. As she explains, "The collective picture [the interviewees] paint shows that Cambodians are not just victims; rather they are survivors who can teach us a great deal about the strength that human beings can call forth in the face of the most extreme deprivations and cruelties." The dozen community leaders interviewed here tell us about their lives and, in most cases, the communities they lead.

They are not representative men. They are highly educated and have managed to succeed, as immigrant leaders have always succeeded, in a culture and in a language that was not their native tongue. Even more important, they show us a largely refugee community as it appears to insiders rather than to outsiders, sympathetic and unsympathetic, who have written most of the previous accounts. *Not Just Victims* is, I believe, not only the most important work yet published about the kind of life that Cambodians are creating for themselves in the New World but it also gives readers a concise account of Cambodian catastrophe in the Old.

Preface

COMPARED TO THE sizable literature on the recent, tragic history of Cambodia, writings on Cambodian refugees now living in the United States are less voluminous. We do, however, have dozens of journal articles and a few books that discuss various aspects of the experiences of this new American ethnic group. These studies reflect mainly the perspectives of non-Cambodian social workers, doctors, nurses, public health experts, psychiatrists, nutritionists, teachers, counselors, and scholars who have either served the needs of or have conducted research on Cambodians while the latter were living in refugee camps along the Thai-Cambodian border and/or after their arrival in the United States.

Such studies provide a useful starting point for exploring the lives of Cambodian Americans, but they tell only part of the story. What we also need, I believe, are studies that reflect "insiders'" points of view. A dozen or so book-length autobiographies and an even larger number of short published memoirs by Cambodian survivors of the Khmer Rouge "killing fields" meet this need to some extent, but they usually end with the narrators' arrival in the United States. In addition, a few journalists, such as Gail Sheehy and Alec Wilkinson, have published moving portrayals of Cambodians whose stories have deeply touched them. Still, by focusing on the most dramatic years of the narrators' lives (that is, their lives under the Khmer Rouge regime), these accounts tell us relatively little about the less gripping experiences of the refugees after they set foot on American soil.

Despite this growing body of writings, three images continue to frame what most Americans know about Cambodia and the Cambodians now living in their midst. First, audiences who have seen *The Killing Fields,* a film

about *New York Times* journalist Sydney Schanberg and his Cambodian partner Dith Pran, made by British filmmakers David Puttnam and Roland Jof-
fe and released by Warner Brothers in the mid-1980s, may remember scenes
of huge piles of skulls and bones and know the names Pol Pot and Khmer
Rouge. Second, in the early 1990s newspaper readers and television viewers
in some parts of the country—particularly in southern California—may have
read or seen brief reports of gang warfare involving Cambodian American
teenagers. In both instances, the controlling image is one of death and dying. A third image has been circulated by psychiatrists and other health professionals, who have documented that a very large proportion of Cambodian refugees suffer from posttraumatic stress disorder, major depression,
anxiety, and other psychological problems. In these writings, too, Cambodian refugees are depicted as severely traumatized and helpless victims.

This book enlarges our understanding of Cambodian Americans in two
ways. First, it offers a nuanced picture of Cambodian ethnic communities in
the United States. The twelve chapters reveal how Cambodian community
leaders themselves view the conditions their compatriots face. The narrators
speak from the perspective of insiders. The collective picture they paint shows
that Cambodians are not just victims; rather, they are survivors who can teach
us a great deal about the strength that human beings can call forth in the face
of the most extreme deprivations and cruelties. Many individuals are trying
their best not only to survive but also to enable other Cambodians to deal
with the problems they face in a manner that maintains the group's dignity
and self-respect. Although the interviews were conducted in 1995 and 1996,
the analyses they contain are still relevant. To bring the stories up to date I
have included information in the chapter headnotes about major changes
that have occurred since the original interviews were conducted.

Second, this book helps to redress an imbalance in the scholarly literature
on refugees from Southeast Asia. The main groups that have entered the
United States since 1975 are the Vietnamese; Sino-Vietnamese (ethnic Chinese from Vietnam); "Montagnards" (a collective name the French gave various ethnic groups who live in the hills of Vietnam); Khmer Krom (ethnic
Cambodians from Vietnam); Lao (the major ethnic group in Laos, who live
in the lowlands); Hmong (an ethnic group living in the hills of Thailand,
Laos, and Vietnam); Iu Mien and Tai Dam (two other hill-dwellers, primarily from Laos); Khmer (the major ethnic group in Cambodia); Sino-Cambodians (ethnic Chinese from Cambodia); and Cham (a Muslim ethnic
group living in Vietnam and Cambodia). Despite this heterogeneity, the existing literature focuses largely on the Vietnamese. In many studies of "Southeast Asian" or "Indochinese" refugees, data on the smaller and lesser-known

groups are combined with those on the Vietnamese so that the former are often conflated with the latter, even though their experiences may be distinct in many aspects. Quite a number of studies are now available about the Hmong, but so little has been written about the Lao (even though they have entered the United States in larger numbers than the Hmong) that they are virtually invisible to the American public as well as in scholarly consciousness. The literature on Cambodians is growing, but it deals mainly with their pre-arrival experiences rather than with their lives in the United States. Next to nothing has been published about the Sino-Vietnamese, Khmer Krom, Sino-Cambodians, Iu Mien, Tai Dam, "Montagnards," and Cham. By focusing on Cambodians—with discussions not only about the Khmer but also the Sino-Cambodians and Khmer Krom—this book not only adds to our knowledge about people from Cambodia but also underlines the fact that the refugee and immigrant population from mainland Southeast Asia now living in the United States is diverse and complex.

Acknowledgments

I thank Audrey Kim for the fine interviews she did when she was a graduate student assisting me in my research. Because I was already suffering from an advanced stage of post-polio syndrome (a progressively degenerative neuromuscular condition) when I began my research in 1995 on Cambodian refugees in the United States, it would have been extremely difficult for me to travel around the country while confined to a wheelchair and in constant need of physical therapy. I was very fortunate that Audrey could travel to different places to do the interviews on my behalf. She has since completed her Ph.D. and is now a counseling psychologist at the University of California, Santa Cruz. I express my profound gratitude to the extremely busy Cambodian community leaders who graciously consented to be interviewed by Audrey Kim in person and who talked to me by telephone and corresponded with me. Each of them responded promptly to my request to read over the edited transcripts and to make additional changes as they saw fit. Without their collegial participation, this book would not exist.

I thank the Cambodian Network Council for providing a list of the major organizations in Cambodian ethnic communities from which I chose the sites Audrey was to visit and the names of individuals she was to interview. I am grateful to the Committee on Research of the Academic Senate and the Interdisciplinary Humanities Center at the University of California, Santa Barbara, for their financial support. I thank Roger Daniels, advisory editor of the Asian American Experience series published by the University of Illinois Press, for the enthusiasm he showed in accepting this manuscript. Thanks are also due the anonymous external reviewer who offered many useful suggestions for improving the manuscript. Finally, I thank Joan Catapano, editor-in-chief at the University of Illinois Press, and Mary Giles, who copyedited the manuscript, for helping to turn a rough manuscript into a published work.

Methodology

BECAUSE THIS BOOK is likely to be read by students and scholars in several disciplines, it is important to discuss the methodology used to produce it, as well as the intellectual orientations that the work reflects, in order to minimize the possibility that it be misjudged by standards meant for works in other disciplines. The twelve chapters in this book are the edited transcripts of interviews done by Audrey U. Kim on my behalf in the summers of 1995 and 1996. We approached these interviews as oral histories, which are akin to but not the same as the products of three other kinds of fieldwork: life histories gathered by anthropologists from key informants, oral traditions collected by folklorists, and interviews conducted by sociologists. I shall discuss the differences between oral history and these kindred kinds of oral evidence after I explain what oral history is.

Allan Nevins, a journalist turned professional historian, is usually credited with carving out a niche in academia for oral history when he set up an oral history program at Columbia University in 1948. As he envisioned it, the task of oral history is to tape record from the lips of living persons—usually persons who have led "significant" lives—information about important events in the recent past in which they have participated or that they have personally witnessed. Such material, preserved either as audiotapes or as transcripts, is meant to supplement written documents. Their existence will enable future historians to tap into a fuller record as they reconstruct the history of a certain era.

Nevins's approach was unabashedly elitist in three senses of that word. First, the individuals he and his colleagues thought worthy of being interviewed are well-known, public figures—that is, society's elite members. Second, it is academic historians who get to interpret the evidence. Oral history interviewers and interviewees are assigned the supportive role of making the evidence available. The latter's function is, therefore, archival rather than scholarly. Third, because oral evidence is collected mainly to supplement written documents, the privileged position that written sources have enjoyed in European and American historiography since the nineteenth century under the powerful influence of German historians remains unchallenged.

In the 1960s, some practitioners of oral history began to veer off in a different direction as more and more historians began to write social histories focusing on the lives of ordinary people and as various radical movements tried to change European and American societies and their allegedly oppressive and hierarchical structures. In such a politically charged environment, some historians attempting to write "history from below" seized upon oral history as a way to give voice to groups that have hitherto been voiceless— people whose existence have been ignored by professional historians because they left few written documents. The voiceless groups whom oral historians hoped to rescue from oblivion include workers (Friedlander 1975; Hareven 1978); women (Anderson et al. 1987; Chase and Bell 1994; Gluck 1977; Sangster 1994); members of ethnic and racial minority groups (Hansen 1994; Okihiro 1981; Rogers 1994; Serikaku 1989; Wyatt 1987); elderly people (Bornat 1989); traumatized individuals, such as survivors of the Jewish Holocaust (Klempner 2000; White 1994); and even unpopular groups such as the Ku Klux Klan (Blee 1993). Oral history was grasped as a means to create a record of these people's lives. Hence, not only would oral history help to enlarge the reservoir of potentially usable information, but it would also provide a way to escape the strictures of professional history.

Those oral historians who emphasize the democratizing potential of their craft treat members of underrepresented groups not just as interviewees who can provide information for historians and other scholars to interpret or analyze but as narrators. Narrators do not simply answer questions passively; rather, they actively tell stories. In so doing they are interpreting their pasts. By reclaiming the right to plumb the meaning of their lives and the times in which they live, they are empowering themselves as historical agents. They are not sources but persons who no longer need to look to scholars to tell them in what ways their lives are significant. Sounds recorded on audiotape, images and sounds recorded on videotape, and words transcribed into a written text on paper can all survive the ravages of time better than the human body can.

In part because oral history took on the characteristics of a social movement, it has encountered stiff resistance. To this day, severe criticism dogs the practitioners of oral history. Barbara Tuchman criticized oral history for making possible the "artificial survival of trivia of appalling proportions." Oral historians, she charged, were preserving "a vast mass of trash" (Tuchman 1972: 9). According to her, the major responsibility of historians is to distinguish the significant from the insignificant. When interviewers with little formal training enthusiastically go about taping the utterances of others, they are not performing the critical function that historians are supposed to perform. Other critics have been less harsh in their appraisals. Instead of dismissing oral history out of hand, they question how reliable oral evidence can be, given the fallibility of memory and the fact that interviewees are sometimes self-serving and may distort what they say or even tell outright lies. Moreover, critics claim, people often tend to say what they think their interlocuters wish to hear. In response, oral historians point out that oral evidence needs to be assessed in the same way that written documents are supposed to be evaluated. Oral evidence is neither more nor less reliable than written sources. There are epistemological problems involved in using both kinds of material (Lummis 1988). Moreover, oral historians have the advantage of being able to challenge or interrogate their interviewees—to cross-examine them as it were (Thompson 1988). Giving primacy to written sources is, therefore, in the words of Ronald Grele, simply a form of "paper or book fetishism" (1985: 130).

As I see it, "scholarly standards" are not the real issue here. Rather, what is at stake is the question of who gets to wield power in the academy. As Michael Frisch has noted, some historians have reacted so negatively to oral history because it threatens the historical establishment. By seeking to "redefine and redistribute intellectual authority" within the profession, oral history is undermining the privileged position that a historiography based solely on written sources has enjoyed for more than a hundred years (Frisch 1990: xx).

To clarify what it is exactly that they do, a number of scholars who practice oral history have tried to define their methodology and to specify the nature of the historical evidence they create through interviews. Michael Frisch calls oral history an "interactive dialogue," while Ronald Grele calls it a "conversational narrative." Both terms underline the fact that such accounts are expository and result from dialogues between interviewers and interviewees. According to Grele (1975), a conversational narrative contains three dimensions that can be analyzed: the linguistic structure of the conversation, the performatory aspects of the face-to-face interaction between the interviewer and interviewee, and the cognitive relationship between the interviewee and his or her own historical consciousness. Carrying out such a multilevel analysis will give those who use oral evidence a more sophisticated understanding of what they are working with.

Eva McMahan (1989) has approached oral history from another direction. She borrows insights from the "new hermeneutics" to help us understand the conversations that occur during oral history interviews. Unlike the old hermeneutics, which assumes that the meaning of a text can be surmised if we can decipher the intention of its author, the new hermeneutics asserts that interpretation can be carried out only within certain linguistic possibilities, that bias is always present, and that communication is, by its very nature, intersubjective. McMahan characterizes an oral history interview as an "interpretive communicative event" or a "hermeneutical conversation." That is, the meaning of what is said is emergent—it evolves as the conversation proceeds. During such a dialogue, both the interviewer and interviewee are constrained by the rules of conversation. They must take turns speaking, they must cooperate with each other in order to carry on an intelligible conversation, and they must agree more or less on what topics are to be addressed. Furthermore, what each person says, particularly what the interviewee says, is constrained by an "imagined audience," that is, by who else besides the interviewer will hear the tape or read the transcript of the interview (McMahan 1987).

It is sometimes difficult to pin down what oral history is and what it is not because it is a mixed medium. In the words of Alessandro Portelli, "oral history shifts between performance-oriented *narrative* and content-oriented *document,* between subject-oriented *life story* and theme-oriented *testimony*" (1997: 6, emphasis in original). In other words, most oral histories simultaneously tell a story, disclose factual information, make references to the narrators' own lives, and discuss (often in a didactic way) various occurrences and the lessons they may impart to future generations.

Oral history interviews also differ from other kinds of historical evidence in that they are products of the age in which we live and not the era we are investigating. They exist only through the active intervention of a historian (Frisch 1990; Futrell and Willard 1994; Grele 1978; Lummis 1988; Portelli 1997). Unlike traditional historians who search for and find documents, oral historians help create them. Such an involvement may render oral evidence suspect, but oral historians need not apologize for the intersubjectivity inherent in and the constructedness of the historical records they help to produce. Such a practice is very much in tune with more recent scholarly developments in other fields.

Under the influence of European (mainly French) social theory, notably poststructuralism and postmodernism, a great deal of scholarship produced since the 1970s has moved away from "objectivity"—a norm that reigned supreme in the 1950s and 1960s. Scientific objectivity in the creation of knowledge through the use of data that can be measured, tested, and duplicated experimentally is the hallmark of positivist social science. Although positivism has not yet given way completely to the new reflexive stance, it has had to share center stage, albeit most uneasily, with works that emphasize self-reflexivity, subjectivity, symbolism, imagination, discourse, rhetorical strategy, and the contestation of meaning. Among social scientists, for example, advocates of the new ethnography have argued that the entire process by which ethnographic texts are produced must be problematized (Clifford 1986; Rabinow 1986 Rosaldo 1986; Tyler 1986) because the ability of anthropologists to write about and, hence to represent, other cultures cannot be taken for granted.

Although the practice of oral history and the new ethnography have much in common in terms of intellectual stance, there are differences between the two. Sidney Mintz points out that anthropologists see key informants not as "historical witnesses" but as "culture bearers." The life histories of key informants reveal "what is typical in that culture, but not how representative that life is within it" (1979: 21). Micaela di Leonardo, who is both an anthropologist and an oral historian, identifies the similarities and the differences between the two fields. Common traits that oral historians and ethnographers share are their attempt to give voice to the voiceless and how they conduct fieldwork involving face-to-face encounters. The biggest gap between the two fields lies in the differential intellectual stature each enjoys. While fieldwork is the "constitutive act of anthropology," oral history is still considered marginal and suspect by fellow historians. There are also procedural differences. An oral history interview is dyadic—that is, it involves two persons—whereas ethnographic fieldwork draws in large groups of people as informants. Oral historians focus on tape recording narratives, but they seldom write down what they themselves observe; ethnographers, however, combine the collection of narratives with behavioral observations.

Whereas ethnographic fieldwork is often done in a different culture and is thus cross-cultural, oral history fieldwork is usually intracultural. A final difference has to do with ethical principles. Anthropologists generally protect the privacy of informants by giving them pseudonyms, but oral historians usually take down and reveal the interviewees' real names for the public record (di Leonardo 1987). Public disclosure, however, does not mean that oral historians are not mindful of the possible impact their work may have on interviewees. A number of oral historians have discussed the ethics of oral history research and the need to ensure that subjects are not harmed in any way (Fry 1975; Yow 1995).

Advocates and defenders of oral history often point out that the use of oral evidence goes back thousands of years. There are differences, however, between oral history and oral tradition. In nonliterate societies, oral tradition has an "institutionally recognized place and purpose in the culture and . . . [it] is structured and presented in specific formulae" (Harevan 1978: 140). Such societies train and groom individuals, often from childhood, to preserve tradition through oral transmission. Oral history interviewees differ from keepers of oral tradition in that they do not recite memorized scripts. Folklorists who study oral traditions analyze their substantive content and examine how legends, myths, folk beliefs, and customs are related to one another (Danielson 1980). While oral historians interview people to obtain information stored in their private memories, folklorists collect what already exists in the public sphere (Dorson 1972).

Oral history interviews also differ from traditional sociological interviews in that they are less structured and predetermined. Oral histories contain more variability than is found in sociological interviews because oral historians try their best not to "pre-order" the material too much, whereas sociologists ask each respondent the same set of questions, given their concern about how representative their samples will be. Sociologists usually code the information they collect in order to analyze it statistically. Oral historians, in contrast, do not try to represent a population or a culture and are not enamored of numbers. As Alessandro Portelli puts it, "[W]hile other social scientists perform the indispensable task of abstracting from individual experience and memory the patterns and models that transcend the individual, oral history combines the effort to reconstruct past patterns and models with attention to concrete individual variations and transgressions . . . oral history does not cultivate the average, but often perceives the exceptional and the unique. . . . Texts do not become representative because of their statistically average quality" (1997: 57–58, 86). James Bennett echoes this point when he discusses the values embedded in the practice of oral history: "Each person has qualities that make him or her not necessarily representative but, on the contrary, unique and worthy of respect as a human being" (1983: 6). In short, oral historians are humanists more than they are social scientists.

The twelve chapters in this book are oral histories and not anthropological life histories or sociological interviews. Not being anthropologists, Audrey Kim and I were not trying to tap into larger cultural patterns by examining exemplary lives. More important, we could not stay in each community for any length of time to engage in participant observation as ethnographers do. Not being sociologists, I did not write out the exact wording of the questions to be asked. Nor did I specify the order in which Kim was to ask them even though I did have topics I wanted her to be sure to cover. These included:

—About how many Cambodians are living in the community served by the interviewee? When did they first arrive and through what channels?

—How are Cambodians managing to survive economically? Of those who are working, what kind of jobs do they have? Among Cambodians who own or operate businesses, about what percent are Sino-Cambodians and what percent are Khmer? Among people who are receiving public assistance, how do they feel about being on welfare? How do other Cambodians perceive them?

—What percentage of households in the community is headed by women? Do these female heads of household have special problems in raising their children? If so, what are the problems and what are their causes?

—How are the children and teenagers doing in school? Why are some doing well and others not so well? Are there intergenerational tensions in Cambodian refugee families? If so, how are they manifested and how are they dealt with?

—Are Cambodian youths in the community joining gangs? If so, why are they joining gangs? What kinds of activities do gang members participate in? Who do they fight against? How are law enforcement officers dealing with the gang problem? How are gang problems affecting other facets of life in Cambodian ethnic communities?

—Are most Cambodians in the United States still practicing Buddhists? How has Khmer Buddhism changed since being transplanted to the United States? Are Buddhist monks helping Cambodian refugees to cope with the past traumas they have experienced and the present challenges of a new land? If some Cambodians have converted to Christianity, what denominations do they belong to?

—How are Cambodians trying to preserve their culture?

—What functions do Mutual Assistance Associations perform?

—To what extent and in what ways are Cambodians in America involved in the politics of Cambodia? What impact does such political involvement have on their lives in America?

—Are people sending money to Cambodia? If so, for what purposes? Are there a lot of Cambodians who yearn to return home to Cambodia?

—Will the interviewee tell us something about his or her personal life?

Although Kim kept these questions in mind, I instructed her to vary the order in which she asked them so conversations could flow as spontaneously as possible. Also, the interviewees, rather than the interviewer, would determine the length of the answers. So long as a question has been answered in one form or another, however briefly, Kim was free to move on if she sensed the narrator did not wish to elaborate further. If the narrator started to talk about a topic other than those I had chosen, he or she could carry on for a while but not indefinitely. I asked Kim to keep in mind that every individual we had chosen to interview is a very busy person, so she should limit each interview to about an hour and a half. Although all forty-nine people she interviewed answered her questions knowledgeably, some spoke at length whereas others were succinct.

The twelve pieces chosen for inclusion in this book are transcripts of interviews with individuals who exhibited the most fluent English and the best narrative sense. Each speaks with a distinctive voice. Their personalities come through even though their intonation, pauses, speech rhythm, and body language are not reflected in the edited transcripts. We can tell, for example, that Sam Chittapalo is a streetwise police officer who has picked up some of the hip beat that characterizes the speech pattern of certain urban-dwellers. We can surmise that Sam-Ang Sam, a musician used to giving performances in front of large audiences, is skilled at presenting himself in public, because his words are measured and polished. We sense that the Rev. Chhean Kong has been deeply touched by the trauma his parishioners and clients have experienced, because when he is recounting the atrocities of the Khmer Rouge (which he himself did not experience) his words flow in an almost stream-of-consciousness way as though the vicarious pain he feels is a poison that has to be spewed out and expurgated.

In terms of interview technique, Audrey Kim's clinical training in counseling psychology, as well as her experience first as a teaching assistant and later as a faculty member, proved very useful. She is an attentive listener. By briefly summarizing what had been said before going on to the next topic, she assured the interviewee that he or she had been heard. Oral historians emphasize the importance of creating rapport, and Kim did so by demonstrating that she had understood the points the interviewees had made. Her feedback played an implicit role in overcoming whatever "interviewee reluctance" might have existed. Her technique is a variant of what Charles Morrissey (1987) calls the "two-sentence format." The first sentence explains why a certain question is being asked so that the respondent can see it is worth answering. The second sentence is the question itself. Oral historians also stress the importance of being well prepared. Audrey Kim had acquired a great deal of information about Cambodia and Cambodian refugees when she served as my teaching assistant in a course that deals with post-1965 Asian immigration and the post-1975 refugee influx from Vietnam, Laos, and Cambodia. In addition, I gave her a lot of additional information on topics that few people know, such as who the Khmer Krom are and what major political parties and/or groups were contesting for power in Cambodia at the time she carried out the interviews.

The narrators, for their part, are highly educated Cambodians who now function as cultural brokers. They are familiar with both Khmer and American cultures and constantly mediate between the two, not only for themselves but also on behalf of their Cambodian clients and the American bureaucrats and members of the public with whom they interact. Therefore, they understand the purpose of an interview. In the interviews they gave Audrey Kim, they followed the "rules of conversation" that Eva McMahan has identified, not only by answering questions clearly but also by elaborating on certain points and bringing conversations back on track when they strayed momentarily off-course. In general, they explained why their fellow Cambodians have certain problems, but they did not sound apologetic about their people's plight. The texts that each of them, Audrey Kim, and I jointly produced contain all four elements that Alessandro Portelli had delineated: narrative, document, life story, and testimony.

Even though Kim and I are not Khmer, I believe the fact that we are Asian Americans did help to reduce the social distance between the narrators and ourselves. Having grown up in China and Malaysia and having visited Cambodia, I knew it would be important for us to show respect to the interviewees/narrators. Thus, I showed Kim how to greet people by holding her palms together and bringing them up to her face while bowing her head forward slightly. I thought such an opening gesture when she first met each interviewee would strike the right "pose." I also asked her to dress conservatively but not to wear black because several Cambodian students had told me how disturbed their parents became when they saw them in all-black clothing—clothing the students thought was "cool" but that reminded their parents of the loose black shirts and pants that the Khmer Rouge made everyone wear. Quite apart from what I know about Asian norms and values, showing respect to those who help us conduct our research is something that both oral historians and specialists in ethnic studies (my field) consider important.

Audrey Kim and I also tried to show respect to informants in other ways. We did not judge the manner in which Cambodian refugees have coped with the American environment. We did not ask many personal questions even though we did seek some information about each narrator's individual life. But Kim left it up to each person to disclose however much he or she wished to reveal. Such personal questions include not only an individual's age, marital status, or income but also his or her political affiliation. In fact, one issue I purposely skirted was factional political conflicts within the community. Given the extremely complex quarrels that I knew existed in most Cambodian ethnic communities in the United States, I did not want Kim or myself to be perceived as siding with one or another faction. Therefore, Kim's questions about political affiliations and activities, when she asked them at all, were superficial rather than probing. Unable to stay in each community for a lengthy period to carry out participant observation, I thought it best that we not broach this subject lest we unwittingly step on people's toes. However, some narrators were surprisingly candid. They made references to sensitive subjects such as the detrimental effects of factionalism, spousal and child abuse, and addiction to gambling without being asked.

I also showed respect by following the wishes of the narrators when I decided to have some of the transcripts published. Readers will notice that only one of the narrators is a woman. Audrey Kim actually interviewed five women, and I had hoped to include four of their narratives in this book. Three of them, however, declined to give me permission to publish their accounts. The outside reviewer for this manuscript wondered why these individuals agreed to be interviewed but would not allow the transcripts to appear in print. If the reviewer were an oral historian he or she would immediately have understood the reasons. When a person is being interviewed, he or she is facing only one person—the interviewer. An interviewee can surmise a great deal about the interviewer by observing the latter's physical and verbal mannerisms, tone of voice, and how friendly he or she seems. From such cues, the interviewee can assess to what degree the interviewer can be trusted. The interrogator is thus a known, if not fully familiar, presence. When an interview transcript is published, however, it becomes available to an unknown audience whose very unknowability poses unforeseeable dangers. Not only is the potential audience unknown, but it also may consist of multiple constituencies, each with its own agenda.

When we first approached the narrators for permission to talk to them, I had no intention of publishing the transcripts. Only after I listened to the tapes and read the transcripts did I decide to publish some of them because the narratives are so compelling. Therefore, I had to ask permission, after the fact, to transform verbatim transcripts into published texts. Had the narrators known that their words might appear in print, some might have shown greater reticence in what they said. The women to whom Audrey Kim talked apparently felt more reticent retrospectively than did the men, none of whom denied me permission to publish their transcripts.

The external reviewer also suggested that I summarize the contents of the women's interviews anyway—that is, against their wishes—but I cannot do that without showing extreme disrespect toward them, and that is something I am unwilling to do. As oral histories, these scripts must be treated with a different ethical standard than the way some sociologists apparently regard their surveys and interviews. I repeat: oral history narrators are not simply sources but persons—individuals whose wishes must be respected.

The material in this book further differs from a traditional sociological study in that the accounts are not community studies per se. When sociologists or political scientists conduct a community study, they usually examine the demographic profile of its residents; their occupational distribution; social relations both within the community and between it and the larger society; the most important institutions within the community, including its political structure and what kinds of people compose its leadership; patterns of conflict resolution; and the probable direction of its future growth, decline, or change. Even though Kim did ask about some of these very topics, I did not want her to explore other aspects that social scientists may consider significant. Even more important, beyond collecting "objective facts" the conversations were meant to tap the subjective perceptions of each narrator. I wanted to hear how Cambodian community leaders are trying to solve the problems that their compatriots face. My hope was that they would provide "insiders' views" of what is going on in Cambodian communities in America. And they did.

Oral historians grapple with the issue of how best to transcribe recorded tapes and how much editing to do. Susan Allen exemplifies one pole of the dichotomous approaches recommended. She insists that "a transcript is by its very nature not an article formalized according to standards applied to written material . . . [therefore,] all atypical constructions, regionalisms, and dialect are to be preserved . . . all words . . . [must] be transcribed, including false starts and exclamations. Laughter, too, is indicated." In her opinion, to "clean up and polish" a transcript would reduce its authenticity (1982: 36, 42). Her concerns reflect those of archivists, whose main responsibility is to preserve documents, regardless of whether their origins are oral or written.

At the other pole are oral historians such as Michael Frisch and Alessandro Portelli, who not only carry out interviews but also write books based on oral forms of research. Frisch believes that "the integrity of a transcript is best protected, in documentary use, by an aggressive approach that does not shrink from substantial manipulation of the text . . . [we should] abandon the pretense of literal reproduction, in order to craft the document into a form that will answer to the needs of successful presentation and communication" (1990: 84). He reminds us that written material is always edited before it is published, so why shouldn't material that originates as oral discourse be edited also when it is published? Likewise, Portelli informs us that some of the people he interviewed "felt that my accurate rendition of their speech was an insult to them" (1977: 69). Drawing an analogy with translating something from one language to another, Portelli observes that "the most literal translation is hardly ever the best, and a truly faithful translation always implies a certain amount of invention" (1991: 46).

With rare exceptions, the way people talk is often more choppy than the way they write. In the case of persons for whom English is not their native language—such as the narrators in this book—to reproduce the grammatical errors and not-quite-correct word usages of their spoken words is to present them in an unfavorable light. In my opinion, oral history purists who transcribe every hem and haw, every nonstandard usage, are not ensuring authenticity but are, rather, fetishizing "exotic" speech. I find such a stance paternalistic and condescending. For that reason, I made quite a lot of editorial changes in the transcripts that became this book, although I tried to retain the flavor of how each person talked. I sent a copy of the pertinent transcript to each narrator and asked him or her to make additional changes as he or she saw fit. Several individuals rewrote many sentences to make them more "proper," in the process transforming the conversational tone that I had left intact into a more formal prose. I did not undo those changes, however, because it is important to present a product they approved of. The Rev. Chhean Kong added pages of written text because he wanted to make sure that readers gain a basic understanding of Theravada Buddhist concepts and precepts. I did not delete these added passages, whose written origins are very apparent, because I wanted to abide by his wishes. I agree with Michael Frisch that the production of oral histories involves a "shared authority." This book, I hope, exemplifies that reflexive and democratic intellectual stance.

Terminology

TRANSLITERATED FOREIGN words are italicized when they first appear in the text but are not italicized subsequently. No *s* is added to the plural form of these words. Following conventional usage in English, "Khmer Rouge" is written in the singular but is treated grammatically as plural. (In French, the term is written in the plural.)

"Cambodians" refers to all people who live or lived in Cambodia, regardless of their ethnicity. "Cambodian" is used either as a singular proper noun or as an adjective for anything pertaining to Cambodia. "Khmer" refers to the major ethnic group in Cambodia, as well as to the name of their language. "Kampuchea" is a closer approximation of how the country's name is pronounced in Khmer. "Sino-Cambodians" are Cambodians of Chinese ancestry. "Khmer Krom" are Khmer living in the Mekong Delta of South Vietnam, which used to be a part of Cambodian territory. The "Cham" are an ethnic group descended from the kingdom of Champa, which the Vietnamese conquered and absorbed centuries ago. They presently live in both Vietnam and Cambodia. The country's name has changed several times since 1970. Before Prince Norodom Sihanouk was overthrown in March 1970, Cambodia was a kingdom even though it had a parliamentary form of government. From 1970 to 1975 it was called the Khmer Republic. From April 1975 to January 1979 it was known as Democratic Kampuchea. Between January 1979 and 1989 its name was the People's Republic of Kampuchea. It became the State of Cambodia in 1989. Then, after the May 1993 United Nations–supervised elections voted in new legislators, the name was changed yet again to the Kingdom of Cambodia. (Sihanouk, who had been king from 1941 to 1955, when he abdi-

cated the throne and became Prince Sihanouk, was recrowned as King Sihanouk in 1993.)

The current official name of Laos is the Lao People's Democratic Republic. The "Lao" or "lowland Lao" are the major ethnic group in Laos, but they
compose only about half of the total population of Laos. "Lao" is also the
name of the language they speak. "Laotians" refers to all people who live or
have lived in Laos, even though non-Lao ethnic groups prefer to be called
by their own names. "Laotian" is used either as a singular proper noun or as
an adjective for anything pertaining to Laos. "Hmong," "Iu Mien," and "Tai
Dam" are ethnic minority groups living in the hills of Laos; they are also
found in the hills of Vietnam and Thailand.

"Vietnamese" has four meanings: the major ethnic group in Vietnam; the
language they speak; all residents of Vietnam, regardless of their ethnicity;
and all things related to Vietnam. The ethnic minorities living in Vietnam,
however, prefer to be known by their own names. "Sino-Vietnamese" are
Vietnamese of Chinese ancestry who call themselves "Hoa." "Montagnards"
is a collective name the French gave to dozens of ethnic-minority hill-dwellers
in Vietnam, but each group should be called by its own name. Between 1954
and 1975 Vietnam was divided into two countries—the Democratic Republic of Vietnam (commonly called North Vietnam) and the Republic of Vietnam (commonly called South Vietnam). There were communists in both
countries. "Viet Cong" or "Vietcong" is the name coined by South Vietnamese President Ngo Dinh Diem to refer to the communists in South Vietnam.
Many people, both in Southeast Asia and in the United States, however, have
colloquially used "Vietcong" as a generic term for all Vietnamese communists. Since 1976 the name of the reunified country has been the Socialist
Republic of Vietnam.

Until 1932 Thailand was called Siam. The "Thai" are the major ethnic group
in Thailand; that proper noun is also the name of their language.

I use the word *refugee* only in its United Nations–defined, technical, legal
sense. Refugees are people who have been persecuted, or who have a well-
founded fear of being persecuted, by their own governments on the basis of
their political beliefs and activities, religion, racial or ethnic origins, or membership in certain social groups. This definition has been incorporated into
the 1980 Refugee Act, which removed the geographic specificity embedded
in pre-1980 U.S. refugee policy that favored escapees from communist countries and the Middle East. In general, people must be outside their countries
of origin but not yet in the United States when they apply for admission into
the United States as refugees. In recent years, however, the U.S. government
has made some exceptions (notably during the international crisis caused by

the "boat people" exodus from Vietnam in the late 1970s and early 1980s) and allowed people who were still in their countries of origin to apply for refugee status. The technical, legal meaning of "refugee" is narrower than its colloquial meaning. In everyday speech we often refer to people who are fleeing any kind of catastrophe—whether caused by natural disasters, famine, war, or some other kind of strife—as "refugees."

To signal the distinction between the technical and colloquial usages of the word, I have coined a more inclusive, generic term, *refuge-seekers*, to refer to anyone looking for a safe haven somewhere, either temporarily or permanently. This term is parallel to "asylum-seekers," which is commonly used. It is important to note that not all refuge-seekers qualify as refugees. Only the latter have the right to apply for permanent resettlement in another country. A further refinement is that according to American law, those who seek a safe haven in America after they set foot on its soil are designated as "applicants for asylum" or "asylees." These two terms are not synonymous with "refugees." I also refrain from using the term *displaced persons* because the 1948 Displaced Persons Act was meant to benefit primarily people from certain geographic areas during the post–World War II years and did not have displaced persons everywhere as its intended beneficiaries.

In Cambodia, a person's family name precedes his or her given name. The narrators in this book, however, have reversed the order of their names in order to conform to American usage. Some individuals, such as Him S. Chhim and Hay S. Meas, have made the second word in their given name into a middle initial; others, such as Sam-Ang Sam, have hyphenated the two words; most, however, have combined the two words into a single given name.

Finally, although Americans who are familiar with the concept *dharma* are used to seeing it transliterated according to its pronunciation in Sanskrit, in chapter 2 the transliteration used is "dhamma," which approximates more closely that word's pronunciation in Pali, the sacred language of Theravada Buddhism—the religion adhered to by a vast majority of Cambodians.

Not Just Victims

Introduction

APPROXIMATELY A quarter-million persons of Cambodian ancestry live in the United States today. A vast majority of the adults—almost 149,700 persons—came as refugees between 1975 and 1994, while only slightly more than 6,300 entered as immigrants during that same period. Refugees are legally defined as persons who are in danger of being persecuted by their own governments due to their political or religious beliefs or membership in certain proscribed groups and who consequently seek sanctuary in another country. U.S. laws controlling the admission of refugees differ from those governing the entry of immigrants, but both sets of laws are subject to the changing winds of politics. Children of Cambodian ancestry born on American soil compose the fastest-growing segment of the Cambodian American population. The number of American born will, in perhaps another decade, exceed the number of foreign born for two reasons. First, the birthrate among women of Cambodian ancestry living in the United States is quite high. Second, compared to other Asian ethnic groups, the current rate of Cambodian immigration is very low. Only about a thousand persons a year have entered as immigrants since the Cambodian refugee admission program ended in 1994.

Cambodia before 1975

Cambodia is a small country in mainland Southeast Asia, lying west of Vietnam, east of Thailand, and south of Laos. Mainland Southeast Asia has been a crossroads of civilizations. Vietnam, which was under Chinese rule for approximately a thousand years, was strongly influenced by Chinese culture, particularly the tenets of Confucianism. The Vietnamese, however, are also extremely proud of the fact that they ultimately succeeded in throwing out their Chinese overlords. Later, they also managed to evict the French and then the Americans. Resistance to colonial rule has thus been a powerful current in Vietnamese nationalism. In contrast, Laos, Cambodia, Thailand, and Burma were more strongly affected by Indian rather than Chinese civilization. Because interactions between these countries and India were more cultural than political, the connections between them and India have not been marked by the kind of conflicts that characterized Vietnam's relationship with its successive colonial rulers. The religious beliefs and practices, mythologies and folklore, written scripts, vocabularies, concepts of statecraft and kingship, classical dances, and music of these "Indianized" states all reflect Indian cultural influences (Chandler 1992b: 9–76; Coedes 1968; Hall 1968: 94–139). Over the centuries, these Indian cultural forms were indigenized as they blended with the local cultures of Burma, Thailand, Laos, and Cambodia. To this day, however, Indian elements are clearly recognizable. In Cambodia, for example, scenes from the *Reamker*—the Cambodian version of the Indian epic the *Ramayana*—are still regularly performed and are extremely popular among audiences of all social strata. Theravada Buddhism, the major religion of the country, likewise had Indian origins, although Buddhism is no longer a major religion in India itself.

The Khmer are the major ethnic group in Cambodia, where they have lived for some two thousand years. The language they speak is also called Khmer and belongs to the Mon-Khmer family of languages. The first identifiably Khmer kingdom, which has come down in history as Angkor ("holy city"), was established in 802. It lasted until 1432. Located near the present-day town of Siem Reap in northwestern Cambodia, the Angkor kingdom left behind many magnificent stone temples, each adorned with intricate bas relief of gods, goddesses, kings, queens, princes, princesses, legendary beings, elephants, smaller animals, fish, leaves, and flowers. There are also many carved scenes of royal processions, festivals, market places, and domestic life. Because Khmer builders did not use mortar or any other kind of bonding material, the stones had to be cut precisely and were held together by sheer weight and exact fit. Angkorian temple architecture was infused with cosmological symbols reflecting what Khmer believed to be the structure of the universe. The most famous temple is Angkor Wat—one of the largest religious structures in the world—built in the twelfth century. In addition to temples, the Angkor kingdom also had a well-planned system of canals and reservoirs, enabling it to be productive enough to support an estimated million persons during its heyday. These waterways not only irrigated fields but also transported people, crops, goods, and the heavy stone slabs used to build the temples. The waterworks served an area of approximately four hundred square miles (Groslier and Arthaud 1966; Higham 2002; Jessup and Zephir, eds. 1997; Krasna 1963; Le Bonheur 1995; MacDonald 1987; Mannikka 1996).

Ironically, the very activities that created the glory that was Angkor also eventually led to its demise. As more and more people were pressed into unpaid labor to build and maintain the monumental structures that sacralized their rulers, commoners were left with less and less time to grow food crops. Moreover, in the country's twenty thousand shrines there dwelled thirty thousand priests who annually consumed thirty-eight thousand tons of rice—grain taken from the peasants (Cady 1964: 95). Thus, the socioeconomic foundation of the Angkor kingdom slowly eroded. In time it became so weak that it was destroyed by its Thai neighbors, who sacked its capital in 1432, forcing the Khmer to abandon it. The Khmer built a new capital at Lovek, but in 1593 three Thai armies simultaneously invaded Cambodia and in 1603 made it into a vassal state of Siam (the old name for Thailand).

Cambodia's other neighbor, Vietnam, also began to encroach upon its territory from the mid-seventeenth century onward, sending thousands of Vietnamese there to settle the land. By the third decade of the eighteenth century, Vietnam had gained full control over all the Cambodian territory in the delta of the Mekong River. To this day, Cambodians continue to think of the Mekong Delta as their land, calling it Kampuchea Krom. The Khmer who continue to live there form a distinct ethnic minority within Vietnam, the Khmer Krom. (The interview with Bunroeun Thach in chapter 12 tells the story of the Khmer Krom.) In later decades, Vietnam also took over provinces in the interior of Cambodia. The Khmer revolted against the Vietnamese in 1840, but the rebellion was quelled within a year. Taking advantage of the turmoil, thirty-five thousand Thai troops marched into northwestern Cambodia. They attacked several garrisons that the Vietnamese had set up but could not win a decisive victory. The stalemate ended with a negotiated ceasefire in 1845. Thereafter, Cambodia became a vassal state of both Siam and Vietnam (Chandler 1992b: 77–136; Hall 1968: 436–43).

The next country to gain control over Cambodia was France, which ruled it as a protectorate for ninety years, from 1863 to 1953. (In addition to Cambodia, France also colonized Cochinchina, Annam, and Tonkin—that today compose Vietnam—as well as Laos. These five colonies became known collectively as French Indochina.) Although the Cambodian king was allowed to remain on the throne, French colonial officials dominated virtually every aspect of Cambodian life. Through a treaty forced upon King Norodom in 1863, the French gained control over Cambodia's foreign affairs; the right to mine its precious metals and minerals; to cut timber; to buy, own, and sell land as private property; to import goods without paying customs duties; to impose and collect taxes and fees; to send missionaries to spread Christianity; and to set up their own courts so the French people who broke the law in Cambodia would not be subject to Cambodian jurisdiction. The French eventually also established a civil service staffed almost entirely by Vietnamese and supervised by a handful of Frenchmen, revised the penal code, and set up some schools to teach the French language to Cambodian children—mostly scions of the royal family, the nobility, and wealthy Sino-Cambodians (Chandler 1992b: 137–72; Hall 1968: 758–66; Osborne 1969: 175–258; Smith 1964: 599–604).

In 1940 the French placed a nineteen-year-old prince, Norodom Sihanouk, on the throne because they thought he would be more malleable than the son of the deceased king. What neither the French nor the outside world anticipated was that as Sihanouk matured he became very much his own man—and a wily politician to boot. During World War II, French colonial administrators remained in power, and no fighting took place in Indochina because the Vichy government (the collaborationist French government beholden to Nazi Germany) allowed Japanese troops to be stationed there. Nor did any fighting occur in Thailand, because its leaders, too, let Japan keep troops on Thai soil. In contrast, Japan militarily conquered the rest of Southeast Asia, which was under British, Dutch, and American colonial rule at that time. In March 1945, aware of its imminent defeat by the Allies, Japan encouraged the indigenous leaders of Southeast Asia to declare their independence. All of them, including King Sihanouk of Cambodia, did so (Cady 1964: 546–57, 563–69; Smith 1964: 604–7).

Very soon after World War II ended, however, France returned (with British help) to recolonize Indochina; Great Britain to reclaim Burma, Malaya, and Singapore; and the Netherlands to reimpose its rule over Indonesia. Among the colonized people, the Vietnamese fought the longest and bloodiest war (the First Indochina War, 1946–54) to regain their independence, which they won after they defeated the French at Dien Bien Phu in early May 1954. When that event occurred, the Geneva Conference was already in progress to work out the political settlement for the Korean War (1950–53). French Indochina was also on the conference agenda. The Geneva Agreements divided Vietnam in two at the seventeenth parallel and stipulated that elections be held in 1956. In the interim, communist leaders would govern the Democratic Republic of Vietnam ("North Vietnam"), while pro-Western leaders would rule the Republic of Vietnam ("South Vietnam"). The intended nationwide elections never took place, however, because the South Vietnamese government refused to cooperate.

Cambodia and Laos gained independence a year before Vietnam did— Laos in October and Cambodia in November 1953. That was ironic, because they did not fight against the French in the same fierce way Vietnam did. Sihanouk has claimed credit for securing his country's independence, because at the beginning of 1953 he embarked on a "royal crusade for independence" to exert political pressure on France. When the French rebuffed his efforts, he publicized his country's dilemma by talking to the world press. What really led the French to give up Cambodia and Laos, however, was that French troops were bogged down in Vietnam. Granting nominal independence to Laos and Cambodia, which they had always considered less important than Vietnam, enabled them to give full attention to the war in Vietnam. The independence Cambodia gained was incomplete because it was given full control over only the army, police, and judicial system. France still controlled other aspects of Cambodian national life, particularly its diplomatic relations. Half a year later, however, the 1954 Geneva Agreements acknowledged the full independence of both Laos and Cambodia. Two provinces in northeastern Laos were set aside for the Pathet Lao (a term meaning "land of the Lao" but which Westerners have used to refer to Laotian communists) to regroup their forces, while Cambodia won the right to keep its territory intact (Smith 1964: 607–19; Smith 1965: 52–186).

From the mid-1950s to the early 1960s, the two Vietnams attempted to undermine one another in multiple ways. Fearing a potential communist victory, the United States sent increasing amounts of economic and military aid to South Vietnam. The first American ground troops landed there in 1965. For the next eight years, the Second Indochina War raged between North Vietnam, on the one hand, and South Vietnam and its ally the United States on the other hand. After the 1968 Tet Offensive, during which both sides suffered heavy casualties, American leaders began to realize that a guerrilla war could not be won easily or quickly, even with the most sophisticated weapons. Moreover, a strong antiwar movement at home stymied Congress, the Pentagon, and the executive branch. To extricate the United States from the quagmire, President Richard Nixon in 1968 announced a program to "Vietnamize" the war. Henceforth, more and more of the actual fighting would be turned over to South Vietnam's own troops, although the United States would continue to supply them with arms. After the United States pulled out all its military forces in early 1973, the two Vietnams continued to battle one another. The war ended when the communists captured Saigon on April 30,

1975. The following year, the victorious North Vietnamese leaders reunified the country and renamed it the Socialist Republic of Vietnam.

Meanwhile, Sihanouk dominated Cambodian life for seventeen years after the country regained independence. Desiring to participate more freely and actively in national and international politics, he abdicated the throne in 1955 and made his father a figurehead monarch responsible for court ceremonies. He formed the Sangkum Reastr Niyum (People's Socialist Community), which he characterized as a mass movement. He insisted that the Sangkum was not a political party because he did not like "petty party politics." However, he actively campaigned on behalf of Sangkum candidates who ran for electoral office, and they won so many seats that they virtually monopolized the national assembly (Cady 1974 [1980]: 370–76; Osborne 1994: 86–122; Smith 1965: 619–31).

By the mid-1950s the cold war was in full swing, with the "free world" led by the United States and the communist bloc led by the Soviet Union vying for the allegiance of countries in the "third world." Sihanouk thought that the best way for a small country like Cambodia to survive was for it to remain neutral during the cold war (Cady 1974 [1980]: 398–407; Leifer 1967). In particular, he believed Cambodia must placate China because, as he said in 1961, "within thirty years, with a population surpassing a billion, China will be without doubt the largest world power and its influence in Asia will certainly predominate. . . . all of Southeast Asia will be at China's mercy" (Smith 1965: 119). Accordingly, just as he juggled the various political parties within Cambodia under a veneer of parliamentary democracy, he played off the opposing superpowers against one another. He accepted aid from countries aligned on both sides of the cold war. The United States trained and equipped the thirty-thousand-strong Cambodian army and built schools and clinics. France built Cambodia an international airport and a new port at Sihanoukville. Japan constructed a bridge, improved Phnom Penh's water supply system, and helped develop agriculture. West Germany contributed a technical high school. Great Britain, Australia, New Zealand, and Canada also offered aid. The communist bloc likewise did its part to help Cambodia's economic development: the USSR, the People's Republic of China, Poland, Czechoslovakia, and Yugoslavia all provided various kinds of technical and economic assistance.

For almost a decade Sihanouk succeeded to a large extent in preventing any of the opposing forces, domestic and international, from challenging his dominant position within Cambodia (Osborne 1994: 139–55). But as the United States became increasingly involved in the war in Vietnam, that conflict soon spilled over into Cambodian territory. Vietnamese communist forces repeatedly crossed the border into eastern Cambodia to escape American bombs as well as South Vietnamese and American ground troops. Not wishing to antagonize the Soviet Union and the People's Republic of China, both of which supported North Vietnam during the Vietnam War, Sihanouk did not try to stop the North Vietnamese from sending armaments, political cadres, and military personnel down the Ho Chi Minh trail—a network of jungle paths that connected North and South Vietnam, the northern segment of which ran through eastern Laos and the southern segment through eastern Cambodia. He also closed his eyes to the fact that communist supplies were unloaded at Sihanoukville and carried by trucks owned by Cambodian entrepreneurs across the southern part of the country to Viet Cong (South Vietnamese communist) bases (Krepinevich 1986: 188).

In March 1970 Sihanouk was deposed by two men who had been very close to him—General Lon Nol, who had served both as his defense minister and prime minister, and Prince Sirik Matak, one of his cousins. Both objected to his flirtations with communist countries, and their followers deeply resented the losses they had suffered in recent years as a result of several of Sihanouk's decisions. Army commanders loyal to Lon Nol had lost a lucrative source of graft when Sihanouk broke off diplomatic relations with the United States in 1967 (the generals had been siphoning a portion of U.S. aid into their own pockets). Wealthy Sino-Cambodian businessmen had suffered when Sihanouk nationalized the country's import-export businesses, as well as its banks, as part of his attempt to establish "Buddhist socialism" in Cambodia (Cady 1974 [1980]: 662–66; Osborne 1994: 202–16). Sihanouk accused the U.S. Central Intelligence Agency of supporting this coup against him, but it will never be known to what extent the United States was involved (Norodom Sihanouk 1973). What is known is that the United States gave the Khmer Republic—the avidly pro-American Lon Nol government established after Sihanouk's ouster—$1.18 billion in military aid and $503 million in other kinds of aid during the five years it existed.

Sihanouk could have chosen a life of luxury in exile. Instead, he joined forces with the Khmer Rouge (the most radical, and by then the dominant, faction among Cambodia's communists) to oppose the new Lon Nol government. They formed FUNK—the French acronym for Front Uni National du Kampuchea (National United Front of Cambodia)—in late March 1970 and a government-in-exile six weeks later. The latter was based in two places: in Beijing, where the Chinese had invited Sihanouk to establish his new residence, and in the jungles of Cambodia. Sihanouk's presence lent legitimacy to the alliance in the international arena, while the Khmer Rouge led the armed resistance within Cambodia. Sihanouk enabled the Khmer Rouge to increase their ranks by sending messages over the latter's radio and by distributing cassette tapes of his talks to peasants, among whom he was very popular. He appealed to his supporters to join FUNK's campaign to oust the Lon Nol government and its American allies. The cooperation between Sihanouk and the Khmer Rouge turned out to be a Faustian bargain, although he had no way of foreseeing its tragic consequences. While in power, Sihanouk had persecuted the Khmer Rouge, arresting and imprisoning some of their leaders and sending the rest into hiding in the jungles. Now he became the ally of these insurgents because they offered the only means for him to possibly return to power.

Soon after Lon Nol installed himself as president of the Khmer Republic, a civil war erupted between his armed forces and Khmer Rouge soldiers and guerrillas. The fighting lasted until April 17, 1975, when the Khmer Rouge entered Phnom Penh, the capital, in triumph and set up a government called Democratic Kampuchea (Burgler 1990: 26–56; Chandler 1991b: 206–35; Etcheson 1984). American bombing raids in support of the Khmer Republic's forces played a significant role in the civil war. The bombing campaign was carried out without the knowledge of the U.S. Congress and the American public. It came to light only when it was exposed in congressional testimonies by American pilots who had participated in the raids (Kiernan 1989; Shawcross 1979).

Unfortunately for the United States, American intentions backfired. Lon Nol's troops were unable to hold the territory they initially controlled. The Khmer Rouge successfully used the rural population's growing distress to persuade more and more recruits to join their fighting units as the massive tonnage of American bombs destroyed crops, work animals, and homes of the peasants and killed an increasing number of civilians. When the civil war began in 1970 they had about four thousand regular soldiers and an estimated four to fifteen thousand guerrillas and controlled about one-sixth of the country's territory. At war's end they had over sixty thousand regular troops, about two hundred thousand guerrillas, and control of all Cambodia. Moreover, the bombing raids gave North Vietnamese troops a pretext to move deeper and deeper into the Cambodian heartland. Ironically, that was exactly what the bombing campaign was supposed to prevent. North Vietnamese military and political support was critical to the Khmer Rouge's victory, even though Khmer Rouge leaders would later vehemently deny that the North Vietnamese had played any role at all in their conquest of the country.

The Rise and Fall of the Khmer Rouge

Who were the Khmer Rouge? To answer that question, we must examine briefly how communism was introduced into Indochina. Among the people colonized by France, the Vietnamese were the first to study Marxism. Ho Chi Minh, the most important Vietnamese anticolonial leader, was both an ardent nationalist and an internationally minded communist. Even though these are supposedly opposite political orientations, in colonized countries such a paradox was not really contradictory for two reasons. First, the achievement of political independence is the goal of all anticolonial struggles; hence, anticolonial leaders are nationalists. Second, after the Bolshevik Revolution occurred in Russia, the Soviet Union offered guidance to and support for "wars of national liberation" in various parts of the world. That made Marxism-Leninism an attractive doctrine in the eyes of many educated individuals in colonized societies during much of the twentieth century. It is not surprising, therefore, that a small number of Cambodian intellectuals also found Marxist doctrine appealing and eventually became communists.

It took two decades for communism to take root in Cambodia. Even though a Khmer section had been established within the Indochinese Communist Party, founded in 1930 by Ho Chi Minh, an independent Khmer People's Revolutionary Party (KPRP) did not emerge until 1951. In 1954 the KPRP had only about two thousand members. Half of them, who felt a strong bond with their Vietnamese mentors, left for Hanoi when Vietnamese troops, guerrilla fighters, and political cadres withdrew from Cambodia as mandated by the 1954 Geneva Agreements. The other thousand who remained in Cambodia formed a political party named the Krom Pracheachon in order to participate in electoral politics. Despite establishing such a legal front, the Pracheachon's ranks were drastically thinned by Sihanouk's police in the late 1950s.

In the midst of this repression, twenty-one Khmer leftists met in a Phnom Penh train station in 1960, changed the name of the KPRP to the Workers' Party of Kampuchea (KWP), and adopted an explicit Marxist-Leninist platform. A faction within the KWP soon coalesced around Saloth Sar, who would later be known by the nom de guerre Pol Pot. Sar and almost all of his allies, who became the core leaders of the Khmer Rouge, came from fairly well-to-do families. They received their college and graduate education in France, where some of them joined the French Communist Party. After they returned to Cambodia, many became teachers in Phnom Penh. In that capacity, they influenced large numbers of discontented urban youths (Chan-

dler 1991b: 125–30; Chandler 1992a: 51–67; Kiernan 1985). As political scientist Craig Etcheson has observed, "Those who would become the masters of
Cambodia's peasant revolution were not themselves peasants" (1984: 49).

The Saloth Sar clique emerged as the strongest faction within the KWP as
Sihanouk's police arrested and incarcerated or killed off many of the party's
key veteran members. In 1966 the KWP was renamed the Communist Party
of Kampuchea. Meanwhile, Sihanouk had dubbed them the "Khmer Rouge,"
meaning the Red Khmer—the moniker by which they have since been
known. After Sihanouk was overthrown by Lon Nol in 1970, the Cambodian
communists who had gone to Hanoi in 1954 returned home. But most of
them soon perished at the hands of the Khmer Rouge, who did not trust them
and had developed a different analysis of what needed to be done to carry
the Cambodian revolution to a successful conclusion (Chandler 1991b: 217–
19). Hanoi loyalists believed that the revolutions in Vietnam, Laos, and Cambodia must be carried out in a coordinated fashion and that revolutionaries
in Cambodia should not engage in armed struggle until the Vietnamese revolution seemed closer to victory (Porter 1983). The Khmer Rouge, however,
thought that the progress of the Cambodian revolution should not be im-
peded by the Vietnamese one (Chandler 1983). Having few ties to either the
Vietnamese or to those Khmer communists who felt great solidarity with the
Vietnamese, the Khmer Rouge did not hesitate to express hostility to the
Vietnamese, even though they depended heavily on the latter's support during the 1970–75 civil war (Chandler 1991b: 171–78; Kiernan 1985).

Eager to implement their revolutionary principles throughout the entire
country, the Khmer Rouge began giving orders to evacuate Phnom Penh on
the afternoon of April 17, 1975—the very day they captured the capital. They
told people that Americans were going to bomb the city, so its two-million-
plus residents, three-quarters of whom had sought refuge in the capital during the civil war to avoid America's bombing raids in the countryside, had
to leave their homes. Khmer Rouge cadres cruised the streets in trucks, making announcements through loudspeakers, and also went on foot from house
to house, asking people to evacuate (Ashe 1988: 25–34; Mam 1997: 11–15; Ngor
1987: 91–94). Told to take only a few days' rations with them, the citizens assumed that the move would be temporary. The Khmer Rouge leaders had
made the decision to evacuate the capital, as well as the country's smaller
cities and towns, two months earlier. They thought that moving the urban-
dwellers into the countryside would enhance their own ability to control
every segment of the population and would reduce the people's capacity to
resist their new rulers.

What the city people did not anticipate was that they would not be allowed to return to their homes; moreover, they would be subjected to unimaginable horror in the months and years to come. The urbanites, including patients lying on hospital gurneys pushed along by their relatives, traveled at gunpoint back to their ancestral villages (Ponchaud 1978: 6–7). During these journeys, tens of thousands of people died from hunger, thirst, exposure to the elements, illness, and executions. The cadres who accompanied the evacuees cajoled the latter to tell their life stories. In this manner, they identified former government officials, military commanders, educated individuals, merchants, and landlords, who were then shot or bludgeoned to death, sometimes in front of family members. Six months later, to further disorient the people, the Khmer Rouge ordered a second cross-country trek. More people died. By now they had been so weakened by hunger, illness, and long hours of harsh labor that they succumbed easily.

The Khmer Rouge divided the country's population into three groups: those with full rights, those with no rights, and those with a few rights. Poor peasants who had resided in areas that the Khmer Rouge had controlled before April 17, 1975, were called "old people" or "base people" or "full rights people." They would hold power from then on. Only they could participate and speak in mass meetings led by Khmer Rouge cadres. The urban evacuees were called "new people" or "April 17 people" or "depositees" and would henceforth be treated as enemies of the revolution with no rights whatsoever. Farmers with relatively large plots of land were also suspect and counted as "new people." However, peasants with only a little land and petty traders were classified as "candidates" and were allowed to attend meetings but not speak (Vickery 1984: 81–82).

Thus, with a few seemingly simple rhetorical changes—categories introduced in an atmosphere of pervasive terror as people were summarily executed—the Khmer Rouge overnight turned their country's social structure upside down. To eradicate all visual cues of socioeconomic hierarchies, everyone now had to wear black clothing. The French-educated Pol Pot and his fellow leaders dubbed 1975 "year zero"—a term they borrowed from the French revolution to signify the beginning of a total transformation of their society.

Other extreme measures they imposed included the abolition of markets, money, banks, private property, Western medicine, schools, and Buddhism. Buddhist monks, the most venerated members of Cambodian society, were defrocked and forced to work in the fields along with everyone else, and Buddhist temples were used to store weapons or as places to house and slaughter animals. Both uses violated the precepts of Buddhism—a religion opposed to violence and especially to the killing of animate beings (a discussion of Buddhist beliefs appears in chapter 2). The Khmer Rouge undermined family life by splitting families, separating husbands from wives and children from parents. Worse, young children were trained to spy on their elders. People became afraid to talk, even to close relatives and friends in case something they said would be reported and get them into trouble (Martin 1994: 157–214; Vickery 1984: 64–188). Even the smallest infractions were punished severely, sometimes by death. To conserve ammunition the Khmer Rouge ended the lives of some individuals by breaking their necks with a hoe or an ax, suffocated others with plastic bags, and buried alive yet others in holes they had been forced to dig themselves (Burgler 1990: 99–154; Quinn 1989a, 1989b).

In addition to exterminating so-called class enemies, the Khmer Rouge also persecuted ethnic minorities, as Ben Kiernan has chronicled (1996). In September 1975 they expelled at least 150,000 of the four hundred thousand ethnic Vietnamese, some of whom had lived in Cambodia for generations. Worse, tens of thousands were massacred en route to the Cambodian-Vietnamese border. An estimated half of the four hundred thousand ethnic Chinese, many of whom had likewise lived in Cambodia for generations, also perished, but more from hunger and illness than from executions. The Khmer Rouge singled out the Cham, a Muslim minority, for cultural degradation. The Cham were not allowed to speak their language or wear their traditional clothing. The Khmer Rouge forced them to eat pork (a food proscribed by their religion, Islam) and used their mosques as pigsties. An estimated one-third of the Cham population died during the Khmer Rouge regime. The regime also forbade members of the various mountain-dwelling ethnic groups to practice their animistic religions and broke up their social organizations, even though some of the Khmer Rouge's earliest recruits had come from these groups.

A year after coming to power, the Khmer Rouge set up a torture and execution center at a former Phnom Penh high school which they called S-21. (*S* stands for *sala* [room], and *21* was the code for the *santebal* [security police].) There, in the following two and a half years, they incarcerated fellow Khmer Rouge leaders whom Pol Pot and his circle no longer trusted (and there were many Khmer Rouge who opposed Pol Pot's bloodthirsty extremism), systematically tortured them to extract "confessions," and killed all but seven persons out of the estimated twenty thousand so incarcerated. The wardens kept meticulous records of their deeds, took mug shots of many of the victims before killing them, and wrote the word *komtech* (smashed) next to the name of each victim after he or she died (Chandler 1999). The bloodletting grew to a frenzy in 1978, when Pol Pot's henchmen arrested and killed somewhere between one hundred thousand and a quarter million Khmer Rouge commanders, cadres, and their family members, all of whom Pol Pot now considered his internal enemies.

The Khmer Rouge turned the entire country into a giant forced-labor camp. Men, women, and children were forced to dig a huge amount of earth and carry it in baskets to work sites where dams and irrigation ditches were being built with their bare hands. People also had to plant and harvest crops, using virtually no implements. To ensure compliance, the Khmer Rouge worked everyone, including children over the age of seven, long hours and fed them a starvation diet of thin rice gruel, thereby depriving them of energy to resist. They accused individuals caught foraging for edible plants or small animals to assuage their hunger of stealing from the state and brutally punished them. Even small children caught stealing food were penalized. Teenaged Khmer Rouge cadres and soldiers, barely out of childhood themselves, beat some of the young thieves. They tied up others and placed them where red ants, whose bites are excruciatingly painful, could bite them. They buried alive yet others. Malnutrition became rampant. Night blindness, beriberi, scurvy, and other illnesses that result from an inadequate diet became common ailments (Ashe 1988; Criddle and Mam 1987; Fiffer 1991; Him 2000; May, ed. 1986; Ngor 1987; Ouk and Simon 1996; Pin 1987; Pran, comp. 1997; Stuart-Fox 1985; Szymusiak 1986; Ung 2000; Welaratna 1993).

Sick people suffered the utmost deprivation when their already meager ration was further reduced. Anyone unable to engage in productive labor was deemed unworthy to be fed. Some seriously ill individuals tried their best to continue working lest they be accused of malingering and be punished. People who had brought Western medicine along when they left their homes were afraid to use it for fear of being charged with engaging in a counterrevolutionary act. The sick usually languished until they died. Those taken to the huts that served as "clinics" were injected with potions the Khmer Rouge had concocted themselves under unsanitary conditions. Often, these poor souls died from infections.

In the three years and eight months that the Khmer Rouge regime lasted, from April 1975 to January 1979, at least 1.5 million people (some estimates are higher) perished. This figure, when added to the half-million who died during the 1970–75 civil war, meant that about two million people out of an estimated 1970 total population of 7.88 million lost their lives during the 1970s. The carnage destroyed such a huge fraction of the population that some writers have called it an "auto-genocide" because it was Cambodians who killed their fellow Cambodians.

Communist doctrine alone cannot explain the savagery of the Khmer

Rouge revolution. Various factors have been proposed to make sense of their behavior. Political scientist Karl Jackson has identified the characteristics that set the Khmer Rouge apart from other communist revolutionaries: "The proclivity to violence, the fear of contamination by outsiders, the moral self-righteousness, and the literal and doctrinaire way of pursuing goals are what separate the Khmer Rouge from comparable revolutionary phenomena" (1989c: 7). Khatharya Um, also a political scientist, has called the Khmer Rouge a "brotherhood of the pure," to signify their obsession with ethnic and political "purity" (Um 1990 and in press). Roel Burgler, a political scientist as well, has pointed out that the use of terror need not be "mindless," but when the terror becomes an end in itself—that is, when it "keeps on extending and intensifying its work out of self-vindication and self-preservation"— then it can be characterized as "terror gone mad" (1990: 271–73). Historian Ben Kiernan has argued that the Khmer Rouge were "racists" as well. They waged not just a class war but a war to exterminate non-Khmer (1996: 26). In my opinion, "ethnic chauvinists" would be a more accurate term, because the killers, as well as their victims, were all Asians, members of the same "Mongoloid race."

In retrospect, Sihanouk has theorized that the Khmer Rouge's heinousness can be explained in part by their reliance on uneducated teenagers to carry out the most gruesome tasks (1980). Some of the interviewees in this book also point to the unschooled youthfulness of the Khmer Rouge cadres to explain why they could be manipulated so easily by veteran Khmer Rouge leaders. This line of analysis seems to be borne out by some ethnographic data. The words of a former youthful Khmer Rouge soldier interviewed by social scientist Marie Alexandrine Martin suggest that the young people were proud to be entrusted with such important functions. At the same time, they constantly feared that they would be mercilessly punished should they fail in their assignments (1994: 167–68). A former guard at S-21 whom anthropologist Alexander Hinton interviewed told him, "I did this [kill the prisoners] so that others wouldn't accuse me of being unable to cut off my heart. . . . When my boss asked me to do this . . . I couldn't refuse" (1998b: 95). Hinton has argued that the Khmer Rouge succeeded in motivating their underlings to kill on such a massive scale by combining communist ideology with deeply rooted aspects of Khmer culture that were "emotionally salient" to many of the soldiers and cadres. These included Khmer concerns about power, honor, face, status, and patronage. Of particular importance was the Khmer tendency to inflict disproportionate revenge upon those who had shamed them—what Hinton calls "a head for an eye" (1996, 1998a, 1998b). Frank Smith, another anthropologist, has discovered that many ordinary

Cambodians now living in the United States as refugees think that the Khmer Rouge could not have been "real" Khmer; rather, they must have been Vietnamese (1989).

Finally, as I see it, the key Khmer Rouge leaders were obsessed with delusions of grandeur. For example, Ieng Sary, one of Pol Pot's closest comrades-in-arms and his brother-in-law, proclaimed grandly that what they were trying to do "has never been done before in history," and Pol Pot bragged about how the Khmer Rouge revolution had leapfrogged over other socialist revolutions to transform Cambodia instantaneously into the world's most advanced communist society. Pol Pot was apparently also extremely paranoid. Among communist revolutionary leaders even Joseph Stalin trails behind Pol Pot in terms of the total number of fellow revolutionary leaders each man murdered as he went about consolidating power after establishing a new regime.

Despite the overwhelming terror, people did attempt to resist, some by escaping, others by organizing. During the Khmer Rouge years, about thirty-four thousand people managed to escape across the Thai-Cambodian border into Thailand, and about three hundred thousand ethnic Vietnamese and an untold number of ethnic Chinese were either forcibly expelled or fled voluntarily into Vietnam. The successful escapees represent only a fraction of those who tried to flee, because the Khmer Rouge did not hesitate to kill anyone caught running away. Escape routes were treacherously dangerous, because the Khmer Rouge planted land mines along the borders and erected walls of sharpened bamboo stakes to hinder the passage of potential fugitives. But many people felt that because they were going to die anyway, they might as well die while trying to reach freedom.

A more potent form of resistance came from thousands of middle-rank Khmer Rouge cadres who did not accept Pol Pot's auto-genocidal policies and practices. In 1977 and 1978, hundreds of these dissident Khmer Rouge, including Hun Sen and Heng Samrin, escaped to Vietnam to seek the aid of the Vietnamese in an effort to overthrow Pol Pot. The Vietnamese were only too happy to help. Ever since communist governments had come to power in both countries in April 1975, Vietnam and Cambodia had been engaged in border clashes, which eventually escalated into large-scale incursions into each other's national territory. A real war was in progress by the time the dissident Khmer Rouge sought Vietnam's assistance and formed a United Front for the National Salvation of Kampuchea. On Christmas Day 1978, the front, backed by 120,000 well-armed Vietnamese troops, invaded Cambodia. They met no resistance along the way. By January 7, 1979, they had driven Pol Pot from Phnom Penh. A new government, the People's Republic of Kampuchea, was established, headed by the youthful Hun Sen (then only in his twenties) and Heng Samrin (in his thirties) and propped up by a Vietnamese army of occupation numbering more than one hundred thousand men (Martin 1994: 215–55; Morris 1999; Nguyen-vo 1992: 96–133; Vickery 1984: 189–252).

The demise of Democratic Kampuchea did not end Cambodia's nightmare, however. The Khmer Rouge remnants decamped in northwestern Cambodia with an estimated forty thousand troops and an even larger number of civilians whom they had forcibly abducted to serve as porters and reserve fighters. For the next twelve years, low-intensity warfare erupted every dry season (from December to April) between the forces of the People's Republic of Kampuchea and a coalition of three groups. The coalition was composed of the Khmer Rouge; people loyal to Sihanouk, who established FUNCINPEC (the French acronym for the National United Front for an Independent, Neutral, Peaceful, and Cooperative Cambodia); and the followers of former prime minister Son Sann, who set up the KPNLF (Kampuchean People's National Liberation Front). In 1982 the alliance formed a government-in-exile called GCKD (the French acronym for the Coalition Government of Democratic Kampuchea).

Because the United States refused to recognize the People's Republic of Kampuchea, branding it a puppet government that had been installed by Vietnam—a country many Americans continued to think of as their enemy—U.S. political leaders began to give military aid to the three-way coalition even though they were quite aware of the atrocities that the Khmer Rouge had committed. The United States justified this policy by pretending that the aid went only to the two noncommunist factions, FUNCINPEC and KPNLF. In fact, as the Congressional Research Service has revealed, the Khmer Rouge received $54.55 million in U.S. aid in 1980, $18.29 million in 1981, $4.57 million in 1982, and smaller amounts in later years.

As I see it, the cynicism shown by the United States can be explained by the politics of the cold war, especially its offshoot, the so-called Sino-Soviet split. In the early 1960s, the USSR and the People's Republic of China began to quarrel. Put simplistically, they disagreed over what to make of Joseph Stalin's legacy. In 1956, at the Twentieth Congress of the Communist Party of the Soviet Union, Nikita Khrushchev denounced Stalin's "crimes"—an act that sent shock waves through the hitherto monolithic communist world. But three communist countries staunchly defended Stalin and opposed Khrushchev's stance: the People's Republic of China, the Democratic People's Republic of Korea ("North Korea"), and Albania. The antagonism between the two communist giants did not abate until 1985, when Mikhail Gorbachev came to power and began making efforts to normalize relations between the two countries. Diplomatic relations were finally restored in 1989, but by then the Soviet Union itself was disintegrating.

The Sino-Soviet split affected Vietnam, Laos, and Cambodia. Vietnam sided with the Soviet Union in the international ideological dispute, while relations between Vietnam and the People's Republic of China grew increasingly cold. These relations were especially frigid during the years when Vietnam was persecuting its ethnic Chinese population. The government of a reunified socialist Vietnam perceived the Sino-Vietnamese as undesirable "bourgeois capitalists" because they were retail and wholesale merchants who controlled Vietnam's economy. Several hundred thousand of them fled as "boat people" in 1977, 1978, and 1979. In contrast, relations between China and the Khmer Rouge were very warm. China was the fallen regime's strongest supporter, in part because Chinese leaders feared the "expansionism" of pro-Soviet Vietnam, whose troops were occupying Laos and Cambodia, just south of China's borders. For that reason, China was more than willing to supply the rabidly anti-Vietnamese Khmer Rouge with arms.

During the 1970s, certain U.S. policymakers, particularly national security advisors Henry Kissinger and Zbigniew Brzezinski, thought it would be advantageous for the United States to "play the China card" in order to checkmate the Soviet Union (Becker 1986: 394–402; Brady 1999; Chanda 1986: 263–96; Sutter 1992). One result of this policy change was the reestablishment of diplomatic relations between the United States and China on January 1, 1979, after a break of almost thirty years. Another was the decision to favor the coalition of which the Khmer Rouge was a component, in part because China, America's new friend, supported the Khmer Rouge. An even more critical reason was that American leaders did not want to become involved in another ground war in mainland Southeast Asia—something U.S. troops would have to do in order to topple the Vietnam-supported government headed by Heng Samrin and Hun Sen. Thus, American foreign policymakers hoped that the Khmer Rouge, who had the strongest fighting force within the three-way coalition, would serve as a U.S. proxy in the effort to oust the Vietnamese from Cambodia. Thailand, for its part, allowed the remnant Khmer Rouge forces to operate on Thai soil so that they could serve as a useful buffer between Thailand and Vietnam. In exchange, China promised to stop aiding Thailand's own communist insurgents and to sell arms to the Thai government on favorable terms.

Due to these Machiavellian political calculations on the part of the superpowers and their allies, the second Cambodian civil war (also known as the Third Indochina War) dragged on for twelve long years. Various international attempts to end the conflict all failed (Burchet 1981; Chang 1985; Elliott, ed. 1981; Evans and Rowley 1990; Haas 1991a, 1991b). Finally, in 1989, Vietnam withdrew all its troops from Cambodia because it could no longer support a huge army of occupation, given the country's poor harvests in the late 1980s and because Soviet aid to Vietnam had begun to diminish as the USSR's own problems worsened. The United Nations succeeded in brokering a political settlement in late 1991. During the next eighteen months, the United Nations Transitional Authority in Cambodia (UNTAC) helped repatriate some 360,000 displaced Cambodians who had endured a precarious, violence-filled existence along the Thai-Cambodian border. UNTAC also partially disarmed the warring factions (but failed to disarm the Khmer Rouge because the latter refused to comply with the terms of the UN truce) and supervised a national election in May 1993. These efforts cost $2.6 billion—the most expensive UN peacekeeping effort to that point (Brown and Zasloff 1998; Findlay 1995; Heder and Ledgerwood, eds. 1996).

FUNCINPEC won the largest number of votes, and the Cambodian People's Party headed by Hun Sen came in second during the 1993 elections. Because Hun Sen still controlled the country's army as well as its administrative apparatus, however, FUNCINPEC's leader, Prince Norodom Ranariddh, one of Sihanouk's sons, was forced to share power with Hun Sen. For the next few years they each tried to outmaneuver the other. Because the Khmer Rouge were still to be reckoned with, both men tried to win over the remaining Khmer Rouge leaders. In 1996 Ieng Sary, Pol Pot's brother-in-law, who was often called "Brother Number Two" to signal that his status ranked below only that of "Brother Number One," Pol Pot himself, defected to the government. He cagily surrendered to both Prince Ranariddh and Hun Sen in order to hedge his bets, because the outcome of the political contest for power between those two men was not yet clear. Calling Pol Pot a liar, a cheat, and "the chief of the cruel murderers" who carried out purges on flimsy pretexts, thereby weakening the Khmer Rouge movement, Ieng Sary denounced Pol Pot for his crimes against humanity as though he himself had played no part in those bloody acts.

Pol Pot made the next move in 1997. He arrested Son Sen (not to be confused with Son Sann of KPNLF), his former defense minister and the chief of his security police, and killed him and his entire family. In response, "Ta" Mok, a top Khmer Rouge leader whose nickname was "the Butcher," seized Pol Pot and put him on trial at a jungle locale. Pol Pot was placed under house arrest and died in April 1998 at the age of seventy-three. The remaining Khmer Rouge leaders then defected to Hun Sen, who had promised them amnesty. Sihanouk, who had been recrowned as king but who continues to spend considerable time in Beijing for medical treatment, refused to approve Hun Sen's generous decision, but there was little he could do. Hun Sen now exercised full control over Cambodia after having pushed Prince Ranariddh aside in a coup in July 1997. At the end of 1998, Khieu Samphan, another paramount Khmer Rouge leader, declared, "We would like to apologize and ask our compatriots to forget the past so our nation can concentrate on the future. Let bygones be bygones."

But neither he nor the other Khmer Rouge leaders, with one exception, accepted personal responsibility for the killings. Not only that, but they are also living comfortable lives as free men. Only two former Khmer Rouge leaders are in jail—"Ta" Mok and Kang Kek Ieu. Kang is commonly known as "Duch" and was the chief administrator of the torture and extermination center at S-21. Both have been charged by a Cambodian court with genocide. Duch, who became a born-again Christian, has called himself the "chief of the sinners" (the allusion is to the Apostle Paul, who, after his conversion, helped to spread Christianity throughout the Roman Empire) and has declared that his life is now "in God's hand." Although Sihanouk signed a law on August 10, 2001, to set up a U.N.-assisted genocide tribunal and Hun Sen agreed to such a "joint tribunal," the U.N. advisers sent to explore how such a tribunal might operate ended negotiations with Cambodia in February 2002, citing inadequate assurance of the tribunal's legal independence. (The preceding account of political developments between 1993 and 2001 is based on articles in the *Far Eastern Economic Review* that are far too numerous to cite.)

Hun Sen's party won a majority of the votes in the 1998 elections. Journalists now often refer to him as "Cambodia's strong man." As a conciliatory gesture, he invited Prince Ranariddh to resume a role in the government, and the prince returned from exile to do so. Today, many international nongovernmental organizations are trying to help Cambodia develop economically, maintain political stability, and practice true democracy. But life for the common people, who have suffered so much for so long, remains extremely hard.

Cambodians as Refuge-Seekers

Cambodians who sought sanctuary during the years of turmoil were given various labels: "displaced persons," "illegal immigrants," "evacuees," "refugees," and "humanitarian parolees." Each label has legal and political implications, so the treatment that different groups of Cambodian refuge-seekers received depended a great deal on what label was pinned on them. The use of such labels reflects how highly politicized the international refugee regime has been and continues to be (Chan, forthcoming; Haines, ed. 1985: 3–16; Jorgensen 1989; Koehn 1989; Loescher and Scanlan 1986: 68–101).

In March 1975, anticipating the imminent fall of the Saigon government, President Gerald Ford formed an Interagency Task Force composed of representatives from various federal agencies to oversee the possible evacuation and resettlement of Vietnamese who would be at risk when communist forces captured Saigon (Strand and Jones 1985). Because it also appeared that the Khmer Rouge would be the likely winners in Cambodia's civil war, five thousand of the 130,000 slots for potential Indochinese refugees were alloted to Cambodians who lived outside their country at the time—"diplomats, high level officials, and others whose lives might be endangered if they returned to Cambodia." The remaining 125,000 places were reserved for the Vietnamese. In addition, in early April the U.S. embassy in Phnom Penh offered to evacuate important Cambodian government officials, military commanders, and persons who had worked closely with Americans and might be imprisoned or even lose their lives when the capital fell to the Khmer Rouge. The embassy staff was authorized to evacuate a thousand persons, but only eight hundred accepted that offer. Of the five thousand slots set aside for Cambodians who were abroad (and would become stateless once the Khmer Rouge set up their new government), only 4,600 were eventually filled (Loescher and Scanlan 1986: 147–69). Hundreds of these slots were used by pilots in the country's air force, who flew themselves, their family members, and their friends to safety in Thailand, and by the officers and crew of Cambodia's small navy. Sokhom Tauch, for example, whose interview appears in chapter 9, fled by sailing into international waters. Relatively few high-ranking officials, however, felt the need to leave their country, because most were convinced that once peace returned, people who had been on opposing sides of the civil war would be able to cooperate with one another and to live, once again, in peace. None of them apparently foresaw the years of agony that would ensue.

Both the ones evacuated directly from Phnom Penh and the stateless persons picked up from various countries around the world entered the United States as refugees. Along with the Vietnamese, they were processed in Guam or elsewhere and flown in U.S. military airplanes to reception centers at Camp Pendleton in California, Fort Chaffee in Arkansas, Fort Indiantown Gap in Pennsylvania, and Eglin Air Base in Florida. By the end of 1975, Vietnamese and Cambodians alike had all been resettled with the help of voluntary agencies on contract with the federal government.

Members of the 1975 cohort were admitted under the parole power of the

U.S. attorney general. At that time, refugee admission was an executive prerogative because Congress had not yet enacted a refugee law. (People admitted into the United States as refugees in earlier years did so under temporary legislation or by executive order.) Moreover, in 1975 the United States had not yet adopted the United Nations' definition of "refugee"—a person who is outside his or her country and who is unable or unwilling to return to it "owing to a well-founded fear of being persecuted for reasons of race, religion, nationality, membership of a particular social group or political opinion." Instead of treating individuals seeking refuge from various oppressive governments equally, U.S. refugee policy definitely had a cold war slant from the late 1940s through the 1980s; most of those admitted were escapees from communism. In contrast, U.S. policymakers had very little sympathy for refuge-seekers from dictatorial right-wing governments, especially if those governments were friendly to the United States (Loescher and Scanlan 1986; Sutter 1990).

Many of the five and a half thousand Cambodians rescued from the horrendous fate that befell their countrymen have played leadership roles in the Cambodian ethnic communities established since 1975 in the United States, France, and other countries. Because the Khmer Rouge killed an estimated 90 percent of the pre-1975 educated upper and middle classes (only individuals who successfully hid their former identities survived), this first batch of refuge-seekers composed the main group of Cambodians capable of helping those who escaped in later years, many of whom were farmers and fishermen with no experience living in non-Khmer-speaking, industrialized, modern societies. Just as important, because members of the 1975 group—sometimes called the "first wave"—did not experience the horrors of Pol Pot's "killing fields," they were not traumatized or physically disabled, which meant they could function normally.

The crucial role played by those who arrived in 1975 becomes immediately obvious when we look at who occupies leadership positions in Cambodian community organizations that interface with the larger American society. Forty-four of the forty-nine community leaders whom Audrey Kim interviewed told her where they were in mid-April 1975. Seventeen were outside Cambodia (seven in Thailand, seven in the United States, and one each in the Philippines, Indonesia, and India); nine left either just a few days before or right after the Khmer Rouge took Phnom Penh; and eighteen lived through the Khmer Rouge period. That is, twenty-six out of forty-four, or approximately 60 percent, of these leaders did not personally experience the brutalities of the Khmer Rouge. Among the twelve interviewees included in this book, six were abroad in 1975. Sam Chittapalo, the community relations officer in the Long Beach Police Department, was in Thailand; Chhean Kong, a Buddhist monk and psychotherapist, was studying in India; Daniel M. Lam, a government official, was studying in the United States; Hay S. Meas, a medical doctor, was in the United States trying to obtain a hospital residency; Samien Nol, an engineer, was in Thailand; and Sam-Ang Sam, an ethnomusicologist, was studying in the Philippines. Among those who fled in April 1975, Him Chhim, an agronomist, went to Vietnam. Dharamuni Phala Svy Chea, a clinical social worker who was young at the time, fled with her family to Thailand. Sokhom Tauch, a naval officer, and Bunroeun Thach, a Khmer Krom intellectual, also escaped to Thailand. Only Samkhann Khoeun, who studied engineering after he got to the United States, and Sambath Rim, the enterprising orphan, lived under the Khmer Rouge. That is to say, members of the 1975 "wave" are overrepresented among the best-educated leaders who are fluent in English. Cambodian refugees have had an extremely difficult time adapting to life in the United States. Without the presence of individuals such as those mentioned, all of whom changed occupations in order to help fellow Cambodians desperately in need, the latter's lives would have been even more difficult.

Aside from the "Westernized" multilingual cultural brokers portrayed in this book, however, there are other kinds of leaders within Cambodian refugee communities. One group may be called "traditional" leaders, who tend to be older, who emphasize the importance of maintaining and perpetuating Khmer values and norms with as few modifications as possible, and who continue to exercise tremendous influence on their ethnic communities. Although the two kinds of leaders sometimes disagree in terms of how to relate to the host society in which they all now live, the more Westernized (usually younger) leaders nevertheless are always careful to show their respect to the more traditional ones. The boards of directors of community organizations usually contain both kinds of leaders. A third group of people who play a significant role are the older women who support the Buddhist temples that have been established. It is they who keep the temple premises clean, serve the monks, chant the daily prayers and participate in other temple rituals, and prepare some of the food eaten during large celebrations on temple grounds. Even though they are deferential to men and possess no formal titles, it is these women who keep crucial cultural institutions functioning. In that sense they, too, can be considered leaders.

The next batch of refuge-seekers—the second wave—were the thirty-four thousand Cambodians who survived their escape to Thailand while the Khmer Rouge were still in power. The Thai government classified them as "displaced persons" and housed and fed them until they could be resettled in France, the United States, Australia, Canada, or elsewhere. About ten thousand of the thirty-four thousand came to the United States, also through the parole power of the attorney general.

Few people left in the months immediately following the fall of the Khmer Rouge, because the first priority of the survivors was to return to their homes or to roam the country in search of relatives who might still be alive. But by the late summer and early fall of 1979, large numbers had shown up at the Thai-Cambodian border for various reasons. Among the third wave, the largest group was on the verge of starvation. Due to the chaotic conditions accompanying the retreat of the Khmer Rouge, which coincided with the usual harvest time in January, much of the 1979 rice crop had not been harvested. As the specter of famine loomed, hundreds of thousands of starving people made their way to the Thai-Cambodian border. At the height of the exodus more than half a million Cambodians were amassed there.

The international relief agencies trying to feed them ran into almost insurmountable hurdles. The Vietnam-backed People's Republic of Kampuchea insisted that all food aid had to be distributed through Phnom Penh, with none going to the border population. International relief workers, however, were adamant that the latter must also be fed. Worse, the food shipped to Sihanoukville piled up on the docks because the country's roads had been so badly damaged that motorized vehicles could no longer be driven over them. Moreover, the trucks that Cambodians had owned before 1975 had rusted in the humid weather and fallen into disrepair because the Khmer Rouge had refused to use modern machinery or vehicles.

During this crisis, the Soviet Union, in its capacity as Vietnam's major supporter, came to the rescue, donating hundreds of trucks and sending a large contingent of technicians to repair the port, the docking and storage facilities, the cranes, and the roads. Vietnam itself supplied a large amount of emergency food to feed people within Cambodia. At the border, meanwhile, Robert Ashe, a British relief worker, persevered against all odds to create a "land bridge" between Thailand and Cambodia. The phrase *land bridge* refers to designated distribution points where people who came to the border could pick up rice and seed grain and carry it by oxcart and on their backs into the hinterland (Mason and Brown 1983; Shawcross 1984). These starving Cambodians were concerned mainly with obtaining food rather than with possible resettlement abroad as refugees.

A second contingent consisted of anticommunist Cambodians who could not stand the thought of living under yet another communist regime. Even though they were relieved and grateful for having been saved by the Vietnamese, many Khmer still considered the Vietnamese as their historic enemies.

As opponents of communist regimes, regardless of whom the leaders of those regimes might be, many of these people hoped to be accepted for resettlement in Western countries. In short, they were aspiring refugees.

A third group was made up of politically minded individuals who wanted to drive the Vietnamese out of Cambodia. They came to the border to set up military camps (Vickery 1990). The Khmer Rouge, followers of Sihanouk, and people loyal to Son Sann all had their own camps. In addition, the Khmer Serei, right-wing guerrillas who had opposed Sihanouk, had operated for decades along the border. They eventually joined Son Sann when he returned from exile and provided the initial sanctuaries for a significant portion of the tens of thousands of Cambodians who flocked to the border. The goal of the resistance leaders was to return to Cambodia to overthrow the Hun Sen-Heng Samrin government and not to leave the country.

A fourth group consisted of entrepreneurs hoping to make money or at least to feed their families by engaging in trade. Given the severe shortage of all kinds of consumer goods in both Cambodia and Vietnam, cross-border traders could make sizable profits if they managed to survive the land mines, bandits, and soldiers who extorted them along the way (Vickery 1990). The soldiers considered these traders to be smugglers and showed no qualms in taking away their goods or shooting them dead. Most traders were not really looking for a chance to move to foreign countries but rather to make a living.

Unfortunately for all four groups of Cambodians gathered at the border, they had reached Thailand during the very years when hundreds of thousands of Vietnamese and Sino-Vietnamese were escaping by unseaworthy boats to Thailand, Malaysia, Singapore, Indonesia, the Philippines, and Hong Kong, which became "countries of first asylum." Additional tens of thousands of lowland Lao and Hmong were also seeking sanctuary in Thailand, which they reached after crossing the Mekong River. Until September 1977, people who had fled from Vietnam, Laos, and Cambodia into Thailand were housed in holding centers set up under the aegis of the United Nations High Commissioner for Refugees (UNHCR) but administered by the Thai government. They were given presumptive refugee status (that is, the very act of escape was considered sufficient proof of their refugee status), interviewed, and eventually resettled in "countries of second asylum"—the United States, Canada, Australia, France, and several dozen other countries around the world.

As the initial trickle quickly turned into a flood, however, this generous policy changed abruptly. In 1978 ninety thousand "boat people" from Vietnam landed at the neighboring Southeast Asian countries of first asylum, while sixty thousand "land people" from Laos entered Thailand. The influx doubled in 1979 when an even larger number of arrivals from Vietnam and Laos was augmented by approximately 140,000 Cambodians who showed up during the late spring, summer, and early fall of that year. The countries of first asylum reacted harshly to a situation getting increasingly out of control. Shore patrols in Malaysia pushed boats back to sea after giving the refuge-seekers food, water, and fuel, turning away more than fifty thousand "boat people" while threatening to deport another seventy thousand who had already been placed into UNHCR holding centers. Indonesia and the Philippines soon followed in Malaysia's footsteps, although on a far smaller scale. Some "boat people" became so desperate that they chopped their boats up with hatchets and tried to swim to shore, drowning those unable to swim (Robinson 1998; Sutter 1990).

To deal with this international crisis, sixty-five nations met at Geneva in June 1979. Participants eventually agreed on three things: Vietnam would stop forcing people out, countries of first asylum would continue to house the "boat people" temporarily, and countries of second asylum would increase their intake of refugees. The Geneva conference, however, did not discuss "land people" at all, probably because their numbers were smaller and they did not have the same kind of sensationalized media coverage that the "boat people" received. Thailand, which was taking in more "land people" than any other country, became desperate. The number of refuge-seekers came to about 1 percent of the total Thai population of fifty-five million. Thailand, a still-developing country without sufficient land for all its peasant population, could ill afford to support the sudden influx. The Thai prime minister moaned that his country was not being "flooded" but "drowned" by the desperate and destitute displaced persons.

Thai officials established a policy of "humane deterrence" to deal with their dilemma. They began with a change in labels. Instead of calling the refuge-seekers "displaced persons," they labeled them "illegal immigrants" or "illegal entrants." Thai immigration law stipulated that illegal immigrants could be arrested, jailed, and deported. The Thai government also announced that, henceforth, the camps housing illegal entrants would be operated at an "austere" level, providing only the barest of necessities. Moreover, new arrivals were not allowed to be interviewed by representatives of foreign countries—interviews to determine whether they could be resettled abroad. Finally, Thailand's borders would be closed (McNamara 1989; Muntarbhorn 1992). Despite these measures, the refuge-seekers kept coming.

During this period, Thailand's treatment of the Vietnamese, Sino-Vietnamese, Lao, and Hmong refuge-seekers diverged from its reception of Cambodians. The "humane deterrence" policy went into effect for lowland Lao in January 1981, for Vietnamese in September of that year, and for Hmong in April 1982. Virtually none of these groups, however, consented to be repatriated voluntarily to Vietnam and Laos. Because many Americans who had interacted with people from those two countries during the wars in Vietnam and Laos felt an obligation toward them or felt guilty about having abandoned them, the United States increased its intake of "boat people" as well as certain "land people." Thus, almost all the Vietnamese, Sino-Vietnamese, Lao, Hmong, and members of other ethnic minority groups who escaped in the late 1970s and early 1980s were interviewed and eventually resettled in countries of second asylum, Thai pronouncements notwithstanding. A rigorous screening process was put into effect only after 1989, when the exodus still continued, seemingly without end.

In contrast, Thai policy toward Cambodian refuge-seekers was harsher because their potential numbers might be in the millions. In October the Thai prime minister visited the border and was so visibly shaken by the utter misery he witnessed among the emaciated Cambodians that he reversed his country's recent decision to close the border to them. But the border remained open for Cambodians for only three months, from October 1979 to January 1980. Then the Thai government, which had a change in leadership during that period, closed it again, terrified by the possibility that the starving survivors of the Khmer Rouge would all find their way into Thailand (Robinson 1998: 68–74).

In June 1979 Thailand had dealt mercilessly with approximately forty thousand Cambodians, many of Chinese ancestry, who had crossed the border in April and May of that year. The Thai army trucked those unfortunate souls back into northwestern Cambodia and forced them at gunpoint to descend the Dangrek Mountains, which were full of land mines. Thousands were blown to bits, including women and children (Robinson 1998: 45–50). The outside world reacted in shock when news of this forced repatriation leaked out. The Thai government was pressured to refrain from using such drastic measures in the future, but it stood firm on not granting refugee status to Cambodians. In time, however, approximately a quarter million Cambodians were resettled in Western countries, almost 160,000 in the United States. How and why that happened reveals how highly politicized the process of resettling refugees from the three Southeast Asian countries has been.

All the Vietnamese, Sino-Vietnamese, Lao, and Hmong who entered Thailand were placed into UNHCR holding centers. At Thailand's request, in October 1979 the UNHCR also built a holding center, literally overnight, for Cambodians. Named Sa Kaeo (also spelled "Sakeo"), it was located in a low-lying rice paddy that flooded every time it rained. The "houses" were mere sheets of blue plastic strung up on bamboo poles. They had no walls. People slept on the bare earth. Whenever it rained, the ground on which they sat and slept turned to mud. Individuals too weak to hold themselves up sometimes suffocated, with their faces in the mud. Worse, because the latrines consisted of open pits dug close to the shelters, flies, mosquitoes, and all kinds of germs bred easily. Many of the malnourished people became sick and died. The appalling conditions at Sa Kaeo was broadcast around the world when television news reporters filmed Rosalynn Carter's visit to the camp in November 1979. The UNHCR eventually remedied the situation by moving Sa Kaeo residents to another holding center nearby that became known as Sa Kaeo 2.

The largest UNHCR holding center for Cambodians was called Khao I Dang. It was built in November 1979 to accommodate those who arrived during the three-month period when the border was open to them. Cambodians were also placed into a number of other UNHCR centers, but all of them closed by the end of 1982 and their Cambodian populations were moved into Khao I Dang or into one of the "border camps" discussed below. When Thai officials decided they must do everything in their power to deter any more Cambodians from coming, they stopped accepting refuge-seekers into UNHCR holding centers (Chan, forthcoming).

Beginning in February 1980, Cambodians who reached the border were prevented from crossing it and were placed into a different kind of camp. Called "border camps," two of the eight established for this purpose housed members of Son Sann's KPNLF, one Sihanouk's followers, and five the Khmer Rouge. The Thai government forbade UNHCR officials from entering these camps. Their residents could not be inspected, much less classified as refugees eligible for resettlement in other countries (Reynell 1989; Robinson 1998: 80–88). In this manner, Thailand hoped to reduce the "magnet effect" that had apparently been created by the UNHCR holding centers, which had drawn a seemingly unending stream of Cambodians to Thailand. However, a problem soon developed. Every year during the dry season, see-saw battles were fought between the troops of the People's Republic of Kampuchea and its Vietnamese allies on the one hand and the guerrillas of the three-way coalition composed of the Khmer Rouge, the KPNLF, and FUNCINPEC on the other hand. During the fighting, the border-camp population was often evicted and driven into Thailand. Thai troops forced them back into Cambodia as soon as fighting abated when the rains began. The Thai-Cambodian border was not clearly demarcated at the time, so it was not always clear which side of the border the Cambodians were on. To deal with that ambiguity, Thai officials created a new label, "evacuees," to signal the fact that these people were being allowed inside Thai territory only on a strictly temporary emergency basis. In other words, they could not become potential refugees (Chan, forthcoming).

Initially, the United Nations International Children's Emergency Fund and the International Committee of the Red Cross assumed responsibility for feeding the border-camp population. They asked the World Food Program to purchase the food, which that agency handed over to the Thai military, which then transported it to the camps. Once the food reached some of the camps, however, self-styled Cambodian "warlords" siphoned off a large portion for sale on the black market. In early 1982 a temporary United Nations agency, the United Nations Border Relief Operation (UNBRO), was set up to support people in the border camps (Reynell 1989). Despite UNBRO's attempts to care for them, the camp residents suffered greatly, in part because they seldom had enough to eat and in part because the very Thai paramilitary force supposed to protect them often abused them, raping women and girls and stealing the camp residents' meager belongings (Lawyers Committee for Human Rights 1987, 1989).

The United States did not object to Thailand's stringent measures, mainly because most Americans did not have the same sense of obligation toward Cambodians as they had toward Vietnamese and Hmong. No U.S. troops were ever stationed on Cambodian soil, and the only time that American G.I.s landed in Cambodia was during a brief incursion following Sihanouk's overthrow. U.S. military advisors who aided the Cambodian army during Sihanouk's and Lon Nol's rule interacted mainly with high-ranking officers rather than with the rank and file. Thus, unlike the situation in Vietnam, few Americans had established personal relationships with ordinary Cambodians. Most Americans therefore felt less obligation to "save" them once the sympathy elicited by their haunting images flashing across America's television screens faded from memory.

In contrast to the border-camp population, the Cambodians in Khao I Dang were eligible to be interviewed as potential refugees because they lived in a UNHCR holding center. The fact that they happened to arrive at the border during the three months it was open, not their personal political history, distinguished their fate from that of Cambodians confined in the border camps. Even though some Khao I Dang residents also encountered acts of violence and all of them experienced extreme anxiety, not knowing when or where they might be resettled, they could hope for a better life somewhere, someday. When the difference between the border camps and Khao I Dang became known, people began to sneak into Khao I Dang at night or to bribe their way in. Thus, the center's population failed to decline as rapidly as expected as the resettlement process progressed, because even as people moved out, others sneaked in to replenish the holding center's population (Chan, forthcoming).

The massive refugee exodus from Vietnam, Laos, and Cambodia spurred Congress to speed the legislative process required to pass a refugee act. Lawmakers had debated various bills for some years. The version that became the Refugee Act of 1980 had two major objectives: to "respond to the urgent needs of persons subject to persecution in their homelands" and to provide "a permanent and systematic procedure for the admission to this country of refugees of special humanitarian concern to the United States." The law also contained six provisions: first, to adopt the U.N. definition of "refugee"; second, to set an annual quota of fifty thousand refugees (although that number could be changed through an annual consultation between the executive branch and Congress); third, to provide a flexible but orderly procedure for dealing with emergencies if refugees of "special humanitarian concern to the United States" could not be accommodated within the fifty thousand ceiling; fourth, to give Congress, rather than the president, paramount control over U.S. refugee policy; fifth, to provide a more clearly defined basis for political asylum; and, sixth, to establish and fund federal agencies to oversee refugee resettlement (Jorgensen 1989; Zucker and Zucker 1992: 62–63).

Even after this law came into effect, it was extremely difficult to determine which Cambodians qualified for resettlement as refugees in the United States. The Thai government's decision to close the border as well as the UNHCR holding centers to people who arrived after the end of January 1980 helped limit the number of potential refugee applicants, but it did not solve the problem of which of those already in the holding centers were eligible for resettlement. The dilemma arose from the fact that many Cambodians in the UNHCR holding centers were Khmer Rouge soldiers or their civilian hostages. The two successive Sa Kaeo holding centers and the UNHCR centers at Mairut and Kamput housed Khmer Rouge affiliates almost entirely. Understandably, no country wanted to admit any Khmer Rouge as refugees. U.S. immigration law specifically denies refugee status to "any person who ordered, incited, or otherwise participated in" the persecution of others. U.S. immigration officials were put in a quandary, however, because everyone placed into an UNHCR holding center had an implicit right to be interviewed for potential resettlement. The Thai military tried to solve the problem by sending about nine thousand Khmer Rouge back to Cambodia, but the Hun Sen-Heng Samrin government did not want them and forced them back across the Thai-Cambodian border. The Thai government then placed them into the five border camps under Khmer Rouge control. However, thousands of Khmer Rouge had also been transferred into Khao I Dang when the other UNHCR holding centers were closed. There, they quietly mingled with the other residents, who still feared them and were consequently too afraid to finger them. Thus, despite their best efforts, U.S. immigration officials who interviewed refugee applicants unwittingly did let some Khmer Rouge into the United States—at least according to other Cambodians now living in this country who claim to recognize them (Chan, forthcoming).

In early 1981 the U.S. refugee admission program alloted thirty thousand slots to Cambodians. The first twenty thousand chosen either had family members in the United States or had some connection with Americans before 1975. That is, prior or current relationships got them into the United States rather than proof of political persecution or potential persecution. Even though the 1980 Refugee Act mandated that persecution or potential persecution be used as the operating principle, that law, as part of the overall U.S. immigration program, nevertheless reflected the twin principles underlying post-1965 immigration law: family reunification and the admission of persons who had skills needed in the American economy.

After the twenty thousand were sent on their way, the selection process became very difficult, and the rejection rate began to increase. The U.S. State Department wanted to admit as many of the Cambodians still left in Khao I Dang as possible in order to salve the anxiety of Thai officials who feared they might be burdened with tens of thousands of unwanted people. In contrast, U.S. Immigration and Naturalization Service (INS) officials interviewing Cambodians in Thailand tried to be far more restrictive. The staff of the Joint Voluntary Agencies, which had been contracted by the State Department to prepare the applicants' dossiers, were quite sympathetic to the Cambodians and criticized INS officials for inconsistencies in the selection process. The disagreements among these various organizations repeatedly delayed Khao I Dang's closing.

The processing of potential Cambodian refugees was also influenced by a number of advocacy groups that had emerged to lobby Congress. Pro-Cambodian spokespersons such as Foreign Service officers Sheppard Lowman and Lionel Rosenblatt, Leo Cherne of the Citizens' Commission for Indochinese Refugees, and member of Congress Stephen Solarz apparently thought the amount of suffering rather than proof of persecution should be the key consideration in terms of whom to admit (Loescher and Scanlan 1986: 151–67). The INS relented in the face of pressure from so many directions. Its field officers in Thailand eventually deviated from the strict guidelines they had initially followed, and several thousand persons who did not qualify as refugees, regardless of how laxly the rules were applied, were allowed to enter as humanitarian parolees.

Consequently, many more Cambodians than the thirty thousand originally intended managed to come to the United States. Between 1975, when the Khmer Rouge seized power, and 1994, when the U.S. Cambodian refugee program was terminated, a total of 148,665 Cambodians entered the United States as refugees; 6,335 as immigrants (mainly people who had family members, some of whom were only distant relatives, already residing in the United States); and 2,518 as humanitarian parolees (Chan, forthcoming). Those numbers have been augmented since 1994 by an influx of approximately one thousand immigrants per year and by the birth of a large number of children of Cambodian ancestry on American soil. A return migration is also in progress. Some well-educated, idealistic individuals have returned to participate in the reconstruction of Cambodia. As for those who now live in the United States, even though outsiders may think they are fortunate, their lives have not been easy.

Life in the United States

Many factors have influenced where the Cambodians who entered the United States as refugees, immigrants, and humanitarian parolees settled and how they have fared. These factors are, first, federal policy that sought to disperse the refugees as widely as possible; second, the location of voluntary agencies, which assumed major responsibility under federal contract for resettling the refugees, and of sponsors; third, the location of the refugees' own relatives and friends; fourth, the magnet effect of emerging Cambodian ethnic communities; fifth, the climate in various places; sixth, the different amount of public assistance ("welfare") offered by the fifty states; seventh, the role played by the Khmer Guided Placement Project (sometimes called the Khmer Cluster Project); eighth, the availability of cheap private or federally subsidized public housing; ninth, the availability of entry-level jobs and vocational training programs; tenth, the location of Khmer Theravada Buddhist temples and monks; eleventh, the initiatives taken by certain individuals who have made extraordinary efforts to help Cambodian refugees; and twelfth, the perceived degree of friendliness versus the extent of antagonism toward refugees in particular places.

As the federal government prepared to resettle the first batch of 130,000 Vietnamese and Cambodians in April 1975, it decided to reduce the fiscal and social impact they would have on any single American community by dispersing them around the nation. Their placement, however, was not entirely random. Rather, where the refugees went depended on the location of the individuals, organizations, or social service agencies that agreed to sponsor them. Sponsorship required a great deal of time, effort, and money. Sponsors provided housing (either in their own homes or in rented houses or apartments), food, kitchen utensils or even major appliances, and clothing for the refugees. They also helped enroll the children in school and the adults in English-as-a-second-language classes or vocational training programs. They even drove the refugees to medical appointments, classes, appointments with social service providers, or grocery stores and helped them in myriad other ways to adapt to life in the United States. Some sponsors treated their guests with extraordinary kindness, others exploited the refugees by making them work for very low wages or without pay in their own homes or business enterprises, still others became burned out and abandoned their wards. Because many sponsors were local churches scattered across the United States, a good number of Vietnamese, Cambodians, Lao, Hmong, and other refugee groups ended up in places where relatively few other Asians lived. Refugees were also sponsored by their Cambodian relatives or friends, but there were not too many of those because fewer than a thousand Cambodians lived in the United States in April 1975 (Coleman 1990: 362–63). Most of the pre-1975 arrivals were college students, military officers and professionals in the United States for advanced training, staff at the Cambodian embassy in Washington, D.C., employees of the Voice of America, and Khmer language teachers at the Foreign Languages Institute in Monterey, California.

Today, the largest Cambodian community outside Cambodia is found in Long Beach, California. The significance of the third, fourth, fifth, and sixth factors listed previously is illustrated by how this community became established and how it grew so fast. In the 1950s and 1960s, before Sihanouk severed diplomatic relations with the United States, several hundred Cambodian students had come to America for higher education. The two largest contingents graduated with degrees in various branches of engineering and agricultural sciences from the Long Beach and Los Angeles campuses of the California State University system (not to be confused with the University of California system, which is also state-supported). In 1958 the students at Long Beach State University formed the Cambodian Students Association of America. Almost all the college graduates returned home, but a few came back to Long Beach in the late 1960s and early 1970s as political instability increased in their country. Seven Cambodian families and some single individuals were living in Long Beach in April 1975, when approximately a thousand Cambodians arrived at Camp Pendelton. The Long Beach Cambodian residents immediately went to the camp to welcome their compatriots. They, as well as some Long Beach State University professors who had taught Cambodian students, sponsored several hundred of these first wave refugees, who, accordingly, settled in Long Beach (Shaw 1989). In December 1975 the Cambodian Students Association of America changed its name to the Cambodian Association of America, incorporated itself, and began to provide needed social services to the refugees. Him Chhim and Samthoun Chittapalo provide details on the growth of the Cambodian community in Long Beach (chapters 1 and 3).

The Long Beach Cambodian community grew slowly in the late 1970s as more people who had successfully escaped from the Khmer Rouge regime trickled in. By the time the Vietnamese army drove the Khmer Rouge out of Phnom Penh, there were perhaps ten thousand Cambodians in the United States. After the United States decided to admit Cambodian refugees, the Long Beach Cambodian population dramatically increased. By the mid-1980s an estimated thirty-five thousand Cambodians called the city home. Even though they lived in the run-down, inner-city area, their presence, especially the dozens (and eventually hundreds) of small businesses they established, became a magnet that drew Cambodians from elsewhere in the United States via a process called secondary migration. At its peak in the late 1980s and early 1990s, the Long Beach Cambodian community numbered more than fifty thousand (Shaw 1989; Tan 1999; Welaratna 1998). Although Cambodians from around the world continue to drift in, others moved away during the 1990s due to their fear of earthquakes and to escape the gang violence that wracked the community from the mid-1980s to the mid-1990s (Chan, forthcoming).

A survey of Indochinese refugees published by Vietnamese American scholar Van H. Nguyen in 1993 showed that 76 percent of them had engaged in secondary migration in search of a warmer climate, 67 percent had moved to join relatives and friends, 33 percent to find better employment and vocational training opportunities, and 20 percent to obtain a larger amount of public assistance (quoted in Hein 1995: 53–54). (The percentages total more than one hundred because people could choose more than one reason.) Although data on the Cambodian respondents in this study cannot be disaggregated, it can be assumed that the motives of Cambodian secondary migrants show roughly the same distribution. The balmy weather in southern California, the nucleus of Cambodians in Long Beach, the possibility of setting up small businesses in that city to serve a largely coethnic clientele, and the fact that California's public assistance is much more generous than that offered by many other states have all helped to draw Cambodian secondary migrants to Long Beach.

Federal officials in charge of refugee resettlement did not like the second-ary migration phenomenon at all because it contradicted their policy, which was to disperse the refugees as widely as possible. To reduce the number of Cambodians flocking to Long Beach, the Office of Refugee Resettlement decided in the spring of 1980 to fund a demonstration project called the Khmer Guided Placement Project. Its goal was to resettle three hundred to a thousand Cambodians each in twelve cities. Various characteristics in-fluenced the choices of location. Each was not yet heavily impacted by the influx of Indochinese refugees, had relatively cheap housing, had plenty of entry-level jobs for people who could not speak English well or at all, and already had a small number of Cambodian residents who could assist the new arrivals. The twelve cities, in alphabetical order, were Atlanta, Boston, Chi-cago, Cincinnati, Columbus, Dallas, Houston, Jacksonville, New York City, Phoenix, Richmond, and Rochester. Altogether, more than eight thousand Cambodians were resettled in these cities during the early 1980s (Chan, forth-coming; Coleman 1990: 371–74).

Several problems plagued the project, but overall it can be considered a success—at least in terms of the federal government's objectives. First, the out-migration rate from all except one of these cities has been relatively low. Second, a very large percentage of the resettled Cambodians have found jobs—albeit at low wages—and a significant number have even bought their own homes. The only unsuccessful site was New York City, where at least one-third of the Cambodians resettled under the aegis of the Khmer Guided Placement Project have moved elsewhere. Social service agencies had warned that non-English speaking and mostly uneducated farmers and fishermen would find it virtually impossible to function in this fast-paced city; unfor-tunately, the project's directors did not listen to their advice (Chan forthcom-ing: chapter 4).

The factors that led to the influx of Cambodians into Long Beach and the various Khmer Guided Placement Project sites were structural. They arose from decisions made and carried out by the government or its contractual representatives and by groups of individuals, some of whom had organized themselves. Such organized groups are part of the institutions that make up a society's social structure. A few idiosyncratic factors have also been at work, however, as illustrated by the growth of the second-largest Cambodian eth-nic community in the United States in Lowell, Massachusetts.

Two individuals, Peter Pond and Kitty Dukakis, played critical roles in welcoming Cambodian refugees to New England. Pond, a graduate of Yale Divinity School, went to Thailand in early 1980, where he helped to estab-lish a Buddhist temple at the Sa Kaeo holding center. When Thai authorities tried to forcibly repatriate the center's residents (almost all of whom were Khmer Rouge or their civilian hostages), they refused to go. The monk at the temple declared it a sanctuary, so thousands gathered there. The Thai arrested Pond for his interventionist role and imprisoned him for a week. When Queen Sirikit heard about how Pond had been mistreated by her country's military personnel, she made amends by offering him three wishes. In response, Pond selected three Cambodian boys to take back to the United States. In time, Pond and his wife adopted more Cambodian youngsters (Sheehy 1984). After returning home, he traveled around New England, talking to church groups and urging them to become sponsors. Moved by his stories, many did so. And that is how Cambodians were resettled in small towns in western Massachusetts and elsewhere in New England (Burton 1983).

Pond also talked to Kitty Dukakis, who had been involved in projects to commemorate the Jewish and Armenian holocausts. Moved by the plight of Cambodians, she added them to her concerns. She, too, traveled to Thailand to witness the miserable situation at the border and testified before Congress after arriving home. More important, she urged her husband, then-governor Michael Dukakis, to make Massachusetts a "refugee-friendly state." He obliged by establishing a Governor's Advisory Council for Refugees and Immigrants in April 1983. A Sino-Cambodian, Daniel Lam (chapter 4), became the refugee affairs director in the governor's office. Later, Governor Dukakis issued an executive order instructing all pertinent state agencies to find ways to help refugees obtain employment. In line with its "refugee-friendly" attitude, Massachusetts did not pressure refugees to take dead-end, minimum-wage jobs as quickly as possible. Instead, refugees were encouraged to attend classes and obtain vocational training before going on the job market so they could qualify for better-paying positions.

When Cambodians first found their way to Lowell, the city was in a depression, but by the mid-1980s a boom had gotten underway as Massachusetts participated in the computer revolution. The corporate headquarters of Wang Laboratories, founded by Chinese American entrepreneur An Wang, was in Lowell. Raytheon and Digital Equipment also had factories there (Kiang 1994). These electronics assembly plants did not hesitate to hire non-English-speaking Cambodians; what mattered to them was good hand-eye coordination rather than language skills. As news spread that jobs were available, more and more Cambodian refugees flocked to Lowell. At its zenith, the Cambodian ethnic community in that city numbered some twenty-five thousand. The population declined in the early 1990s due to a recession that hit the electronics industry, but it grew again in the late 1990s as Lowell's non-Asian citizens realized the critical role that Southeast Asian refugees play in revitalizing certain areas of the city and consequently developed a more friendly attitude toward them. (The oral history of Samkhann Khoeun, a community leader in Lowell, appears in chapter 5.) Lowell was also attractive because a Buddhist temple had been established there as early as 1984.

The extraordinary importance of Buddhist temples as a determining factor in the settlement pattern of Cambodian refugees is best illustrated by the growth of a sizable Cambodian community in Providence, Rhode Island. The first temple established on the East Coast was in that city. Although it was housed in a dilapidated tenement, its first monk was a world-renowned Buddhist scholar whose presence drew many Cambodians to Providence (Lind 1989: 9). As devout Theravada Buddhists, Cambodians from all over New England, and even the mid-Atlantic states, visited the temple during major Buddhist celebrations. Some individuals even moved to Providence so they could attend the temple every day. By the mid-1990s, however, the temple had lost many adherents, in part because the head monk was thought to be too actively involved in the factional politics of the homeland (Chan, forthcoming).

Detailed statistics on specific Asian ethnic groups are not yet available from the 2000 census of population. (The preliminary statistics list Vietnamese, but not Cambodians, as a separate group.) According to the 1990 census, the states that had the three largest numbers of Cambodians were California, Massachusetts, and Washington, with, respectively, 68,190, 14,050, and 11,090 persons of Cambodian ancestry. Next-ranked were Pennsylvania and Texas, each with five to six thousand persons of Cambodian ancestry. Between one and four thousand each lived in thirteen states: Virginia, Minnesota, Rhode Island, New York, Illinois, Ohio, Georgia, Oregon, Maryland, Connecticut, Florida, North Carolina, and Colorado (in descending numerical order). Substantial Cambodian communities probably would not have materialized in Florida, Georgia, Illinois, New York, North Carolina, Ohio, Texas, and Virginia had the Khmer Guided Placement Project not existed and selected cities within them as resettlement sites. The remaining thirty-two states had fewer than a thousand Cambodians each. Community leaders, state refugee coordinators, and knowledgeable social service providers all agree, however, that the census figures are much too low.

In terms of how they have fared, Cambodians who live in the United States in the early twenty-first century can be broadly divided into three groups. The first is a small, middle-class community whose members make up about 5 percent of the population. They include older professionals who received their training before the Khmer Rouge came to power, younger professionals educated in the United States, and people who have established their own businesses. Even though many have experienced downward social mobility, and even though in terms of American standards their socioeconomic status is only middle class, they are the elite in today's Cambodian ethnic communities. As cultural brokers between their compatriots and the larger society, they try their best to formulate solutions to the most intractable problems that their communities face. As the narrators in this book attest, their concern for their fellow countrymen is genuine, and they live daily with the profound sorrow of being Khmer—a people who have suffered one catastrophe after another.

The second group, about 40 percent of the total Cambodian-ancestry population, is made up of lower-middle-class people who live in medium-sized or small cities in states that have relatively small Cambodian populations. As individuals they earn low wages, but as families they have managed to become economically self-sufficient because many families have two or more wage-earners. Despite certain cultural differences, their lives are not too different from those of America's working poor. Some hardworking individuals hold two jobs in order to earn enough money to buy homes of their own. Even though they enjoy little social prestige, most seem satisfied with their lives.

The third and largest group (about 55 percent of the total population) is made up of those who live in inner-city neighborhoods within large metropolitan areas in states that have the largest numbers of Cambodians. These people are not doing well at all. Three-quarters to four-fifths of the Cambodians in Long Beach were relying on welfare for survival in the mid-1990s. The percentage has not declined much, even after welfare reform went into effect in 1996 and limited the receipt of benefits to a life-time total of five years. That is because many welfare recipients are physically or mentally disabled. Thus, even though they may no longer be eligible for Temporary Assistance to Needy Families (TANF, which replaced AFDC, Aid to Families with Dependent Children, the major component of welfare), they continue to qualify for Supplemental Security Income (SSI). Very poor families, as well as widows raising numerous children, still qualify for food stamps. Before welfare reform, the dependency rate in Massachusetts hovered around 60 percent, and about half the Cambodians in Washington and Minnesota were also on public assistance. There are no reliable figures on how many have left the welfare rolls since 1996, because states do not collect data according to ethnicity. It is likely, however, that the percentages are still very high. The lives of welfare-dependent Cambodians are filled with helplessness, hopelessness, and despair. Living in environments filled with crime and violence, many of their children drop out of school, join gangs, or even become hardcore criminals. Thus, the conditions that keep them down are passed on to the second generation (Chan, forthcoming).

The socioeconomic status of the Cambodian American population as a whole is low. Statistical data are available from the 1980 and 1990 U.S. censuses of population. According to Chi Kwong Law (1988), who analyzed data from the 5 percent Public Use Microdata Sample of the 1980 census for each of the Southeast Asian refugee groups (*n* for Cambodians = 596) for a doctoral dissertation in social work completed at the University of California, Los Angeles, only 2.2 percent among those gainfully employed held managerial or administrative positions; 6.5 percent were professionals; 13.5 percent were technicians, salespersons, and clerical workers; 18.3 percent were service workers; 17.2 percent plied various crafts; 34.4 percent were machine operators or common laborers; and 8.1 percent were farmers and fishermen. Some improvement had occurred by the time the 1990 census was taken.

My computations using the 1990 published census data for the entire self-identified "Cambodian" population in the United States (*n* = 147,411) show that 9.8 percent of those gainfully employed had managerial and professional jobs (a 1.1 percent increase); 23.3 percent held technical, sales, and clerical positions (a 9.8 percent increase); 17.9 percent were service workers (a 0.4 percent decrease); 17.2 percent were in the various crafts (no change); 30 percent were machine operators, fabricators, and common laborers (a 4.4 percent decrease); and 1.7 percent were farmers and fishermen (a 6.4 percent decrease). (The total percentage for both censuses do not total 100 due to rounding.) Thus, approximately two-thirds of the gainfully employed were blue-collar workers in 1990, compared to 78 percent in 1980. But these statistics do not paint a complete picture due to the fact that unemployed, welfare-dependent Cambodians outnumber the gainfully employed in both census-enumeration years. It is not surprising, therefore, that the percentage of Cambodians who live below the official poverty line is almost double that of African Americans.

In addition to their daily struggles to put rice on the table and to deal with many aspects of acculturative stress that other authors have analyzed at length (Canniff 2001; Hopkins 1996; Mortland 1994a, 1994b; Palinkas and Pickwell 1995; Smith-Hefner 1999), Cambodians in America face three especially heartbreaking problems. First, their efforts to preserve the integrity of their religion, Theravada Buddhism, are being undermined by Christians, who are trying to convert them. Second, many Cambodian families in America are experiencing intense conflicts. Third, some refugees have found it well-nigh impossible to overcome the effects of the multiple traumas they suffered during the civil war, the Khmer Rouge regime, their perilous escapes, and their anxiety-filled days in refugee camps.

Compared to other groups of refugees from Vietnam, Laos, and Cambodia, relatively few adult Cambodians have converted to Christianity. Their Buddhist faith remains steadfast even though Khmer monks in America have had to modify some religious practices in order to keep them alive. Many families, however, are having a hard time trying to interest their children in Buddhism. Even when the children and teenagers are willing to attend temple events, Buddhism is not something that infuses their daily lives, because its precepts are not being reinforced by the values and norms of American society. In Cambodia, Theravada Buddhism is the official religion, and its teachings underlie all behavior. Thus, many adults worry, rightly so, about whether Buddhism has a future among second-generation Cambodian Americans (Chan, forthcoming; Mortland 1994b; Smith-Hefner 1994, 1999).

The problems within many Cambodian families in America are similar to those faced by other Asian immigrant and refugee families, but they are much more intense. (Similar intrafamilial dynamics existed in European immigrant families when large numbers of old world Europeans entered the United States in earlier centuries.) The problems arise from the fact that gender roles and the age hierarchy in the United States differ considerably from those in Asian or other old world societies, and different individuals within a family acculturate at different rates, with children becoming Americanized much faster than adults.

Even though the lives of Cambodian, lowland Lao, Thai, lowland Burmese, and Filipina women have not been as restricted as those of women in traditional China, Japan, Korea, and Vietnam, Cambodian women and girls must nevertheless follow strict rules with regard to the gendered division of labor. Although they are greatly valued for bearing and raising children, cooking, doing laundry, cleaning house, and contributing to their families' economic well-being by planting and harvesting crops, raising farm animals for household consumption and for sale, spinning yarn and weaving cloth, selling goods in the public market, or working for wages, they are expected to respect male authority and privilege at all times. Many Cambodian women manage their families' budgets and thus, from an American point of view, seem relatively powerful, but they cannot contradict their fathers, uncles, husbands, or even grown sons in public. At home, if they do not agree with the male members of their families, they are supposed to use gentle persuasion rather than confrontation to influence the men. The ideal Khmer woman is expected to be soft-spoken, calm, obedient, generous, chaste, and beautiful yet modest in dress and comportment (Ledgerwood 1994). Men, in contrast, are supposed to be strong both physically and morally; to work hard if they are self-employed or to earn enough money to support their families if they are wage-earners; and to abstain from excessive drinking, gambling, and cavorting with prostitutes in order to minimize the potential financial drain such activities might cause.

Given such ideals, Cambodian women in America who work outside the home, where they often mingle with men, are liable to become subjects of gossip. Cambodian men unable to support their families—either because they cannot get a job at all or because the wages they earn are insufficient—often become demoralized. In welfare-dependent families, wives rather than husbands now hold the key to their families' economic well-being, because the American welfare system is female-centered. It is mothers, not fathers, who receive the government checks that feed their children. The American legal and law enforcement systems, too, have created problems for Cambodian families. The divorce rate, although still comparatively very low, is rising because women can divorce more easily in the United States, suffer relatively few negative social sanctions for doing so, and are able to find jobs to support themselves and their children. Women who are victimized by domestic violence can, at least theoretically, go to temporary shelters in cities where such shelters exist, or they can call the police. In reality, however, very, very few women do so because they are too ashamed to let anyone, much less strangers, know about such incidents.

Although there are tensions between husbands and wives due to cultural and institutional differences between the United States and Cambodia, there are even greater conflicts between parents and children as a result of differences in how the concept of age hierarchy is manifested in the two societies. In Cambodian society, children are socialized to obey and respect everyone older than they (Smith-Hefner 1993, 1999). This hierarchical relationship is expected to continue even after children reach adulthood. In the United States, however, parents are supposed to be "friends" with their children, to consult them with regard to important family matters, to encourage them to speak up, and to refrain from corporal punishment. Cambodian children who grow up in the United States and imitate the behavior of their American peers can get into real trouble. In many families, children who express their opinions and feelings are sometimes punished for daring to "talk back." There are known instances of parents beating sons for wearing baggy pants and daughters for wearing tops that expose too much skin (Chan, forthcoming).

Cambodian American girls who wish to act like American teenagers lead especially difficult lives. Most of them are not permitted to date or attend parties. Although some parents do allow their daughters to go out if they are chaperoned, others forbid them to leave the house at all after they come home from school. Girls are expected to help with or even to assume major responsibility for all the household chores, while their brothers can go out with their friends or sit and do nothing. Some truly strict parents prohibit their daughters from participating in sports, even though athletics are a part of the school curriculum, because yelling and body-contact activities are offensive in the eyes of traditional Cambodians. Sex education, not surprisingly, horrifies many refugee parents. Teenagers who refuse to accept this kind of control fight with their parents, or become sullenly defiant, or rebel by running away. In search of an alternate family and lifestyle, some of these unhappy young people end up joining gangs—a fact that has caused despair among the refugees (Chan, forthcoming). To "lose" their children in this manner, after enduring the unimaginable horrors of the Khmer Rouge regime and the many hardships during their flight from their homeland, is something that breaks the hearts of Cambodian refugee parents.

To reduce the chances that their daughters' reputations might become tarnished, some Cambodian parents in America are marrying off their daughters at increasingly younger ages (Holgate 1994). Girls are forced to drop out of school and to marry boys with whom they have been friendly, even though some of these young men are not, according to American social mores, "real" boyfriends. Unfortunately, such a practice has negative consequences. Girls who do not complete their high school education cannot go to college, or help their children with homework, or find well-paying jobs.

Parents also try to control the behavior of their sons, but Cambodian boys are no exception to the rule that boys everywhere enjoy more freedom than do their sisters. The strict behavior of Cambodian parents is understandable if we remember two things. First, they are trying to protect their children from what they perceive as dangers in the environments in which they live. Second, every Cambodian who lived through the Khmer Rouge period is painfully aware that Khmer culture was almost wiped out during those few short years. Cambodians, therefore, are even more determined than other Asian immigrants to preserve their culture in whatever way possible.

Unfortunately, those whose bodies and minds have been permanently scarred by atrocities find it virtually impossible to meet the challenge of holding their families intact (D'Avanzo, Frye, and Froman 1994b; McKenzie-Pollock 1996). A large body of research has documented that the Cambodian refugee population has higher rates of posttraumatic stress disorder, major depression, dissociation, and anxiety than any other ethnic group in the

United States (Boehnlein 1987a; Carlson and Rosser-Hogan 1991, 1993; Chow et al. 1989; Clarke, Sack, and Goff 1993; Hubbard et al. 1995; Kinzie 1989, 1990; Kinzie and Boehnlein 1989; Kinzie et al. 1984, 1989; Realmuto et al. 1992; Rozee and van Boemel 1989; Sack et al. 1986; Sack et al. 1993; Sack, Clarke, and Seeley 1995, 1996; Strober 1994; Uba and Chung 1991; van Boemel and Rozee 1992; Wilkinson 1994).

Yet culturally relevant therapy for torture victims—people who have suffered what psychotherapists call massive trauma—is seldom available (Boehnlein 1987b; Frye 1991; Frye and D'Avanzo 1994). Cambodians in America have to rely on other means to deal with their nightmares, panic attacks, and startle responses (Herbst 1992; Kuoch, Miller, and Scully 1992; Lipsky and Nimol 1993). Some talk to Buddhist monks, where they are available, whereas others remain silent, keeping their distress to themselves. The interview with Chhean Kong (chapter 2) illustrates his creative attempt to merge Buddhist concepts with therapeutic techniques; in chapter 11, Phala Chea describes how the agency in which she works attempts to deal with the problems faced by Cambodian clients in a holistic way.

Some adults who are unable to manage the demands of daily life in America stay in their homes all day and seldom socialize with anyone, Khmer or non-Khmer, relying mainly on their English-speaking children to deal with the outside world. Such role reversal, however, can become yet another source of intrafamilial tensions. Among the better-educated, some cope by committing their lives to serving their ethnic communities (the interviewees in this book are examples of such individuals) and others by teaching the Khmer language or classical ballet and other arts to their children in order to preserve and revive Khmer culture.

Hundreds of refugees who have professional and technical skills have returned to Cambodia to help reconstruct their homeland. They play a multiplicity of roles and stay for varying periods of time. Some hold dual citizenship in Cambodia and in the United States and have become transnational citizens of the world. During the 1990s, almost a hundred young Cambodians who grew up in the United States went to Cambodia under the aegis of the Cambodian-American National Development Organization (CANDO) to participate in the rehabilitation of their ancestral land (chapter 8). In a country struggling to recover from years of devastation, the technical skills the CANDO volunteers have acquired in the West were put to good use. Even though the young people who grew up outside of Cambodia experienced culture shock when they first set foot on Cambodian soil, they tried to contribute in whatever ways they could. Sad to say, the CANDO program lasted only six years. It ended in 1997 when it lost its funding.

The words of the Western-educated bilingual/multilingual and bicultural/multicultural individuals contained in this book will enable readers to glimpse how Cambodians are dealing with the traumatic memories of their past, struggling with the multilayered challenges of their present, and searching for ways to create a more peaceful future for themselves and their descendants. In myriad ways they are trying their best to ensure that Cambodians will not remain victims forever.

1. Him S. Chhim
Long Beach, California,
the Capital of Cambodian America

MR. HIM S. CHHIM is the executive director of the Cambodian Association of America (CAA)—a position he has held since the beginning of 1992. Audrey Kim interviewed him on July 24, 1996, in his office at CAA located in the heart of "Little Phnom Penh" in downtown Long Beach. Mr. Chhim first came to the United States in 1962 with a scholarship from the U.S. Agency for International Development to study agriculture at the University of Georgia. He received both a bachelor of science degree and a master of science degree from that university before returning to Cambodia in 1967. He worked in the Ministry of Agriculture from 1967 to 1974. Then he left his government post to take a job with World Vision International, which was providing aid to people within Cambodia who had been displaced from their homes during the 1970–75 civil war.

He and his family fled to Vietnam when the Khmer Rouge came to power in 1975 and remained there until January 1979, when they were resettled in Flordia. At the end of 1979 he came to California and found a job with Catholic Charities in Los Angeles helping to resettle Cambodian refugees. After working at Catholic Charities for a year, he became a social worker in the Orange County Social Services Department. He stayed at that job for twelve years until he became the executive director of CAA. While working, he attended evening classes and earned a master's degree in public administration from California State University, Long Beach, in 1993.

When I talked to Mr. Chhim by telephone on September 24, 2001, he told me that CAA had bought a building and moved into its new quarters on Pacific Avenue in July 2001. Even though the new location is about two miles from Little Phnom Penh, it is easily accessible by public transportation. CAA's budget has increased to almost $3 million a year, with funds from the federal, state, and county governments as well as grants from private foundations. The CAA had thirty-five staff members in 2001 and planned to hire more. On October 1, 2001 its family preservation program would begin to handle non-Asian (that is, European American, African American, and Latino American) cases in addition to Cambodian and Vietnamese ones. The new initiative is funded by the Department of Children's Services, which named CAA as the lead agency in this multiethnic effort. CAA has also begun a mental health outreach program in an attempt to help Cambodians understand the importance of seeking professional help.

When asked what major changes have occurred in the Long Beach Cambodian community since the mid-1990s, Mr. Chhim replied that the population had stabilized, and relatively few Cambodians were moving into or out of the area. Welfare reform has made life even more difficult for about 80 percent of the city's Cambodian residents. When a family's lifetime eligibility of five years runs out under the Temporary Assistance to Needy Families (TANF, which replaced Aid to Families with Dependent Children, AFDC, in 1996), parents are cut off from public assistance, thereby reducing each family's allocated amount by $225 a month. As was the case before welfare reform, children who reach the age of eighteen are no longer eligible for public assistance. Even though the amount a poor family receives in food stamps may increase a little, destitute people are barely able to put food on the table, especially as rents continue to increase. Some Cambodians previously on public assistance have found part-time menial work, sometimes earning less than minimum wage, often at businesses operated by fellow Khmer or other Asian entrepreneurs. The gang problem has abated somewhat, but it still plagues the community. The main improvement that has occurred, Mr. Chhim observed, is that more Cambodians now know something about American society and have learned to survive in a complex institutional environment. Despite the problems they face in the United States, very few families have returned to Cambodia because their children are thoroughly Americanized and do not know Khmer well enough to attend school there.

Mr. Chhim still hopes to return to Cambodia some day to participate in its reconstruction. He visited his homeland for several months in 1998 but could not remain there because he had not found anyone to take over his job at CAA. Before he retires he would like very much to contribute to the rehabilitation of Cambodia—a country ravaged by decades of war and revolution.

*   *   *

AK: Because you have limited time, I'd like to focus on certain topics. Scholars and social service providers have often compared Vietnamese and Cambodian refugees, especially in terms of how their children are doing in school. In your opinion, is it fair to make such a comparison?

HC: No, it is very unfair. Among our people, those who survived the "killing fields" were physically the fittest. They were farmers with an agrarian background and very little education. They had little exposure to urban society and urban life, let alone a Western, capitalistic society.

AK: Can you tell me about your organization, the Cambodian Association of America, what it does, how it's different from other Cambodian organizations? I'd also like to hear about your impressions of the Cambodian community in Long Beach. For example, what are the adults doing? The children doing? Then, if there's time, I'd like to ask you something about yourself because it's always interesting to see how someone like yourself got to be in this sort of leadership position.

HC: CAA is the first nonprofit Cambodian American organization to be recognized in the United States. We were incorporated in December 1975, after the first wave of just a few thousand Cambodian refugees had arrived in the United States. Camp Pendleton was the camp that housed these first Cambodian refugees. The first wave consisted of professionals who were on training assignments abroad. They were outside of Cambodian borders in April 1975—diplomatic personnel, their civilian staff, high-ranking military officers, and navy men on battleships. Some had fled the country all of a sudden, such as the pilots who left with their planes.

AK: You mean, originally, the organization was set up by students who were here who helped that first wave?

HC: In April 1975, there was a small group of Cambodian students in the United States who had not returned home, perhaps one or two dozen people. Perhaps close to two hundred students from Cambodia came to the U.S. for training in the 1960s; many studied at Cal State Long Beach and Cal State L.A. I myself came to the United States as a foreign student in the early 1960s.

AK: Why were those universities so popular with Cambodians?

HC: There was an agreement between the U.S. and Cambodian governments. The United States was to promote vocational training, such as mechanical engineering and so forth, in Cambodia. The U.S. was also to build an engineering school in Cambodia. That was the original plan but it was not realized any further after the rupture of diplomatic relations in 1967.

AK: Does that mean if all those students hadn't been in Long Beach, Long Beach wouldn't be the center of Cambodian America?

HC: That's true. The embryo of Long Beach was the group of Cambodian students who had been studying there in the 1960s. There was a Cambodian Students Association, which held weekend social gatherings, but among them was a group of students looking for more structure to provide some kind of mutual assistance. When the former students found out that their fellow countrymen had come to Camp Pendleton, they rushed to help their own people. At the time, they sponsored their friends, families, and other Cambodians out of Camp Pendleton. Former professors and acquaintances [also] sponsored our people out of the camp. Thus the Long Beach Cambodian community grew.

AK: Do you know about how many Cambodians originally settled in this area in 1975? Two hundred students plus how many out of Camp Pendleton?

HC: No, there were not two hundred students. Out of the original two hundred or so students who had come to the U.S., 80 to 90 percent had already returned to Cambodia; only a dozen or two still remained. This small group was responsible for receiving and cooking for their own people at Camp Pendleton. I can't pin down the exact number of Cambodian refugees who originally came to Camp Pendleton at that time, but I guesstimate it to be no more than a thousand or two at first. We're talking about trainees abroad and the military personnel who had fled on the military aircrafts or the small battleships. We didn't have a big air force or navy at that time.

AK: So, in 1975 maybe about a thousand Cambodians were settled here?

HC: Yes, at most maybe two thousand. They composed the first wave, who did quite well, considering that they had been educated, had professional backgrounds and work skills. For example, the French-speaking military officers did not have a hard time learning English and finding jobs. The first wave did OK.

AK: What kinds of jobs did they get?

HC: They could not be choosey in the beginning; they did all kinds of work. Many among the first wave did not have the patience to learn English and other skills. Most middle-aged people went into small businesses; doughnut shops were one of the first businesses they chose. Cambodians followed the footsteps of the Koreans and the Japanese into small businesses, such as the food industries, gas stations, groceries, liquor stores, and the like.

AK: Mostly in Long Beach or in other parts of L.A.?

HC: Mostly in Long Beach; a very few resettled in the Chinatown area of Los Angeles.

AK: One thing I noticed just walking around here is that there are lots of jewelry stores, which I didn't see when I went to other Cambodian communities. Can you tell me about that?

HC: There is a very high concentration of various Cambodian-owned businesses along the Anaheim Corridor: souvenir shops, restaurants, groceries, clothing stores, jewelry stores. Jewelry stores are not representative of our community of fifty thousand–plus people. No more than two-thirds of the businesses are jewelry stores. We also have pawnshops because gambling is a big problem in our community.

AK: You're saying that maybe some of the jewelry stores—not a lot, but some—are associated with pawnshops. And the pawnshops are getting goods from people who are gambling.

HC: That's correct. Gambling is one big problem in our community, and there is no program to address that. We have talked to the police department; they say there is nothing much they can do.

AK: What kind of gambling?

HC: Blackjack. We Cambodians have our own kind called French-style blackjack. There are all sorts of card playing, a game with numbers, etc.

AK: It's so easy to get sidetracked because everything you're saying is so interesting. Back to the organization . . .

HC: The idea of the organization came from the former students of the 1960s. The idea, the embryo, was born in Camp Pendleton. Out of the camp grew the idea that we needed to have our own Cambodian association. CAA got incorporated in 1975. There was no funding at all, not even an office; somebody's garage had to be used. Later on, from the Cambodian members' contributions, we did succeed in raising enough funds to rent a storefront space.

AK: When was that?

HC: I was not here to witness all of those occurences, but I've heard of them through word of mouth. That's why I cannot pinpoint the exact year. Maybe 1977, 1978, when a few hundred people were helping to manage our agency. We did have storefront office space; we had ESL [English-as-a-second-language] classes taught by volunteers. We had volunteers to teach our people about American society, helping to orient us. Children got to continue learning our Khmer script. I volunteered in the early '80s to teach children the Cambodian language Saturday and Sunday mornings. After that, [the Department of] Children's Services gave us a small grant of a couple of thousand dollars.

AK: You weren't getting money from ORR—the Office of Refugee Resettlement?

HC: No, not during that early period. We didn't receive federal government funding until 1980 or 1981, when we received one big grant from the Office of Refugee Resettlement. We had a nationwide program to help resettle additional refugees during the Carter years, with twelve sites across the United States—from the state of New York to Florida.

AK: You mean CAA was involved with resettling people all over the country?

HC: At one time, our agency was, yes.

AK: Was that related to the Khmer Guided Placement Project?

HC: Yes, we were the soul of that program. We were the only [Cambodian American] office that was involved in that. We helped to establish and incorporate other groups. We were going to various states and settling several dozen families in each city. We tried to define leadership and to get the potential leaders together. We helped them form their own MAAs [Mutual Assistance Associations]. To get started, they could use our charter so that they became a chapter of our principal organization based here in Long Beach. Later on, they got to incorporate on their own, inside their own state, under their own state law. We did that in Illinois, Florida, New York, all over.

AK: You mean, you helped resettle people and establish communities, and that some of the MAAs started under your charter?

HC: Yes, community organizations for empowerment. Later, they created their own organizations.

AK: Until you got money from ORR, did you have only ad hoc contributions?

HC: Yes. That nationwide resettlement project was based on one-time-only funding. It was a model project; it was not designed to continue. The urgency was due to the many refugees who were left behind in the Thai border camps, and the U.S. government felt, at that time, that there must be some measure to relieve the strain over there. That's why we brought in a larger number of Cambodian refugees at that time.

AK: My understanding is that the program wasn't wholly successful because a lot of those people ended up coming to Long Beach eventually anyway.

HC: A small component of the program entailed counseling our people and settling them away from Long Beach. To tell you the truth, there was too much pushing and pulling. There were many magnets, many attractive points, connected with Long Beach. We cannot disregard the people's welfare. The weather is better here. The warmth comforts our own kind. Chinese people, no matter how successful they are, try to live within their own communities. They feel better; they have a sense of belonging; they feel comfort in having the opportunity to talk Chinese among themselves. The Japanese lived among themselves as well. They have Little Tokyo and Japantown.

There are also concentrations of Russians and Poles living together all over. It's nothing new. But the unique experience of our people must be remembered—the trauma we have suffered; the need for a community is therefore stronger for us. There is a comfort and convenience in having our own grocery stores here; we have a lot more here than in any other town. I lived once in a small town in Florida; I could not even find soy sauce, let alone fish sauce, or the other ingredients we use a lot and enjoy in our cooking. We could not even find soy sauce anywhere. We kept longing; we have survived being killed, but we cannot enjoy life when a community of our own is lacking. Here, in a new environment, it's too strange. If we find some soy sauce, we find some comfort already. There are many explanations for the growth of Long Beach.

AK: It seems like it's natural that in a strange country, you want to come together. But the fact that Long Beach was the place was probably because of those early students?

HC: Yes, the early students and the snowballing effect.

AK: Do you find that Cambodians are continuing to move to Long Beach?

HC: No, I don't think so now. It has pretty much stabilized now. I sense that there are as many moving out of Long Beach as coming in. At one time, we participated in a program that moved families from, say, here to Colorado, where it's calm and peaceful with less crime and with good-paying jobs. A couple of years ago, they started to build a new airport in [Denver,] Colorado; there are many industries and much manufacturing there.

AK: Your organization was involved in moving people to Colorado?

HC: We were involved. They called it the secondary migration program. ORR funded an association in Colorado, but we were the partners in Long Beach that helped people to go that way. Welfare is not the best system for all people. Every group has had that experience.

AK: Do you find that a lot of Cambodians are receiving public assistance?

HC: Yes, too many of us are receiving public assistance. Pol Pot, during the "killing fields" years, killed too many Khmer men. In Cambodia, the whole family depended mostly on one person who was the male breadwinner. After the men were killed, women were left alone to head the family. They had never worked for wages, had never been to school, and had no employable skills whatsoever. In addition to the traumatic experience, and the posttraumatic stress syndrome, having to raise their children all alone is quite a hardship for Cambodian women and they don't know what to do. The opportunity and the hope to learn English, as well as a skill in order to get a job, is a very remote possibility. I don't say all, but some Cambodians have to rely on welfare since there is no other choice.

AK: So, a lot of the hardship has to do with the fact that many of the households here are headed by women and women aren't used to being the breadwinners in Cambodia?

HC: That's true. Women have not been, in our traditional environment, the heads of households. It is not customary for as many girls to go to school as boys. Survival of the fittest. The Cambodian refugees who are here now are from rural backgrounds. You have to remember that they have a farming background and a low educational level.

AK: You mean physically they're the fittest but not in terms of fitting into this society?

HC: Yes, they experience great difficulty in fitting into this environment.

AK: What percentage of the households here in Long Beach are headed by women?

HC: Between 65 and 70 percent. Very high. Men have been eliminated or killed. Former military men or policemen, government employees and the like have been eliminated by the Khmer Rouge.

AK: What percent of families are on public assistance?

HC: Close to 70 percent, I guess. I'm afraid to say for sure—there are no statistics or fresh data available. I would guesstimate over 50 percent is the benchmark. They are not employed nor skilled. They have not found work and are on public assistance.

AK: But are the people who came during the first wave all working?

HC: Most of the refugees who composed the first wave, maybe 90 percent, are working.

AK: What is the attitude toward public assistance? Is it OK or is it stigmatized?

HC: It is a stigma. After welfare reform began, I feel for my people. I worry for my people when we hear about or talk about welfare reform. Many of the programs [to ease the transition] are not well designed to serve our people, including ESL classes; perhaps they are good for the mainstream—people who have a better educational background.

AK: From what I understand, many Cambodians aren't even literate in their own language.

HC: That's true. The average education of a Cambodian refugee would be no more than two and a half or three years. They're barely literate in their own language. They may read, but they cannot write their own language. The majority of them neither read nor write their own language. That means English is a difficult skill for them to acquire. We don't even use the same alphabet. Even the Hmong use the same alphabet as English: A, B, C. We have our own script so they would have to start all over again with English. Many of them haven't even learned Khmer. And what about self-esteem? What about mental health, what about loneliness, depression, and all those kinds of things that come up in their lives? They have to survive; they have to live from day to day. They have to think about what to do to help their children. Plus, role modeling is a problem. I didn't quite finish talking about our organization, so let's get back to that topic. Our organization is a small agency with a grant here and there.

AK: It seems like it was quite successful in getting the first wave resettled.

HC: We now help troubled families and children with problems. In domestic disputes, we have to go into each home and talk to the parents and children about how to get along to preserve the family, to increase their self-esteem.

AK: Were you involved with families in the beginning, too?

HC: Yes. Now, one of the missions of our program is to preserve the family. Children who are not doing well, who skip school, who don't come home, are on their way to foster family placements. To do a complete turnaround, there is one program we call Family Preservation, and it is funded by the Department of Children's Services, through the lead agencies inside the city of Long Beach, such as Family Preservation Services or Long Beach Youth Center. We have social worker–type employees with bachelor's degrees to counsel and deal with the families. The main component is home counseling. We want to talk to the parents, all the adults, and all the children in the families in order to do a turnaround in five or six months. It's a very successful program.

AK: How many families have you worked with in that way?

HC: We have three counselors. At any one time, one counselor cannot manage more than eight families.

AK: That's a lot.

HC: That's a lot because for each family we have to go see the family twice a week in their own home in order to provide the right counseling. It's hard work, but we are seeing results.

AK: Would you say that most of the family problems are caused by intergenerational differences?

HC: Yes. I'll give you a scenario typical of our people. The mother does not speak English. The mother-child bonding relationship was exemplary among our people. From day one to about one and a half years of age, the child is on mom's lap all the time. Much physical bonding took place—something that cannot be achieved even among the mainstream folks. There was the best bonding possible between mother and baby. Up to about age two or three, the child knows Khmer, the mother tongue back home, because the mother doesn't speak anything else besides Khmer. Then, the infant starts kindergarten and learns some English very, very fast in school. The same infant forgets Khmer at about the same rate.

AK: I thought maybe here it would not be as big a problem because there are so many Cambodian students in the schools. I thought they would speak Khmer to each other and maintain their knowledge of the language. You're not seeing that?

HC: No. From age four or five on, they forget Khmer completely. All of a sudden, we find they are very comfortable speaking English. They forget Khmer altogether. All of a sudden, the mother and child do not communicate. There's a complete barrier; there is no communication whatsoever. That's when the problem starts. Mother doesn't know what's happening with the child's education. How can mothers help with the kids' homework? They cannot even read to their babies. Before long, there's a complete communication barrier between parents and children.

AK: I've heard other people also say that the parents' authority is undermined because they can't speak English. The children have to translate.

HC: That's right. That results in child abuse.

AK: You see child abuse, too?

HC: Yes. For example, the parents say, "I'm still your mom. I'm still your dad. Although I don't speak English, I can still beat you up." Even between husband and wife, it works that way. "I used to bring home the bread; I used to bring the paycheck home back there. Now, even though I am not the breadwinner, I can still beat you up because you are still my wife. I can get from you that welfare check issued in your name."

AK: Do you see a lot of domestic violence?

HC: Yes. That's one of the reasons our agency has to tackle all those problems.

AK: So, in this in-home counseling, do you deal with both parent-child conflicts and spousal issues?

HC: Yes. Domestic violence, alcohol, gambling, child neglect, those are the four areas we deal with. The problems have been blown so much out of proportion that our capacity to deal with them is stretched to the limit. Many of our small programs are overwhelmed. Funds are not very plentiful out there. Competition is very, very strong. Being a small agency, we don't have the resources for grant development or for a grant-writing position. We don't have money to fund that position even part time. So you can tell how discouraging it is to survive in this type of competitive environment. The needs are enormous; the funds and programs are not there to address those needs; the gap is getting wider and wider. After four years and a few months in this job, I feel exhausted. I feel like I cannot last any longer. I have burned out. I have learned how to slow down. I have to remind myself to slow down for my own health. I have to take care of my family also. I need to live longer in order to take care of my community and the needs of Cambodia—Cambodia over there.

AK: It's hard when you see so many pressing needs.

HC: It's hard, very, very hard.

AK: You said you have grants from the city to do in-home counseling. What other kinds of programs do you have?

HC: We have parenting training. But parenting training is no longer funded by the Department of Children's Services because when we submitted a proposal for renewal, we were turned down. But we have to keep the staff position in order to keep the class running. That particular class, the parenting program, supports our other programs. It is very pertinent. We cannot do family preservation without a parenting class. So, funds from other sources have to be spread out thinner in order to support the non-funded components. I tell my staff, "This is not the place to make money. Social work is not where you make a lot of money. If you like money, there's business school—you can earn a business degree. But if you want the opportunity to serve our people, then, yes, we want you to stay."

AK: Are you still doing things like vocational training or ESL classes?

HC: About a year ago, we lost the employment program although we met all the goals. But we didn't do well the first half of the year. We did well during the second half of the year, but, unfortunately, the County Office of Refugees evaluated us based on the first and second quarters. We lost that grant about a year ago. It's very, very hard to find a job developer in our own community. You have to be bilingual and know the job market, as well as our people. You have to know about culture and things like that. Unfortunately, we don't have employment or job development any more.

AK: Where are you getting your funds? Is it all from the Department of Children's Services?

HC: Children's Services is one. They give us about 30 percent of our budget. Another part comes from the County Alcohol Program; another from the Office of Refugee Family Strengthening. We now have these three pillars—about $100,000 apiece.

AK: Your budget is approximately $300,000 a year?

HC: Yes. A little bit more than that.

AK: And it's mostly focused on in-home counseling?

HC: Yes, family preservation. Family strengthening—that's another. The alcohol prevention and recovery program is the third. These cost about $360,000.

AK: What is your relationship with other Cambodian organizations?

HC: UCC [United Cambodian Community] is another major Cambodian organization. Some time ago, they went mainstream. They opened wide with all kinds of activities and programs. Not just for Cambodians—they also serve the Lao, the Vietnamese, and the African refugees. Being mainstream and getting a federal source of money, they cannot deny service to anyone. At one point, they had a multiethnic board of directors. CAA also has a small number of Vietnamese cases because our family preservation program is so successful. The needs are there because there is no Vietnamese community agency to help the Vietnamese families with problems. UCC, at one point, had about ninety staff and maybe a $3 million budget a year. We have more Cambodian staff now than UCC does.

AK: Do you work together with other organizations or is each working separately?

HC: We are working pretty much together. When I write a proposal, I write them in as a partner. I can see that they are also having problems; they are also being challenged by budget cuts. All kinds of cuts. It we don't work together, then all the needs and demands are put on us alone. The load would be even heavier. I do see the need to have a greater variety of agencies.

AK: What is UCC doing? Does it have a different focus from what you're doing?

HC: At one time, yes, but now they are being reduced to only two components—one focused on youth, the other on substance abuse prevention and mental health. CBA, the Cambodian Business Association, was a pet project of CAA originally. We gave birth to CBA; we did the incorporation, the bylaws, and helped elect the first board of directors. Before CBA was born, we had been doing the activities CBA was designed to do, like workshops to educate our businesspeople, such as how to start a business, how to give an accounting inventory, how to get loans, how to get financing, banking, and things like that. We had been doing those things, but after we created CBA, we stopped doing them.

AK: If someone comes to you with those kinds of questions, do you refer them to CBA?

HC: Yes. We work alongside CBA, but CBA had some problems and went through several presidents and directors. From the vantage point of the businesspeople, they don't think that CBA helps them to the extent that they would like, so they retreat. CBA, in turn, says, "We don't get support from businesspeople and from the community, so what can we do?"

AK: How many Cambodian businesses are there in Long Beach?

HC: There's no specific data. Maybe between two and three hundred; no more than that.

AK: I know that in a lot of Cambodian communities, the businesses are run by Cambodians of Chinese descent. Do you find that true here, too?

HC: Yes. Again, that's culture. Some people are predisposed to do certain things. With the background and the educational level of our people, we don't find too many lawyers, engineers, or doctors in our community. About 80 percent, if not more, of our people have farming backgrounds. In the traditional village environment, there were no businesses. All the shops and businesses were owned by Chinese who came from China originally. Our people are artisans and artists; they do farming and fishing. They do small things here and there, but not business.

AK: Are most of the businesses here owned by Chinese Cambodians?

HC: You can say that—the majority of them are. The Chinese Cambodians have more knowledge and more of a predisposition to do business. Back in Cambodia, they used to live in an urban environment.

AK: Do they interact mostly with other Cambodians or do they consider themselves part of the Chinese community?

HC: They consider themselves Chinese Cambodians, except for a few who consider themselves Chinese and live in the central part of [Los Angeles] Chinatown where their businesses are located. [In southern California,] they live in Echo Park, talking Chinese among themselves. The ones in Long Beach consider themselves Cambodians.

AK: You said that a large percentage of Cambodians are on public assistance and some own businesses. Besides those two sources of income, what are other people doing to support themselves?

HC: Some find work as civil servants in the welfare department or in city hall. Some are employees of businesses, a few are engineers, some work in manufacturing.

AK: All sorts of things.

HC: All sorts, all sorts of occupations.

AK: It seems like there's a pretty big distinction between the first wave of Cambodians who came and the people from more rural backgrounds who came later.

HC: That's very true.

AK: Is there much mixing between the two groups? Have members of the first wave moved out of Long Beach or are they still living here?

HC: Most of them still live here. They are established and have bought homes here. They are happy here. To tell you the truth—I cannot lie—no generalizations can be made. There are many who believe that there is a class structure in our community. But, everywhere in the whole wide world, there is some kind of class structure—economically, intellectually, or professionally speaking. There is no neat demarcation between the two groups [of Cambodians] but there is something observable. There's one class made up of business and professional people. They are well-behaved and can function easily in the mainstream. The other ones, the larger group, are lagging behind and not doing so well. They are poor, falling below the poverty line. Unfortunately, this is a very large group of people. The larger group face[s] the greatest challenges: gang involvement, children who are not doing well in school, children who are dropping out, with no role modeling, living in family environments that are not nurturing education, much less higher education. Too many of our children quit school.

AK: Are children in families from the first wave mostly going to college and getting jobs?

HC: I can say that, yes. But many families in businesses like doughnut shops leave their teenaged children at home alone. Leaving children home alone is not a good solution; having latchkey children is not a good situation for any family. Many businesspeople, although they are economically successful right now, have children who may fare poorly due to a lack of supervision, leadership, and role models.

AK: Are you saying that even in families where the parents are from educated, urban backgrounds, because they are so focused on making a living here, their kids may be neglected? Are they as lost as families from rural backgrounds?

HC: Yes, that's the case.

AK: Can you comment further on what's going on with the kids these days? You alluded to the dropout problem, gangs . . .

HC: Remember, due to the lack of a nurturing home environment, the lack of role models in the home, too many of our children drop out of school and join gangs by the thousands.

AK: About what percentage are dropping out?

HC: I made an attempt to find out the dropout rate for our children, but I have not been successful at all. The figures are not available. The school system is not mandated to collect that kind of data [broken down by ethnicity].

AK: Would you guess maybe 50 percent?

HC: No, maybe not that high, but I suspect it's quite high. According to a study in San Diego [by Professor Kenji Ima of San Diego State University and his research associates], Cambodian youth are the most likely to drop out of school, the most likely to get into trouble with the law. They have the lowest career expectancy. They rarely talk about wanting to be a doctor, lawyer, or engineer.

AK: Are the youth who are dropping out of school joining gangs?

HC: You can say that; that would be a fair statement. They don't find comfort, love, or anything interesting for them to do inside their homes. They live in crowded neighborhoods, crowded apartments, unsanitary conditions, and spill over into the streets. That's where the gangs recruit them.

AK: Are the gangs just people hanging out together or are they involved in serious criminal activities?

HC: Cambodian gangs started out with good intentions—to protect their own kind from other youth. Small children get beat up or somebody stole their bicycles or something like that. Some protection is needed. That's how it started. The limited-English-speaking students, the very shy Cambodian students, they are not taught to stand up for themselves—for example, like reporting to the school counselor. And sometimes the good guys get punished. Some of these children come to us and say, "I need help. I must do something." Anger turns into hate. They have to do something to express their anger.

AK: Are you saying that actually, at first, the gangs were defending fellow Cambodians, but later on, they started beating up others?

HC: Yes, that's true. At a later stage, they get involved in all kinds of violent activities.

AK: Are they mostly preying on the Cambodian community?

HC: Yes, preying on their own kind.

AK: Are the businesses dealing with extortion from the gangs?

HC: I suspect they are; I don't know the extent. I would guess there's some level of activity still going on. People need to report more to the police department. It doesn't take a lot of English to open up a business, but it takes a lot of English to report to a police department that does not have many Cambodian speakers. We meet with the chief of police almost every month. We have been pushing, we have been very vocal about the lack.

AK: The Cambodian youths who are making it through high school, are they going to college?

HC: Some are, but there's a lot of room for improvement. Too few of our children get through high school and go on to college. Too many of them spend too much time in the community colleges. They end up spending several years in a two-year college because they don't understand the system, such as how many units are needed, etc. Nobody's there to guide them, to hand-hold them, to show them the way. It seems the community colleges enjoy keeping our youngsters with them because they make money out of them being enrolled there. But there's no support system to guide them and to help them transfer to four-year colleges. There's some good news in that

Cal State Long Beach is the first university to be open to the Cambodian community's needs. We have been cooperating with Cal State Long Beach, especially with the School of Liberal Arts. They have a support system now, including an orientation for parents and new students. We were involved in setting up some of those activities outside of our funded programs.

AK: I get the sense that, compared to other Asian ethnic groups, Cambodians, especially the ones from rural backgrounds, are not as big on education, so they're not pushing their kids as much. Are the kids who are making it defying all kinds of odds?

HC: Unless the kids find peer support among themselves, they have a hard time because the parents are not there to help them. We have to be there, every one of us who is able to help.

AK: So, some of them *are* making it through the system and graduating?

HC: That's right.

AK: What kinds of jobs are they getting?

HC: All kinds. At one time, electrical engineering was in very high demand, and many of them went to engineering school. But now these jobs have really dried up due to the cutbacks in defense spending. Hundreds of Cambodian youngsters have engineering degrees but no jobs. People are coming in to social work like crazy now. It is the responsibility of the university to guide them. An educational institution must not only graduate our children but must also bring them to jobs. There must be some system, some transition, to channel them into jobs. You can't just graduate people. Your mission should be to get them hired—make the graduates successful professionals. In turn, you'll have graduates as tax payers, as contributing members of society.

AK: It must be so disappointing to make it all the way through college and not be able to get a job.

HC: Yes! Many of our children have neglected English, communication skills, interview techniques, and writing skills. Many finish all their coursework but cannot get a job because of their poor English proficiency. Cambodian culture teaches us to look down when talking to higher-ups. When talking to our own people, young people must look down and not straight at the other person. It's disrespectful to look someone straight in the eye in our culture. Many of our youngsters fail at interviews because of this habit.

AK: Basic cultural differences.

HC: Yes, basic cultural differences.

AK: You mentioned that when you talk to the police, they haven't been real responsive to the needs of the community. Do you find that the city of Long Beach is recognizing the Cambodian presence?

HC: Yes, now the city is starting to recognize our presence. I used to be very shy myself; I have changed my nature due to this job here. I used to be very calm, passive, and shy, not talking much. Now I almost turn aggressive sometimes and make very blunt statements in front of the elected officials. You have to make your needs known and demand action or these needs will not be met. If you wait for Cambodians to become eligible voters, then it'll be too late. We may never become voters. Cambodians need a lot of training in order to become voters. Elected officials should be concerned about all the residents of Long Beach, not just the ones who have voted for them. Now they are opening their eyes more and more. For example, during the term of Mayor David O'Neill, who was president of Long Beach City College, I applied for a commission seat. I was turned down because I didn't meet their residency requirement. I understood that, so I didn't protest. Ironically, now that I no longer apply, I am always being asked to serve on different committees. I have been waiting for so long; it's overdue now.

AK: You mean the politicians are starting to realize that they've got this potential bloc of voters?

HC: Yes, and they are tapping into that. Alongside that, CAA participates with other voluntary agencies to promote citizenship. We do citizenship education, etc. We want to encourage our people to become citizens; we want our people to be involved in American politics. It takes a lot of hard work to do this.

AK: One thing I've heard some people say is that Cambodians are still so focused on what's going on in Cambodia, especially the politics there, that they aren't paying attention to what's going on here.

HC: That's kind of true. Remember, two million people were killed during the "killing fields" years. Those killed were mostly educated males, so our leadership is stretched very, very thin. From Long Beach, we have to cover the whole nation also. I am on several national boards, such as the Cambodian Network Council, which sends some of our young college graduates to help our people in Cambodia. As for myself, I am committed [to the reconstruction of Cambodia]. Without being in Cambodian politics or American politics, I want to give myself a higher mission, which is to help the people of Cambodia. I don't want to be involved in Cambodian politics, but I want to help people in Cambodia who are dying of hunger. I want to be an agent of change over there. Somebody else can take the reins of my job here. I hope America will not let my people die over here. But the world community may let my people die in Cambodia.

AK: I know we are running out of time, and I want to make sure that we have some time to cover your personal background. Can you tell me something about your personal background?

HC: The first time I came to the U.S. was in 1962 as a student with a scholarship from the U.S. government—specifically, the U.S. Agency for International Development. President Kennedy had signed an agreement with Cambodia. The United States promised to build an agricultural college for Cambodia. The U.S. trained about twenty to thirty students in all kinds of agricultural science—agronomy, horticulture, animal husbandry, forestry. However, diplomatic relations were broken off [in 1967] by Prince Sihanouk, so the U.S. government would not let us finish school. My advanced education was in agriculture. I studied agriculture and earned a bachelor's degree and a master's degree in five years from the University of Georgia in Athens. Upon my return to Cambodia, I joined the Ministry of Agriculture. But in 1974, I left my government post because government pay could not keep up with inflation at that time. I joined World Vision International, which was helping to resettle displaced people within Cambodia. There was an influx of people at that time from the rural areas into the urban centers. I escaped to Vietnam when the Khmer Rouge took over.

AK: Was your family from an educated, urban background?

HC: Yes. My father-in-law was a member of the supreme court. My wife was a high school teacher. I was a government official. Everybody in the family qualified to be killed [by the Khmer Rouge]. Ten members of my family escaped to Vietnam where we were stranded for several years. We came to the U.S. in January 1979.

AK: Were there a lot of people who went to France and then came to the U.S.?

HC: No, very few, because those who went to France didn't have ties in America, so they couldn't be resettled here. I was resettled by a small church in Florida and stayed there for about nine months. I went to work right away doing minimum-wage jobs and did not get any sort of cash assistance. Later, I received a temporary teaching credential in Florida. Then I got a job with Catholic Charities in downtown Los Angeles. I specifically came to California to be with other Cambodians. At that time, the end of 1979, there were relatively few Cambodians in Long Beach. It wasn't until the mid-1980s that a large influx came to the area. I was with Catholic Charities for one year. After that, I worked as a social worker for Orange County for over ten years. Soon after my arrival in California, I became involved in the Cambodian Association of America. I was basically drafted to become the executive director of CAA. I tried to take a leave of absence from my job with Orange County but was told either to stay or to quit, so I retired. At the time, I was also finishing a master's degree in public administration at Cal State Long Beach in the evenings.

AK: When you first came to California, how many Cambodians were in the Long Beach area?

HC: No more than two or three thousand.

AK: Were you resettling Cambodians for Catholic Charities?

HC: Yes, I was hired to do that.

AK: I think you mentioned that there are now more than fifty thousand Cambodians in Long Beach. How many of them are people who were originally settled here by the resettlement agencies and how many are people who are secondary migrants, such as yourself?

HC: I think a majority was originally resettled here, perhaps 70 to 80 percent.

AK: So, only about 30 percent came from other places?

HC: Again, there are no figures set in stone. I could be making a big mistake. There are no statistics nor any kind of hard data.

AK: One interesting thing I've seen is that a lot of the leaders whom I've talked to are either people like yourself who didn't go through the "killing fields" or they're people who were in the refugee camp at Khao I Dang. I can understand why people like yourself, who are from educated backgrounds, assume leadership roles, but I don't understand why so many people [who had been housed] in Khao I Dang are leaders.

HC: Many people from Khao I Dang indeed are leaders. The people who were leaders in Khao I Dang remain leaders today. Khao I Dang was the largest refugee camp by far and housed primarily Cambodians, whereas the other camps contained other ethnic groups. Most Cambodians who came to the U.S. as refugees were held in Khao I Dang. Remember, our leadership is stretched very thin. There are very few people in Cambodian communities who are qualified and available for leadership roles. The same people end up doing everything. It's a Catch-22 because it's hard to just walk away from the community's problems, knowing how great the needs are.

AK: The topic we haven't touched on yet that I want to ask about is Cambodian culture. I know that a lot of the dancers, artists, and musicians were killed by the Khmer Rouge. Are you doing anything in the Cambodian community to preserve culture and the arts? Who is teaching them, given the fact that so many artists and musicians were killed?

HC: As a hobby, I wrote a small book on Cambodian culture for the Orange County Education Department back in the '80s. Cambodian culture is one area that is enjoying a lot of progress; we are doing well in terms of preserving our own culture. We did not do well in politics, government, or much else, but we have preserved our culture. Many of our artists have indeed been eliminated, killed, or died from starvation and illness. But from inside Cambodia and outside Cambodia, we have tried very hard to find those who are still alive and to support them. At UCC, there's an art gallery, and children are being taught to play the traditional instruments. We have been involved in teaching our children the language; we still have a Khmer language class. We are also teaching the traditional folk dances. Every year, we try to preserve our culture through our New Year's festival. Last year, we gathered forty thousand people, most of them Cambodians, for the New Year's celebration.

AK: It sounds like a lot of the Cambodian organizations are making efforts to have cultural programs.

HC: Yes, and we pool our resources to have activities together. Sometimes, when the opportunity arises, we bring a performance group from Cambodia or even from somewhere else in the United States to perform here.

AK: Is there anything you want to add before we conclude?

HC: A sizable percentage of our people have severe mental [health] problems. Those problems tend to exacerbate our adjustment problems. Many people are not successful in adjusting [to] and coping with the new environment. There are some mental health programs that are targeted for the Cambodian people, but more should be done in that direction. There are no outreach activities nor programs related to the mental health needs of our people. Again, when we talk about Asians, they care a lot about reputation and the family name. A person with problems would rather not talk to a stranger. We don't just walk into a counselor's office to talk. That's our problem. If they don't sleep well for many nights, the mainstream people will walk into a counselor's office to talk about their problems, but that's not the case among Asians. Spousal abuse, child abuse, and gambling may all be [partly] due to the underlying mental health problems.

AK: Do you think that in dealing with such kinds of mental health issues, Cambodians may be more inclined to talk to Buddhist monks?

HC: I think that's true. Being more traditional and conservative in their background, they would rather use the more traditional ways to deal with their mental health problems.

AK: I've taken up a lot of your time, so we better stop here. Thank you very much.

July 24, 1996

2. Chhean Kong
On Buddhism and Psychotherapy

THE REV. DR. CHHEAN KONG is the chief executive officer of Wat Khemara Buddhikaram [Cambodian Buddhist Temple] in Long Beach, California. He is also the community services coordinator of the Long Beach Asian Pacific Mental Health Program, a component unit within the Los Angeles County Department of Mental Health. Audrey Kim interviewed him on July 25, 1996, in his office at the mental health agency. Although he was working in his secular office, he was attired in the saffron robe that all Theravada Buddhist monks wear.

Reverend Kong is very much at ease in several worlds. To reduce the cultural distance between himself and Khmer Buddhists, on the one hand, and the American public, on the other hand, he refers to himself as "Reverend," even though "the Venerable" is the English term most commonly used to address Buddhist monks in Asia. He calls the classes he holds for children at his temple on Sundays "Sunday school," even though Theravada Buddhist temples in mainland Southeast Asia do not have Sunday schools. Instead of being known as the "head monk" of his temple, he is its CEO.

Reverend Kong entered the monkhood when he was still a boy. After completing his studies at the Buddhist University in Phnom Penh in 1968, he went to India for further education. He received an M.A. from Bihar University in 1972 and a Ph.D. from Banaras Hindu University in 1975. In 1979 Cambodian refugees in the United States invited him to establish a Khmer Buddhist temple in Long Beach. He is the only one among the interviewees in this book who entered the United States as an immigrant rather than as a refugee or political asylee. Recognizing the refugees' need for culturally sensitive mental health services, Reverend Kong returned to school and obtained an M.A.

in counseling psychology from Pepperdine University in 1986 and a Ph.D. in clinical psychology from American Commonwealth University in 1989. He also completed the Certificate Program in Serving the Severely and Persistently Mentally Ill at the University of Southern California in 1991. He is fluent in Khmer, Pali, and English and has a reading knowledge of French. In addition to establishing and managing his temple, he has worked at the International Institute and the VISTA program in Los Angeles. For many years he has been on the board of directors of the Cambodian Association of America, the Long Beach Health Advisory Committee, and the Long Beach Police Department Chaplaincy.

Now an American citizen, Reverend Kong remains deeply committed to the preservation of Khmer culture. In addition to ensuring that Cambodians in the United States can continue to practice their faith, he also teaches the Khmer language to many young Cambodian Americans. He and a volunteer teacher hold language classes for about two hundred children at his temple. He also has classes for adults who were born in Cambodia and can speak Khmer but do not know how to write the script. He is very pleased that Khmer-English bilingual programs are now available at four or five elementary schools in the Long Beach School District. California State University at Long Beach has also begun to offer Khmer language courses.

In a telephone conversation with me on September 27, 2001, Reverend Kong said that between three and five hundred people visit Wat Khemara Buddhikaram regularly, but approximately five thousand people flock there during Cambodian New Year, which occurs in April, and for the major Buddhist festival that commemorates Buddha's birth, enlightenment, and death (all of which occurred on the same date, although, of course, in different years). The faithful come from all over southern California. There are now eight monks at his temple, all from Cambodia. Five of the monks are relatively young—in their twenties—and he has enrolled them at Long Beach City College to study English and to learn how to use the computer so they can help him administer the temple.

The mental health clinic where Reverend Kong works has grown since 1996 and now serves approximately nine hundred clients, about five hundred of whom are Cambodians, with Vietnamese, Hmong, Lao, Filipinos, and other Asians making up the rest. The clinic is funded by Los Angeles County, so its financial situation is relatively secure. When I asked whether a lot of clients still suffer from posttraumatic stress disorder (PTSD), he replied that in the weeks following September 11, 2001, he treated many Cambodian clients whose trauma symptoms were reactivated by what they saw on television. He maintains that PTSD is not a condition that can be "cured" easily.

Compared to the mid-1990s, he sees an increasing number of younger clients, some of whom were traumatized in childhood, and others who did not experience the atrocities of the Khmer Rouge regime directly but grew up in households with adults who did. The transmission of PTSD to the second generation is a phenomenon that psychiatrists treating Cambodian clients in clinics in Oregon, Minnesota, and Massachusetts have also observed and discussed in professional journal articles and doctoral dissertations.

*   *   *

AK: Could we start with some background information about yourself? It's interesting to get a perspective on where you're coming from.

CK: I was born in 1945 and raised in a Buddhist family in Cambodia; I was committed to a Buddhist temple when I was a child. In 1968 I finished my studies at the Buddhist University in Phnom Penh, Cambodia. I then left Cambodia to study Buddhism and psychology in India, where I stayed until 1979. I came to the United States in 1979.

AK: Can you give me your impressions of what the Cambodian community was like when you came to this area in 1979?

CK: When I came to the United States in 1979, I learned that the Cambodian people had been forced by the most cruel circumstances to resettle in third countries such as the United States. The immigrants who comprised the first wave in 1975 had high educational and occupational backgrounds in Cambodia. Most people in this first group were government officials such as ministers, ambassadors, members of parliament, professors, medical doctors, and generals. In the United States they were no longer able to pursue their professions; they faced a lot of problems. What were they going to do? How could they survive? They had no properties with them and no money from home. They entered a new society, [met] new people whom they had not known before, and [faced] a new cultural environment. They tried to work at whatever employment they could get, although they had been highly educated and highly trained at home. But others were not even qualified for jobs at a minimum wage because they had no relevant vocational skills, no degrees, and no work experience in the United States. When they wanted to acquire some kind of vocational skills or get a degree in the United States, they were told, "You are not qualified because you have no work experience here, no school record or any kind of document to certify that you have a degree or any work experience from your own country." When they tried to go to elementary school, they were told, "You're too old." The only thing open to them was English-as-a-second-language [classes].

AK: They didn't fit anywhere?

CK: Well, most of them accepted whatever jobs they found, even if they received low pay. These jobs were not like the jobs they had in their own country. Because of the war in Cambodia, they could not go back there to get their old jobs back. I have heard that some Cambodians did return to Cambodia in 1975, but they were killed by the Khmer Rouge, even though some of them had been members or supporters of the Khmer Rouge in earlier years.

AK: In 1975, was there any Buddhist temple or monks in this area?

CK: Well, we had Chinese, Thai, Japanese, Sri Lankan, Burmese, and Vietnamese Buddhist temples, but there were no Cambodian Buddhist monks or temples in this area. Although there were several Buddhist temples in America, unfortunately communication between Cambodians and those other Buddhist temples was poor because of language barriers and different practices. It is for these reasons that the Cambodian community in southern California sponsored me to come from India to build a Cambodian Buddhist temple in southern California. By creating the Cambodian Buddhist Society and Temple in southern California, particularly in Long Beach, the new home of Cambodians, the Cambodians hoped to preserve their cultural heritage and to revive their community spirit. The new temple was built to provide the Cambodians with a mechanism for holding on to their Buddhist way of life and to discuss the conflicts or problems they face in their new society as they attempt to preserve the past and adapt to the present. For many of the Cambodians, especially the adults, it is Buddhism which helps them [to] cope with both their past and their present.

AK: When you came to the U.S. in 1979, the first wave had already come and tried to get adjusted, maybe gone to night school, that sort of thing. But you saw that the stress was building up. Were family conflicts, divorce, problems with children already occurring?

CK: Yes, the stress of adjusting to the new cultural environment was building up for most Cambodians. Cambodians have been subjected to the stresses caused by the breakdown of traditional roles, the rapid Westernization of the children, the lack of appropriate roles for the elderly, a lack of employable skills, the employment of women (which results in a reversal of the former roles of husbands and wives), and the assumption of a lead role in the family by the children—due primarily to their quick acquisition of the English language. Many Cambodians have experienced difficulty in solving financial and other economic problems and face a possible breakdown of the family unit. They experience a loss of trust that can result in child abuse, divorce, and domestic violence. While young people have their problems, the elderly face an even less potentially optimistic future. Most of the Cambodians know they have to adapt to survive in this new society. The slower process of acculturation among the elderly Cambodians often leads to physical and emotional difficulties, including depression, headaches, sleep disturbances, recurrent nightmares, outbursts of anger, anxiety, and stress.

AK: Can you tell me about the foundation of your temple? How did it get established?

CK: A firm belief in Buddhism is that "those who do good deeds will reap good results; doing bad deeds will lead to bad results." A willing resolve to preserve and foster the Buddhist religion is characteristic of Cambodian Buddhists. Therefore, the Cambodian Buddhists in southern California unanimously decided to create a Buddhist society and to purchase a property on which to build a Buddhist temple. In order to raise enough money to cover the cost of this property, we decided to divide the property into twenty thousand shares at $50 a share. We solemnly appealed to all generous individuals to purchase these shares according to their means so that we can have a Buddhist temple to serve as the cradle of the Cambodian soul and culture in America. We will abide by the following bylaws:

1. This property will be named Wat Khemara Buddhikaram (the Cambodian Buddhist Temple), and all of the shareholders will be the owners of the temple regardless of color or race.
2. Wat Khemara Buddhikaram cannot be transferred or sold to anyone without the consent of a majority of the shareholders.
3. Wat Khemara Buddhikaram will be used solely for the purpose of practicing Theravada Buddhism and to preserve the Cambodian cultural heritage.
4. The individual whose name is on the purchase agreement is only a symbolic figure. He/she does not have any rights or prerogative to dispose of this property at all.

AK: About how many Cambodians were in the area in 1979?

CK: I don't know exactly how many Cambodians were in southern California in 1979, but approximately six or seven thousand or more.

AK: And almost all of them donated money to the temple?

CK: Well, only those who are Buddhists donated money to support and build a Buddhist temple.

AK: You were the only monk for all these people in 1979?

CK: Yes, I was the only Cambodian Buddhist monk in southern California in 1979.

AK: How does the temple support itself? Do people contribute money regularly?

CK: Well, some people donate regularly and some donate from time to time and others do not give at all. We conduct a mass ceremony on every Buddhist holy day, which occurs on the eighth, fourteenth, and fifteenth days of the waxing and waning of the moon of the lunar calendar. We organize at least seven traditional religious and cultural ceremonies a year in order to raise money to support the temple. These are:

1. In February of each year, we hold a Buddhist ceremony to commemorate the spontaneous gathering of Buddhist monks to listen to the Buddha's preaching.
2. In April, we celebrate our Cambodian New Year with Buddhist ceremonies.
3. In May, we celebrate the birthday, enlightenment, and passing away of the Buddha.
4. In July, we perform our religious ceremony at the beginning of Lent (which occurs during the rainy season in Cambodia) for the Theravada Buddhist monks. It means that all Theravada Buddhist monks must retire to their own monasteries for the period of Lent, which lasts three months.
5. Between September and October of each year, we honor our ancestors.
6. In October, we perform a special religious ceremony to mark the end of Lent. Some Buddhist temples give a sermon about the prince who was the next to the last incarnation of the Buddha (we call this the Vessantara Jataka).
7. Between October and November, we hold an annual ceremony during which the laity gives clothing to the Buddhist monks.

AK: Would you say that most of the Cambodians here go to the temple in Long Beach?

CK: As far as the Cambodian people are concerned, 85 percent of whom are Buddhists, the need for a Buddhist temple is placed above everything else in their lives and is a must. Before the events of 1975, Buddhist temples played a powerful role in Cambodian society. They were not only places of worship where people came to organize social, cultural, educational, and religious activities, but also places where depressed, distressed, frustrated, and sorrowful people came to receive blessings and relief from their burdens. Cambodian Buddhists here as well as elsewhere look to their Buddhist temples for solutions to their problems in every aspect of life. The need for a Buddhist temple is valued above all else except physical survival. It ensures the mental health of a people resettled on American shores. Therefore, most of the Cambodians both in southern California and from elsewhere in the U.S. or even other countries come to the Buddhist temple here.

AK: Is everyone a member?

CK: Not all of them, because some Cambodian people were invited to join

Christian churches by their sponsors. But we have to work with everyone we can in order to protect our Buddhism and cultural heritage.

AK: Do people place their trust in you and the Buddhist temple?

CK: They don't trust the individual. The Cambodian people were victims of repeated waves of violence which took place in Cambodia year after year. They became physically, mentally, and spiritually sick and almost lost their souls. Even family members were unable to trust one another for fear of being killed. By resurrecting Buddhism, they are making a gesture to symbolize renewed trust and their gradual reunification as a people.

AK: What kinds of services do you provide at the temple?

CK: We created in southern California a Cambodian Buddhist center for the celebration of religious ceremonies and to provide educational programs as well as a forum for Cambodian community issues. We provide counseling services to Cambodians through Eastern psychotherapy, prayers, and meditation. To preserve, maintain, and foster Cambodian arts, culture, and tradition, we provide to Cambodians the support they need in order to re-build their self-esteem, dignity, and identity. We hold a religious ceremony on every Buddhist holy day. When Cambodians have a problem, like stress or some other kind of problem, they express a strong desire to talk about their problems with the Buddhist monks. American mental health practice makes little sense to these people who do not understand much about Western notions of mental illness or the common Western method of discussing prob-lems as a form of treatment.

AK: When did you start to sponsor the Buddhist monks who are now at your temple?

CK: In 1990, our Buddhist Association here in Long Beach started to spon-sor Buddhist monks from Cambodia to come to the U.S. Some of them like to stay here a long time, while others prefer to return to Cambodia after a short period. When they go back home, other monks will come.

AK: They're like visiting Buddhist monks?

CK: Yes. As I said earlier, most Cambodians express a strong desire to talk about their problems with their Buddhist monks. They come to visit Bud-dhist monks quite often, so we need to have several here at one time.

AK: Are you the only permanent monk here?

CK: In 1979, I was the only permanent Cambodian Buddhist monk here.

AK: I know during the Pol Pot period they killed many of the Buddhist monks, so these monks whom you're bringing over from Cambodia, are they people who were monks before or are they recent monks?

CK: Yes, during the Pol Pot years among the first to be killed were the

Buddhist monks. The Cambodian communist regime forced Buddhist monks to resign from the monkhood and sent them to forced-labor camps. Those who survived the Cambodian holocaust began to hide themselves. Some Buddhist monks managed to escape to the Cambodian-Thai border for safety. Many of these Buddhist monks were admitted to the U.S. and other countries. After the trauma of genocide, there are some Cambodians who firmly believe in Buddhism. Some who were monks before became monks again, but most of the young ones have become monks only recently.

AK: It sounds like there's been a real revival of Buddhism within Cambodia.

CK: Well, since its inception, the Buddhist temple is looked upon by the Cambodian people as a treasure-house in and under which their religion, culture, education, social, mental and spiritual health, and well-being are stored and preserved. During the decline of Cambodia, Cambodian Buddhists suffered indescribable humiliation and misery, which seriously hampered their ability to survive and rebuild their country. Yet, despite this downfall and misfortune, the Cambodian Buddhists who know and practice Buddhism have made untold sacrifices to rebuild Buddhism. We have a well-known proverb: "It is better to die than to give up the teachings of Buddha." Based on this firm belief in Buddhism, the number of monks and temples is growing very fast. For many of the Cambodians, especially the adults, Buddhism is an integral part of people's daily lives. The Buddhist monks care for the sick, give shelter to the homeless and the poor, including the aged.

AK: My understanding is that, for a time after the Vietnamese invasion, only men over fifty-five were allowed to be monks. Is that still the case?

CK: No, it has changed. In 1990 the Cambodian Supreme Patriarch came from Cambodia to visit my temple here in Long Beach, and he reported that he has ordained a lot of young Cambodians aged twenty-one to twenty-five years old. Here at my temple in Long Beach, during summer vacation, we have some boys who become novices.

AK: Oh, really? Are they Cambodian Americans?

CK: Yes, most of them are Cambodian Americans.

AK: You have four young boys here this summer?

CK: Yes, I have four or five.

AK: My understanding is that it's typical for boys to become monks temporarily and then do other things, right?

CK: Spending time in a temple is not compulsory, it's not a law, but it is our tradition. Cambodian boys were raised in Buddhist families and committed themselves to Buddhist temples. Most of them lived in the countryside; they used to be admitted to Buddhist temples in order to learn the teachings of the Buddha, morality, and only after that did they start to do other things. In the cities, most of the Cambodian families don't abide as closely by this tradition.

AK: These young boys who are coming, I'm curious, are their parents sending them or do they really want to become monks?

CK: As I said earlier, the cultural influence begins at birth; from the very first day of life, the family begins to socialize the child. Cambodian culture shapes the Cambodian child's behavior from the day he or she is born. Parents cannot force their children to become monks. They must themselves decide to shave their hair, wear saffron robes, learn morality and spirituality, and stay in the Buddhist temple, whether temporarily or permanently.

AK: That's very interesting, because I hear so much about young Cambodians rebelling against Cambodian traditions, but it sounds like with these boys, they're not doing that.

CK: No, not at the moment, I have not seen any young Cambodian monks rebelling against their traditions yet.

AK: One thing that I'm really interested in is whether the Buddhism practiced by the Cambodians in the U.S. is any different from the Buddhism practiced by Cambodians in Cambodia.

CK: We practice Theravada Buddhism in the U.S. the same way as we did in Cambodia.

AK: It hasn't been modified in any way?

CK: No, the doctrine is the same. Our goal is to practice Theravada Buddhism here just as we practiced it in Cambodia.

AK: In terms of the doctrine, what are the differences between Theravada and Mahayana Buddhism?

CK: There are differences between these two sects in terms of beliefs, practices, and observances, but the teachings of the Buddha are the same.

AK: The religion hasn't become a little Americanized? You see no difference?

CK: Yes, there are some differences in practice due to the different cultures in the various countries where Buddhism is practiced.

AK: Do you see a lot of people who talk about the trauma they experienced during the Khmer Rouge years?

CK: Yes, many survivors of the Cambodian holocaust have come to the temple or attended community meetings to talk about their extreme sufferings during "Pol Pot time." They talk about how Pol Pot's soldiers began a forced march of the entire urban population of three million people into the countryside. They talk about separations or losing their children, wives, husbands, parents, siblings, aunts, and uncles. They talk about walking over dead bodies, sleeping with dead bodies, and witnessing people being shot and hanged before their eyes, seeing people buried alive, witnessing the Khmer Rouge soldiers tying women with ropes and cutting off their breasts, pulling out people's toenails and fingernails, executing politicians, Buddhist monks, intellectuals, killing babies, killing anyone with education, including the students at the university, and forcing starvation on almost half the population. They always talk about their trauma experiences of deprivation, physical injury, incarceration or [political] reeducation. All Cambodians who were put in forced-labor camps witnessed such torture every day. When Cambodian refugees here today meet for breakfast, lunch, or dinner, or attend any meeting, they always talk about their memories regarding the lack of food or water, having to drink dirty water, sometimes even cow urine. They recall how they ate whatever they found, such as dogs, cats, earthworms, snakes, monkeys, rats, lizards, crickets, the stalks of banana trees, banana leaves, and lemon grass. They remember their ill health, lack of shelter, imprisonment, sexual abuse, and being near death or witnessing murder. They also talk about how Thai soldiers bused them three hundred kilometers north to Preah Vihear and forced them to walk down the steep Dangrek Mountains back into Cambodia. Thousands of Cambodian people have died from mine injuries, malaria, and dehydration. The Cambodian people in the United States and in other countries, as well as those inside Cambodia, continue to talk everyday about the war trauma they experienced.

AK: Do they come to the temple to talk about that or do they come here to your office?

CK: As I said earlier, either at the temple or at my office or wherever they meet; they always talk about their war trauma in Cambodia, along the way to the Thai border, and in the refugee camps. This war trauma of genocide has caused profound pain for the Cambodian people. Pain is both physical and emotional because they remember these tragedies forever. Pain is the result of the most cruel circumstances known in the history of human civilization that were imposed upon them. They have been uprooted from their soil, their homes, their ancestors, and made to move from one place to another, to new environments, new atmospheric and climatic conditions unknown to them before, in order to rebuild their lives afresh without any means of subsistence or any implements or tools provided for the purpose. Under such harsh conditions, no life could possibly thrive. Though most unwilling to abandon their native land, in order to save their lives they have been forced to flee to the neighboring countries with just what was on their bodies. This is a true picture of the circumstances under which the Cambodian people have been placed. Being suddenly swept away by the whirlwind of terrific waves of violence, torture, murder, and destruction, the Cambodians are still in shock over the horror which has taken hold of their lives.

AK: They're having nightmares?

CK: Yes, approximately 85 percent or more of the Cambodians still have recurrent nightmares about their time under the Khmer Rouge regime.

AK: How does Buddhism help people to deal with what happened?

CK: Since its inception, Buddhism is strongly opposed to any kind of war, violence, and murder. Buddhism helps people to deal with war trauma through great compassion and great wisdom. Great compassion refers to love, charity, kindness, tolerance, and rational speech, rational action, and rational livelihood. Wisdom refers to rational effort, rational mindfulness, and rational concentration (meditation). [These concepts comprise the Buddhist eightfold path to Enlightenment.] Buddha gave his teachings for the good of the many, for the happiness of the many, out of compassion for the world. Buddha's message is one of nonviolence, peace, rational understanding, truth, wisdom, respect and regard for life, and freedom from selfishness, hatred, and cruelty. Buddha explained that "hatred is never appeased by hatred in this world; it is appeased by non-hatred." Buddha also said, "One should win over anger with kindness, wickedness with goodness, the miserly with liberality, and the liar with truthfulness." But the Khmer Rouge regime under Pol Pot did not understand these ideals of Buddha's teaching. There is no peace or happiness for a man as long as he desires and thirsts for conquest and to kill people. The only conquest that brings peace and happiness is self-conquest. Buddha pointed out that "one may conquer in battle a thousand times a thousand men (that is, a million), but he who conquers himself, only himself, is the best of conquerors."

Buddha's teachings are very beautiful, noble, and sublime, but they were not practiced by the Khmer Rouge. Pol Pot's practice was to hate one another, to kill one another among his own people, to live in eternal fear and suspicion like wild animals in a jungle. According to Buddhism, the troubles and strife that engulfed Cambodia for nearly four years arose as little personal quarrels between individuals but grew into great wars over the whole of Cambodia. They arose out of personality disorders, irrational livelihood, irrational speech, irrational action, irrational effort, irrational mindfulness, and irrational concentration. This high incidence of personality disorders became manifested as killing, torture, and destruction of the whole country. From the Buddhist point of view, each of these factors was rooted in thirst, ignorance, desire, greed, craving, which gave rise to all forms of problems. According to Buddhist psychology, this thirst or greed is the cause or origin of personality disorders. Western psychiatrists have described many kinds of personality disorders: antisocial, paranoid, passive aggressive, schizoid, schizotypal, and self-defeating. It is such personality disorders on the part of the Khmer Rouge that led them to brutally slaughter more than a million of the Cambodian people in a crazed genocide. Buddhism aims at total integration of the personality at a high level. According to Buddhism, people are commonly deranged. The whole purpose of Buddhism is to apply mental therapy to a condition which, accepted as the norm, is in truth nothing but a state of universal illusion. The terms *volition, illusion,* and *delusion* denote the same thing [to Buddhists]; they denote the desire to accumulate more and more. Buddhism helps people to eliminate mental and personality disorders completely. The goal of Buddhism is the extinction of volition, desire, ignorance, delusion, and thirst. Buddhism helps people to deal with traumatic war through meditation. Meditation is a technique, a method, employed by Eastern psychotherapists for reducing stress, for coping with the posttraumatic stress disorder experienced by depressed, distressed, and sorrowful people. Meditation is a well-known exercise, connected with our body, for mental development. There are several other ways to develop attentiveness in relation to our body. The aim of meditation is to help the person who is suffering to restore his balance, and in this sense meditation is related to personal experience. Meditation aims at promoting a happy and harmonious life both for the individual and for society.

AK: It sounds like a lot of people are talking to you about loved ones they lost; are they still mourning the loss of loved ones?

CK: Yes, as I said before, wherever the Cambodian people meet, at the temple or some other place, they're always saying, "I lost my children, I lost my husband, wife, parents, brothers, or sisters during the Khmer Rouge regime." They always recall, "My son, daughter, grandchildren, husband, or wife was dutiful, beautiful, intelligent; I loved them." There are many Cambodians who have difficulty thinking, concentrating, and remembering. But they still remember the names of their [dead] children, wives, or husbands. They remember how the Khmer Rouge tortured and killed their family: "I can still see how the Khmer Rouge killed my parents. I still remember how the Khmer Rouge tortured me by beating me over my head and knocking me unconscious on numerous occasions."

AK: So, their memories are still vivid.

CK: Yes, they are. When Cambodians tried to escape to the Thai border, on their way they met robbers and bandits who robbed, raped, and sometimes killed them. I've heard many women who come to our temple or clinic report that at least 80 or 90 percent of women aged thirteen to forty-five years were raped. They report that many women who were younger than fifty shaved their hair and wore white clothing, acting as Buddhist nuns for safety. Some women were raped by bandits many times until they passed out. Some women escaped with their husbands and children, but the bandits arrested the husbands and separated the children and then three or four men raped the women.

AK: Were the 80 percent of the young women raped along the way violated by other Cambodians or by Thai soldiers?

CK: According to the Cambodian women who have immigrated through various refugee camps to the United States, some women and girls were raped in Cambodia during the traumatic war in the 1970s. There are many other women who were raped by Cambodian bandits along the way to the Thai border. Most of the women and girls were raped again in the refugee camps by Thai soldiers.

AK: Do you think that the trauma has affected people in terms of their being able to work? I've heard that many Cambodian refugees are still in shock, and that's one reason that they aren't working.

CK: More than three years of violence and aggression have taken a terrible toll on the people of Cambodia. Most of the Cambodians are still shocked at the horrors of Khmer Rouge annihilation that left more than one million Cambodians dead through execution, starvation, exhaustion, and pain. Suffering appears mostly as physical and mental pain. These, in turn, affect Cambodians in such a way as to lead to problems at home, at work, and in society. Sometimes such suffering causes them to make irrational decisions and to encounter problems, such as wishing to leave a job or spouse, or trying to kill themselves, or to explode in anger outbursts against their families. Even the Cambodian people who immigrated during the first wave in 1975 have problems. They come from a higher educational background and a higher occupational status in their country, but now they have a lower occupational status than they did in their homeland. This lower status in the country of resettlement can produce severe shock.

AK: You must have heard so many awful stories.

CK: Yes, I've heard so many awful stories from the Cambodian people. First, within hours of entering Phnom Penh, the capital of Cambodia, the Khmer Rouge soldiers began a forced march of the entire urban population of more than three million people into the countryside, including women who had just delivered babies. The Khmer Rouge soldiers started to kill Buddhist monks, executed all high-ranking officers, especially military officers, destroyed Buddhist temples, including Buddha's statues, books, killed intellectuals and medical doctors, and separated them from their families and children. Then in December 1978, the Vietnamese attacked the Khmer Rouge.

A decade of violence, destruction, and dislocation followed. These misfortunes created in Cambodia a population whose need to survive has become intimately intertwined with a necessity to migrate. Pressured by a massive outpouring of international sympathy, Thailand temporarily agreed to an open-door policy for Cambodian refugees. For three months, Thailand accepted thirty-five thousand Cambodians into Thailand. Other Cambodians were turned back. For those who were permitted to cross the borders, Thai soldiers robbed them, raped women and girls, and sometimes killed them. Some people told me that either Cambodian bandits or Thai soldiers plunged their hands into women's vaginas and men's anuses searching for gold, diamonds, or other precious stones. Let me quote the words of William Shawcross who wrote of the appalling condition of these refugees: "Daily, awful creatures, with no flesh and with wide vacant eyes stumbled out of the forests and the mountains into which the Khmer Rouge had corralled them. They had malaria, they had tuberculosis, they had dysentery, they were dehydrated, they were famished, they were dying." The above describes the awful experiences that caused the Cambodians to live in constant fear, sickness, and tension. They won't trust each other; there is no trust between even wives and husbands, children and parents. It's difficult for them to live or work together. They are having conflicts and suspicion within the family and the community.

AK: Even within families, the Khmer Rouge pitted children against their parents. Is that right?

CK: Yes, as I said before, for more than three years the Khmer Rouge regime ruled Cambodia. Its brutal policy of separating families, training children within the Khmer Rouge forced-labor camps, and sending them back to their homes where they were pitted against their parents caused children to distrust and suspect their parents. Some even arrested and killed their parents.

AK: Do you think Buddhism can give any sort of an explanation for what happened during "Pol Pot time?"

CK: Well, Buddhism explains how such happenings could occur among all people, not only during the Pol Pot regime but also during Buddha's time. Here is a lesson for Cambodians and the world today: to turn the country back from war and violence, we must embrace the Buddha's message of nonviolence, peace, justice, and happiness for all. Buddhism explains that the institution of kingship (that includes presidents, prime ministers, and other political leaders) must rely on *dhamma* (law), honor and esteem dhamma as the standard and mandate. Buddhism explains that kingship or leadership is created by man as an imperfect embodiment of dhamma, which realizes that punishment is only a preparation for self-discipline. This is the fundamental nature and essence of man, as well as of the universe, because man is inseparable from his environment. Dhamma guides the relations of man to his fellow men; it rules all. The king or leader as an embodiment of dhamma must demonstrate it in his own life and deeds and be [an] example to his people. The king or leader does not set himself over and against either his realm, his people, or dhamma, but stands with them under the rule of the law. Buddhism also explains that if we want to change or improve our society or country, we need first to change or improve the individual. According to Buddhism, it is man who corrupts the society/country and not vice versa; therefore, we must analyze the human condition which leads to a need for reorientation on the part of the individual to act in accordance with dhamma. The king/leader should promote liberality, generosity, charity, and the welfare of his people. The king/leader should not kill, cheat, steal, exploit others, commit adultery, or take intoxicating drinks and drugs. The king/leader sacrifices everything for the good of the people; he must give up all personal comfort, his name, and even his life for the good of his people. The king/leader must have honesty, integrity, and sincerity in his intentions and not deceive the public. The king/leader must show kindness and gentleness, he must possess self-control and austerity in his habits. The king/leader must avoid hatred, ill-will, enmity. He should not fight against the majority of his people. The king/leader should be nonviolent and promote peace, justice, fairness, and try to avoid war. The king/leader should show patience, tolerance, forbearance, and understanding; he must concentrate his mind without losing his temper. The king/leader should protect his country and rule in harmony with his people.

To sum up, Buddhism explains the democratic origin and basis of the state, the idea of a social contract that gives the people the right to oust a government which is not working for the promotion of both their material and spiritual welfare, and the ideal of a common humanity. These ideals would find their fulfillment in a worldwide network of democratic and socialist countries, each acting in accordance with dhamma. Unfortunately, the Khmer Rouge leaders forgot these great ideals of Buddha's teachings. The result of the Khmer Rouge regime was the mutual annihilation of humanity in Cambodia—an unthinkable Cambodian holocaust.

AK: You mean what happened was that leaders were not following Buddhist doctrines and becoming corrupt?

CK: Well, as I said earlier, the Buddha's teachings of great compassion and great wisdom are excellent, beautiful, noble, and sublime, but they were not practiced by the Khmer Rouge. The Khmer Rouge practice was to promote hate between Cambodian and Cambodian, to kill one another, to live in eternal fear, tension, and suspicion, like wild animals in a jungle. Is this behavior more practical, peaceful, and comfortable for the Cambodian people? Was hatred ever appeased by war? According to Buddhism, hatred is appeased by love and kindness, evil is won over by goodness, and war is appeased by non-war. The Khmer Rouge's politics and propaganda were deceptive and blind. My understanding is that there is no way that Cambodia will be able to recover from these multiple disasters without following the Buddhist doctrine of nonviolence, great compassion, and great wisdom.

AK: That may explain how the leaders were evil and brought these disasters on the country, but for the average Cambodian who wasn't corrupt and had all these horrible things happen to him, how does Buddhism explain why all these awful things happened?

CK: Buddhism explains to everybody in the world that leaders of each country must rely on dhamma and follow it. Dhamma is above everybody, it rules all. I heard that there were a few noncorrupt Cambodians fighting against the Khmer Rouge, but it did not work out. Since the Khmer Rouge leaders did not abide by dhamma, a bad atmosphere was created for everybody, including noncorrupt Cambodians. The Khmer Rouge policy toward Cambodia was abetted by foreigners. Foreigners taught the Khmer Rouge leaders to execute all Cambodian intellectuals, to separate families. When the whole population was very weak, it became possible for foreigners to invade Cambodia very easily. What I mean is, this internal violence in Cambodia was compounded by a foreign invasion and occupation.

AK: Weakening the country so that it's really susceptible to invasion from foreigners?

CK: Of course! First foreigners advised Khmer Rouge soldiers to begin a forced march of the entire urban population into the countryside and admitted some uneducated people from the countryside into the city. Then they started to execute intellectuals, politicians, businessmen, social workers, Buddhist monks. People also died from starvation, exhaustion, and disease. Disease and illness made the whole population of Cambodia very weak so that we could not protect our country, our people. That is why in late 1978, Vietnamese attacks against the Khmer Rouge drove more than two hundred thousand Cambodians toward the border of Thailand.

AK: So, the horrible things that happened under Pol Pot can be seen as a lesson in what happens when corruption reaches a dire level? And this is a lesson for people to live in a just way and to abide by dhamma so that kind of thing doesn't happen again?

CK: Well, the war trauma of genocide which occurred in Cambodia from

1975 to 1979 is not only a lesson for Cambodia, but it is a lesson for the world today as well. As I said before, Buddhism recognizes the fact that kings/leaders must abide by dhamma, which rules everybody. Buddhism explains that sovereignty in the sense of supreme legislative power is vested in the people as a whole. If the king/leader fails to fulfill the social contract, which is presumed to exist, and instead of providing good government betrays the trust that the people have placed in him, the people have a right to change the king/leader. In order to protect Cambodia and not allow the Khmer Rouge atrocities to recur again, we must maintain law and order for the welfare of the Cambodian people as a whole.

AK: It seems like Buddhism is very strong in Cambodia and is very strong in California right now.

CK: Well, so far as I knew, it's not just in the state of California; it's in the whole United States. A lot of Buddhist monks from Cambodia have been admitted into the United States and have set up Buddhist temples throughout the United States.

AK: Do you know how many Cambodian Buddhist temples there are in the country right now?

CK: So far as I knew, across the country, there are approximately sixty or more.

AK: And how many in California?

CK: There are fifteen or more.

AK: And in Long Beach?

CK: There are two Cambodian Buddhist temples in the Long Beach area. We have one Cambodian Buddhist temple in Orange County and another one in Los Angeles County.

AK: Do people here send money back to Cambodia to support the temples there?

CK: The Cambodian people visit their families and donate some money to support Buddhist temples there.

AK: I'd like to go back to the topic of Buddhism among young people. You mentioned that there are boys who come to the temple. In general, what is the attitude of young Cambodians toward Buddhism?

CK: The rapid Americanization of Cambodian children enables them to adapt to a new cultural environment in the U.S., so it's very difficult for them to retain their adherence to Buddhism as they become adults. But Buddhist monks in each Cambodian temple give important counseling to young Cambodian children in matters relating to Buddhism. Buddhist monks teach them to avoid misuse or destruction. Buddhist monks discipline their moral character, increase their awareness of shame and misdeeds, help them to grow with a knowledge of the consequences of wrong-doing, to gain not only knowledge but how to acquire wisdom that transcends mere knowledge. The Buddhist monks need to build a good relationship with the children.

AK: Do the kids come with their parents?

CK: The young Cambodians in the U.S. come with their parents to the temple. According to our tradition, Cambodian Buddhists send their children to the temple school which provides education to children from all walks of life, from the royal family down to the peasantry.

AK: But they're not listening to the teachings, or they're not interested?

CK: You know the attitude of children. Even when they attend church with their parents, they do not know how to listen to prayers and are not interested to learn religion. The Cambodian American children do not know how to chant nor are they interested in studying Buddhism. Nonetheless, the Buddhist monks still try to educate them. Education and communication will help the young Cambodians to become interested in learning Buddhism.

AK: If the young people aren't really following it, what do you think is going to happen to Buddhism?

CK: During the decline of Cambodia, as I told you before, the Cambodian people suffered indescribable humiliation and misery, which seriously hampered their ability to rebuild Buddhism. Therefore, it is an urgent and important task for the world Buddhist community to organize adherents and admirers of Buddhism for manifold actions. The training of young Cambodians through networks of mutual consultation and confidence-building is essential, particularly in grappling with problems of newly converted young immigrants who are thrown into alien surroundings. As long as Buddhist monks continue their truly excellent traditional role in this respect, Buddhism may not die out. At the same time, our Cambodian community leaders must work hard to improve our young Cambodians' ability to learn our culture, traditions, and religion.

AK: Are you doing anything currently to try to attract young Cambodians?

CK: First, I have deliberately built a Buddhist temple, which serves as a social-cultural community center in the greater Long Beach area. The Buddhist temple provides a community school for young Cambodians. This Sunday school teaches the Cambodian language, culture, and Buddhism. Occasionally, there are young Cambodians receiving ordination as Buddhist monks.

AK: Are there some Cambodians who become Christians?

CK: I have heard there are a lot.

AK: A lot? About what percent?

CK: I don't know exactly how many percent, but maybe approximately 25 percent. They were invited to attend church through their sponsors. They established the Cambodian Baptist Church right in front of the United Cambodian Community [a social service agency] in Long Beach. At the moment, the Cambodian Christians are giving aid to Cambodia. They are opening Christian churches in Cambodia also.

AK: Are there Cambodian missionaries from America going to Cambodia?

CK: It's not only from America, but also from France, Australia, and other countries.

AK: What Christian denominations are popular? You had mentioned Baptists.

CK: I have heard of the Baptist church, but I don't know what other Christian denominations exist among the Cambodian population.

AK: You're talking about the missionaries who go to Cambodia. But in the U.S., in Long Beach, Cambodians who are Christian, what denominations are they in?

CK: I don't know exactly.

AK: Do most Cambodian Buddhists here belong to the Thammayut or Mahanikay sect?

CK: Most of the Cambodians both here and in Cambodia belong to Mahanikay. According to Cambodian history, the Thammayut was born in Thailand and was brought into Cambodia by a Cambodian king. Thammayut came from Thailand.

AK: The terms refer to where they came from? Thammayut came from Thailand. Where did Mahanikay come from?

CK: Mahanikay was born in Cambodia.

AK: I've asked you most of the questions I have about Buddhism. I'm curious about the work that you're doing here as a mental health professional. Can you tell me a little about that?

CK: In 1986 Supervisor Dean Dana, a member of the Board of Supervisors of Los Angeles County, approved the inception of the Long Beach Asian Pacific Mental Health Program in response to the critical mental health needs of the growing Asian population in the community. Meantime, in order to bring more Cambodians to this clinic, the Department of Mental Health hired me because I'm a spiritual leader and most of the people know me. When the department hired me, at first they probably hired me only temporarily in order to bring the patients to this clinic. Treating Southeast Asian patients is not an easy task. Most of these patients have no formal education and many of them are illiterate. They have difficulties in keeping clinic appointments, following the psychiatrist's treatment. Therefore, we need to telephone to monitor the patients to encourage them to cooperate with the psychiatrist's treatment and to keep clinic appointments.

AK: Are you the only Cambodian counselor or are there others?

CK: In 1986 I was the only one, but due to the fact that the clinic has an increasing population of psychiatric patients, the Department of Mental Health hired three more Cambodian community workers. The program currently has twelve staff, including psychiatrists, psychologists, psychiatric social workers, nurse counselors, community workers, and a community services coordinator. Our staff can speak English, Khmer, Lao, Thai, Vietnamese, Chinese, Korean, and Filipino. [Eighty-eight languagues are spoken in the Philippines, but Tagalog is the national language and likely the one to which he refers.] We help the patients to learn to cooperate effectively with the psychiatrist's treatment. We provide Rational Emotive Therapy to help them abandon their irrational beliefs, such as the belief in supernatural, malevolent, spirits or winds, etc. Most of our patients frequently visit traditional herb doctors and folk healers who know little about Western medication. In our clinical practice, it has been helpful to explore the patients' and the family members' conceptional orientation to mental illness, their health-seeking behavior, and their expectations of treatment by Western psychiatrists. Of course, we are not going to abuse their traditional beliefs. But in terms of Western psychiatrists, believing in supernatural intervention by demons is irrational.

AK: You said you use Rational Emotive Therapy?

CK: Well, Western psychiatrists call it Rational Emotive Therapy, but Eastern psychotherapists use meditation and the Buddhist Noble Eightfold Path: namely, rational understanding, rational thought, rational intention, rational speech, rational action, rational livelihood, rational effort, rational mindfulness, and rational concentration. These techniques are used as tools to treat psychiatric symptoms.

AK: How do you get them in here in the first place? Are you still doing home visits?

CK: No, I no longer can walk from door to door to invite them to our clinic. When they have emotional difficulties, including severe headaches, anxiety, depression, stress, recurrent nightmares, nervousness, sleep disturbances, poor appetite, anger outbursts, and act confrontationally within their families nearly every day, they need the psychiatrist to treat them. They hear my name and say, "Oh, I know him."

AK: Word has spread that you work here, so people are more willing to come here?

CK: Yes, the people are willing to come here. Some people call to make an appointment and others just walk in. When they come in, we have to evaluate them. Then we escort them to see the psychiatrist to get medication. We provide interpretation for either the psychiatrist or for the patients because the patients cannot communicate effectively with the psychiatrist in the English language. At the moment, we have no Cambodian psychiatrist.

AK: What is your degree in? Is it in psychology?

CK: Yes, I have a master's degree in psychological counseling from Pepperdine University and a Ph.D. in clinical psychology from American Commonwealth University.

AK: So, it's mostly people coming of their own free will to see you?

CK: All patients are coming here of their own free will.

AK: Is anyone who lives in Long Beach eligible?

CK: Most of the patients live in Long Beach, but people from the whole Los Angeles County are eligible. It is difficult for this clinic to accept patients from other counties.

AK: What sorts of problems do you see in the people who come to you?

CK: As we have discussed earlier, almost all our patients are victims of repeated waves of events that took place in Cambodia one after another—that is, traumatic experiences under the Khmer Rouge regime and the Vietnamese invasion of Cambodia in 1978. The majority of patients, approximately 85 percent or more, have posttraumatic stress disorder, depressed feelings. All of them have frequent recurrent nightmares of traumatic events. They complain of having bad dreams in which they see Khmer Rouge torturing them in Cambodia; they never have good dreams of their lives in the United States. Nearly half of them admit hearing voices (usually their children or parents calling for help) and noises (usually a buzzing sound). More than one-third of them have hyperactive startle reactions and visual hallucinations (usually seeing their dead children, husbands, wives, and parents). Some others have Bipolar I Disorder, schizophrenia paranoid type and other psychotic symptoms.

AK: Are you doing long-term treatment with people or short-term?

CK: Some patients we treat long-term and others short-term.

AK: I'd like your general impressions of what's going on. You've told me a little bit about the kids. With the adults, how are they doing, besides the mental health issues? Are they working? Are most on public assistance?

CK: There are many Cambodians working. Public assistance is used only by those who have kids and who cannot go to work. The people who are single and have higher education, most of them are working.

AK: What percent do you think are on public assistance?

CK: I cannot tell you exactly, but maybe 25 to 35 percent.

AK: For the people who are working, what kinds of jobs do they have?

CK: The people are encouraged to work at whatever jobs they can get even if they receive low salaries. Some people work in their own business, such as restaurants, auto [repair] shops, and grocery stores. There are some people who work at the Welfare Department, Department of Children's Services, hospitals, hotels, other government jobs, as well as private jobs.

AK: What kinds of business?

CK: There are different kinds of business—whatever they can do, such as doughnut shops, insurance, and other businesses.

AK: The businesses owned by Cambodians, are most of them owned by Chinese Cambodians?

CK: Most of them are owned by Cambodian Chinese.

AK: What percent do you think?

CK: I don't know exactly, approximately between 80 and 90 percent. In Cambodia, most of the businesses were owned by Cambodian Chinese. The Cambodian Chinese, they seem to prefer to run businesses rather than hold government jobs.

AK: Do Chinese Cambodians think of themselves as more Cambodian or more Chinese?

CK: They think that they are more Chinese.

AK: They don't really associate much with Cambodians? For example, there is a Cambodian Chinese Association in Los Angeles. Its members do not associate much with other Cambodians; they meet and perform ceremonies among their own ethnic group. Are these Cambodian Chinese coming to your temple?

CK: They do come to my temple. But most of them speak Chinese and perform religious ceremonies according to Chinese style. The Cambodian Chinese kids also speak Chinese rather than Khmer. They send their children to Chinese school on Sunday rather than to Cambodian school.

AK: What percentage of the households here are headed by women?

CK: A very large percentage is headed by women due to the fact that their husbands were killed by the Khmer Rouge. Men are the heads of families in our country, women are expected to stay at home, run the house, raise the children, and support their husbands' work. But here, women are troubled by changing family roles. The Cambodian community leaders try to help them to take responsibility in their homes, to learn how to be heads of their families. These suggestions may not be fully understood by the single mothers; they can cause marital and family problems. The problem is frequently that the single mother is not yet prepared to learn to take care of her whole family.

AK: Is there a large percentage of families where there are no fathers?

CK: Well, during the Khmer Rouge regime, most of the people killed were men, especially military men. The remaining women and their children immigrated through various refugee camps to third countries. Some women have eight or more children without a husband.

AK: One thing I've heard is that although women may be running the households in Cambodia, they are not used to being the breadwinners. So, families here who don't have fathers often end up on public assistance. Is that something that you see?

CK: Well, let me tell you: first, the Khmer Rouge forced people to abandon their homes, their ancestors; they could not bring anything into the countryside. Second, at the time of the Vietnamese invasion in 1978, they escaped to the Thai border without any properties or money, so they arrived in the U.S. without any properties from home. Most of these women, in general, are not well educated. This low education makes them less confident about joining the mainstream society and succeeding in English-as-a-second-language courses or in job-training programs. Many women withdraw and limit themselves to the traditional role of homemaker and mother. Many women find the public assistance application process, cashing checks, or negotiating the food stamps process beyond their comprehension.

AK: What percentage of families do you think has just the mother?

CK: I cannot tell you exactly, but maybe 30 to 45 percent.

AK: That's all?

CK: Well, I think so.

AK: That's not as large a percentage as I've heard. Would you say that most of them are on public assistance?

CK: As I said, they came from home with empty hands. They have no education from home, no skills, and do not understand the English language. They need public assistance to support their families for survival.

AK: Do you think those families have a harder time dealing with the kids?

CK: Before I answer you questions about whether such Cambodian families have a harder time with their kids, let me tell you about the parent-child relationship from the Buddhist and Cambodian culture's point of view. There are five ways that parents should bring up their children: They should restrain children from committing wrong-doing, they should teach children about virtuous deeds, they should educate children in good schools, they should provide their children with suitable wives or husbands, and they should give children their inheritance at the proper time. There are also five ways children should honor their parents: Children should support and protect their parents and supply them with what they need, children should show devotion to their parents, children should maintain the good name of the family, children should conduct themselves in such a way as to deserve the inheritance of the parental property, and children should support and protect their parents when they are old. These traditional concepts are what most Cambodian parents believe in. Therefore, Cambodian parents in America fear that their children, fast becoming Westernized, will not care for them in their old age. The Cambodian children in the United States, in general, are indeed rapidly becoming Americanized. Many children were born in the United States and are less tied to their ethnic backgrounds. The children go to American schools and they speak English as their first language and lack fluency in their parents' native language and knowledge of their parents' native culture. Parental authority with strict discipline is part of the Cambodian culture. Frequently, Cambodian American children have a hard time accepting that authority. The kids see greater latitude given their White peer groups, which provokes conflicts with their parents. At the same time, the Cambodian parents are involved in a difficult transition adjusting to their new cultural environment and new home. The adjustment problems, combined with discipline problems, result in an inability to maintain the Cambodian traditions and culture, as I mentioned above. But I'm not surprised, it's not only Cambodian families that are having such problems, but also the Chinese, Japanese, Korean, Lao, Vietnamese, Thai, and others. They all have the same problems.

AK: What about domestic violence?

CK: The employment of women is resulting in a reversal of the former roles of husbands and wives. According to the former roles, the duty of the husband/father is to work to support the whole family. In return, wives and children are supposed to give total obedience to their husbands and fathers. Wives in Cambodia are expected to stay at home, run the house, discipline the children, and support their husbands' work. This role is no longer appropriate in the United States. Husband-and-wife conflicts within the family structure are inevitable. Such factors have caused physical abuse within Cambodian refugee families.

AK: It sounds like some of it is cultural difference, but I also imagine that all of the other stressors that build up exacerbate the violence in the family. Do you agree?

CK: The significant social disruption, dislocation, and resettlement as aliens in a new, strange, and different culture have resulted in a very difficult and stressful adaptive process. The cultural differences and culture shocks that are inherent in such circumstances have added confusion to the already existing feelings of depression, anger outbursts, sleep disturbance, fear, and loneliness. Their traditional roles and patterns of authority are no longer appropriate. New roles in the new culture of the resettlement country have not yet been learned. Parent-child conflicts and the erosion of the family structure can therefore be expected. These are some of the stresses and trauma inflicted upon Cambodians as they escaped from their homeland and immigrated to the United States. The loss of family members left behind and the powerlessness of fathers and husbands, all these leave their marks deep in the emotional fabric of Cambodian refugees. Moreover, while they are in the United States, the loss of status, identity confusion, generational conflict, cultural difference, homesickness, and so on all plague them. These are the major sources of stress that need counseling in Buddhist temples.

AK: What about substance abuse, drug abuse, alcoholism?

CK: Substance abuse is not so prevalent in Cambodia, but after more than twenty years of association with American culture, some Cambodians have become substance abusers. These abusers cause many problems in their families. In Cambodia, drug abuse is relatively rare—they use marijuana, opiates, amphetamines, and barbiturates. In the United States, they use cocaine. Alcoholism is a problem for the male Cambodian adult population but is a rarity for females. Gambling is a big problem that brings misery to innumerable individuals and causes many families to divorce and to have child abuse. Buddhism prohibits substance abuse, alcohol, drug abuse, and gambling. Buddhism explains that all people should refrain from taking intoxicating drinks and drugs and be mindful of their duties to others. When they have intoxicating drink and drugs, they attempt to kill, to steal, to indulge in sexual misconduct, and to lie. That is the reason Buddhists are opposed to any kinds of intoxicating drinks and drugs.

AK: What kinds of drugs are they using?

CK: I have heard they are using mostly cocaine.

AK: Do you see gambling as an addictive behavior?

CK: As I said, gambling is a big problem frequently leading to child abuse, spouse abuse, sexual misconduct, lying, and other social problems.

AK: Besides the temple, are there other organizations working to preserve Cambodian culture?

CK: Yes, we do have the United Cambodian Community, the Cambodian Association of America, the Cambodian Business Association, and the Cambodian Women's Association here in Long Beach. We have a Cambodian Chinese Association in Los Angeles to preserve Cambodian Chinese culture.

AK: Do you see many young Cambodians finishing high school and going on to college, getting good jobs?

CK: Yes, I've seen many young Cambodians finish high school and go on to college and the university. As we've discussed, in general, Cambodian women were less educated than men. Most of the Cambodian parents did not allow their daughters to get educated. But here in the U.S., many Cambodian girls are going to college and the university. According to Buddhism, parents should educate their children from a young age because good begets good and evil begets evil. It means that parents must provide their children with a proper education for academic studies, personal development, [the] learning of new skills in the U.S., and the ability to engage in humanistic pursuits, so that they can think and act rationally and wisely. The gift of education is the greatest gift that any parents could give to their children. I tell Cambodian parents to train or educate their children for a good profession. I explain to young Cambodians and their parents that if both the parents and children perform their good duties as advised by the Buddha, then there will be happiness and peace in the family and in society.

AK: Are the other less-educated youth ending up on public assistance like their parents?

CK: No, I don't think so. Second-generation Cambodian Americans have no interest in applying for public assistance. The young Cambodians get only limited guidance in the field of educational interests. I tell parents to encourage their children to achieve higher education and get good jobs.

AK: Do you have a sense of why Long Beach has become the central gathering place for Cambodians?

CK: Well, Long Beach has been favored by most Cambodians because the climate is similar to that in Cambodia and it is the site of the Cambodian Buddhist temple. It is easier for them to practice their own culture and to communicate and interact with each other effectively.

AK: I can understand why people want to come together, but why Long Beach and not some other place?

CK: That is a good question. Let me ask you why are Vietnamese living together in Westminster? In downtown Los Angeles, one side is a Chinatown, one side is a Little Tokyo, and the other side is a Koreatown. I think it is human nature; it is not just the Cambodians who choose one place, like they choose Long Beach as their headquarters with the largest concentration of Cambodians outside of Cambodia, but also it is the behavior of all the people in the world to choose one place as their headquarters or site of the government offices. Each country in the world chooses one place as their capital, such as the American people chose Washington, D.C., as their capital, etc.

In Cambodia, they set up Phnom Penh as their capital. For the Cambodian people who immigrated to third countries, they need to choose one place as their center.

AK: Someone said to me that Long Beach became the center because there were a number of students from Cambodia at California State University, Long Beach. They helped to start a community here. Does that ring true?

CK: Yes, it is true. Because of those Cambodian students who came to Long Beach first and then their friends, their family members followed. They preferred to live together with their ethnic group. But some Cambodians have moved out of Long Beach after they earned some money to run businesses or to buy houses elsewhere.

AK: The Cambodians who are a little better off financially are probably not going to stay in Long Beach. They're going to move out to the suburbs. Is that right?

CK: Well, I have seen some people move out step by step. Some Cambodians decide to move out to the suburbs because they don't want their children to be involved in gang activities.

AK: Have you seen a lot of Cambodians come here from other parts of the U.S.?

CK: Yes, I have seen a lot of Cambodians move to Long Beach from different states in the United States. But some people have moved to other states as well.

AK: Right now, what do you think the population here is?

CK: Well, I cannot tell you exactly.

AK: What percent do you think are people who came here originally versus those who came from other places in the U.S.?

CK: I think maybe about 30 percent came here originally. Most of them, perhaps 70 to 80 percent, came from other places, like Texas, New York, and other states in the U.S.

AK: So, only a minority of the people here were initially resettled here?

CK: Yes, they arrived here in 1980 when our Cambodian community leaders started to sponsor the Cambodian people from refugee camps at the Thai border to the U.S. At that time, if I remember correctly, the U.S. government advised us: "Do not come to the state of California," and we agreed with that point. Later on, after they had settled down in the United States, they moved to the state of California, particularly southern California, to join their family members, friends, and close relatives.

AK: I've taken up a lot of your time, so we'll end now. Thank you very much.

July 25, 1996

3. Samthoun Chittapalo
Law Enforcement Issues

MR. SAMTHOUN CHITTAPALO (Sam to his non-Cambodian acquaintances) was a community liaison officer in the Asian Affairs Division of the Long Beach Police Department when Audrey Kim interviewed him on August 15, 1996, at the police station. He then drove her around to show her the different sections of the city. When I tried to contact him in September 2001, I discovered that he is no longer at the address or telephone number he had given me in 1996. My contacts in Long Beach informed me that he is no longer working at the Long Beach Police Department and that he has experienced some personal problems. Moreover, his wife had died, so I decided not to impose upon him and made no further attempts to find him.

Mr. Chittapalo was educated in Cambodia, France, and the United States. He returned to Cambodia from Paris around the time that Gen. Lon Nol deposed Prince Sihanouk. In 1970 he joined the Cambodian army and was trained by American military advisors in Vietnam. After fighting for a number of months in the civil war then raging in Cambodia, he escaped to Thailand because he did not want to continue killing fellow Cambodians. He remained in Thailand, where he supported himself by singing and playing guitar in a nightclub and working part time for the U.S. Central Intelligence Agency until the Khmer Rouge took over Cambodia on April 17, 1975.

Mr. Chittapalo and his wife entered the United States as part of the first wave of Cambodian refugees in May 1975. He worked at the Los Angeles office of the Immigration and Naturalization Service, the Los Angeles County Health Department, and the American Council of Nationalities Service (a voluntary agency that resettles refugees) before joining the Long Beach Police Department as its first Cambodian employee. He took evening courses while he was working and obtained an M.B.A. In 1988 he formed the Asian Advisory Council to the Police Chief, which meets regularly with the chief to discuss the law-enforcement needs of all Asian ethnic communities in Long Beach. Although the following information is not current, Mr. Chittapalo's account remains valuable for the insights it provides into some of the most heart-wrenching problems that affect Cambodians in the Long Beach area.

* * *

AK: I'd like some information from the police/law enforcement perspective about the gangs, about domestic violence, and whatever information you have about the Cambodian community. And some information about your personal history because it's always interesting to hear how people got to where they are.

SC: My personal background, I'm from Cambodia. My dad's from China, and he married my mom who's from Cambodia. I was born in Cambodia and got educated in French. The country was colonized by the French. Vietnam and Laos were also colonized by the French. When I was sixteen years old, my dad sent me to Paris, where I studied for a couple of years. And then the government got troubled by communists. I came back from Paris to Cambodia, which had become a republic. They let the king out of the country. The king went to China, then North Korea, and stayed there. In 1971, I joined the military; it was coordinated by the U.S. military. They sent me to Vietnam in 1971. I underwent training for almost nine months and then came home. I felt sad about communists fighting, Cambodians fighting other Cambodians. I asked my dad to let me go to Thailand and he took me to Thailand. At that time, I was only nineteen, twenty years old.

AK: You went to Thailand so that you wouldn't have to take part in the fighting?

SC: Yes. First I went into the jungle in Cambodia to fight for a couple of months, but I thought, "If I keep fighting like this, how am I going to have a future? I would have no future." I kept telling myself I have to be someplace else besides Cambodia. So I went to Thailand. I escaped. I said to my dad, "I'm not going to fight anymore, Dad, I have to go to Thailand." He gave me some money. I went to Thailand and I couldn't get a job at all. But I could sing, I could play the guitar. So I found a job at a restaurant in a nightclub.

AK: Were there a lot of Cambodians at the time who had gone to Thailand?

SC: Oh, sure, yeah, a lot of Cambodians fled to Thailand because only Thailand was safe. No bombing, no shooting, nothing like that. If you went to Laos or Vietnam, it was all the same: fighting. I actually wanted to go to

France. My brother was in France, but he didn't want me to go there. So I said, "OK, fine, I'll go to Thailand instead." I enjoyed living in Thailand very much. I enjoyed working with the American military until '75. I worked with the CIA.

AK: You were in Thailand when the Khmer Rouge took over?

SC: Yeah, the Khmer Rouge took over in '75. My boss said, "You go to America." "How come I don't go to France?" "You go to France, no future." He gave me some address to go to in California. I didn't know anything but I ended up in Hollywood.

AK: As an aside, I heard that a lot of Chinese Cambodians went to France because France was more receptive to them. Is that true?

SC: Right, right. Normally, Cambodian Chinese have a lot of money because they are businesspersons. They have a lot of gold, diamonds. But now, from Paris they're coming to the United States.

AK: Why are they coming to the U.S.?

SC: This is the land of opportunity, of freedom, more than France. Land of everything, you name it. I don't talk about France or Japan; I've been to Japan and I really don't like it too much; there's too much discrimination, more than in America. I don't see any Cambodian person there who can work in an office, be in the Japanese military, be a police officer. Here, they give you opportunities. If you are good enough, if you have ability, if you got a good education, you can do whatever. But not in Japan or France, I don't think so.

AK: What happened to your family when the Khmer Rouge took over?

SC: Spread all over. All tried to escape. Half of them died. I went to Cambodia last year; I cried. I went to the village where I was born; I went to my dad's village, I paid him respect. I still think about him sometimes. I never had anything to pay him back with; I feel so sorry.

AK: Was he killed by the Khmer Rouge?

SC: He was killed by the Khmer Rouge. My brother, my sister, they were also killed. What can we do, it's not only me. A lot of people got killed. However, I think that I'm lucky. I got here with my wife. My wife worked for the American embassy in Laos. She's a trainer, a cultural trainer. When your military was sent to Laos, they had to learn the culture.

AK: I've heard that a lot of people who didn't live through the Khmer Rouge also had lots of problems because they didn't know what was happening to their families. They experienced survivor's guilt.

SC: Right. In 1977, two years after the Khmer Rouge took over, I wrote a letter to the American Red Cross; they found out about my dad in Cambodia; he had already been killed. I cried; I couldn't do my job. What can I do?

You never see your dad again; you expect your dad to be alive. They fired me from my job. I went back to school and I passed a test, an immigration test.

AK: Let's back up a little bit. You said the CIA person gave you some addresses and you came to Hollywood.

SC: Some addresses, yes. I went to Hollywood and lived there for two years. I was working and going to school at the same time. When they fired me, I had around $2,000. I looked for another job and passed a test as an immigration agent. I worked at Immigration and also in the Health Department.

AK: When you came to Hollywood in 1975, how many other Cambodians were there?

SC: I think around five families. I didn't know them well; we were too far apart. And then I found the Long Beach area because I knew a lot of people here. Around 1965 the government had sent 125 Cambodians to study at Cal State Long Beach in engineering, in agriculture. The Cambodian community had its origins here.

AK: Do you think the students were instrumental in building the base of the Cambodian community here?

SC: Yes. The word spread to Cambodia. The first person who came here in 1965, I think he's still here. The people who have been here since 1965 are still here. I got a job in Long Beach ten years ago because I felt Long Beach didn't have enough Cambodians who've been active, who can serve. I was in L.A.; I got very good pay in L.A. working for Immigration and for the American Council of Nationalities Service. I left that job with good pay; my wife got so mad at me. I had to convince my wife that it was OK to take the pay cut and work for the police department here.

AK: You felt that the Cambodian community here needed to be served?

SC: Yes. Need to be served; need to be directed. Cambodians need someone who can do things like write letters asking for things from the government.

AK: One thing that I've heard about Cambodians is that, because many of them aren't from educated backgrounds and because of the cultural differences, they're not willing to ask for things, demand things from the government.

SC: That's correct.

AK: That's why they're underserved compared to other groups.

SC: They don't know how to ask. They don't know how to bargain. They're born to suffer, you know, quiet, in the corner. They're always like that. When I first came here, I was the same way, but I learned the American system. We must do something; we must be active. Otherwise, people don't know what we want. I keep writing letters, sending this and that. When I came to this department ten years ago, I was the only one, the only Cambodian working here.

AK: How many Cambodians were there in Long Beach in 1986?

SC: I think around twenty thousand to thirty thousand.

AK: Did they hire you because they wanted a Cambodian presence on the police force? Or did they hire you and you just happened to be Cambodian?

SC: They were pushed to hire a Cambodian by the leadership people. They had a lot of young people applying; I don't know why they chose me. When I got a call from them, when I went there to interview, I passed. When I passed, I questioned myself, "Why are they hiring me?" My wife didn't like that: police get killed. I've been here ten years and I like my job very much.

AK: Can you tell me about your work with the Long Beach Police Department?

SC: When I first came to work, they put me in the Neighborhood Watch section.

AK: Was this sort of like outreach to the community, letting them know that the police department was there for them?

SC: Outreach, yes. My picture was on all sorts of police advertisements. I don't know why, but I committed myself too much at that time. I worked long hours, including Saturdays and Sundays. Then I joined the reserve officers in the Police Academy I think six or seven years ago. At first, they didn't want to hire any person who doesn't speak good English. My accent I don't think is good enough to talk to American people. I agree I don't speak good English because I was not born here. My daughter speaks like an American; I'm not like my daughter or my son; I was grown up already when I came. So, they assigned me to Asian Affairs. The chief said, "You take care of all Asian problems." Asian Affairs means all Asians: Japanese, Koreans, Filipinos, Lao, Thai, Vietnamese, Samoans also. I formed an Asian advisory council to the chief, called AAC, in 1988. We also work with the U.S. Department of Justice. In Long Beach you got a lot of problems, you should have something. So we have an Asian advisory council. Every three months, we go to the chief and talk about what we need.

AK: So, this came from a federal directive?

SC: Backup. The problems come to Long Beach: always shootings, always killings or robberies, a lot of big problems.

AK: Can you tell me about the history of crime in Long Beach? How did it develop? When did it peak? What is it like now?

SC: Long Beach, you got approximately a half million people, 450,000 or almost five hundred thousand. Breakdown according to minorities: you got a hundred thousand Latinos, Spanish-speakers; you got almost a hundred thousand Asians; you got around thirty-five thousand Blacks; and the rest is Caucasian. Now breakdown of the hundred thousand Asians: fifty to fifty-five thousand Cambodians; we got around fifteen thousand Vietnamese; we got around eight thousand Filipinos; around four thousand Koreans; around four to five hundred Hmong. You combine all these together, almost a hundred thousand Asian population. But the big majority is Cambodian. It's number two or number one in the United States right now; I think number one. Lowell is second. I went to Lowell; I think it has thirty to thirty-five thousand. I don't believe [the numbers given by] the U.S. Census Bureau.

AK: Do you think the Cambodian population here is growing or staying the same?

SC: It's growing, it's growing. Why do I say growing? People come from Paris, Cambodians from Paris, from Australia, from Canada, from all over the world they come to Long Beach. Even from Cambodia they now come to Long Beach.

AK: I sense that there's a lot of secondary migration from other states and it seems as though that has somewhat slowed down, but now you're saying that there are Cambodians from Paris, Australia, and other countries who are coming to Long Beach.

SC: Cambodians from Japan come to Long Beach, too.

AK: When did that start?

SC: It started because this is the land of freedom. You can buy a house easy here, down payment only $10,000.

AK: So, when did people from France, from Australia, start coming here?

SC: Five, six years ago. We had one Cambodian [Sichan Siv] working in the White House with the Bush administration. It pops up; he is referred to all over the country, even in Japan, even in France, even in Australia. Cambodian people are starting to see if a guy has ability, he has a chance to work in the White House. Why shouldn't I come here, bring my daughter, my kid, my son to study here?

AK: You think that having this person working in the White House was what brought international attention?

SC: Right. This led some other Asian groups to express jealousy, to want their own representation in the White House, but this Cambodian person has a graduate degree and is well qualified. Starting in 1986 or 1988, more Cambodians have come here, there are now more problems.

AK: The population has grown a lot since 1986 or 1988?

SC: Yes.

AK: Was most of that secondary migration?

SC: Right. In 1990, the Census Bureau reported that we have around seventeen thousand Cambodians in Long Beach. I don't believe it. You count. You go to the Welfare Department, it's about 80 percent Cambodians. The U.S. Census Bureau should check with the Welfare Bureau, with Social Services. The Cambodians have more problems than anybody else. Before I talk about the gang problem, I'll talk about the family problem first.

AK: Who's making the calls to Children's Services? Is it neighbors, family members?

SC: All over, from the schools, from the police, from neighbors. Right now, you have six, eight Cambodians working with DCS [Department of Children's Services] to handle those cases; 90 percent are in Long Beach. It's higher than Vietnamese. Why are we a small community yet we have more problems? Because of a lack of leadership, a lack of direction, a lack of support.

AK: In your opinion, what are the child abuse cases like? Do you deal much with them in person?

SC: I deal with a lot of them, especially four or five years ago. I also deal with the gang problem. Let's talk about how it began. In the 1980s, when the Spanish, Latinos—young and old—started to get jealous, the problem started to grow. It cropped up overnight in the Cambodian community and also affected other businesses like [those owned by] Vietnamese, Chinese. Anaheim Street was abandoned by the city. Now, we call it the Anaheim Street Corridor. We try to develop more and more businesses, especially from the freeway up to Redondo; it's all Cambodian businesses around there. And then the Spanish people, they don't like it. Koreatown [in L.A.] is a similar example. Around the country, they're aware of the Black problem, of the Latino problem. The Asians start to be picked on by both groups; so they formed gangs to protect themselves. The kids reported to the parents, the parents didn't know what to do. The kids cannot go to school because other kids are throwing rocks at them. And the kids start to pick up the gangster clothing style; now, the Asian style looks exactly like the Hispanic.

AK: I've heard the same thing in the East Coast in terms of rumors being started that Cambodians were getting money from the government to open up businesses, things like that. Is that kind of thing happening here too?

SC: The same. A guy said to me, "How can you guys open the store? Who gave you the money? It must be the government." We worked so hard; we earned it. Latino people, they don't like that. Asian people, we support each other.

AK: Cambodians were getting money from family, from friends?

SC: Right. We share the money. I opened three businesses when I came. I sold my diamond ring to open the business, borrowed money and paid back later. But they don't do that in that community, they don't do that.

AK: Most of the businesses here, are they operated by Cambodians of Chinese descent?

SC: Mostly Cambodian Chinese. However, a lot of Cambodians now try to learn more about business, especially businesses that cater to other Americans. Going back to gangs, when the Cambodians form a gang, the gang is always led by Vietnamese because Cambodians are not as knowledgeable as Vietnamese about such things.

AK: Cambodians and Vietnamese are getting along OK?

SC: The kids, OK. The kids OK, but not the older ones. The older ones still hurt.

AK: They were probably being picked on equally by the Blacks and Hispanics?

SC: They got three types. What we call the Asian Boyz, that group combines all Asians.

AK: So, when the Cambodian gangs first got started, they were led by the Vietnamese?

SC: Yes. Vietnamese are the Asian gang organizers, mobilizers. Not just in Long Beach and L.A., but all over the United States: Chicago, New York. After they form the gangs here, Cambodians became stronger. When you're the teacher, and I'm the student, if the student learns faster than the teacher, then later on, I can take over. You teach me but later I beat you up. From 1988 to '90, or '92, the Cambodian kids started to form their own gangs: TRG [Tiny Rascals gang], Cambodian Boyz, Lazy Boyz.

AK: First, it was just a bunch of Cambodians led by Vietnamese, but then they broke up into different Cambodian gangs?

SC: Right. But now, ABC, the Asian Boyz Club, doesn't have Cambodians at all. No Cambodians, just Vietnamese, Koreans, Japanese, Filipinos. But TRG is all Cambodians; they don't want nobody else.

AK: How many gangs are there right now? Cambodian gangs?

SC: I think there are about 1,800 gang members. But for all the Asian gangs, there are maybe five thousand Asian gang members. There are about seven thousand Latino gang members, around three thousand Black gang members. But they're divided. The gangs that are powerful, the hard-core gangs, they have eight hundred.

AK: It sounds like the gangs were originally formed to protect themselves against other groups, and then a small percent of those became real hard-core criminals.

SC: Right. The kids who went to school and at nine years old started to learn the gang signs. Cambodian families don't take care of their kids very well. The kids learn a little faster than the parents. When you go to school, every teacher, every school, will tell you about child abuse. The Cambodian kid, when he comes home, he doesn't speak Cambodian, he speaks English to his mom and dad. His dad speaks Cambodian back but the kid doesn't know Cambodian. Big gap already. Blacks, they speak English to their mothers. The Latino situation is similar to the Cambodians' situation. When Cambodians go to school, when they come home, they speak English. They say, "My mom is stupid, she does not speak good English." They do not obey their parents; they try to rule the parents. The parents cannot understand English; when they go to the welfare office, when they go some place, they don't want the kids to know about confidential matters but they need the kids to translate for them.

AK: The language gap exacerbates the gang problem?

SC: Right. Culture shock. When the kid asks the parent to help him with homework, I don't think the parent can help him. Even me, I cannot help my kids. There's some English I don't understand, too. Now, 85 percent of the Cambodian females don't have husbands because the husbands were all killed in Cambodia. They brought the kids here to Long Beach, and the kids grow up and the moms don't know how to cope.

AK: Do you think the households headed by women have a harder time?

SC: Harder time than other people. Even when they have husbands and wives, it's still hard.

AK: Do you think the gang problem is related to child abuse because they're both an outgrowth of parents and children not getting along?

SC: Gangs, we all know, come from the atmosphere of the community that we live in. If they live in Beverly Hills, I don't think we're going to have a gang problem. If you're on welfare, welfare doesn't give you enough food to eat, barely enough day by day, month by month. And the kids, like you and me, want good cars and want good clothes, want to get out there and live, and the parents cannot support that.

AK: The children are being tempted by all these material goods that their parents can't give them. They think that their parents are stupid because they don't speak English and can't communicate. So the gangs become their support and provide a way to get money for the things they desire?

SC: Right. The Vietnamese gangs, they start with money: "Friend, you have no money. Come to my team. You join me, I buy you good clothes. You can buy a good car. You can drink whatever you want." But one day, the gang leader says: "I have no money. You have to pay back."

AK: So, at first, they're nice. They give you money, but then you have to pay back.

SC: "Oh man, I have no money; I'm broke now." You're spending for a robbery, for a home invasion, for a home burglary, for auto theft. City of Long Beach, 750 cars every month have been stolen from Long Beach. Two hundred cars are stolen from Cambodians every month. Two hundred Cambodians stealing, two hundred Blacks stealing, and two hundred Latinos stealing, and the rest is Caucasian.

AK: It sounds like if I'm a gang member, probably, I didn't originally intend to become a criminal; I was hanging out with these guys who seemed nice, they were giving me things and money, and then one day they said: "Hey, I need money, will you do this for me?" And you get lured into it.

SC: Yes. Two hundred cars a month, as I told you. What kinds of car? You got Toyotas, Hyundais, Datsuns. These cars, it could be chop, chop. Chop up and you sell the tires, the engine. All the rest, you send to New York. Or they're put on the boat and shipped to China. After that, you got two hundred cars from Latinos. What kinds of car? You got Chevrolets, around '87 or '88; they go to Tijuana. Or from Tijuana to someplace else, like El Salvador or Central America.

AK: The ones that are going to New York, it sounds like you need to have a network to ship them.

SC: Network. Organized crime. You talk about Asian organized crime. I give you some examples. You got two hundred cars a month from Blacks. Blacks stealing BMWs, Cadillacs. Each ethnic group specializes in stealing certain makes of cars. The cars stolen by Blacks are sent to Compton.

AK: Do Cambodian gangs fight with one another?

SC: Right now, yes. Cambodian gangs right now still fight each other and fight with Vietnamese gangs, fight with Latino gangs, fight with Black gangs.

AK: Has the gang problem gotten worse or is it the same?

SC: I think right now it's better; it's much better than two, three years ago. At that time, you got around five gang details, five detectives. Now, you got forty, compared to four years ago, three years ago. In 1992 there were around fifty-six homicides a year. But now there are about thirty-six homicide gang problems a year.

AK: The gangs are fighting with one another, they're stealing cars. What else are the Cambodian gangs doing?

SC: Besides the car stealing, we have the home invasions. Your gang leader says, "I have no money now, we got to find another house that has money." Asian families don't put their money in the bank. They put it in the house: $10,000, $30,000, $100,000 in the house. So they're looking for someone who has a good car, who has a good business, and they follow him around. And later, home robbery, home invasion.

AK: Are Cambodian gangs robbing other Cambodians?

SC: Yes, other Cambodians. Asian gangs, Cambodian gangs, never rob Latinos, never rob Blacks. They know they don't have money inside the house, they don't have jewelry, they don't have diamonds, anything expensive.

AK: It seems like the community's relatively small. You're robbing your parents' friends, your friends; you're robbing from yourself.

SC: That's right. The gangs, they don't care. They don't respect anybody. They don't obey anybody. The kids ask other gang members to rob their own parents. They do that!

AK: Are Cambodians getting better about reporting crime? I have the sense that they have been very hesitant.

SC: They still do not report, they underreport.

AK: How many home invasions do you see per month among Cambodians?

SC: I think at least five.

AK: And that's an underreported figure?

SC: Four, five years ago, every day there were sixteen robberies, home invasions.

AK: One way of fighting the gang problem has been to increase police activity. But are there other problems at the root of the gang problem?

SC: When they reported more homicides by gangs, the police department started to work with the schools, to work with the social service programs, to work with other communities. The curfew in Long Beach now is 8:00 in the morning until 2:30 P.M. and 10 P.M. until the morning. At first, the curfew was only at night, but we later installed a curfew during the day and kids who aren't in school are put in holding centers.

AK: Are there a lot of kids dropping out of school, not going to school?

SC: Cambodians have a 65 percent drop-out rate from high school.

AK: Are they all joining gangs then?

SC: Drop out of school, no place to go. Fooling around someplace, got no place to go. If you don't go to school, the kids tend to enjoy themselves. Like my son, he cannot stay at home; it's boring, boring; I have to find something for him to do: buy him a game or let him play basketball. When you have a group of kids with nothing to do, talk about problems. They never talk about school; they talk about bad things.

AK: What about child abuse?

SC: The mother has three or four kids; the mother always wants her way and the kids want their own way. When you go to school, if you got a blue eye or a red arm or whatever, the police calls the social worker. You don't want the kid to go home and be hit by the parent again.

AK: Do you think some of this has to do with cultural differences in disciplining?

SC: Right, right.

AK: In terms of discipline, are there differences between traditional Cambodian versus American standards?

SC: I think a lot of Cambodian parents don't agree with the American way; they don't agree with that. The parents don't have power here. Kids have more power than parents in the family.

AK: What about domestic violence? Do you see a lot of that?

SC: Cambodians have more problems than other minorities now.

AK: More domestic violence?

SC: Yeah, I see a lot of cases. I see a lot of cases where the parents fight. When parents fight, kids suffer also. When the father is fooling around outside, goes to gamble, plays games, comes home and tries to get money from the wife, the parents fight, sometimes the kids get scared and call the police and this is reported as domestic violence. Or sometimes the kids call the police to get back at their parents, or husbands and wives make false reports against each other. About 25 percent of the cases are false reports. There are about 30 runaway cases per month.

AK: Are Cambodians going back and forth to Cambodia to visit?

SC: Everyone goes to visit, do business. Go to do this and do that. Some Cambodians from the U.S. have gone back to Cambodia to take up positions in the government there. Now, let's talk about when you go back to Cambodia, as a man, you leave the wife behind, you leave the house behind. You don't take care of the house, whatever.

AK: A lot of the men are going back and forth?

SC: Yes. And then the economic situation here is a little bit down because money is spent in Cambodia. When I went to Cambodia with my wife and my kids, I spent $20,000. If you spend $20,000 in Long Beach, Long Beach could grow. But now, they sell a house here, they sell this, sell that, to go to Cambodia.

AK: Do a lot of people send money back to Cambodia to their relatives?

SC: They send every penny to Cambodia right now. That's why the savings is not increasing here, it's always sent to Cambodia.

AK: There's an outflow of money.

SC: The Vietnamese, too, the same, it's sent to Vietnam. It's $30 million a month, I think. The businesses here cannot pick up.

AK: How are the businesses here doing? Are they surviving OK?

SC: A lot cannot survive long.

AK: Do a lot of businesses open and close almost right away?

SC: Yes. A lot of people close; 25 percent close almost right away.

AK: You talked about gangs being involved with auto theft, home invasions. Are they preying on businesses as well?

SC: They have what they call gang protection. We've arrested a lot of people already. Gang protection; before, yes, a lot; now, no more. Before, they came, knocked on the door, asking for protection money, grabbed the gun and shot on the wall, something like that. But now, no more.

AK: How come they stopped doing that?

SC: Because we arrest a lot of people. Now, it's escape to Lowell, Massachusetts. Escape to Stockton, Fresno, Modesto, Oakland.

AK: It seems like the police here have really cracked down.

SC: Forty police officers are detectives on gang detail.

AK: Do you see gambling as a problem among Cambodians?

SC: Yes. I would say the gambling is around 30 percent. Cambodians, Chinese Cambodians, like gambling too much. See the Bicycle Club right over there? It's a place to gamble. The problem with gambling is they don't have time to take care of their own kids. When they play games, it's going to be overnight, two, three nights. They're tired when they get home.

AK: So that indirectly feeds into the gang problem?

SC: Yeah, everywhere, it's all directed at the kids. The kids lose a lot of family. So I don't blame them. Some of them say, "OK, I'm old enough; I should enjoy myself also."

AK: What are some other things you see as problems in the Cambodian community? It seems like the chief one that you've identified is the parent-child relationship having all sorts of problems.

SC: Another thing that I see is the leadership's concerns. The leadership should focus on Long Beach instead of on Cambodia.

AK: Is that what the leadership is doing right now? Focusing on Cambodia?

SC: Right. Too much politics.

AK: Do you see a lot of political factionalism here, people fighting amongst each other?

SC: Right. I'm in the middle; I can see. If you cannot solve your own family problems, how are you going to do the politics? How are you going to solve Cambodia's problems? You better serve your own family, your own daughter and son, teach them to be independent, you be a role model, but you go to Cambodia instead. You've got a broken home here, your kid is in a gang. But you go to Cambodia, you focus on something in Cambodia, you are going to do something corrupt in politics over there. Right now, it's focused over there.

AK: One thing I heard is that because a lot of the men are focusing on politics, even when a family has a business, it's the wife who ends up running the business. Do you see that kind of thing going on?

SC: Normally, the man is too much into politics. He leaves the kid far behind, leaves the wife far behind. For me, if I cannot take care of my own kid, my own wife, I'm not going to go to Cambodia to solve any problems. You can solve the problems here first. If you give your kid a good education, get yourself established, become independent, you'll have a little bit more brains to solve problems. But if you leave the kids behind, by the time you come back, the kids are in gangs.

AK: I hear 70 to 80 percent of the Cambodians in Long Beach are on welfare?

SC: Yes.

AK: What's the attitude toward welfare? Is it considered OK to be on welfare or is it something to be ashamed of?

SC: They're not educated, that's why. If you educate them, they will find jobs, they will do something. Nobody educates them, nobody tries to help them. Now, I think it's around 70 percent, because a lot of the new immigrants from France, from other countries, are hiring them to work. They don't hire other minorities, they hire their own people. That's why Latinos and Blacks, they don't like it.

AK: So, these [Cambodian] immigrants from France, from Australia, they're actually revitalizing the economy?

SC: Yes. They invest many million dollars here.

AK: What kinds of business are they opening?

SC: Normally they buy buildings, they buy jewelry stores, they buy hotels.

AK: What kinds of jobs do Cambodians have, the 20 percent or so who are working?

SC: Teachers' aides, engineering, service providers, social workers. Very few Cambodians work with the American government. I see more young Cambodians who are getting medical degrees. We have no Cambodian lawyer yet, but we will soon. The lawyers must understand the culture.

AK: It seems like so many of them aren't even making it through high school.

SC: The government has tried to help, to educate more Cambodians. Like at this school [California State University, Long Beach], we have a lot of Cambodians attending to get diplomas.

AK: Do a lot of those who are in gangs go back to school when they get older?

SC: Not all of them go back to school. They end up with low-paying jobs somewhere. Cambodians are suffering more than other minorities because our leadership here is not strong enough.

AK: What is the relationship between the Cambodian community and the city government? Is the city responding to the Cambodian community's needs?

SC: Five years ago, no. But since we have a new mayor, the new mayor here is very good. I have consulted with her a couple of times. She's very sensitive and she's very helpful to the Cambodian community.

AK: You mentioned that you're a Cambodian but you have some Chinese blood in you. Do you think most Chinese Cambodians tend to identify themselves as Chinese or as Cambodian?

SC: A lot of Cambodian Chinese identify themselves as Chinese. I feel my Chinese blood, but I cannot forget my hometown in Cambodia. But a lot of Chinese people say: "I'm Chinese, I'm not Cambodian." But the Chinese Cambodians coming from Cambodia are making money because of our people. They should understand that. The Chinese people here have businesses because of Cambodians. Without Cambodians to buy your products, your business is going to die.

AK: At the same time, didn't they suffer a lot under the Khmer Rouge, even more than other Cambodians?

SC: Right. They suffer and suffer, five generations suffer and suffer and suffer.

AK: What do you think is going to happen to the Cambodian community in the next ten, twenty years?

SC: I think in the next ten, twenty years, my daughter and my son [that is, the younger generation] will take over.

AK: Another question I have is, what happened to the Cambodian students who came in the '60s? Are they still in the Long Beach area? What kinds of jobs did they end up getting?

SC: I know a couple of them. They work with the State Department. They work at Cal State Long Beach. They work with the C.I.A.

AK: So, they're in pretty good jobs?

SC: Good jobs. They have good jobs; they have a good life.

AK: Do you think people like that have the same kinds of problems with their kids? Are their kids joining gangs, that sort of thing?

SC: A couple of them, the kids have joined gangs. I'm glad my kids have not gone into the gangs. If they go to the gangs, I'll kill myself.

AK: It seems like there's such peer pressure on Cambodian youngsters. Even if the kids want to go to college, it's hard.

SC: A couple of years ago, we had a Cambodian attending Cal State Long Beach who was a gang member. At night, he committed crimes to get money to go to school.

AK: Are drugs a problem?

SC: The kids try to pick up drugs now after they've been involved with gangs for so long.

AK: They're taking drugs, but are they selling?

SC: Buying drugs, selling drugs. Started a few years ago. If you're an addict already, you got to do something to feed your addiction. You got to do everything: kill or shoot or rob, whatever.

AK: Do you think that's going to be an even bigger problem?

SC: Bigger problem. I see many Cambodian young ladies who have a drug problem, and they cannot study. They come to my office, a lot of them. Some of the Cambodian kids, their parents send them back to their hometowns [in Cambodia]. They start crime over there! In Cambodia, we never had home robberies, we never had kidnappings but now it's started. The gangs took those problems from here to Cambodia.

AK: Why do the parents send the kids to Cambodia?

SC: They got no choice.

AK: They don't know what to do with the kids?

SC: That's right. You buy an airplane ticket, ship them over there. But after they go over there, there's still a gang problem. Motorcycle robbery, car robbery, highjacking.

AK: Are there kidnapping, carjacking among Cambodians here too?

SC: Yes.

AK: It sounds like the problems you are dealing with are almost overwhelming. The Long Beach Cambodian community is fortunate to have you in the police department. Thank you for sharing your insights with me.

August 15, 1996

4. Daniel M. Lam
How Massachusetts Became a Refugee-Friendly State

DR. DANIEL LAM is the executive director of the South Cove Community Health Center in Boston. When Audrey Kim interviewed him on August 25, 1995, he was working as a special assistant to the Norfolk County district attorney. In that capacity he directed the Peace Project—an initiative to prevent hate and bias-motivated violence. The interview took place in his office in Quincy, Massachusetts. We sought him out for an interview because he was the director of the Massachusetts Office for Refugees and Immigrants for seven years—during a period when a very large number of refugees from Southeast Asia entered the United States.

Daniel Lam grew up in the Chinese-Cambodian enclave in Phnom Penh. A high school dropout, he straightened out his life after converting to Christianity in his late teens. After receiving a bachelor of theology degree from Alliance Bible Seminary in Hong Kong in 1970, he came to the United States, where he obtained a second B.A. from Toccoa Falls College in Georgia in 1971. He returned to Phnom Penh and became the assistant minister of the Chinese Alliance Mission Church in that city. He came back to the United States in 1973 and obtained an M.A. in cross-cultural communication from Wheaton College in 1974, an M.Ed. in counseling and psychological services from Georgia State University in 1975, and an Ed.D. in higher education from Highland University in Tennessee in 1977. When the Khmer Rouge came to power in 1975, he was granted political asylum. (He was considered an asylee rather than a refugee because he was already in the United States at the time.)

From 1976 to 1978, Dr. Lam served as the associate minister in the Community Baptist Church in Milwaukee, Wisconsin. He went to Hong Kong in 1978 to become the director of counselor training, research, and evaluation at the Breakthrough Counseling Center there. He also taught part time at the Hong Kong Baptist College. Dr. Lam crossed the Pacific Ocean once again in 1980 to become the director of mental health and social services at the South Cove Community Health Center. In November 1983 he was appointed as the director of the Massachusetts Office for Refugees and Immigrants. He served in that capacity until 1990. In 1992 he served as the director of the Quincy Coalition for the Prevention of Alcohol, Tobacco, and Other Drug Problems. He has been a part-time director of the Asian American Marriage and Family Institute in Quincy, Massachusetts, since 1993. He has taught at Wheelock College in Boston, Brown University in Providence, Rhode Island, and the University of Massachusetts, Boston. In addition, he has had a private practice in marriage and family counseling and mediation since 1978.

For some two decades, since he became a U.S. citizen in 1980, Dr. Lam has actively participated in the civic affairs of the state in which he lives. He has served on the board of directors, often as president, of numerous community organizations, including the Boston Chinese Evangelical Church, the Lam Family Association of New England, the Massachusetts Governor's Advisory Council for Refugees and Immigrants, the Massachusetts Asian American Forum, the International Institute of Boston, the United Way of Massachusetts Bay, the Randolph Chinese American Parents' Association, the Randolph Peace Committee, and the Randolph Credit Union. He lives in Randolph, Massachusetts.

*   *   *

AK: Can you start by talking about your work in the Massachusetts Office for Refugees and Immigrants? What kinds of activities were you involved in?

DL: At the state refugee office, basically we have to implement policy in an even-handed, across-the-board way. One cannot single out any group. Just because I am from Cambodia, I cannot give Cambodians special treatment. You probably know that in 1984–85, around that time, the federal Office of Refugee Resettlement provided money to start an initiative called the MAA [Mutual Assistance Association] Initiative that generated a whole series of activities. Instead of saying, "OK, you write a proposal and you compete, just like anyone else," we realized that no way are we going to have a group of refugees, a group of Cambodians, to whom we can say, "You are going to have to compete. You are also going to have to demonstrate for us your track record." So what we did was to incorporate leadership training and wrap it into the whole proposal-writing process.

AK: Was that what the federal government asked you to do?

DL: I don't think the federal government told us what we could do. We felt strongly at that point that the survival of the community, both short term and long, would have to rely on the leadership. We knew that sometimes the official spokesperson may not be the real leader. So what we did was have a group of people go through a training program on how to survive in the United States. We identified experts who knew about community development and so forth. And then we asked each of the communities to identify a team of people. At that time, the refugee communities were Cambodian, Vietnamese, Lao, Hmong, and ethnic Chinese. You probably know about the ethnic Chinese, they don't organize by country, they organize by their ethnicity. They had a name like Organization of Chinese from Vietnam, Cambodia, and Laos. For more than three months, once a week, one evening a week, we got the whole group together, let's say about forty people. In order for people to do proposal-writing, they have to first identify what they want, right? One has to first develop a program idea before one can write a proposal. But these people probably did not know that in fact we in the state refugee office had a hidden agenda. That is, we're going to identify, we're going to open this process and see how the leadership emerges.

AK: I see. You asked the Cambodian community to identify a team of people, then you started to groom those people for leadership by training them.

DL: Right. The first set of leaders included people like Ly Y. Ly was instrumental later on in building the Buddhist temple, the one in Chelmsford. So we had this group of people. As in any Cambodian community, you have people who were identified very much with their national politics, also their politics here.

AK: It seems like Cambodians are very tied to the politics back home and also there are factions here based on those alliances.

DL: Exactly.

AK: [Massachusetts State Refugee Coordinator] Tom Ford mentioned that in Chelsea the leadership keeps changing depending on the political alliances.

DL: Yes, on who won the elections.

AK: I'm going off on a tangent here, but do you see the MAAs as being almost like fronts for political organizations?

DL: I don't know if they can be called fronts, but if what you mean by a front is that a certain leader has some kind of political agenda, then one would have to say that the MAA is a vehicle, yes. The Cambodian leadership in Long Beach also does those things. And for them, that's not a surprise. The Vietnamese leadership, same thing; American leadership, same thing. One's personal political alliance becomes obvious. But I think what's important for Cambodians is figuring out how we are going to survive here.

AK: Can you back up and describe for me the different ways and different types of people who were coming over?

DL: Yeah. Before the MAAs, Cambodians did not really come here in any significant numbers.

AK: Did they start coming here in 1979?

DL: Not really.

AK: So was Massachusetts a later resettlement site?

DL: Yes. I went to work in 1983. The significant arrival of Cambodians did not occur until the mid-1980s.

AK: Why did so many Cambodians come in the mid '80s?

DL: Remember that Vietnam invaded Cambodia. Although the Khmer Rouge came to power in Cambodia in '75, Pol Pot's genocide was not well known then to the world. If you can recall, when the Khmer Rouge entered Phnom Penh, people were lining the streets to welcome them. "The war is over! The war is over!" At that time, the attitude of most Khmer was, "We don't care whether this government is Khmer Rouge or Sihanouk. All we want is a hut, a transistor radio, a motorcycle, and a plot of land that we can work on." It was not until 1979 that people started coming out in large numbers. They probably felt that Cambodia was going to be colonized by Vietnam when Vietnam invaded Cambodia. So that was the push. As for the pull, the pull, the then-first lady of Massachusetts had a lot to do with it.

AK: Really?

DL: Oh, yeah. Kitty Dukakis. Kitty is active in the Jewish community; she's Jewish herself. She was involved in Jewish Holocaust memorial projects, that kind of stuff. She's one of the national leaders in that effort. She somehow transferred her personal commitment to publicizing the Cambodian genocide. Every year, in the state house, there's a memorial service for victims of the Armenian genocide and the Cambodian genocide. She knew a person by the name of Peter Pond. Peter is a Protestant minister, the stepson of a former diplomat. Peter, at the early stage of Cambodian resettlement in the United States, was one of the strong advocates for refugees, to the point where he campaigned to resettle them here. Peter met Kitty and, knowing her commitment to commemorating the Holocaust, Peter talked to her. Kitty asked, "How can I be helpful as the first lady?" At that time, we had the Cambodian Minors Project, the Refugee Minors Project, which involved children who didn't know where their parents were. They were brought here to be resettled in the United States. So then Kitty got involved with the sponsorship and resettlement of those children. That was her first contact with Cambodians. And somehow, I don't know, her heart—it's a personal thing—her heart identified with this. She went to the camps in Thailand, and then she began to lobby.

AK: About what year was this?

DL: '84, '85, around that time.

AK: Before that, Massachusetts was just like any other state?

DL: Not just like any other state. I think very few Cambodians had come here. You know that volags [voluntary agencies] tried to distribute people wherever their offices were. Although they said there was no quota, if you count the number of refugees going to each of the states (I'm referring to the first distribution, not secondary migration), if you figure out the total population of the state, perhaps with the exception of California, the percentage of refugees going to that state is almost exactly the percentage of people from that state in the United States. For example, in Massachusetts, we've got about 4 percent of the total population of the United States. In all the years, on the average, about 4 percent of the refugees came to Massachusetts.

AK: Was there some sort of unwritten federal policy to do that?

DL: Yes. Anyway, Kitty began to lobby, and then she and Peter Pond made a trip to Washington, D.C. [to testify in Congress]. The Cambodian community nationwide is basically a small community. At that time, Lowell was unknown. But all of a sudden, in about four years, you have this large number of Cambodians here. At that time, Lowell was a depressed city. Lowell was almost bankrupt.

AK: In the mid-eighties?

DL: Yeah. That's before the so-called Massachusetts miracle. We had a depression and then all of a sudden, a boom. The areas where refugees go to are mostly depressed areas with relatively inexpensive housing or housing that no one else wants. The resettlement agencies place people there because rent is cheaper in those areas. Later on, how they transform that into another kind of community, that's a different chapter of the story.

AK: You mean, in resettling refugees, volags were more interested in cheap housing than in whether jobs were available in the area?

DL: I think any volag or the local affiliate of a volag usually would ask, What are the basic needs? Housing, jobs, and education. Now, at that point, working in computer companies, assembly work, was one of the most popular jobs for refugees. We have several companies out there in Lowell and Lawrence.

AK: I understand that Wang Computers started some businesses in Lowell.

DL: Wang's international headquarters is in Lowell. Kitty has been blamed by some of the people who didn't want to see refugees coming in. I believe that at one point there was a demonstration in front of her home, saying, "OK, why don't you take these refugees into your home?"

AK: I want to make sure I understand. Kitty Dukakis was really instrumental, both in lobbying at the federal level in Washington and in saying, "Massachusetts will take you."

DL: Yeah, at that point the economy was picking up in Massachusetts while the economy in other areas, in other states, was going down. Massachusetts was booming.

AK: Oh, really? I thought Massachusetts has been in a recession for a long time.

DL: No. During '85, '86, '87, those were the golden years. That's why we had plenty of secondary migrants. The large number of Cambodians in Massachusetts resulted not just from direct resettlement but also from secondary migration. Not only that, I believe in 1986 the state legislature enacted the Gateway City Initiative: $15 million going to cities that had significant numbers of newcomers. The chairwoman of the Ways and Means Committee in the [state] senate was from Lawrence. Lawrence has a significant number of Hispanics. Her definition of newcomers is Hispanics. You had $15 million from the state to do the Gateway City Project, which had very few requirements. All you had to do was document how many people were newcomers. And then you decided, you the city, since you knew the community, decided what you wanted to do with the money. Because of that, specialized education and other so-called luxury items became available. For example, the library would have special sections of certain kinds of books, tapes, or whatever. In there, too, was a citizenship training program. At that time, twenty-some localities, cities and towns, qualified for this. The mayor's office hired a person to be coordinator for the newcomers. Fall River at that time was not even a place that Khmers went to.

AK: Massachusetts was doing really well economically and you've got Kitty Dukakis lobbying for the refugees. People were feeling generous because there was all this money. The cities in Massachusetts said, "We want a piece of this pie since we've got newcomers." So they started setting up more programs and that became a draw for the secondary migrants.

DL: Yes, definitely a draw. Not to mention that I think one of the most significant developments at that time was a comprehensive refugee service plan. Basically, the governor wrote a memo to all the state agencies saying they would have to develop, as part of their agencies' policies for the future, a section on how they intend to serve refugees. So we're dealing with accessibility issues. That's how we became a refugee-friendly state.

AK: How many Cambodians were settled in Massachusetts initially, that is, not through secondary migration?

DL: I think in any given year, even a booming year, in any given year, it was less than two thousand.

AK: So most of the Cambodians here are from secondary migration?

DL: Yes, secondary migrants. But when the economy crashed, many of them left.

AK: At the peak, how many Cambodians were in Massachusetts, that is, before they left?

DL: At one point, people were saying there were more than forty thousand Cambodians in Lowell.

AK: I think now there are about twenty-five thousand.

DL: Once you kind of put down your roots, it's hard for you to pick up and move. I think the most mobile people are single men without children. They can pick up and move. Twenty-five thousand at this point is not surprising.

AK: When I went to Lowell, I asked the new executive director of the MAA there what percent were secondary migrants; he said everyone there was originally resettled there. It seems there's some confusion [with regard to the definition of "secondary migrants"] because my impression is that a lot of those people were secondary migrants, people who, literally the minute they were resettled somewhere else, left and came to Lowell. But I guess some people don't count that as secondary migration.

DL: Yes, in fact, at that time, there was the public perception or misperception that Lowell had become a draw, that everyone wanted to go to Lowell. There's even a saying, though I'm not sure how accurate it is, that someone went to the camps in Thailand and did an informal survey, asking the Khmer, "If you go to the United States, where do you want to go?" "I want to go to Lowell." "Why do you want to go to Lowell?" "Number one, I'll have a good job there. Number two, I and my children will have better educational opportunities."

AK: The Lowell school system had set up special programs?

DL: No, but they've heard of Harvard, MIT, and all this kind of stuff.

AK: That's very interesting. Are you saying that in the camps, they were already thinking about sending their kids to college?

DL: I don't know about that, but at that time all these accusations were flying all over the place. Kitty Dukakis and another person, a Congressman named Chet Atkins—his district includes Lowell—Atkins, Dukakis, and Pond were asked: "Why did you bring them over and dump them here?"

AK: Tom Ford seems to think that the presence of the venerable monk in Lowell was a big draw for people.

DL: I would agree, yeah. It was the temple, though the first Buddhist temple is not here, it's in Providence. You know the Cambodian Buddhist system is organized much like the Roman Catholics. Cambodian Buddhism has two branches, Thammayut and Mahanikay. Ly and his group established the temple.

AK: Is the Lynn temple older than the Chelmsford one?

DL: Yeah. the Lynn temple was the first one. You know, Long Beach is the largest Khmer community in America. Some people are saying Lowell is the Long Beach of the East Coast.

AK: How were Cambodians doing when they first got here, and how are they doing now in terms of jobs and the rate of dependency on public assistance?

DL: Just like the Vietnamese, the first arrivals had direct connections with Americans, either public or private. So this group's adjustment has been relatively easier. People like Ly Y was a reporter.

AK: Is he in this area?

DL: Yeah, working at the *Boston Globe.* He was a reporter but he can't report here; he's doing something else. His relationship was with, I believe, Greenwell, who is now associate editor at the *Boston Globe.* Greenwell, at that point, was a reporter in Cambodia for the *Globe,* covering the war. Ly Y was his interpreter. You saw the movie *The Killing Fields,* much like that relationship.

AK: So the first Cambodians who came out were probably educated people who had some ties to the U.S.?

DL: Yes. They left all of a sudden. They came totally unprepared. You're talking about three waves. The first wave adjusted relatively easily because they already had connections. The second wave came between '75 and '78.

AK: I didn't even know that there were any Cambodians who got out between '75 and '78.

DL: Oh, yes, there were.

AK: I thought they were trapped in Cambodia.

DL: I know, but some were walking out. We had a number of "boat people" at that time. The larger number of boat people was Vietnamese, but there was also a small number of Cambodian boat people. The large push, the third wave, was after the end of 1978, after the Vietnamese invasion. This group of people were mostly country folk, farmers.

AK: They're people who would have had a hard time in Phnom Penh probably.

DL: Exactly! During the war, I was in the capital for two and a half years, '71 to '73.

AK: What year did you come to the U.S.?

DL: I came in 1970.

AK: So you weren't in Cambodia during the Khmer Rouge?

DL: No. I came in '70, I left in '71 to go back to Phnom Penh, and I returned again in '73. But even during the time I was living in Phnom Penh, the refugees were already running to the capital because of the fighting in the outskirts. Before that, Phnom Penh had probably around five hundred thousand people. But in a short two years, it swelled to more than one million.

AK: Lots of people escaped to the capital?

DL: Yes, because it was safer there. There was fighting in the countryside, but Phnom Penh was not affected initially. The people from the countryside came in and most of them became laborers. But that influx was not unusual. You can harvest two times a year in Cambodia. But some people do only one harvest and then they come to get odd jobs in the city. From my observation, it was difficult for them to function in Phnom Penh. Imagine how much more difficult it is for such people to function in the United States. I still remember this group of people arriving some time in the middle of winter. I was so angry because the volags should not have allowed that to happen. You cannot have this Khmer family arrive in the middle of winter at Logan Airport, wearing sarongs and beach flip-flops. The staff in the volags didn't think about all those things. They just picked up the people and dumped them here. I'm not saying that all volags are like that. No, within a certain agency, you have different people. But still . . .

AK: One explanation I heard was that a lot of Cambodians were settled in the Boston area because there are a lot of volags there, and they were independently bringing over Cambodians, so there wasn't good coordination. Is that true?

DL: True. The Khmer themselves, some of the early leaders, scouted different locations. And whether or not Kitty Dukakis had anything to do with it, people mention Kitty Dukakis. At one point, people even alleged that the volags were actually recruiting Khmer directly from the camps. People asked the Khmer, "Where do you want to go?" "Want to go to Lowell." I don't know how accurate that is. The government in this state is very cooperative. You have a government that is really working together. Everyone has a lot of input. And maybe a policy developed out of those discussions. It's not a traditional bureaucracy saying, "You do this." There's a lot of input.

AK: You're talking about the State Refugee Office?

DL: The State Office. Every year, during those several years, we even had town meetings or hearings, depending on how you want to name them, in different regions in the state. Refugees could come directly to share in what's going on in that community. So they're at least acting on the perception that we welcome them here.

AK: How did the Cambodians do when they first came? Did they start to work right away?

DL: I don't think they worked right away. The State Refugee Office was the leader at that time. We felt it would be better to invest; we even had a term at that time, we called it "front-end loading." I believed strongly, I still believe now, if this group of people is better prepared or at least has minimum skills to go into a minimum-skill job, the likelihood of their returning to public assistance will be reduced. So, take whatever time was allowable, give them training, make sure that they are really ready for the job market, and make sure that there are wage-earners in the family. Don't be too concerned about whether it'll take three months or six months. Think in terms of the family, instead of simply looking at the head of household. If you recall, U.S. refugee policy at the beginning stage focused on the head of household, and the head of household is the husband. But we in Massachusetts had this front-end loading approach.

AK: That philosophy seems to have really changed. In talking to various state refugee coordinators now, they're all saying, "We don't care about learning; just get them working."

DL: Yeah.

AK: Do you think that policy was successful?

DL: I think so. If you were to do some research, if you were to take the group of people who actually went through the training, you'll see the difference. If you recall, to begin with, the refugees were allowed thirty-six months of cash assistance and medical assistance, and then the eligibility period was gradually reduced, and now it's only eight months; pretty soon, it's going to be three months. If you were to take that group of people and you examine whether or not training had any impact on their rate of job retention and their earnings, you will see the people who are now doing much better financially are the people who arrived first. The condition in which they arrived was not better than that of those who arrived later, but the later arrivals did not have the same training. Supposing I arrive and I get a job right away. I earn a wage. What happens? Unfortunately, six months later, I lose my job. My only job. I was a poor farmer, and certainly I cannot do farming here. So the only thing I can do, know how to do, is to do something where I make minimum wage. I have, let's say, a typical family, I have three kids, my wife has to take care of my kids, so everyone relies on my forty hours a week at $4 an hour. Meanwhile, you're saying, OK, you do your work, everyone who comes to this country, they learn English on their own. They learned English at night. It would take a person with strong, strong motivation to mop floors for eight hours, not to mention taking care of the other needs of the family, and then go study English at night. So, not only philosophically, but in terms of fiscal management, from the state's selfish standpoint, it's not that we want to milk more federal dollars . . .

AK: Rather than paying for these people later, have the federal government pay for this up-front?

DL: Pay now or pay later. Even when these people later on become AFDC [Aid to Families with Dependent Children] recipients, at least 50 percent of AFDC [funding] comes from the state. So, why not do it now? I've heard the saying that the state of California is making money off the refugee business.

AK: How are they making money?

DL: Well, if you look at the federal allocation of refugee dollars to California, at one point I think it was more than all the rest of the states combined. Certainly a lot of refugees have gone to California.

AK: You mean California is probably making more money than it is providing in services to refugees?

DL: That's basically what people say.

AK: It sounds like a lot of Cambodians who came to Massachusetts were given time to learn English and job skills. But after thirty-six months, what happened? Did they end up working?

DL: They end up working. I remember a man by the name of Win Su among the first group of people. Win Su came with barely any English. But Win Su actually became a social worker, he got training from the community college, and then he got a degree, and then he worked as a counselor for Metropolitan Indochinese Children and Adolescent Services. And later on, he was recruited by a bank.

AK: Related to that, I've seen a pattern where it seems like a lot of the leadership in the Cambodian communities are either pre-'75 people or they're men who are now in their thirties who came over in their late teens. I think Tom Ford mentioned that a lot of those people started by working in the community, maybe at an MAA, and then if they're good, they're recruited by places like banks.

DL: I have mixed feelings about that. On the one hand, I feel that, oh geez, a lot of investment was put into training this person to enhance what he can do for an MAA. And then after so many years of nurturing, he gets recruited by a money-making business. If you're going to continue to work in a human services agency, the pay is low, so why on earth won't you go to work in a bank? By working at the bank, there are better opportunities for you. This trend is not unique in the Khmer community; I think it occurs in all immigrant communities—being recruited by the bureaucracy, that is. But if their hearts and souls remain devoted to the community, then it's good. Otherwise, you become a tool of the oppressor.

AK: Along those lines, in your opinion, do you think MAAs and the leadership are really there for the benefit of the community?

DL: The MAAs, when they first started, they got their name from ORR. ORR, at one point, to begin with, was kind of simple-minded. Hearing that we don't want to have volags monopolize the whole thing, that we would like to have refugee communities serve themselves, they wanted to groom people within the ethnic communities to become service providers. But the volags viewed the MAAs as competitors. Even now, the resentment still exists. Some sabotaged the whole thing. There are only three Khmer MAAs in Massachusetts that are still functioning: the one in Lowell, the one in Chelsea, the one in Fall River. Are they merely surviving, or are they doing well? It's debatable. Are they really helping people? In any given situation, regardless of the motivation of the leadership, the MAAs more or less serve someone in the process. But if your question is, Have the MAAs played a key role in developing new leadership in the community? that is a question that cannot be answered easily. Giving help is easier. How come? I receive this letter from public welfare, for example; I don't know what it is. It has only one line in Khmer saying this is an important document, make sure someone reads it. Now, I live in Chelsea; I know there is a Khmer MAA here. So I go over there and say, "Would you tell me what's going on here?" That's how the MAA can help. But has the MAA helped develop new leadership? Has the MAA really helped people to be self-sufficient? It's hard to say. Self-sufficiency is the key word in the whole refugee resettlement process. From ORR's perspective, anyone who gets off public assistance is self-sufficient.

AK: What do you think is the rate of dependency on public assistance at this point? Or is that an irrelevant question for Cambodians? There is a high percentage on public assistance, I've been told.

DL: Yes.

AK: You were talking about the definition of self-sufficiency. I'm wondering if this is even a helpful way to look at the situation.

DL: It certainly is one of the criteria; it's not the only criterion. I think it should mean not only that someone no longer has to rely on public assistance but who also knows how to manage [the environment one lives in], who, in the longer term, becomes a participant in the community. The Chinese have lived in this country for a long time, but how many Chinese Americans actually participate in the larger society they live in? I think we cannot afford, we, as a country, cannot afford that kind of nonparticipation. For example, registering to vote; they simply don't do it. I think the willingness to participate is more important than the skill. Skill you can learn; you can pick up the skill, but the willingness or the feeling that, "Hey, look, I can do this, too," the right or the desire to be involved, is harder to come by. The majority of these people still feel that this is not their country.

AK: Isn't that sort of attitude more true for refugees than for immigrants?

DL: I haven't really studied it, but I don't think there's a significant difference between the two. For example, the newer immigrants from Hong Kong simply say, "The reason we would like to have permanent resident status is it's more convenient." As for the sense of belonging, even if we really want to belong, whether or not the system really embraces us, that's another thing. I believe Massachusetts was one of the first states, if not the first state, at that time, to push for naturalization and citizenship for refugees. We began to do this about '86.

AK: What was the impetus for that?

DL: It's based on the belief that part of self-sufficiency depends on a sense of belonging in the community, and nothing can be more concrete to demonstrate one's sense of belonging and desire to participate than by becoming a citizen and learning how to work in that process. At one point we said, "OK, encourage the MAA purposely not to schedule the meeting in a home, but to schedule it in one of the government's public buildings, like, for example, schedule the meeting in the town hall." Because you and I know, psychologically, the Khmer want to stay as far away as possible from the government. Knowing that the government is yours, and people who work there are, in fact, your employees, is an alien concept to them.

AK: It sounds like what you're saying is that even though some Cambodians are self-sufficient and have jobs, as a group, they're still marginalized because they're not really part of the mainstream society, participating, feeling like this is their own government.

DL: Yeah, I would stand by that statement. Is that behavior exclusively Khmer? No. You know that prior to the Refugee Act of 1980, there was a program called the Indochinese Refugee Assistance Program. Vietnam, Cambodia, and Laos collapsed in 1975. There was no public policy for refugee resettlement, so for humanitarian reasons Congress quickly said, "OK, this group of people needs to be rescued." It was truly a rescue mission at that time. So Congress quickly put together the Indochinese Refugee Assistance Program. We needed to have something in place to provide cash assistance and medical assistance to these people, so immediately they were given welfare benefits. Looking back at this, the immediate convenience created a long-term repercussion with a negative impact.

AK: You mean setting up a system that was aid-oriented has become problematic?

DL: Yes, using welfare as a vehicle for refugee resettlement has had unanticipated repercussions.

AK: But wasn't that consistent with what was going on in the Thai camps? I've heard some people say that it's hard for Cambodians to work because they've been dependent on the U.N. [and other international relief agencies] in the camps, and then they come here and they get aid. In other words, it's a behavior that is perpetuated.

DL: True. I've argued that refugees, most of them, or the majority of them, the large majority of them, are self-sufficient people. They have worked, they have raised families—the majority of them. OK, so they are displaced. The reason that they cannot take care of their families any more is because they have been displaced. So, why don't we treat them as displaced workers? I'm a displaced worker; I need help now because I am in transition. But I'm not in this situation forever. We have a federal unemployment program. If I were to get a check from unemployment instead of welfare, that reminds me quite quickly that the reason I get the check is because I'm unemployed. And therefore, my goal should be to make sure I get employed. It's desirable for me to get employed. In fact, the welfare program, when it started, was also transitional, but that transitional program has become a tool that perpetuates dependency.

AK: That analysis could be applied to everyone on welfare, not just the refugees.

DL: Exactly.

AK: So you're saying, from a psychological standpoint, it's a kind of mindset that people get habituated to.

DL: Yeah.

AK: A lot of people I've talked to say that for an uneducated Cambodian who doesn't speak English, if you have a choice between making minimum wage and trying to support a family of five or going on AFDC [the main component of welfare until welfare reform went into effect in 1996], anyone would choose AFDC.

DL: Anyone! If I have three kids, my wife and myself, we have five people. So figure it out. You get not just AFDC; you also get food stamps and medical assistance. How much do I have to make? I would have to get a job in the $40,000 range to have all this stuff. [But if I'm on welfare,] I don't have to do any work, yet the check will come.

AK: I've heard that, too. Do you have any idea what percent are on public assistance?

DL: I don't know. I think Tom Ford should have those numbers. Shortly before I left the State Refugee Office, the dependency rate became an issue, almost to the point of saying because the dependency rate is so high, we're not going to give you any more money or something like that.

AK: Can you comment a little bit about how the kids are doing? Are they mainstreaming?

DL: I would say much more so [than the adults].

AK: In some ways, that seems to be creating a lot of conflicts.

DL: Of course. I used to go to schools to do talks. In Chelsea, I went to this sixth-grade class to talk about what it means to be American. I share my story. In the middle of my presentation, I notice a Cambodian kid, he has hair this side is short, the other side is long, this side is green, that side is purple, wearing a leather jacket with studs. I asked the question, "What's democracy?" This kid says, "It means there is no king. But big deal; we have no king, but we have a president." If a kid is not acculturated, blue hair and all, and behaves more American than Americans, if this kid is not acculturated, he probably would not have answered, "No king." So, we have to take the good, and we also have to tolerate the bad.

AK: With other immigrant groups, there's a desire for upward mobility. Kids go to college, get better jobs, etc. With the Cambodians, somehow, it seems the kids, a lot of them, are dropping out of school and ending up working in factories like their parents. They seem trapped in a cycle rather than moving beyond where their parents are.

DL: I don't think that observation can be applied across the board. For example, I know of a youngster who has graduated from college, even got her M.D. When she first came to my office, she was in high school. We sat down and we talked, and at one point, she said, "I want to go to medical school." I said, "Good, these are the steps you need to take to get to medical school." She ended up in medical school in Pennsylvania with a full scholarship. She just graduated last summer. We have people like that. We also have people at U Mass, Amherst; we also have a group of people who graduated from Boston with college degrees. So I don't know if that observation is really true across the board.

AK: But in terms of the parents, I don't get the sense that they're moving into better jobs. Are they pretty much still in factory or service jobs?

DL: Right. You know the doughnut phenomenon, right? L.A., I think, is the doughnut capital of the world. Forty-eight percent of the doughnut shops in the city of L.A. are owned by Khmer. I viewed this tape—I'm teaching a course at U Mass—it quite surprised me. I saw one of the doughnut shop owners by the name of Bu Na. I almost dropped dead. Bu Na was a social worker here in Massachusetts. He was one of the strong advocates for providing service to refugees. But even more interestingly, in the tape a street-person asked Bu Na to give him a doughnut. And Bu Na's saying, "No way, get out of here." Later on, the reporter asked Bu Na, "This man's hungry and needs to have a doughnut; how come you're not willing to give him even one doughnut?" Bu Na said, "Hey, look; I'm not a shelter here, I'm not a food center, I'm not the Salvation Army either. I pay my rent. I'm doing business and paying taxes. Why do I have to pay taxes twice?" Bu Na was one of the persons who was more educated. I don't mean to suggest that running a doughnut shop is no good. But I can't help but wonder why he was doing this. When a person seems to have ideals and commitment and conviction and wants to do something—Bu Na was in social work; Bu Na was in human services; Bu Na was working at a couple of volags—when you see him ten years later, Bu Na is now doing doughnuts and making a livelihood for himself. Bu Na also said in that tape he always wanted to have a Jaguar and now he has one. In one scene, he was driving his Jaguar to the carwash, a red Jaguar. He said he always wanted to have a Jaguar. OK, who am I to judge? So, I think anyone in human services would have to maintain faith in human beings. But also, at the same time, we should not get too disappointed when ideals get conquered by reality.

AK: Are there many Cambodian businesses in this area?

DL: You probably saw shops in Lowell, some shops in Fall River.

AK: Are those mostly run by ethnic Chinese?

DL: They're Cambodians, but they have a little ethnic Chinese connection.

AK: When I went to the Chelsea MAA, the executive director told me that there are actually a number of Cambodian-owned businesses: travel agencies, insurance, that kind of thing.

DL: Smaller businesses.

AK: I think that's interesting because in the other areas I've been to, there aren't many Cambodians operating any kind of business.

DL: How about Long Beach, have you been there?

AK: No, I haven't been there yet. I'm talking just about the East Coast. Do you have any ideas why there are more Cambodian businesses in this area?

DL: You probably already know that the majority of them are small shops: video stores, little grocery stores.

AK: Are the grocery stores mostly catering to Cambodians?

DL: I think so. It's difficult to imagine a non-Asian going to an Asian grocery store in Lowell. I think if you look at this group, most of them are catering to their own people. The desire of most Khmer, similar to most other Asians, is: "I want to be my own boss." And if you look at those people who are running businesses, with the exception of one or two small restaurants that are owned by people who are a little bit older, the majority of them are younger people.

AK: People who came here in their late teens?

DL: In their late teens or their early twenties. Some of them probably had a job somewhere; for example, working for a sewing company or something like that. In the history of Cambodia, for a long while, most of the businesses, if not all, were owned by ethnic Chinese. The majority of the Khmer were not trained or did not even develop the kind of thinking that says, "I can do this too." Fishermen caught fish, never thinking, "I can sell the fish myself." They took the fish and sold it to the ethnic Chinese. The farmers never thought, "I can sell rice myself." They went to the mill to sell the rice to the ethnic Chinese. So I think there's a new generation of entrepreneurs coming along, but it will probably take a long, long time for Khmer to really learn how to do business.

AK: One theory that I heard is that if Cambodians are catering to other Cambodians, then you need to have a sizable Cambodian community for the businesses to stay afloat. In this area, since there are so many Cambodians, it seems that businesses can be more viable. Do you think that's true?

DL: No. If we have people who are learning how to move around, their language ability improves. Then their need to rely on Cambodian-owned businesses is reduced. Let's take a travel agency, for example. The likelihood of having people like myself go to a Chinese-owned travel agency in Chinatown is small. If they give me a better deal, I probably would go to them, not because they're Chinese but because I'm a consumer who compares prices. My loyalty to doing business with the Chinese is almost nonexistent. There were two grocery stores, Asian grocery stores, that opened here. Neither of them lasted long.

AK: Because there's not a large enough immediate community?

DL: No. From Quincy, for example, the red line [commuter train] takes only about ten, fifteen minutes to get to Chinatown. Now, the Chinese are extremely practical people. If I can buy a head of bok choy here for 72 cents a pound, and if I can get a head of bok choy in Chinatown for 65 cents a pound, not to mention I have a lot of other reasons—the store is larger, the supply is more abundant, you get fresher produce—since I have to go to Chinatown anyway, why pay 7 cents more? So I think ethnic businesses mostly cater to the first generation.

AK: In Philadelphia, there's a large Cambodian community, but there are no Cambodian businesses.

DL: Right.

AK: So, you're saying that it's the younger people who are starting up their own businesses? I'm trying to understand why something happens in one place but not in another.

DL: I believe that the Khmer community in Philadelphia isn't concentrated, is it? Cambodians are all over the city. But if you're looking at Lowell, if you're looking at Chelsea, Revere, you see concentrations. In Revere, they're concentrated on Shirley Avenue for four or five blocks with two or three shops. So I think proximity has something to do with it.

AK: We've talked a little about the ethnic Chinese. I want to find out more about the ethnic Chinese in Cambodia. I've heard different stories about what happened to the ethnic Chinese. One person told me that 90 percent of the ethnic Chinese were killed and only a very small number escaped, and that those who escaped went to Vietnam. Can you tell me whether this is true?

DL: I'm not sure; I have no idea whether or not the majority of ethnic Chinese were killed, but what I can share is that the Khmer Rouge viewed the Chinese as oppressors. I only know that my name was on the list of people to be eliminated, not only because I'm Chinese Cambodian but because I'm educated.

AK: Luckily, you weren't in the country, right?

DL: Yeah. I have relatives who went to Vietnam because at the time when the Khmer Rouge were in power, I think the Vietnamese policy was less harsh. The Vietnamese government was not destroying everything. The Khmer Rouge government wanted to start a whole new society.

AK: One last question, do you think the ethnic Chinese self-identify more as Cambodian or Chinese, or does it depend on the person?

DL: I think it depends on the person, it depends on the situation, the context, whatever they feel is advantageous to them. For example, there is an Organization of Chinese from Vietnam, Cambodia, and Laos in Boston. The majority of the people who are participating have stores, they're doing business. They behave impartially. Although some people know they are Chinese, they behave impartially. It's part of survival, I guess.

AK: Also, I heard that many of the ethnic Chinese Cambodians who escaped from Cambodia ended up going to France and that a lot of the ethnic Chinese here are from France. Is that true?

DL: Not a lot, but I think the first part of the statement is correct. There's a huge community of ethnic Chinese from Cambodia in Paris. In fact, I have at least a dozen friends in Paris. They behave very much like they're still back in Phnom Penh.

AK: I heard that Fall River and Lowell were conducive to many Cambodians coming over because historically they are towns that have received immigrants.

DL: No. The majority of the refugees are Vietnamese. Why did they go to Dorchester? The living is cheaper there, that's why.

AK: Fall River is a really interesting phenomenon because the Cambodians there came all of a sudden.

DL: The majority of the people in Fall River are of Portuguese descent. The Portuguese came as fishermen. A volag initially brought Southeast Asian refugees to that locality. I believe the volag that resettled the first wave was Lutheran.

AK: Were the Lutherans big players in this area?

DL: Back then, but no more. You have to have available housing. If you say that refugees came because Lowell or Fall River is a traditional immigrant town, you must remember we're a country of immigrants. So why didn't the refugees go all over?

AK: That's a good point. I think we better stop now because I've already taken a lot of your time. Thank you very much for allowing me to interview you despite your busy schedule.

August 25, 1995

5. Samkhann Khoeun
Lowell, Massachusetts, the "Long Beach of the East Coast"

MR. SAMKHANN KHOEUN is the executive director of the Cambodian Mutual Assistance Association (CMAA) of Greater Lowell, Inc. in Massachusetts. He was only in his late twenties when he was chosen for that job in 1995, making him one of the youngest executive directors of a Southeast Asian mutual assistance association in the United States. Audrey Kim interviewed Mr. Khoeun on August 23, 1995, in his office, 1.5 miles from the Acre area of Lowell where many Cambodian refugees live and a location difficult to reach for those without cars. In early 1998, the CMAA moved to the more centrally located Courier Building in downtown Lowell in order to better serve the Southeast Asian refugee communities in that city.

Mr. Khoeun and his family lived through the Khmer Rouge period, during which they were separated from one another and forced to work in different labor camps. A seven-year-old in 1975, Mr. Khoeun was placed into a youth brigade. He and some members of his family escaped to Thailand in 1980, where they were confined in several refugee camps while awaiting resettlement. They were finally admitted as refugees into the United States in 1984. A church in the Greater Chicago area served as their sponsor. A year and a half after arriving in America, Mr. Khoeun's father became a Buddhist monk, leaving him and his older sister to support the family. He had to earn money not only to pay for his schooling but also to assist his mother and younger siblings. He studied electrical engineering, first at a junior college and then at the Illinois Institute of Technology. He received a bachelor of science degree in engineering in 1991. While in college, he helped to establish the Illinois chapter of the Cambodian Students Association and did volunteer work in the Cambodian community in Chicago. After working as an engineer for several years, he moved to Lowell to assume the directorship of the CMAA. He has completed the Certificate Program in Non-Profit Management at Northeastern University.

When I talked to him by telephone on September 26, 2001, he had exciting news to report: Rithy Uong, a Cambodian American guidance counselor at Lowell High School, successfully ran for a seat on the nine-member Lowell city council in 1999. He ran for reelection in 2001 and won. Even though approximately one-third of Lowell's population is now of Cambodian ancestry, Mr. Uong won by gaining support from mainstream voters in a citywide election. No Cambodian candidate can win on the basis of Khmer ethnic solidarity, because relatively few foreign-born Cambodians have become naturalized citizens. Moreover, the number of Cambodian American voters is small because most American-born people of Cambodian descent are still too young to vote. Rithy Uong is the first Cambodian American elected official in the history of the United States. (Some individuals in Long Beach have also run for office but they did not win.) Encouraged by his effectiveness in the political arena, a second Cambodian American, Vesna Noun, campaigned for a seat on the Lowell school board, but he did not succeed in his bid.

The new possibilities are the result of two developments. First, many Cambodian refugees now realize that they are in the United States to stay and must, therefore, do something to empower themselves. Second, racial antagonism toward Cambodians has declined as more and more people in Lowell see their positive contributions to revitalizing the downtown area by occupying run-down residential buildings, many of which had been boarded up, and opening new stores.

The CMAA has grown since 1995 and has forty staff members. Its programs continue to focus on education, job training, health, youth, and the elderly. It is involved in two collaborative projects to serve the mental health needs of Cambodian residents in northeastern Massachusetts: the Harvard Program in Refugee Trauma and the Mental Health Association of Greater Lowell. Welfare reform has had a negative impact, mainly on the elderly and on families that have a large number of children. To ease the transition, the CMAA has trained and placed about 250 individuals in assembly, factory, and service jobs since the late 1990s. The subsidized-employment initiative was funded by the federal Office of Refugee Resettlement, which paid part of the wages earned by the refugee workers whom the companies hired.

The Cambodian-ancestry population in Lowell has increased through birth and secondary migration. People are moving to Lowell from California, as well as from the Midwest, the South, and elsewhere in New England.

Mr. Khoeun thinks the fact that Lowell was, once again, designated as an All-America City in 1999 improved its image. It is now recognized as a city that fosters cultural diversity. Its Cambodian residents are happy that the contributions they are making are finally being recognized and appreciated.

*   *   *

AK: Can you start by telling me a little about yourself, what your background is and how you became executive director of this MAA—the Cambodian Mutual Assistance Association?

SK: I came to the United States in November 1984. When I arrived, I went to college directly, to junior college. After studying there for two and a half years, I got my associate's degree in engineering. And then I went to a four-year college, stayed there for three and a half years and got my B.S. degree majoring in electrical engineering and minoring in corporate management.

AK: So you had technical and business training.

SK: Right.

AK: Can you tell me about your background in Cambodia, whether you were living in the city or the countryside?

SK: I was living in the second-largest province in Cambodia, in Battambang, close to Thailand. I was very young at the time, so I was just a student before 1975. After 1975, everyone was forced to work in labor camps, and I was one of them.

AK: What was your father's occupation?

SK: My father was a farmer and business person. Along with my mother, they farmed during the farming season and they also had a year-round business at home. It was a home business, not a big business.

AK: When the Khmer Rouge took over, was your family on the list of people being targeted or were you not much affected?

SK: Well, we were affected. In different locations, from one zone to another, there were different degrees of severity, depending on who was in charge there. The place where we were, it was severe but not to the point where they killed everyone. The people they targeted were those who had been linked with the former government and intellectuals; those were the people who got it really, really bad. My family was pretty much middle-class farmers, so we weren't eliminated. However, it was bad for everybody. People were led away almost every night [to be killed]. My aunt and my uncle, their whole family was led away; they never returned.

AK: In your family, were you all put into work camps?

SK: We were all separated. My father was sent away to work in the forest digging tunnels. My mom was allowed to stay home to take care of the smaller children. All my brothers and sisters, those who were old enough, were put into labor camps. At the time, I was at the prime age to be put into what's called a youth brigade; my older sister was in the women's mobile team. We didn't have any opportunity to live together.

AK: Then what happened? Did you end up going to Thailand after the Vietnamese invaded?

SK: Yes. By the time the Vietnamese invaded, it was late 1978, early 1979. Some of us were killed. But there was also an opportunity for many of us in the labor camps or those who had been separated from their families for years to go back to their villages to find, to reconnect, with some members of our families. I lost some of my immediate family members to starvation.

AK: It sounds like when the Vietnamese came, a lot of people looked for their families and then went together to Thailand.

SK: Yes. In a lot of cases, they first looked for their families and if they couldn't find anyone, they would go towards Thailand. The Cambodian-Thai border, we were there for a short period of time.

AK: Which camp were you in?

SK: I was in Nimet first. Then we were transferred to Sa Kheo 2 camp due to the overcrowding. The trip took one month from our village to Thailand. We were bicycling, riding on an oxcart, and walking barefoot through the jungle, minefields, and battlefields.

AK: Even though you were pretty close to the Thai border?

SK: Even though we were close to the border. At that time, there was a lot of traffic and there were a lot of patrols; they were checking everybody, they didn't want people to leave and go to the Cambodian-Thai border. It was the harvest season, so we camouflaged ourselves as farmers and carried farm implements on our shoulders. "We're going to reap our rice crop," that's what we told them. And sometimes we bribed them, gave them some pieces of gold and some rice.

AK: It must have been a very difficult trip. What year was it when you got to Thailand?

SK: We got to Thailand in 1980, December 1980; it was a few days after Christmas. That time of the year was the chilly season. We didn't have snow but we had the cold air from the North.

AK: How long were you in Khao I Dang?

SK: I was there for close to a year and then they transferred the whole section to another camp, the Sa Kheo 2 camp. We were there till 1982.

AK: Was that because your section of Khao I Dang was getting too full?

SK: Right, it was getting too big. They could not accommodate all the people.

AK: What was your impression of the refugee camps? I've heard some people say that they were almost as awful as the work camps under the Khmer Rouge. Living conditions were dangerous and very poor.

SK: Right; that is very true. The word I would use to describe the camp is that it was like a prison. We were surrounded by barbed wire, two or three layers of barbed wire, and we were guarded by Thai soldiers. Anyone who dared to cross the barbed wire [fence] would be subject to death; they were killed.

AK: By Thai guards?

SK: By Thai soldiers. There were also a lot of robberies by Thai soldiers. There were a lot of rapes and other crimes committed against defenseless refugees.

AK: Was this mostly done by the Thai soldiers or was it Cambodians robbing, raping other Cambodians?

SK: The majority of the cases that I heard about was [committed] by Thai soldiers. Sometimes, the Thai soldiers could speak Khmer and camouflage themselves. In the daytime, they went from place to place, so at night, after the UNHCR staff went back to their residences [outside of the camps], the Thai guards knew who had daughters and possessions. They took the girls and robbed the refugees at night.

AK: How were you finally able to get to the U.S.?

SK: Well, through a letter asking for asylum. I didn't know English, so I just copied from others.

AK: Were you learning English in the camps?

SK: Right, in the camps. I learned English and furthered my education in the camps. My wait was longer than most other people who had relatives in the United States. When I got here, I found out I had an uncle here, but he had left Cambodia before 1975; he had gone to Thailand, and from Thailand he went to the United States. He was looking for us, and we were looking for him, but we just couldn't find each other.

AK: So you applied for asylum and you were waiting in the camp. How long did you wait?

SK: We were there two and a half to three years. It was a long time, a long time to wait. At some point, I was so fed up, so upset, so discouraged, thinking that maybe we wouldn't be able to leave that miserable place.

AK: Who were you with? Were you with your family members?

SK: I was with my family. At that time I had a grandmother—I started out having two grandmothers with me but one left; she couldn't wait any longer so she went back to Cambodia. I also had a cousin who went back to Cambodia with her.

AK: Because they got so discouraged waiting in the camps?

SK: Right. We felt so helpless at the time. My parents wanted to go back but I said, "Well, I don't think we can go back." I wouldn't let them take my brothers and sisters. I said some strong words to them.

AK: You knew there was no food in Cambodia. People were starving.

SK: Well, at the time, people had no seeds to sow, they were short of manpower, short of equipment and everything. There was a lot of poverty in Cambodia, plus the heavy fighting between the Vietnamese soldiers and the Khmer Rouge guerrillas. In the camp, we were fed, given food, water, and other supplies. It was enough for us to live on from day to day. Then, finally, in September 1983, we were called for an interview. The interview process went very smoothly. But the waiting period before that was long.

AK: Were you admitted technically as a "free case" [people with no family members already in the United States] or through family reunification? As I understand it, those were the two different ways to get admitted into the United States.

SK: I'm not sure what we were but we must have been a free case. We could not go back. We would have no freedom. If we had stayed in Cambodia, we would not have been given any freedom to do farming or whatever we wanted to do. It took us over a year to get to America, from September 1983 until November 1984.

AK: What took so long?

SK: Well, we have an extended family. My grandmother was ill at the time. And the processing was lengthy as well.

AK: Just coordinating everyone coming over took time?

SK: Right. We had to go through a screening process: health screenings. And then we had to go through cultural orientation. That took six months. In Thailand, they moved us from Khao I Dang to Phanat Nikhom, where we stayed for six months. That was pretty much for health screenings, for teaching us American culture and everything. Then from Phanat Nikhom, we were transferred to another refugee [processing] center in the Philippines for cultural orientation, English [as-a-second-language courses], and so forth. We were there for another six months.

AK: You finally made it in November '84.

SK: We finally made it in '84.

AK: Where did you go?

SK: Chicago, Illinois. There were some Cambodian families there.

AK: About how many Cambodians would you say were in the Chicago area in '84?

SK: Probably between four and six thousand Cambodians.

AK: That's a pretty large number.

SK: Cambodian families were settled all over the place. Some people were sponsored by their families. Others were sponsored by a combination of their families and resettlement agencies and churches. We were sponsored by a church and a resettlement agency. During the wait in Thailand, when we got the OK from the U.S., I was working in a small outpatient clinic. I was sort of a supervisor there, in charge of the whole office. There was an American nurse who volunteered there for three months. I had a chance to meet her and during the three months we got to know each other really well. I told her about our plight, our situation. We didn't have any sponsor, we didn't have any family living in America. We didn't know where in the United States we were going to be resettled. She and I became really good friends. She adopted me as her brother and I adopted her as my sister. She had friends in Evanston and in Chicago.

AK: This nurse was from Chicago?

SK: She was from Evanston, which is just outside Chicago.

AK: Did she arrange for the church in the area to sponsor you? Is that how you ended up in Chicago?

SK: Right. She had a friend who's a member of a church. She presented our story to the officers of the church. They had sponsored a Cambodian family before us. They made all the arrangements for us to come; they had clothing and everything for us.

AK: You mentioned that you were too old to go to high school, so you went to a community college and then you went on to get your engineering and management degrees. What did you do after that?

SK: I got out of school in 1991 and went to work in the engineering field. [When I was in college,] in the summer I had jobs with different engineering companies. I got paid and that enabled me to pay for my schooling and everything.

AK: You were working during school?

SK: I worked in a furniture company, one of the most reputable furniture companies; it's been in business for more than a hundred years.

AK: Someone told me that for Cambodians who do make it through college, sometimes it's really hard to get a job because they don't have any work experience. Cambodians apparently think you can just go to school and then at the end get a job. That's very different from the way Americans approach work experience, school, and all that.

SK: Really true, very true. I have a number of friends who have children. They want their kids to concentrate only on school because they think they cannot keep up with both work and school.

AK: Different rules.

SK: Right. I was fortunate enough to keep up with both. I worked really hard, but compared to what I had gone through, it was nothing. Under the Khmer Rouge, you worked at gunpoint. You didn't have enough to eat. You were starving to death, yet you had to work in order to earn that food ration. Here, in the United States, I had a small car. I had to keep a schedule and make time available for both my work and my studies. Because I'm the oldest [son], I had to play a big brother role, a father role, and help tutor my younger brothers and sisters.

AK: Did your father work when he came to the U.S.?

SK: He didn't work. After he had been in the States for about a year and a half, he decided he didn't want to live a normal life like ordinary people. He decided to become a Buddhist monk. He's right now in California. At the time, I was sort of upset with his decision because I needed someone to take care of the family so that I could continue with my schooling and have some time to work and so forth.

AK: You didn't want to be a grown-up parent. Do you know of many others who became Buddhist monks after Pol Pot?

SK: There's a number of them. Most of the Buddhist monks who are in the United States, most of them had become Buddhist monks either in the refugee camps or after they arrived in the United States.

AK: They weren't people who were monks before because the Khmer Rouge killed the monks?

SK: They were disrobed during the Khmer Rouge and afterwards they became Buddhist monks again by going to the Thai temples. There are also some other monks who were fortunate enough to get out of the country before the fall of Phnom Penh. They were in Thailand, they were in India, they were in the United States, they were in England on the way to further their education and so forth. They went to the border camps, the refugee camps. The former Buddhist monks wanted to continue their monkhood, so they held the religious ceremony to make them become Buddhist monks again. It's sort of like being baptized here. My father had been wanting to be a Buddhist monk for a really long time and he felt that after he had brought the family here, he could choose to go into the monkhood instead of being unemployed on the streets. It was hard. I was eighteen years old and I needed a father. I needed to catch up with my schooling because I had been away from school for more than ten years. From 1975 to 1985, all those years were filled with war, destruction, labor camps, starvation, separation, hate, anger, and longing to be free, to be educated, and especially for peace.

AK: So, you were going to school and you were working. Were you supporting your mother and your siblings? Were they getting some public assistance?

SK: At the time, they got some sort of public assistance. After a few months, my older sister started to work, and I worked, so we were able to help the family. And then later on, one of my younger brothers worked. And then in the summer we all worked after school.

AK: When you graduated and got your degree, did you work as an engineer for a while?

SK: I worked as an engineer for a while; I was an associate engineer, they didn't give me a full title yet. I also did volunteer work in the Cambodian community. I worked with a student organization when I was in school. I helped start up the Cambodian Students Association [of Illinois].

AK: Even in Chicago, you were doing things in the community?

SK: Right.

AK: By the way, when you were in college, were there any other Cambodians you knew of?

SK: In the community college, there was, I think, one other Cambodian. His family had been in the United States since 1975. He had become quite Americanized. His family didn't go through the "killing fields" of the Khmer Rouge. We didn't have a chance to become friends, because he had no time and I had no time. At the Illinois Institute of Technology there were ten to fifteen other Cambodian students.

AK: Did you all come from really different backgrounds?

SK: Right. All the English that I knew was pretty much learned in the camp. And it was broken English. I can write and I can read but I still speak with a heavy accent. People still have a hard time understanding me. I get really, really upset with myself. Engineering was my choice because it required a lot of science courses but not a lot of English courses.

AK: It's so hard to learn a new language after a certain age.

SK: That's true. Plus, I had not been in an educational institution for such a long time. I was so isolated, so alienated from any educational institution.

AK: It seems like there are a number of people like yourself who are leaders in the Cambodian community, who are maybe about your age, who went to college here. Is that common?

SK: Yes, in many cases. When we were in school, we always felt that the education we had would put us in a better position financially. At the same time, we have another obligation—the responsibility to help others. We didn't really look at ourselves as leaders; we looked at ourselves as sort of like a big brother or a big sister.

AK: Because of your language skills?

SK: Language skills and the understanding of both cultures. We've been educated in this country in technical and scientific subjects. We were educated about our culture at home or by the community itself. So, we were able to understand both cultures, plus the ability to speak, read, and write fluently both languages. The whole thing is sort of the reverse of the traditional relationship within the family. It used to be the parents were the leaders of the family. Due to the language barrier and the slowness of adults to learn the new language, to adapt to a new culture, and the fact that the children, due to their youth, can learn the new language and pick up a new culture faster, they become the so-called spokespersons of the families and later on, pretty much the leaders of their families because they are the one who understand the language, who know the system, and so forth, so they make a lot of the decisions pretty much based on what they think would be best for their families.

AK: Just as the teenagers are the intermediaries between their families and the outside world, when they get older, these people become the intermediaries between the Cambodian communities and the larger society.

SK: Right. And what really struck me at the time was that so many networks, so many connections, were among people who had gone to the same schools. We were really happy that, for some reason, we have achieved, our families are really proud of us. Yes, we got our college degrees. And we all got jobs in x, y, z companies all over the country. And some of us work in the state, work in the city. We are spread all over the United States.

AK: Are you in touch with other Cambodian college graduates?

SK: Yes. But not very regularly any more.

AK: How did you know these people?

SK: Well, when we were in school together, we had an association called the Cambodian Students Association of Illinois. And then there was the Cambodian Association of America; it's pretty much covering the United States. They have an eastern regional chapter, a midwestern regional one, etc.

AK: That must have been a good support group.

SK: Right. So that's how we know each other. Conferences are being sponsored by other Cambodian agencies such as the Cambodian Network Council. We are able to meet one another on a national level. It's true that most of us in my generation are the ones with more opportunities. We're not too old or too young; we're in just the right age group in terms of becoming really successful at school and at work and so forth. At the same time, we have a strong connection with the family, with the community. There are a lot of us who were not able to stay in the city or town that we were originally in. We were employed somewhere outside of the town, of the city. We had to reestablish ourselves. Most of the time, we are out there by ourselves, living in the mainstream community. Some have no connection, no time to get involved with the Cambodian community. Because of the language barrier, most of us are able to work well in math and science, a lot of us went into technical, engineering fields, such as computer science, etc.

AK: In those fields, you don't need to be as proficient in English.

SK: Right. Originally, I didn't really want to go into engineering, but I had no friends who went into other fields. Plus I was good at it. On the other hand, one of my own brothers, after seven years in the United States, became the spelling champion in the city of Chicago, which has more than half a million students. I wanted to be a role model to other families who might not be fortunate enough to have a strong support or good role model in the family, which, in many instances, was the case. Many of the Cambodian families are headed by single mothers.

AK: I was going to ask you questions about Lowell, but since you had this experience in Chicago, I want to ask you about both places. You said most of the families are headed by women in Chicago. Is that also true in Lowell?

SK: Pretty much true throughout the Cambodian neighborhoods.

AK: About what percent?

SK: I would say close to 30 percent in some neighborhoods. In some areas, some communities, more than 30 percent. Because, as you know, most of the men, if they were in the war, in the government, they were killed during the Khmer Rouge years. That left more women. Women had to become both the mother and the father here in the United States. So there's a gender imbalance in Cambodian families.

AK: Do you find that those families have more trouble dealing with their kids? Are there more problems when there's just the mother raising the family?

SK: A majority of them, yes. A majority of kids who have problems are from those Cambodian families.

AK: Is that true in Chicago as well as in Lowell? Are there any differences?

SK: It's almost the same. Both locations are pretty much the same. The youth have their peers, their friends, and they want to be accepted by their friends.

AK: Having two parents doesn't mean that everything will be perfect.

SK: Right. If you have two good parents, maybe there's a difference. For families where the living standard is OK, then maybe the parent or parents have more time to spend with the kids, to educate the kids, and to establish strong bonds with their kids.

AK: My impression is that in a lot of the families headed by women, the women aren't working. They are staying home being supported by AFDC [Aid to Families with Dependent Children, which has been replaced by Temporary Assistance to Needy Families (TANF) since welfare reform in 1996]. So wouldn't those mothers actually have more time to spend with the kids than if both parents are working?

SK: That doesn't make a big difference really. Even though some mothers might not be working or are on welfare, it is not easy to be both mother and father at the same time and to deal with a new culture, deal with a new system. Even though she's physically there, it's a hopeless situation, a helpless situation. In some cases, they're being abused by their children. If they raise their voice or threaten to beat the kids up, the kids can pick up the phone and call 911. Parents need to relearn parenting skills, especially the skills practiced in the mainstream society.

AK: So the kids know about the child abuse laws and all that.

SK: They know all that. They may not know it very well, and they may have just heard about it from someone, but they understand they can call 911.

AK: You've seen that happen in Chicago and in Lowell?

SK: In Lowell, there've been even more cases, just because there's a larger number of Cambodians living here.

AK: The children know how to manipulate the system to get their parents to do what they want?

SK: True. Some parents feel they have no control over the children. They just let the children do whatever they wish to the point where it's so extreme, so bad, that all they can do is to just keep praying that everything will be all right. But they have no way of knowing when, how, or what. And to ask for assistance from others may not be helpful because they wouldn't understand. They have a completely different way of disciplining the children. And so you get no support from the mainstream community. They come to the Cambodian agency for help but we can only do so much to help. We are helping with ESL [English as a second language], with day care, with the elderly, but disciplining the children, we're not in a position to do that. However, we can do some counseling. It's important to find a way to help them mediate between the two cultures and be able to discipline effectively for the benefit of their families. Back in Cambodia, before the war, we had sort of global family values and a support mechanism. Wherever you go, there's reinforcements of family values everywhere. But the school system in this country and the school system in Cambodia are completely different. And so are the cultures of school and family.

AK: My sense is that in Cambodia, the teachers are responsible for school. But here, the teachers expect the parents to help with homework, but the parents here are saying, "We can't control the kids; we need help, too." So everyone's looking to someone else to help them.

SK: Right. Not only with the homework, but with the cultural education as well, with the family values, with other issues or concerns. You know, the schools here are not responsible for teaching family values or morality because these are so diverse. How are they going to teach the culture of one group and not the others? How are they going to understand the Cambodian culture when we are the most recent group of people to arrive in this country? They don't know. All they know is that these people had gone through hard times, the "killing fields" and so forth.

AK: The schools don't really understand the kids either.

SK: They don't really understand the cultural aspects. Sometimes, they're helping, but they're helping in *their* way. Instead of helping the whole family to grow, they only empower the children. The children become so empowered that they use it against their parents. As a result, there's conflict within the family. And that is not helping.

AK: Also, you mentioned earlier that the children tend to acculturate faster than the parents. You've got these generational and cultural differences. So, how are the kids doing? What was your experience in Chicago and what are your observations in Lowell?

SK: Well, there are different generations. The different age groups, they have different problems. In my generation, in my age group, there wasn't any problem in terms of dealing with family conflicts because we grew up and spent more than half our lives in Cambodia. The younger kids had less connection, contact, or experience in Cambodia; it [their childhood] was all [spent] in Thailand in the refugee camps. So, even though they are Cambodians, they have no idea what Cambodia is like. And they are being put in these neighborhoods, put in the schools, that's who and what they see. They act and talk the same way as most of their American friends—White, Hispanic, you name it. So they're having values different from their families. The younger they are, the more problems they have in terms of conflicts with the family. They have less ambition in terms of trying to help themselves become a better person and so forth.

AK: Why do you think that is?

SK: I think it's because of the social contact they have with their peers in this society. For us, for Asians or Southeast Asians, especially for the Cambodian people, we divide life into different stages. When you are young, there are certain duties and responsibilities you have, and there's reinforcement from the family, from the community, from the school, from the cultural centers, the Buddhist temples [with regard to those values and norms].

Wherever you go, there's reinforcement. You have to behave in a certain way in order to become a good son or a good daughter or a good Cambodian. You got to study hard, do well in school, whether you like it or not. And when you are home, you got to be helpful at home and so forth. You have to do x, y, and z. That's part of the unwritten rules you're expected to follow.

AK: The expectations are very clear. You know what you're supposed to do.

SK: Right. That's one aspect of our culture. On the other hand, kids want to be kids. They want to have a good time, they want to experience a whole bunch of other things that are going on, and they're so conscious right now of all these things, sexual and material things.

AK: Do you think Cambodian culture is more disciplined in terms of how kids should behave and the farther the kids are away from the traditional Cambodian culture, the more Westernized and loose and undisciplined they become?

SK: That's what it is. Five days a week, the kids, all the kids, all the children are in school being exposed to different aspects of Western ideas and concepts, way of living, way of talking, doing this and that. They don't see their parents until 5, 6 P.M. in the evening for dinner. And after that, the kids are left to do their homework. So, they don't really have much chance to talk to one another at all. They are busy with their homework, with watching TV, listening to the stereo, and playing computer games.

AK: Do you see any differences in the children or the parents in Chicago versus those in Lowell? Are they people from different backgrounds? Are there any differences?

SK: The major difference is the number—the size of the community.

AK: Is it about double here?

SK: At least triple. There are almost twenty-five thousand here. In Chicago, there's probably less than five thousand. Here, the Cambodian population represents one-quarter of the whole city's population, whereas in Chicago, the whole city's population is three million or something like that. You cannot even compute a percentage; the Cambodian population is so, so tiny in Chicago.

AK: Does that mean that the children in Chicago are more Westernized, acculturated, because there are fewer of them?

SK: No, not necessarily. Even though there are fewer of them, there are close bonds there. They're living in so-called neighborhoods.

AK: You mean, in Chicago, they only live in certain neighborhoods?

SK: Right. People tend to gather together when they are few in number, when they are the minority.

AK: Are those the areas where they were resettled originally or are they areas where the families moved to afterwards?

SK: Some of them were resettled there originally; some of them moved to places where they can be close to other Cambodian families in case they need help, so they can come to one another, help one another, provide mutual assistance in case there's some emergency, and so forth. For those who are in the mainstream, they become pretty much Americanized. The problem is rather complex in the family. It's not just a single thing. What you have here is a completely new culture whose language and way of living are so completely different it feels like we were just dropped down in a certain place and then were left to grow up by ourselves. Prior to that, these people had gone through a lot of hard times; they have gone through a holocaust, a genocide; they have gone through so much hardship. And being without any culturally sensitive assistance other than public assistance is not sufficient. They're not going to be able to grow up strong. With the war trauma and everything, there's no healing process for them. OK, you get a job, you work and make money. But that may not help you heal the war trauma that you have gone through. Either you can stand up on your own two feet or you get abused by the system. You have no way of explaining your case or asking the system to help you, to understand your problems and so forth. It's just not possible. Parents expect the schools to do all the educating of the children, whereas the schools expect the parents to do their job as the primary teacher, to help the children with the schoolwork. So you got two completely different expectations. And yet, the two [groups] cannot speak to one another because of the language barrier. The cultural aspect is so complex. Here in Lowell, it's even worse because we have a larger Cambodian population here. In the city, I would say there are a lot of racial things going on. Even though we've been here for ten years, and we assumed that the city will accept us as one of their people, as one of them, the older residents haven't. They still consider us outsiders, the ones who come and try to steal all their jobs—jobs that, most likely, these people would not want, factory jobs. We don't mind [having such jobs]; we work at all those things. Yet, we are being blamed for stealing the jobs.

AK: Can you back up and tell me the history of Cambodians coming to Lowell? Why were Cambodians placed in Lowell, and how many came through the initial migration, and how many came through secondary migration?

SK: A majority of them came during the first migration; they were initially resettled here because there were a lot of factory jobs here in the early 1980s.

AK: What kinds of factories are here?

SK: Some electronics, some manufacturing. They put these people here, taught them some English, some vocational skills, and then placed them in jobs. They were expected to figure out ways to survive by themselves.

AK: Did the resettlement agencies think that Lowell was a good place because there are a lot of factory jobs and so they placed a lot of Cambodians here? Was that their thinking?

SK: I'm not sure what the mentality was at the time. I assume that was the case. They try to resettle the Southeast Asians, all the Cambodian refugees, in areas where they say they can find jobs, in the industrial cities: here in Lowell, in Chicago, in big cities.

AK: One thing I'm curious about is the Vietnamese weren't really resettled in the Boston area, I don't think. In the early '80s—I don't know about Lowell specifically—Massachusetts and Boston were suffering from a recession. Were there still a lot of jobs in that period?

SK: The recession in the early 1980s affected the community drastically. That's how come this agency was established in 1984. During the time the Cambodian population started coming in, until the early 1990s when the settlement of all Cambodians stopped because of the political changes in Cambodia, there was so much to be done. Right now, we don't have anyone coming in at all. But even without that, we have enough things to do here. The details have changed dramatically, have changed two times. First, when we were simply trying to survive, all we needed were the basic necessities: shelter, food, and clothing. But now, after we've been here for a while, there are more needs. So our agency changed our programming so that we can meet all the needs of the community: ESL, job placement and training, programs for the elderly.

AK: What kinds of services do you have for the elderly?

SK: Making medical appointments and providing language assistance because they can't communicate with the doctors. Nor are their family members able to do that because family members are either working or they are going to school and cannot take time off from work or school. We make sure they have proper medication, know when to take it and so forth. We also have a youth program where we help the youth with their homework, where we keep them busy with activities instead of letting them loose on the streets.

AK: Isn't it hard for the kids to get here though?

SK: It is a little bit hard. We're in the process of moving to a place where we'll be more accessible.

AK: I want to back up a little bit. In '84, when this organization was started, how was it funded?

SK: At first, it was funded by the Office of Refugee Resettlement and a number of state government agencies. It was established by a group of Cambodian leaders who felt that an agency should be established in order to help the growing Cambodian population in Lowell. We had help from some American friends.

AK: Someone told me that you had implemented a very successful youth program in Chicago before coming here. Can you tell me about the Chicago program and then tell me more about what you're doing here?

SK: It's pretty much a program where we're trying to educate kids about both their cultures—their own history and the American one—so they can have a better understanding of the two instead of a misunderstanding of both. We teach them that Cambodian culture is like this and like that. We try to tell them about aspects of what has been going on in Cambodia through the decades. Cambodia has gone through a lot of changes, and one of the worst things Cambodia has been through is the Khmer Rouge regime, and you see a lot of bad visuals, bad feelings from this. Most kids say they don't want to be Cambodians because there are so many bad things happening. They say, "Well, if we identify [ourselves] as Cambodians, other people will make fun of us." [They don't know that] what is so beautiful about Cambodia is [that] it's four thousand years old, much older than America. We have a lot of things to offer to this world, all the beautiful aspects of Cambodia. We try to develop the culture for the kids so that they can feel comfortable in this country having a dual identity: Cambodian and American. Say it with pride. That's how it is. This program is a cultural and mentoring program. We're trying to do a number of things. One is to promote positive role models by having successful Cambodian adults as the mentor-instructors; we teach them the Cambodian language, the arts, music, dance, history, and social behavior.

AK: I thought a lot of the dancers were killed during the Pol Pot period.

SK: A lot of them were, a lot of the master dancers were killed. But there were some survivors. These are students or amateurs who do research and are able to retrieve the dance repertoire, lyrics, and music.

AK: This program you're describing, is it the one you implemented in Chicago and now are trying to recreate here?

SK: Right. Right.

AK: It seems to have two purposes: one, to preserve Cambodian culture and heritage, and, two, to help the kids feel better about themselves.

SK: There's a number of things we want to get out of it. One is to promote their self-esteem. We teach the kids about their cultural heritage, the goodness of it, what's in there, have a true understanding and appreciation. This is also geared toward families. You know there's often conflict in the families, due not just the language but the cultural differences. Kids want to be

American. Cambodian parents want to be Cambodian parents. They live in different worlds even though they're living in the same house. What we want to do is to foster [the parent-child] relationship. By having this kind of program we get the adults and the children together. The more time they spend together, the more they can understand one another and they can understand both cultures. If you don't have this, they're not going to be able to learn, they're not going to be able to know. It's not in the TV or the [other] media. There's not enough printed materials. The schools will not do the job for us, so we have to do something at any cost, I felt, in order to prevent youth delinquency. We have to use this proactive approach. If the kids know who they are, where they came from, then they know where they want to go. If they don't know where they came from, they're confused. How are they going to make up their minds where they want to go? I believe all of us want to have love and affection, want to be accepted.

AK: What were the results of this program?

SK: There are a lot of positives. I was so amazed! I worked there pretty much five days a week and then volunteered there another two days a week, pretty much seven days a week I'm out there.

AK: Were you working for the Cambodian MAA in Chicago?

SK: Yes, the Cambodian Association of Illinois. What we want to do depends on the resources in the community itself. We have so many resources out there: artists, former teachers, musicians, dancers, you name it, they're out there. And when they come here, for so many years they have had to put everything aside in order to work in the factories and so forth. I felt so sad about that. Why can't an artist make a living as an artist? Why can't a dancer make a living being a dancer? Why can't they have an opportunity to share their skills with the younger generation in such a way that their education, their knowledge, is recognized and appreciated? I created an environment that the adults feel comfortable in and everyone benefits. And on top of this, we teach family values, the cultural aspects.

AK: How did you get kids to come to this program?

SK: Well, first of all, the kids come to the after-school program for assistance with their homework: reading, writing, math, and science. We want them to do well in school. However, there are other aspects they need to be educated in as well because they spend five days a week in school. If we were to help them to understand both cultures and be comfortable about who they are, be able to speak their language and be able to read and write their language, be able to express themselves in their own way—wouldn't that be nice? So the method is that I go around and talk to the parents and community leaders and Buddhist monks and students, and they say, "Wow, that is wonderful." So everyone wants to help. Some artists say, "I know how to do art work; can I come and teach the art?" Or the dancers say, "I know some of that." If you just have enough room and a tape recorder, you can dance. Some people, they want to teach the language. All of a sudden, I get more than a hundred students coming in and wanting to join.

AK: How many students?

SK: A hundred and fifty students or so.

AK: What about here? How many students do you have here?

SK: Here, we have sixty-eight, sixty-seven.

AK: It's only been around a month or so?

SK: Two months. All this good knowledge needs to be made visible. We need to bring all these things out again.

AK: I imagine that a lot of these artists spend their days in the factories, so it's a labor of love for them to do something like this.

SK: Right. They must still work because this art work, it's not enough to make a living. So if they can do their job on the weekdays and just do this on the weekends, everyone benefits. The kids benefit, the whole family benefits knowing their children are developing skills—bicultural, bilingual skills, able to understand both cultures and to appreciate their own culture.

AK: You mentioned the juvenile delinquency rate earlier. What is the high school dropout rate in Chicago and what is it here?

SK: There's a higher rate here because of the fact that there's not so much assistance here. Plus, there's a larger Cambodian population. Even if there are services, most of these kids will not benefit from those types of assistance. Whereas in Chicago, there are fewer of us, but there are more services and programs to help us. In other words, there are more help mechanisms in the larger cities.

AK: I thought in a place like Lowell, because there are so many Cambodians, you'd have more specialized services. But that's not really the case?

SK: That's not the case. I don't know for what reason, but probably it's economic. We're working very hard to get to a point where we'll be visible to the community. Clients pretty much have to live near here or they have to drive here. I don't have statistics on the dropout rate, but I heard that the educated . . .

AK: Do you think it might be 60 percent in Lowell?

SK: Probably close to that.

AK: Is it much less in Chicago or just a little less?

SK: It's much higher here than in Chicago.

AK: What is contributing to the high dropout rate? For example, I've heard that those Cambodian kids who haven't been in school for many years because of the camps, they're placed in grades that are really not appropriate for them because they look old. Plus, they're not getting the support at home with homework, that kind of thing. So they get discouraged. They drop out, they join a gang.

SK: That's really true. That is one of the most alarming facts, the dropout rate. Because they don't have early educational preparation, they're not prepared to be in the proper grade, at the proper educational level they're supposed to be in according to their age. As a result, they are running behind. Plus the schools don't really have a specialized program to help them. Therefore the children, these students, have to catch up with their level on their own. Meanwhile, the parents at home aren't able to help with the homework. Most of the time, they aren't able to afford a bigger apartment or house. The study area is in the living room, in the dining room, so if you have the TV going, the kids have a hard time trying to concentrate on their homework. So you have a lot of factors. But the most alarming factor is that they do not have early educational preparation to help them succeed. Only those who are really committed, whose parents, whose families, really support them, can make it. Other than that, most likely when they drop out of high school they would either get married or go to work in the factories or in other places. There is another factor. A major reason has to do with the fast cars, the nice cars, the electronic gadgets out there. If you don't work, you're not going to be able to get those.

AK: You mean it's easier to just get a job and start buying those things.

SK: Pretty much the idea is to make money.

AK: So they're not willing to make a special effort to finish school?

SK: Right.

AK: One thing that I've heard is that, oftentimes, how a child does in school depends on the parents' educational background, because parents who have a lot of education usually push their kids. Kids from such families are the ones who graduate from college. A lot of the Cambodians who came over are people from more rural, uneducated backgrounds. So, sometimes, when comparisons are made between the Vietnamese and Cambodian kids, you're comparing apples and oranges because they're people coming from very different backgrounds. If you look at people from similar socioeconomic backgrounds, you'd probably see similar levels of achievement.

SK: That is very true. The majority of the Cambodian people came from rural areas. Most likely, they make a lesser effort in terms of pushing their kids. They don't know how even when they might want the kids to become well educated. For example, in my case, my mother had a fourth-grade education. She doesn't have much education, but she has wisdom, she has knowledge, she has experience. That's the thing that was really helpful. She can read and write, do some calculations and things like that. But the most important thing is she has a big heart. She has an ambition and her ambition is to get her children to be well educated. Because she has not been well educated, she has had to work so hard for so many years. People look at her as a nobody, so she doesn't want her children to be that way, to work so hard and yet not make much money, working seven days a week and not having any extra. I promised myself that I would do whatever it takes.

AK: Sometimes, parents who don't have an education do have these ambitions for their children. But do you think that's the exception or the norm? Do you think there are many parents like your mother?

SK: All of them want the best for their children, to educate them and to do everything for their children. They say they want it but they don't know how. In other families, they really mean it. They will do everything, make sure the TV is off, make sure when the kids come back from school, they have proper food to eat, a place to study and so forth. In my family, we pretty much turned our three-bedroom apartment into an educational space. There are books in the living room, there are books in the dining room, in the kitchen. There's a TV and stereo, too, but they're only allowed to be turned on at certain hours.

AK: I agree the environment is very important.

SK: It is very important. Some kids and their families have gone through real problems because they cannot get rid of their nightmares, their trauma. They are drinking, they are seeking assistance from other places probably. It's not really helpful to drink just to forget, to forget their nightmares, forget their trauma. Drinking alcohol doesn't cure the mental illness. They do not know where to go, or they cannot afford to have any counselors, psychiatrists, or doctors. After they've been drinking for some time, they become so addicted. Of course, drinking helps them to forget, that is true; they get drunk, they sleep. But whatever they forget, they not only forget their past, they forget their responsibilities as well. Others, they have so much time but nothing to do.

AK: Someone said to me that one reason Cambodian children aren't doing that well is because sometimes they're resettled in areas that are low-income because the housing is affordable, but the schools in those areas are often not that good and they're with other kids who aren't that motivated, so it's a vicious cycle.

SK: Very true, very true. Unfortunately, we were settled or placed in neighborhoods which are infested with drugs and with crime, all the negative aspects of American culture. The best skills that Cambodian people learned throughout these years, the past three decades or so, are survival skills. They had to learn how to adapt to the system, you know, because within the last twenty-five years, there have been five governments in Cambodia: first a royal government, then a republic, then the Khmer Rouge, and then another communist—a Vietnamese communist—government [as well as a government-in-exile]. On top of that you have the process of being a refugee. Cambodians always have a strong attachment to their homeland. Cambodians tried to get out of the country only because there were so many bad things happening. We have pretty much been victims of the Big Powers, of capitalism and communism fighting each other. Cambodia has been the battleground for Vietnam and China and the United States. Being a battleground, the place was not livable, so we had to get out. One government came in and said, "This is sensible, this is what we should do," and they got all the educated people, those who had any knowledge of a foreign language or culture, who were considered to be against that government, and they killed all these people. You get mixed messages. The consequence of being a well-educated person was we ended up in the "killing fields" and not in a free land. So we don't know what is the message. For us, the adults, that's the lesson we had learned. It's like an old saying, you have to go along with the river, flow along with the river; it's not going to change for you. You're in a boat in the river, you have to move according to the currents. Otherwise, you're going to sink to the bottom of the river. That's one of the goals of the Cambodians: you have to go along with the river. The Khmer Rouge soldiers were young boys, teenagers. But gangs, we had never been exposed to them before. We had been exposed to violence because Cambodians have been in the battlefield for so many years, but it was not street violence. It was not personal violence, it was sort of structured. After some time in America, Cambodian kids pick up the skills to defend themselves because they are being intimidated. They have been robbed; they have been harmed. So they defend themselves. Then they go further and do others harm.

AK: What is the rate of gang activity among kids? What percentage of kids are involved in gangs?

SK: I would say very small, probably 5 percent at the most.

AK: About how many?

SK: I don't know. The number that I get from the probation officer, about a hundred or so from Lowell.

AK: That's interesting because everywhere I go, they all say to me, "We don't really have a gang problem; the gangs are all coming from Lowell." Is that just a misperception?

SK: Yeah, that's a misperception. You have to understand that gangs are mobile. They move around. They move from Lowell to Chelsea to Chicago to California to other places. This is a heartbreaking situation for the community, for the parents. Imagine being a father, being a mother. They brought their children here, hoping to have the best education, the best opportunities for their children. Unfortunately, because of the environment itself, the children don't live up to the parents' expectations.

AK: What do the gangs do? I've heard that in some areas they're not really gangs, they're just kids who don't fit in, who just hang out together. Are these gangs that really kill and rob, get involved in real violence?

SK: A number of them have turned to violence, turned to robbing and gambling and drinking. But the majority of them just want to hang around. It is socially acceptable in Cambodia for a number of people to come together, chatting, talking, playing, and so forth. To socialize is a cultural aspect of Cambodians. After work, they come together. Those who play music will play music. Those who can dance will dance, and so forth. That is our entertainment because there was no MTV in Cambodia in the old days. There's no TV, there's no telephone, so they build fires under the moonlight and create their own entertainment. Here, if more than three or five [young] people get together to talk, yeah, that's called a gang.

AK: Are they fighting other gangs or fighting one another?

SK: Mainly the fighting is between Latino kids and Cambodian kids.

AK: So it's not one Cambodian gang against another Cambodian gang?

SK: Most likely it has to do with ethnic or racial issues.

AK: So is it racially based fighting?

SK: Yes.

AK: It's not that they're extorting money from each other?

SK: No. I believe that law enforcement looks at these kids as non-persons. They abuse them. You know, when you're oppressed, you rebel. That's what it is. You're not accepted. When you're not given any recognition as a person, you rebel. That's why African Americans rebel against white men. Even when they want a peace march, they are not given the opportunity to do that. The same thing is happening to us. We're the new arrivals, and we are blamed for so many bad things happening here for which we're not responsible. We're actually contributing a lot of good things, and we're not being recognized for that.

AK: You mentioned that Cambodians have been blamed for taking away jobs.

SK: Not just the Cambodians, but other refugees and immigrants.

AK: Besides factory jobs, are Cambodians in other types of jobs?

SK: There's a number of them in technical fields in Lowell and the vicinity of Lowell; in educational fields, as bilingual teachers, or in secretarial work, something like that. Three of the Cambodians now are policemen, in law enforcement. There used to be four, but one of them got into a fight. He couldn't hold his temper, so he got into a fight. So there are only three of them left now. We're talking about twenty-five thousand Cambodians here, a quarter of the city's population, and we have only three Cambodian police officers. Within the city government itself, there's no city councilman, there's no school board member who's Cambodian. Not only that, worse than that, there are those on the council who are racially antagonistic towards foreigners, who publicly argue against ESL or bilingual programs, who believe that when we are here, regardless of where we come from, we have no choice but to be Americans. We're not given the opportunity to be both [Cambodians and Americans]. They just use us to get money from the federal government, saying that they will serve us, when, in fact, they're not really trying to help us. [Instead,] they're trying to treat themselves. And that's the thing that hurts us. That's the thing that we are trying to work on. We have been here ten years. If they are really serious about helping us, they should empower us. But they're not really good at helping us. So we've got some good friends and some not-so-good friends in this community.

AK: Are there certain parts of Lowell where there are a lot of Cambodians, or are they all over?

SK: Pretty much all over. Most of them are in the Acre area. Belvedere has a number of them, but the majority are in the Acre and low highland areas, I think, because of the cheaper housing.

AK: So they were settled there by the resettlement agencies back in the '80s, or have they moved from other areas?

SK: Well, they settle in their neighborhood and then they move around.

AK: Move around within Lowell?

SK: Within Lowell, to better neighborhoods. For those who can afford to buy their own houses, who can afford better housing, they move. That's how it is. The secondary migration, I think that is very small.

AK: So, of the twenty-five thousand or so, almost all of them are people who were originally resettled here?

SK: Most of them.

AK: When I went to other areas, people said to me, "Oh, we have people leaving this area to go to Lowell." So I've heard a lot about secondary migration to Lowell.

SK: Well, when people are moving within the state, from city to city, I consider that to be still primary migration. But I myself am a secondary migrant.

Related to this, a lot of people have been moving in, but a lot of them have been moving out, too.

AK: Where do they move out to?

SK: Some of them find a better place to live. They want a better school for their children. Or they have a better job someplace else, so they move out. Or they have relatives in some other places.

AK: Are they usually just moving within Massachusetts, or are they moving out of the state?

SK: Some of them move far away. A lot of them move within Massachusetts. A number of cases, people are moving in and people are moving out, but not really out of state. Because within this large Cambodian population there's a number of other places where they can go for assistance. There are two Buddhist temples in Lowell where they can go for religious gatherings. There are grocery stores where they can get ethnic foods and vegetables; there are restaurants. There are also associations and agencies with this and that kind of service. They also have friends who will help them with the welfare office or other offices. So there's a number of contributing factors.

AK: You mentioned that Cambodians are pretty diversified in terms of the type of employment they have. Are there some, though, who are still on public assistance?

SK: Yes. I know that there are a number of them. A lot of them are not able-bodied: the elderly, women with a lot of other problems who cannot work. They cannot read and write, not only English but not even their own language. So, it's really hard for them to work. Most companies would not want these kinds of people to work for them.

AK: What is the attitude in the Cambodian community toward people who get public assistance? Is it something that's OK, that's acceptable? Or is there stigma associated with it?

SK: There's a mixed feeling. Because the beliefs, the culture, the tradition in Cambodia, the Buddhist beliefs—most Cambodians are Buddhists—the teachings of Buddha, are quite opposite to what is being practiced here. We're supposed to be self-sufficient, be your own boss, do the right thing, do not lie, do not steal, do not commit any adultery or drink alcohol, and so forth. The majority of individuals do really believe in that. To depend on someone else is not really well accepted. It takes away their pride. But they're willing to close their eyes because they have no other choice. So they think they'll accept public assistance temporarily—until their children grow up to support them or until they themselves learn enough English, learn enough to be on their own. Being on welfare takes away all their pride.

AK: I've heard some people say that for older Cambodians, it's considered OK because they don't really have any other options. But there is the expectation that their kids will work, that their kids are not going to be on welfare.

SK: That is very true. The older people have no choice, they have no skills. How are they going to survive without the public assistance?

AK: Is there any feeling that the U.S. government owes them anything for all its action in Cambodia?

SK: Oh, yes. That is very true. The Cambodians are humble people. Unless a situation gets violent, gets uncontrollable, a lot of them are willing to forgive, they are willing to forget the past. Most of them who were in the countryside were directly affected by the bombs and chemicals. Their homes, their villages, their schools, their temples were wiped out by the bombs dropped by the American B-52s. We're talking about people whose land has been passed from generation to generation. That's the only piece of land they have. It was the only way they could make a living—by doing farming. When they were being bombed by B-52s, how could they do farming? There were all those chemicals, the forests were being defoliated. They themselves were also affected—their health, their skin, their hair, their environment. Yet, there were no experts, no doctors, to help them. Plus they lived in an underdeveloped society. They were not being trained to deal with this high-tech debilitation, this chemical kind of thing. All they had was their faith, their karma, their beliefs. They thought to themselves, maybe they had not done enough good in their previous lives. Cambodians believe in reincarnation. But being bombed has nothing to do with what you did in your previous life! It has nothing to do with that, but the Cambodian people do believe in that, a majority of them, particularly those from rural areas.

AK: You've mentioned the importance of Buddhism several times. Are most of the Cambodians in Lowell Buddhists?

SK: They are. A majority of them are Buddhists. Whether they are serious Buddhists or not, they all go to the temple. If they don't go on a regular basis, at least they go on the religious holidays.

AK: Do most of the Buddhists support the temple financially as well?

SK: Yes. Financially, the temples are stable. They bought both of the temples with cash. Because people do believe that is their culture, they believe if you do the good deeds, if you do make sacrifices for your family, you're earning your merit. And then hopefully you'll go into a better life in the next life. People do believe in that. That is one reason they donate so much money [to the temples], knowing that it's going to lead them some place, lead them to a better life. Also, they like having a place where Cambodians can go and call home.

AK: How many monks are there at the two temples?

SK: The old temple has more than ten Buddhist monks. The new one, I think, has probably four or five.

AK: Were those monks in the old days?

SK: A few of them have been monks for their entire lives. They were able to get out of the country before the Khmer Rouge. A majority of them were disrobed during the communists. Some of them are young; they want to dedicate some part of their life not only to study the Buddhist philosophy but to help people.

AK: The young ones, are they refugees who came to the United States after 1979?

SK: Yeah.

AK: Are the monks sort of therapists for the Cambodian people? Do Cambodians talk to them about their trauma?

SK: Traditionally, Buddhist monks are counselors, teachers, advisors, the community's spiritual leaders. That's their job; that's what they do for their living. They don't get any salary; they don't have any money. They don't carry any money with them. They will go beg in the morning for their lunch. In the evening, they study and go out and teach the people. Cambodian people give them food. Unlike doctors and lawyers here, the Buddhist monks have no charging rates. They get only food, not alcohol or any other things. They're supposed to possess nothing materially.

AK: So they do serve a counseling role?

SK: They do that. They have been really helpful because they're able to combine religious aspects and cultural aspects of Cambodia to help in the healing, particularly with mental illness and depression.

AK: Do you think the temples and Buddhism are also mechanisms for the preservation of Cambodian culture in general, not just the religious aspects?

SK: That's true. When we talk about culture, when we talk about religion, when we talk about Buddhism in Cambodia, they are mixed together. You cannot separate them. It's not like here, religion is different here. But in Cambodia, that's not the case. Cambodian culture and Buddhism are intertwined.

AK: How else are people dealing with the trauma of surviving the Pol Pot years? I suspect most Cambodians aren't going to see counselors and psychologists and people like that. Are they usually just holding it in?

SK: True. Very true. There's a number of things. One of the things is, they were able to struggle, to help themselves, because they have gone through so much, not only Pol Pot, but the refugee experience. So their life has become sort of immune to all these things. They have gone through so much hardship; what else can be worse?

AK: Are they sort of hardened?

SK: Right. Just like people who got no feet, they use their hands. They're emotionally strong. Other than that, Buddhism helps a lot. And, of course, their friends, their families, their extended families, their elders, help them a lot. For the elders, they also depend on their children. They try to forget, not totally forget but at least they try to balance it. We work with others in the family; we keep them busy.

AK: You mentioned earlier that one good thing about Lowell is that it has all these Cambodian restaurants, groceries, and businesses for other Cambodians. Who owns these businesses? Are they Cambodians or ethnic Chinese?

SK: They are Cambodian or Cambodian Chinese who were raised and born in Cambodia. Some of them don't even speak Chinese. They just know that their great-great-grandparents came from China.

AK: Do you know what percentage of the businesses are Chinese Cambodian owned versus ethnic Cambodian owned?

SK: The majority of them are Cambodian.

AK: Where do people get the money to start up businesses?

SK: A lot of times, it's from their savings. They work in a factory, save up the money. Same thing with their family members. They save up money and then they have enough money to open a small business. They have a few tables, start a restaurant. They do that by themselves. The children serve as the busboys, clean up and everything, the mother does the cooking. As enough time goes by, the business grows. Also they have friends who loan them money, they help each other. It's pretty much a family-oriented business. Many businesses, whether it's a grocery store, restaurant, beauty salon, jewelry store, or whatever, started with this kind of arrangement. And, of course, we could not sell this idea to the bank because they do not understand our language; we do not know what kind of language to use to speak to the bank. And a lot of the banks ask the applicants for credit history. It's just so many headaches.

AK: I've heard that for some young people, it's hard to finish school and go to college because there's pressure from their families to work in the business or work at some other job to support the family. Do you think that's one reason for the high dropout rate?

SK: That is very true because it all comes down to economic roles in the family. Each and every one of them has a responsibility to do x amount of

this, y amount of that. Some are able to handle both; some just can't. Again—
I like your analogy—you cannot compare oranges and apples. We've come
from different backgrounds. Most of the educated people during the communist rule were put in jail, or in reeducation camps, or in graves under the
ground. It was so extreme. That's the thing that frustrates me all the time:
sometimes, Cambodians can be so gentle, so humble; at other times, they can
be so violent, so cruel.

AK: Cambodians can be extreme?

SK: Most of the people in the countryside were not given the opportunity
to learn. We had different social classes.

AK: Do you think most Cambodians in Lowell dream about going back
to Cambodia? Do they think about Cambodia a lot?

SK: They do think of Cambodia a lot, but dreaming of returning and living there permanently, that's another story. A lot of the adults always think
about Cambodia: their families, the politics in Cambodia, the social development and economic development in Cambodia. At times, they forget
where they are. They are here. I find it alarming that they are not focusing
on what is going on right here in front of their face, right in front of their
nose, particularly with their children, the development of their children, the
education of their children, their community's development. Instead, they're
putting more emphasis, more thought, more time, into what's going on in
Cambodia, which is thousands of miles away with a situation that is uncontrollable, that is beyond their reach. It's disturbing. All their life, they have
been in Cambodia. They live here maybe not even one-fifth of their lives, so
there's not a strong attachment yet. You have a foreign system, a system that
is so alien that they cannot feel connected to it. Adults or youth alike want
to be accepted by someone, want to be recognized by something, by the system. They don't get that here, so they're ready to find some other way. It
happens that the majority of them do have one thing in common: their experiences, things [that happened] in Cambodia.

AK: Do you find that there's political factionalism here based on who they
support back in Cambodia?

SK: Very true. We have many political parties in Cambodia. But have they
done anything significant to help the people here or in Cambodia? The answer is no. They only talk.

AK: Did you or anyone you know vote in the '93 election?

SK: Only a very small number did. That is the thing we want to educate
our community about, the importance of voting, democracy.

AK: Actually, I was referring to the election in Cambodia.

SK: Well, there was a large turnout, one of the largest turnouts we ever had in the history of Cambodian elections. The majority of the voters were women.

AK: But did people from Lowell go to the U.N. or to Cambodia to vote?

SK: They were not allowed to because they don't have Cambodian citizenship. When they live here, they're viewed as foreigners [by the Cambodian government].

AK: I thought that Cambodians in the U.S. were allowed to vote.

SK: Only a very small percentage who were in Cambodia at the time. They had to be in Cambodia to register. There were a few hundred at the most. People here, I don't think they voted. We had to fly there, and we're not that rich. We could not afford the airfare just to vote, knowing that it's not going to change anything.

AK: Do people here send money back to support the political parties?

SK: Many of them do. Well, maybe not the political parties, but relatives, yes. Supporting the political parties, I don't think it's a large percentage. When they were still at war, they were trying to raise money.

AK: Besides your organization, is there any other organization servicing the Cambodian community here in Lowell?

SK: There's a number of them. There's the Cambodian American League of Lowell. They are focusing on business development. They are newly established; I don't think they have done much yet; they don't have the budget to do so. There's also the Cambodian American Voters League; they're trying to educate the Cambodian community about the importance of the [electoral] system in this country. There's also the Khmer Cultural Institute, where they're focusing on cultural and educational aspects. All these are newly established, and they don't have the manpower, they don't have the financial resources. So far, each one is just another club. Although their names sound so big, each one has only a few members.

AK: So I guess your organization, having been established the longest, is the most active. You've given me a lot of insight into the situation in Lowell. Thank you very much.

August 23, 1995

6. Sambath Rim
Getting Established in Fall River, Massachusetts

MR. SAMBATH RIM is the executive director of a mutual assistance association named the Cambodian Community of Greater Fall River (CCGFR) in Massachusetts. Mr. Rim's most valuable asset is his ability to get along with all kinds of people. Almost all members of his family died during the Khmer Rouge years. He stayed alive by helping strangers, who, in turn, were moved to share their meager food with him, a starving "orphan child." (As it turned out, he was not a real orphan, because his mother also managed to survive, but Mr. Rim did not find that out until years after he had resettled in the United States.) Alone, he escaped to Thailand in 1979 after the Vietnamese invaded Cambodia and ousted the Pol Pot regime.

When Mr. Rim first arrived in the United States as a refugee in 1981, he lived with an uncle in Stockton, California, where he enrolled in Delta Community College even though he had never attended high school. But he did not like Stockton, so after he completed his associate of arts degree he moved to Massachusetts, again alone. He first worked as a nutritionist's assistant and then found a job at Citizens for Citizens, a social service agency. Having relied on his wits for survival since 1975, when he was only eleven, he does not hesitate to take whatever initiatives are needed to improve the lot of other Cambodians. He helped establish the organization that he now directs. When Audrey Kim interviewed him at Angkor Plaza—a business enterprise sponsored by the CCGFR—on August 22, 1995, she was impressed by his "jolly, outgoing nature."

When I talked to Sambath Rim by telephone on October 17, 2001, he told me that Angkor Plaza now has eleven stores including several grocery stores, a laundromat, a beauty salon, a video rental store, a restaurant, a goldsmith who specializes in making Cambodian-style jewelry, a jewelry store, a karaoke studio, and a karate studio. All the stores except the karate studio are owned by Khmer merchants. The karate studio is operated by a martial arts teacher who is both African American and Native American. The customers and clients are largely Cambodians, although Mr. Rim hopes that the number of customers from all over Fall River will eventually increase. Whether that happens will depend on how well the businesses develop marketing skills. To ensure that customers have enough income to buy the goods and services, the MAA has focused on job training and placement. The largest number of gainfully employed Cambodians in Fall River work in textile mills, with a smaller number working in the electronics industry. Mr. Rim believes that self-sufficiency should be not just an economic concept. He would like to see Cambodians become "truly independent," that is, able to function in American society without reliance on anyone.

The population of Cambodian ancestry in Fall River has increased to nearly six thousand. Part of the increase comes from births on American soil and part from secondary migration. Cambodians are coming to Fall River, mostly from California, Washington state, Rhode Island, and other places within Massachusetts. They come because they have heard about Fall River's affordable housing and the fact that people can live there peacefully because the gang problem is absent.

The new arrivals feel that Fall River is the "right place" for them, Mr. Rim says. People in Fall River have become "a little more friendly" toward refugees since the early 1990s because they recognize that the Cambodian presence has benefitted the Flint area, where most refugees live, by sprucing up the neighborhood and keeping it clean. Sambath Rim has worked hard to improve interethnic relations in his adopted city. He speaks at meetings of various groups and points out to his audience that although it is indeed regrettable that more than fifty-eight thousand Americans died during the U.S. involvement in the war in Vietnam, an even larger number of Cambodians perished, in part because the war spilled into Cambodia. Thus, Cambodians should not be blamed for the fact that many of them became refugees, some of whom ended up in the United States. As that idea sinks in, the wounds inflicted by the Vietnam War, as they are experienced in such places as Fall River, seem finally to be healing.

*   *   *

AK: Will you please tell me why you decided to buy this building?
SR: We think that the Cambodian community should own some type of

business. When they were back home, some people had business skills. How can these skills be used in this country?

AK: Were these shops located in other areas and then relocated here or are they new businesses?

SR: They're new businesses. Only the restaurant and the grocery store already existed.

AK: Is it mostly Cambodians who are patronizing the stores or is it all kinds of people coming to the stores?

SR: All people, but the majority is Cambodian.

AK: Are the shopowners ethnic Cambodians or are they ethnic Chinese?

SR: Cambodians.

AK: A lot of the ones who own the businesses elsewhere are ethnic Chinese.

SR: Yes, yes, yes, some of them are ethnic Chinese.

AK: But here they're all ethnic Cambodians?

SR: Yeah, except for one business owner of Chinese descent.

AK: Do you know how the store owners got the capital to start their businesses?

SR: They all borrowed from friends.

AK: You mean they rely on a rotating credit system?

SR: Yes.

AK: So your MAA [mutual assistance association] bought this whole space and you're leasing out the stores. And, in addition, you provide technical assistance to the store owners.

SR: Right.

AK: Does the MAA actually own the property?

SR: No, the two [Angkor Plaza and the MAA] are separate legal entities.

AK: About how many Cambodians live in Fall River?

SR: Twenty-five hundred to five thousand.

AK: Just in Fall River? Wow. And you don't have a temple?

SR: Well, there was a proposal from people here that we really need a temple. But we told them that in order to have a temple, we have to have a strong community base.

AK: You don't want to have too many things going on.

SR: Right. We would like to have this as an on-going project. Then we can have a temple. This building is not owned by any particular person. Community Development owns it. It consists of a majority-Cambodian board of directors. They respond to what the needs are and how resources should be used.

AK: So is this a nonprofit corporation that was formed to own the building?

SR: Yeah.

AK: The MAA provided the leadership in starting the project, but the two are technically not the same.

SR: No. We are different. The MAA cannot own this property because it is nonprofit.

AK: Maybe you could tell me about the MAA and how it got involved with Angkor Plaza.

SR: Cambodian people started to come to Fall River in 1979. At that time, it was only a few families. Up until 1983, we had only about eight families.

AK: Did the resettlement agencies start placing a lot of people in this area? If not, why did Cambodians come to this area?

SR: We have some volunteer sponsors, the churches, they're working very closely with the social services. Two, three Cambodians families came; that was in 1979. And whoever came in 1979, they had friends or relatives in the camps. That was the time the American government started to get people to come to the United States. Until 1982, '83, we got more families to come, about eight families or so.

AK: I just want to clarify: before '79, you had no Cambodians.

SR: No Cambodians.

AK: In Washington and New York, there were some pre-1975 people.

SR: None here. By '84, we had about thirty-five families. The eight families had some families they wanted to bring in, some relatives across the country. And the thing is, we are a very, very united community, we always get in touch with others from one city to another. Most of the time, we do know each other. The leaders across the country, like Dr. Sam-Ang Sam in D.C., like Him Chhim in Long Beach, we know the leaders of the people across the country. Somehow we respond to each other. What are the needs there, what are the needs here?

AK: Do you know which resettlement agencies brought in Cambodians?

SR: Catholic Social Services.

AK: I think in the early '80s, this area was not doing that well economically, Boston and this whole area. So why were people brought to this area?

SR: Well, I think in the '80s, there were jobs in Fall River.

AK: Really? What kinds of jobs?

SR: Factory jobs and jobs that the state can help the refugees to get with no problem.

AK: What happened when Cambodians started arriving?

SR: In 1985, I cried for help from the different agencies: a Cambodian community exists in Fall River! We would like to be a part of the larger community. We would like to be recognized. Well, due to the language barrier, my broken English, sometimes people were not patient enough to listen what I was trying to say. Some of them did but because not much attention was paid at the time, we were not much recognized. But the press and media have focused on us since 1985.

AK: The Cambodians who were here in the early '80s, were they getting services from Catholic Charities to learn English, to be placed in jobs, and that kind of thing?

SR: We did get some services. But do we get enough services? No. Because we don't know our way around. We are just starting to learn. Even though I had been here for a few years, I still didn't know the way around until about 1987.

AK: You're talking about just Fall River, not Providence, right?

SR: Just Fall River. At that time, Providence seemed very, very far away to us because we didn't have transportation. We were using public transportation. So, it seemed very far away. Somehow, since '87, we have been recognized by the mainstream agencies. People now like to serve us.

AK: Was the Cambodian community united in terms of trying to gain recognition?

SR: I always feel I belong to the community. You see, I used to be an orphan child supported by the community. So when I came to this country, I always feel that it doesn't matter where I go, the community always helps. That's why when I realized the community needed help, I tried to find ways to see how I can help the community better. At the time, a lot of people didn't speak English. Just me and a couple of other people could speak English. I put a lot of commitment into trying to help them. That's how I got the job over here when they started to hire staff. They already knew me and what I have done. So, in '87, we got recognized by the mainstream community which saw we were trying to help Cambodians. I used to work for Citizens for Citizens, it's one of the agencies providing services for Cambodians. The mainstream agencies are trying to help Cambodians, but do they know what are the needs of Cambodians? Some of the needs they do know but some of them they don't. Do they know us well in terms of culture? Some of them do and some of them don't. Those who don't know about the culture, sometimes instead of helping they're hurting us. We, because we are the new arrivals, we just don't want to cause any problems for the agencies. Whatever problems we have due to our misunderstanding each other, we don't want them to think the problems arose because of their attitude, their misinterpreting. One example: some parents coined their children when the children got sick.

The neighbors didn't know what this practice was. It was very lucky that one of the policemen was a veteran, he had gone to Southeast Asia at one time, and he knew about coining [a method Southeast Asians use to draw blood to the skin by rubbing the skin vigorously with a coin in order to expel the poisons that they believe cause illnesses]. What would have happened if the police didn't know? He tried to talk to the parents but the parents didn't speak English. I mean, these parents could have been locked up. So we try to prevent that kind of thing from happening. In the hospital many times when the people go in to see doctors, the doctors see all kind of strange marks, they're not used to touching hands and all those kinds of healing.

AK: So, there are a lot of cultural misunderstandings.

SR: Right, right. And, one time, the police was talking to one of the guys. The guy smiled, put his face down, because this was his very polite salute to the police. But the policeman was thinking, "Who is this man? This guy is not even listening to me, not paying attention!" When I saw that, I asked him, "What is the problem, officer?" "You know this guy I'm trying to talk to him and he didn't even listen!" That's why I always talk to the police chief: "We are trying very hard to learn about your culture, but it would be a good thing if you can learn some of ours. Otherwise, you cannot serve the community." I mean, Fall River is a diverse community and whoever is working for the city, especially the police department, should understand the basics of the diverse backgrounds of the residents so they can provide better service to the people.

AK: So, at that time, the MAA did not yet exist.

SR: No, it did not exist. Because all these problems arose, we established it.

AK: The problems were the impetus for the creation of the MAA?

SR: Right. I figured that out. I said to people: "You know, Cambodians need a space. Cambodians need a staff." Cambodians should have their own community, their own community that can serve them. If we ourselves don't serve the needs of our people, we are not going to get our needs satisfied because they don't know anything about us. If we feel this need, we should form a nonprofit organization, what we call a[n] MAA, to help ourselves. I've always had a strong feeling myself that before I ask for help from somebody else, I should help myself first. Then it's easy to ask someone to help and it's easy for them to help. I went to other agencies to talk about setting up the MAA; they were not happy about the competition. Angkor Plaza was part of the five-year plan for the MAA.

AK: In places like Lowell, there are a lot of Cambodian businesses, but they don't own their own buildings. In your opinion, what is so important about owning the building, rather than just having the businesses?

SR: It's important because we can pull the community together, that's one thing. Here, people can talk to each other in a second language without fear. After they get out from class, they can go without fear to the laundromat, the grocery store. I think you should have your own center so that you can perform your cultural activities and also business activities there, like in Chinatown. When you are united in one place, the people feel more confident about themselves and proud of who they are.

AK: It seems like, for you, it's important not just to have the building and community together, but you really wanted to own the building.

SR: Why do we want to own the plaza ourselves? Because if we rent from somebody else, what happens if they don't like Sam Rim?

AK: You have more control as the owner.

SR: Yes. It's our own plaza, we can serve the people better: "People, this is your plaza."

AK: There's a clear sense of ownership and control.

SR: Right, right. When you talk to the owner of a business, you can say, "It doesn't matter where you rent the space, you can get a business of your own. But if you pay the rent here, you're paying to your own community. A year from now, this building will be fully owned by your community. So please help your community." Right now, even though we own it, the bank is the one that owns the equity. The people do understand that. I say, "Why don't you, the business owners, sit down together and talk about which direction we should go, and then propose it to the board of Angkor Plaza?" We created a business management team.

AK: Can we back up a little bit? In '91, you submitted a proposal to the state refugee coordinator for funding to start the MAA.

SR: Right.

AK: And even then you had the seed of the idea to start the Plaza. In the beginning, what sorts of things were you doing at the MAA before you got this building?

SR: We had human services, employment services, educational services. Those are the things that we do. And we would like very much to do business development.

AK: In '91, not that many Cambodians were coming into this area, were they?

SR: In '91? In '91, we had almost two thousand.

AK: Before the secondary migration, about how many Cambodians were in Fall River? How many people were originally resettled in Fall River?

SR: Around forty families. Approximately three hundred people.

AK: So the number you gave me, most of that is through secondary migration? Where were people coming from?

SR: They're coming from Washington state, they're coming from Long

Beach, from Boston, from Sacramento, from San Jose, Oakland, San Francisco. They're coming from Houston, Texas.

AK: Are they coming for jobs or to join families? Why are they all flocking here?

SR: The first intention of the family is to get a job here. Because, at that time, in California, they could not find jobs. Some of them, they have families over here.

AK: Do people move here because of the public assistance?

SR: I think in terms of public assistance, if they want that, they would move to Boston or Lowell. Public housing is one of the draws there.

AK: So were people coming to Fall River because they wanted to work in the textile factories?

SR: They did not specify what kind of jobs they really wanted. But a lot of textile companies are here, so there's more chance that such jobs are open to them.

AK: It's just a lot, three or four thousand people all coming here through secondary migration.

SR: Some of them really wanted at first to be fishermen, to do fishing. We are the number one or number two fishing state.

AK: Oh, really? I didn't know that.

SR: I used to drive around at night to follow the fishermen from here to Cape Cod. The fishermen are mostly Portuguese Americans. So we talk to the Cambodians. We don't have any experience with the sea, only with freshwater fishing.

AK: Are you saying that, initially, people were drawn to this area because they thought they might become fishermen?

SR: Yes. They would like to come over here if they can do fishing. But when they did come, some of them changed their minds, and some of them went into farming. Some of them are working in the textile factories. Some are doing painting jobs. Also, at the time, when we compare rents over here to the rents in other communities, like Providence, we have very cheap rent. So that's one of the reasons they came. They are trying to get away from the problem of gangs and they feel it is better to bring up their kids here.

AK: I want to make sure I understand the big picture. Cambodians came here through secondary migration for a lot of reasons, including the fact they had a vague idea that maybe they could go into fishing. There were textile jobs, housing was cheap. In other areas, there were gang problems, and they thought that by coming here, they could get away from all that.

SR: Yes. So, for us, the agencies over here were formed according to the needs of the refugees. We prioritize what the needs are. Health is one of them;

employment is another. At one time, there was a depression; unemployment was really high: 18, 19 percent unemployment.

AK: This is the early '90s you're talking about? Did many of the Cambodians who were working in the mid- or late '80s lose their jobs?

SR: Yes. We figured out that we haven't used our own skills yet to run businesses. We asked how can we adapt better to the American way. Then, we said, "Well, why don't we set up our own place, a mall which is owned by Cambodians, like Chinatown?" We also wanted a place where we can get our human services and our cultural services.

AK: You mentioned that the adults when they first came here ended up doing things like fishing, textiles, factories. Are they still in those jobs? Have they moved on to other types of work?

SR: Yes, yes. Some of them have. Whatever they can get, they will do it.

AK: What percent are on public assistance at this point?

SR: About 30 percent, AFDC [Aid to Families with Dependent Children] and GA [General Assistance].

AK: I'm wondering, are most of the families on public assistance ones that are headed by women?

SR: Large families are the ones on public assistance. A lot of them are headed by women. Some of them have men, but they've been through the Khmer Rouge regime; they're so depressed.

AK: Right. I've heard that from other people, that the trauma makes people unable to work.

SR: Yeah, even me. Last night, I still had a nightmare; I dreamed Khmer Rouge were chasing me around.

AK: I'd like to hear your personal story but before you talk about that, I'd like to continue our discussion of families. What percentage of the families here are headed by women?

SR: Good question but I cannot give you the figures.

AK: As high as 50 percent?

SR: Maybe about 40 percent.

AK: Do you find that those families have more problems handling the kids or that more of those kids end up in the gangs?

SR: Well, it's not just the families headed by women but also those with both parents whose kids have problems.

AK: So it doesn't really matter whether the family has two parents or one?

SR: The kids are smarter than the parents. Let me tell you a story. One of the kids told me he never went to school. The school sent a letter to the parents saying, "What happened to this kid? Why isn't he coming to school? Why is he absent?" The parents told the kid, "You know, we got a letter from we don't know where; can you translate it?" The kid says, "Oh, it's a letter from school saying that I'm a very, very good kid doing a really good job in school." The parents, hearing their own kid is doing very well, are proud and tell their neighbors, "You know, my kid is very smart, he's doing very good in school. The teacher, the school, sent us a letter." The parents are very excited until the police calls from the police station: "This kid is locked up; he was shot," and they tell the reason why he got locked up. So, you have to be smarter than the kids in order to control them. Otherwise, they just do whatever they want.

AK: What kinds of youth programs do you have for the kids?

SR: Well, we're counseling them, we are trying to let them have fun, and also to understand what is the role of their parents, what is the role of themselves. What is the role of the school? How can we help them do better? What is the role of the Cambodian community? What do you want to be in the future? A doctor? What is the problem that you face? If you cannot do the homework problem or the math, how can we help? This is a program we just started.

AK: It sounds like rather than have a formal type of program, you sort of become friendly with the kids and counsel them.

SR: Right. And we are also friendly with the parents.

AK: About how many people do you serve here? Do all the Cambodians in Fall River come to you at one point or another?

SR: When they have a problem. I'm not talking about when they have a party, but when they have a problem.

AK: It sounds like you're a general troubleshooter for Cambodians in this area when they have any questions or problems.

SR: Yes. Sometimes they divorce.

AK: What is the rate of divorce?

SR: About 20 percent.

AK: Is it mostly the younger people getting divorced or the older ones?

SR: Younger. The older ones, they love each other very much.

AK: Are people in the Cambodian community here still active in politics back in Cambodia?

SR: Yeah, but it's not like Long Beach, San Francisco, Lowell, or Boston. Over here, we try to understand what's going on, but we're not really active.

AK: So you don't have political factionalism here?

SR: No, we don't.

AK: Do you think people here have a desire to go back to Cambodia? Do they dream of going back to Cambodia?

SR: Yes, a lot of them. There's no place like home. A lot of people right now are living here but hope to go back to Cambodia when they retire. But that can change.

AK: I think some people speculate that it's harder for Cambodians and other refugees to move ahead in American society because when your heart and your mind are elsewhere, it's hard to focus on the here and now. Is that true?

SR: I don't see it that way. What I see is we're starting, not from zero, but below zero. For example, if you come from some other part of Asia, like Thailand or Hong Kong, the standard of living and the standard of education there are high. But in Cambodia, after the collapse of the communist regime, never mind about education; if you can get food to survive for a day, you're lucky. So, the mind is preoccupied with that. Plus, we were in what I call the world of darkness. We were forced to work eighteen hours, sixteen hours, a day under the Khmer Rouge. And without seeing the outside world. So you're lost, trapped. Before 1975, even though you were in the country-side, you knew what was going on in the outside world. We had information—radios, newspapers. But under the Khmer Rouge, you didn't have time to read newspapers. They were always strict and watching you all the time. You could not go from one place to another. Even if we wanted to go only one or two kilometers from here, we had to ask permission. Otherwise, we would just get killed. So this experience keeps the minds of people really closed, just like a dark place. And when you emerge into the outside world, you have trouble seeing.

AK: Cambodians were closed off from the rest of the world for a long time and then thrown back in and expected to land on their feet. And they can't do that easily.

SR: That's why those in the United States are starting not from zero but from below zero.

AK: You've told me a little bit about your involvement with the MAA and with Angkor Plaza and your later life. Can you now tell me a little about your life in Cambodia and how you came to the United States?

SR: Well, I was an orphan child. My father was killed when the Khmer Rouge took over. My father was the intelligence investigator for the president of Cambodia. I was eleven years old when the Khmer Rouge took over. I tried to live without having any relatives. Somehow, I got support from other people. Of course, you have to make people like you in order for them to share their food with you. That's why I have very good public relations. I always think in terms of what can be done better in the community.

AK: In '75, when the Khmer Rouge took over, they killed your father and you were left alone. You had no other relatives or family members? Or you didn't know where they were, so you had to scrounge for yourself as a child to find food? You weren't put into a children's camp or anything like that?

SR: Yes, I had to work very hard, just like the other children. Later I shared some of the ideas I had after the Khmer Rouge were gone. I shared the ideas I had with the adults on how to secure the village better.

AK: This is after the Vietnamese invasion?

SR: During the Vietnamese invasion. I said, "We need to protect ourselves from the Khmer Rouge coming back but we also have to watch out for the Vietnamese. Somehow we have to secure ourselves." They got knives and guns to secure the village. I think I'm somewhat outstanding. Under the communists, if you're outstanding, you're not very safe. Never mind if you're still a child. Here, in the United States, when you're fifteen, sixteen years old, you're not a child anymore. But if you were living in the world I used to live in, you cannot act the way you act when you live in this country. Back home, if the community doesn't like how you act, you're not going to survive. What happened was that when there was fighting between the Vietnamese and the Khmer Rouge, I decided to escape. I had no food, no pants, just underwear and one long-sleeved shirt. I left and I walked one full day.

AK: Did you escape by yourself?

SR: By myself.

AK: And you were, what, maybe fourteen years old?

SR: Fifteen. I went to a village and I told them I came from another village. "I don't have any food or any place to sleep. Can you give me some food and a place to sleep?" I stayed there for one night and then I left. When I got to the camp, I asked myself, "What is going on in my country?" When I was not even close to the border yet, I already kept asking: "What kind of games are they playing? Who is Vietnamese? Who is Khmer Rouge?" I'm very thankful to the people who have given me food and shelter every night, and I kept thinking how can I pay them back. In the refugee camp, I was put in the children's center; still no relatives. I thought, "Well, I should learn English." You know the paper that they wrapped the chicken in and they threw away? I put the pieces together to form a notebook so I could learn to write. I went to see a Japanese medical team and they sent me to work as a nurse's assistant. I performed more than the nurse's assistant's role. I kept thinking of the future. "What is my future going to be? Do I have to stay in the camp for years and go back home without knowing what to do about my life?" So I wrote a letter to the American embassy [in Bangkok] because of my frustration that the war in Cambodia was not just a war between different factions in Cambodia. The world got involved. The Vietnam War spilled over into Cambodia. That was the intention of the Vietnamese. So the border country became a war zone. When the Americans pulled out their troops from Vietnam, they never thought of what would happen to Vietnam's neighbors. So millions of people got killed. People got killed because they supported the Americans.

AK: You wrote this in your letter?

SR: Yes. I wrote a letter to the American embassy and said, "I have been victimized. My father was killed because the Khmer Rouge said he support-ed the Americans. Now, I'm all alone and I'm in this orphanage, this chil-dren's center. I would like to ask if the Americans can get me to the United States where I can learn more, understand more. Then I can go back to my country and teach others and direct my country better. Right now, Ameri-cans seem to have forgotten us. Never mind the people who already died. How about their relatives, their children who are still alive?" A month later, the American embassy sent two people to talk to me. At first, I had decided to write in English, broken English. My English is not good; what happens if they cannot understand me? My writing is very poor, so it'd be better if I write in Khmer. Even though the American embassy cannot read it, maybe they can find someone who can read Khmer and can understand fully. So when they sent people to see me, I thought I was in trouble. I had been trying to escape for years. If I hadn't, I would have died. The people from the Ameri-can embassy said to me, "Sam Bath Rim, congratulations!" I didn't even know what congratulations meant. They told me I would be sent to the United States. I was very, very excited. About three months later, they posted the names [of people who] have been selected to go to the United States. On the last day of posting, I saw my name.

AK: Where in the U.S. did you first arrive?

SR: California. Stockton. My father's cousin is there and I wrote a letter to him to ask him if he could do a sponsorship. So I was sent to where he lived and I became a translator for the community.

AK: How long did you live in Stockton?

SR: Two years.

AK: Then where did you go? Were you going to school at that time?

SR: Yeah, I was going to a community college.

AK: So you didn't go to high school at all?

SR: No. After I came here, a few days later I turned eighteen.

AK: What happened after two years in Stockton?

SR: I was thinking, "I'm still an orphan child. Somehow I can be self-sufficient if I make my way around. If I live in Stockton, I'll have no future. I have a lot of friends who are just going out a lot. And when I tried to find a job, I cannot find a job. Immigrants got started in the East." One of my adopted brothers, my godbrother, was living in the East Coast. He came to the United States several months after I got to the United States. I decided, "Why don't I go east, too?" So I came to Fall River. When I came to Fall River, I liked it.

AK: I'm not sure I understand, why did you decide to come to Fall River?

SR: My godbrother was living here.

AK: And you thought this would be a good place to start your life?

SR: Yes. I had read in the history books the immigrants had gotten started in the East, so why don't I myself start in the East too? When I came to Fall River, I just liked it. There were only a few families, eight families, here. Still, people needed help. So, when I came I made myself available.

AK: Did you have a job at that time?

SR: I didn't. I always lived just supported by the community. I didn't have a job at the time, so I registered to go to school. I got work-study. And because I helped people, sometimes they bought food for me.

AK: When did you move to Fall River? What year?

SR: February 29, 1983.

AK: Right before the big influx of Cambodians.

SR: Yes. And then I found out that my mom was still alive in the camps. So I tried to sponsor her to come. I asked some American friends to be a co-sponsor with me. I brought my mom and my stepfather and my stepsisters and stepbrothers here. In 1985, I was given a job as a nutrition assistant. I told my boss, "I am always running around helping my people. Can you give me time to run around?" She understood my situation and said, "No problem, keep helping your people." Then Citizens for Citizens had a job opening. A lot of agencies have tried to help my people, but somehow there are cultural differences they don't understand. So, some of the help they are trying to give is hurting instead of helping Cambodians. I thought of establishing a better nonprofit organization. That's why we started the MAA.

AK: It sounds like you really were the major force in creating the MAA and the Plaza. It's a big achievement.

SR: Well, you know, believe it or not, when we started, we had a lot of opposition. If you compete against people who have the pie, they're not really going to be happy about that. The thing is, if you don't fight for a piece of the pie, you'll never get it. We feed the baby who cries for milk. Whoever doesn't cry, we think they're OK. We feed the one who's crying.

AK: Let me ask you about that. Some people say that because of Cambodian values and culture where people don't ask for things, where it's not polite to ask for or demand things, Cambodians often get lost in the shuffle of receiving social services. Is that something you see as a problem?

SR: It's true.

AK: You are very different because you are willing to ask for things.

SR: I don't know. I used to be peaceful and quiet; that's what we have been taught, to be peaceful and quiet. During the Khmer Rouge, if you were peaceful and quiet, you survived. Also, if you can do something yourself, why ask for help from somebody else? Unless you are really desperately in need, you don't ask. But over here, we're in a new country. Strange people around. Ask them for help? How, with our language barrier? But when I observe and see what's going on, I see North America, the United States has not existed for thousands of years. The first immigrants were people from Europe, different countries. Then they formed the government. Whoever was working in the government, even though they are supposed to represent all the people, they serve whoever is the first priority for them, which is their own people, their own community. If you are from a different world and you don't fight for your share, people will say you are a very nice guy but they don't give you your pie.

AK: Indeed.

SR: Right. That's why I fight. For example, the money for AIDS prevention, we all know that in Southeast Asia, there's a very high rate of positive HIV. This has been written in the reports of the World Health Organization. It's also true in Africa. I'm not trying to accuse other people, but I'm talking about reality here. The people who get funding to prevent AIDS here are Latinos. I ask myself, "Why do the Latinos get the money?" I know that it's needed in their community, there is no question. But why so much? When I see people working in the Department of Public Health, I try to let them know the needs in my community, I beg for funds, but they deny my proposal. They say, "You don't have statistics for that. You don't have charts. So how can we help you?" I said, "If you don't give me a chance, you'll never, never, even ten years from now, never get any charts. If you give me a chance, I will have the statistics." Cambodians almost didn't get a penny until I started to fight very hard.

AK: Obviously, you've learned how to function very well in American society and to serve your fellow Cambodians. Thank you so much for sharing your ideas and your own story.

August 22, 1995

7. Samien Nol
Cambodians in Philadelphia

Mr. Samien Nol is the executive director of the Southeast Asian Mutual Assistance Associations Coalition (SEAMAAC) in Philadelphia. Audrey Kim interviewed him in his office on Market Street on August 8, 1995. SEAMAAC is a coalition of five mutual assistance associations (MAAs): Cambodian, ethnic Chinese, Hmong, lowland Lao, and Vietnamese. Its board of directors consists of the presidents of the five MAAs plus four other individuals. The position of the board president rotates annually in order to ensure that no single group dominates the organization.

Mr. Nol studied engineering in Japan. When he returned to Cambodia, he worked for the Lon Nol government and was sent to Thailand in 1974 on an assignment. When the Khmer Rouge came to power in 1975, he, his wife, and young son were flown to Camp Pendleton in June 1975 and admitted as refugees. Within two weeks he found a job in a heating and ventilation company. He eventually moved to Philadelphia, where he became active in the Cambodian refugee community. He served as president of the Cambodian MAA before becoming executive director of SEAMAAC in 1989. When I talked to him by telephone on September 25, 2001, he said that he will probably remain at his job until he reaches retirement age, which will be in a few years.

SEAMAAC has grown substantially since the mid-1990s. Its annual budget is now almost $2 million, with funds coming from the federal, state, and city governments as well as private foundations. At present, Mr. Nol observes, SEAMAAC is the only Asian community organization in Philadelphia that is a United Way agency. This affiliation is very helpful, because it provides SEAMAAC with a stable source of funds for some of its programs. The organization has twenty full-time and twenty part-time staff who, together, speak the languages of all the Southeast Asian groups SEAMAAC serves. Its main programs still focus on health care and mental health counseling, adult education (with English-as-a-second-language classes being offered at easily accessible locations), the needs of the elderly, and tutoring and mentoring young people, especially those deemed to be "at risk."

In response to welfare reform, SEAMAAC submitted a grant proposal to the federal Office of Refugee Resettlement (ORR) to set up a program to train and place Cambodians in jobs. ORR funded the proposal. Before the contract period ended in June 2001, SEAMAAC trained some three hundred persons and placed more than two hundred of them in a variety of occupations. The employed trainees work for nurseries, in meatpacking plants, and at old-age homes; they also do home repair as private vendors. Not knowing English has not been an impediment in such jobs, especially because some employers now hire English-speaking Cambodians as foremen or supervisors. Many gainfully employed Cambodians work the night shifts that members of more established groups shun. Most Cambodian women with little education, however, remain unemployed. In some families, children have been under pressure to earn money after school, but that has negatively affected their academic performance. They have no time for their homework after getting off work, sometimes around midnight.

The Cambodian-ancestry population in the greater Philadelphia area has increased since 1995, when Audrey Kim interviewed him. Mr. Nol estimates the number is somewhere between fifteen and twenty thousand. SEAMAAC staff worked hard to persuade Cambodians to fill out the year 2000 population census form, but many never did so because of their fear of the government—any government—given their terrifying experiences under the Khmer Rouge. The population increase is due in part to births on American soil and in part to secondary migration from other areas, mainly California and the New England states. A few elderly Cambodians have returned to Cambodia to visit families and friends and, more poignantly, to wait for their own deaths.

Youth problems remain the most important challenge facing Cambodians in the Philadelphia area. In families with two parents, if both of them work, very young children are left at home alone or are watched by older siblings because parents on minimum wage cannot afford childcare. Mr. Nol said that "intergenerational friction" remains high, because children are quite Americanized. Given the low rate of immigration from Cambodia, most young children of Cambodian ancestry in the United States are Americans by birth. They have no memories and little acquired knowledge of their parents' homeland and its culture. Meanwhile, parents still expect them to behave according to the values and norms of that culture. Families that continue to rely on public assistance live in neighborhoods where children are exposed to crime and violence from a very young age. Their parents do not attend school events because they do not know English well enough to feel comfortable at such meetings. SEAMAAC staff members, however, often attend PTA meetings in order to sensitize teachers and school principals to the problems Cambodian American children face but "cannot be replacements for the parents," Nol insists. The primary improvement in more recent years, in Samien Nol's opinion, has been that more Cambodians have become aware of how to obtain help when they need it.

*   *   *

AK: Could you start by telling me a little about yourself, how you came to Philadelphia and became the executive director here?

SN: That's a long story! In 1975, the war ended in Vietnam [and Cambodia]. Cambodia was taken over by the communists. I was on a mission in Thailand. I wanted to go back home but people at the border said that I could not go back. "They're killing everybody," they said.

AK: What kind of background did you come from? Were you from the city or countryside?

SN: I was born in the country, raised in the city, and went to college in Japan. Then I went back to Cambodia and worked for the government. In 1974, I went to Thailand.

AK: You were very lucky to be out of the country.

SN: Yeah. In 1975, I asked for political asylum. The original idea was to come for maybe a few months or a year or two. But I got stuck here. When I first came, I arrived in California.

AK: You mean you applied for political asylum in Thailand and you were accepted and came to California?

SN: Yes. I was flown to California.

AK: How did you end up in California?

SN: I was taken to Camp Pendleton. That was in June 1975. I had a choice at that time to stay in this country or to go to Canada. Both places accepted me, but I decided to stay in this country because my wife didn't like the cold weather.

AK: So, you and your wife both came to California?

SN: Yeah. And I had a small son. My wife's sister was here. She had come as a student; she had just finished school at that time. We wanted to be close to her. At the same time, I had an older brother in New Jersey who was working for the United Nations. So, there were two places I could choose, either the East Coast or the West Coast.

AK: At that time, there weren't that many Cambodians in this area, were there?

SN: No, no, just three, four families. I didn't have much problem. I spoke English; I'm actually an engineer by training. After two weeks here, I got a job. It was not a very good job but it was a job.

AK: Were you receiving refugee cash assistance and medical assistance at that time?

SN: I didn't receive that. I got a job.

AK: Did the resettlement agencies help you much?

SN: I think they helped me. I came and stayed with my sister-in-law. Maybe they gave me some money; I forget now.

AK: You were relying mostly on family support?

SN: Yeah. And I had some money of my own. Then after two weeks, I got a job. I rented an apartment for my wife and myself.

AK: What kind of job did you get at the beginning?

SN: I was a heating [and] ventilation engineer. After a few months, I wanted to go back home; I was so homesick, so I worked at night. That way, I just forgot about what's going on.

AK: You're so homesick you just worked constantly?

SN: Yeah. And hoping that I could go back.

AK: Was the rest of your family still in Cambodia at this time?

SN: Yeah, at that time, some of my family. I had one younger brother in France; my parents, my sister, and my younger brother were in Cambodia. I had no news. They didn't know where I was.

AK: They never heard anything?

SN: Yeah. It was really . . .

AK: Very stressful?

SN: Yeah. Sometime around 1978, more Cambodians began coming.

AK: To this area [Philadelphia], you mean?

SN: Yeah. Since I was more or less established, I started helping people.

AK: Can you tell me more about those people who came in 1978? Why did they come to Philadelphia? What parts of Philadelphia did they settle in?

SN: They didn't have a choice. They didn't know anything about the United States. The settlement agencies put them where they pleased, they put them in poor neighborhoods in Philadelphia.

AK: Because there was affordable housing?

SN: Affordable, but the conditions were bad.

AK: So the people who came to Philadelphia were just brought here by the resettlement agencies?

SN: Yeah.

AK: In those poor neighborhoods, how were the people received, the new Cambodians?

SN: Most of the neighborhoods, as you know, the poor neighborhoods, they kind of resented it. Nobody asked them first or told them who were coming to their neighborhood. That is one of the causes of the friction. The other is that there were rumors spread that refugees had a lot of money. Another rumor is that the government gave refugees start-up money to open businesses. Also, there was no support system in the schools or in anything. And the people who were here were not prepared to receive us. Some of them hated us. They were fighting with the young people, the adults too. But those first few years, the refugees were doing well, especially the kids.

AK: Oh, really? Those who came in '79, that group?

SN: Yeah, '79.

AK: What kinds of backgrounds were these Cambodians from? Were they rural or city people?

SN: In '79, a lot of them were educated. The kids had some education back home, so when they got here, they went to high school, they worked very hard. That kind of Asian thing. However, the ones who came in the early '80s were mostly rural people.

AK: It's incredible that the kids did well because I know a lot of them didn't get schooling in the refugee camps and it sounds like the schools here weren't really set up to receive and deal with the new refugees.

SN: They worked very hard. For the first few years, in the high schools in those areas where there were a lot of Asian students, Cambodians and Vietnamese made up the top twenty of most of the graduating classes. The Blacks and Hispanics resented that, too. They said we got scholarships that were meant for them. When these new people came, they took most of the scholarships.

AK: It sounds like there is still some resentment and conflict between the African Americans and the Southeast Asians. Is that still the case here?

SN: Oh, the conflict is still there! There are some high schools where the Asian student population declined to almost nil. They don't want to go there; they get beaten up.

AK: Did a lot of the first group finish high school and go to college?

SN: Yeah, most of them went on to college. They have good jobs now; they make money.

AK: What kinds of jobs do they have?

SN: Some of them are pharmacists, doctors, lawyers.

AK: A lot of professional jobs?

SN: Yeah. Asians are good at . . . they don't speak very good English but they can go to engineering school and are good in math and physics. But there were not a lot of them.

AK: There weren't that many at the beginning but the ones who were there did very well?

SN: Yeah.

AK: What about the parents? What kinds of jobs did they get?

SN: Well, most of them worked very hard to get retrained. A lot of them were professionals before. However, most of them or all of them didn't speak English. Some of them tried to go back to college to get another degree. They were mostly educated families. They did pretty well. Some of them were on public assistance but now most of them aren't.

AK: What kinds of jobs did they retrain for?

SN: Any kind of job. Most of them went into one-year, two-year training programs. But in the end many couldn't use their training. After they've been here for a while they know what they want to do.

AK: You mean they spent time going to school but it didn't really help them?

SN: Not academically, not if they want a job in a particular field. But going to school opened them up to other opportunities that they wouldn't have thought of. Some people were trained in plumbing but went into business, that kind of thing.

AK: So what kinds of jobs did they end up in? I'm talking about those who came before 1980.

SN: Jobs that pay between $8 and $15 an hour, those kinds of job. Some stayed in their jobs for a long time. But a lot of them switched careers after they've been here a while.

AK: In Washington, D.C., I heard that there are a lot of Cambodians who are taxi drivers. What kinds of jobs do Cambodians have here?

SN: It depends. We don't have taxi drivers. But the people went to work in factories, heating and plumbing. Also because Philadelphia is near the South Jersey agricultural area, people work a lot in the fields.

AK: Oh, really? Picking vegetables?

SN: Vegetables, fruits. Doing a lot of that. Even people on public assistance, they do that all the time. It's not the best work.

AK: It's very hard work.

SN: It's hard work and one problem is the pesticides. You know, you are from California where the Mexican workers are working in the fields; there are pesticides and the owners don't care very much.

AK: Are there health problems for people working in the fields?

SN: Yeah. We have those kinds of problems. I saw on TV the same kind of thing in California or in the South; we have that kind of problems, too. But we are trying here at SEAMAAC to educate people about their rights. They should not go to work when they spray the fields. We came from a country that did not have pesticides. You can drink the water from the fields.

AK: Different ways of doing things.

SN: Right. Here, if you do that, you get sick. So, people are not used to that. They get an apple, they eat it. Back home, we don't have pesticides, we don't have chemicals. But here, you have to wash your hands after picking the fruits and before eating. People working in the fields back home, they don't care about hygiene. But here you have to.

AK: It's a very different way of operating.

SN: Yeah. And people forget to wash their hands.

AK: So, are there a large number of Cambodians who are involved in agriculture?

SN: Oh, yes, there are a lot. A lot of them are women. Their husbands are working and they don't want to stay home. We try quite a bit as an organization to help them.

AK: What other types of jobs are possible for women? Do a lot of women work or do most stay at home?

SN: A lot of them work. We have what we call a crew leader, like a factory leader. If the factory contracts out to the group leader, they get workers from the community.

AK: So if the leaders are Cambodian, they'll recruit other Cambodians to work under them?

SN: Yeah. Vietnamese recruit Vietnamese, Laotians Laotians. These people are not illegal either. These people have the right to work. The thing is they get paid cash for that. We try to get them some protection.

AK: You mean, they don't get social security deductions, that kind of thing?

SN: Yeah. But as you know, that's the old American style. The laws apply on demand. But if you make too much noise, it hurts them more than it helps.

AK: It's a fine balancing act.

SN: Yeah.

AK: You mentioned earlier that there was the perception that Asians were getting money from the government to open up businesses. Does that mean there are a lot of Cambodian businesses around here?

SN: There are people of Chinese descent; there are quite a lot of them in business.

AK: So, most of the business owners who are Cambodian are of Chinese ancestry?

SN: Yeah. They speak Cambodian, it's different from Chinese; they cannot mix with the people in Chinatown here.

AK: Do these Chinese Cambodians consider themselves part of the Cambodian community or more a part of the Chinese community?

SN: I would say that they consider themselves Cambodian. But it depends on the circumstance. Sometimes they would say they are Chinese. But most of them have never been to China. They celebrate Chinese New Year, they celebrate Cambodian New Year.

AK: They're both [Chinese and Cambodian]. I heard that not too many Chinese Cambodians escaped directly from Cambodia but they went to France first and then some came here. Do you know anything about that?

SN: Some of them might do it that way but that's the long way.

AK: Most came directly from Cambodia?

SN: Yes.

AK: How did they get the money to open businesses? We know that the government didn't give them a lot of money.

SN: They work together a lot. They borrow from the community.

AK: Rotating credit among friends and family?

SN: Yes. I would say Cambodians, Vietnamese, we do that.

AK: It's a common Asian practice. What percentage of the Cambodian families here are headed by women?

SN: I don't know the percentage, but it's quite a bit.

AK: Fifty percent?

SN: I would say less than that, but might be close to that. Cambodians, their husbands were killed. Women in Asia need men. So the women usually marry some eligible men along the way.

AK: You mean although they may have been widowed, they oftentimes get remarried?

SN: Yeah, so if you have a man or if you are married along the way, then piracy is way down. You are likely to be safer along the way. If you are not married, somebody might harm you. But still there are women who are not married or just with children, or maybe a woman with a few children but the oldest son may be sixteen, seventeen years old, so they have some man in the family.

AK: I know that in general, there are a lot of intergenerational conflicts between parents and children—in all societies—but especially, I've heard, with the Cambodians because of the really different cultural expectations. Do you think that's maybe even more of a problem in families headed by women? In terms of controlling the kids, making sure they don't get involved in gangs, that kind of thing.

SN: I don't think that's necessarily true. I would say that it depends on the sociocultural class status. Farmers, or merchants, or poor farmers, some have their value systems intact, others have lost that.

AK: What determines whether you lose it or are able to maintain it?

SN: They can control their children if it's still intact, although there is always conflict between the new and old generation. The parents want to be in control of the family, but some parents just lose that battle. Nobody knows for sure but I would say that if you are at a certain step in the social hierarchy, you are likely to be able to control your children.

AK: Versus someone who is of a lower socioeconomic status? Why is that?

SN: I would say that the people who are not educated enough, those adults are in a crisis themselves. They cannot get support from anybody for the problems they have. But if you have a certain status, you tend to be able to have friends you can talk to, friends with a certain standard, ideals still there, or cultural values still intact. But let's say some of the people who came from the poor rural areas, they have never been to a big city even in Cambodia. Once they are here, they are lost, completely lost.

AK: So, along they way, they lose control of the children?

SN: Yes. They have never been to school themselves. They don't read or know the language. Even people with education have problems, like myself, I have a son.

AK: How old is your son?

SN: Twenty-four. He's in California. He's at Cal State Long Beach, doing anthropology at school. He originally wanted to do Asian American studies but for some reason he went into anthropology last year. He has problems with one of the teachers and he switched.

AK: What percentage of the youths here are involved in gangs?

SN: We don't know that. We have no statistics. We estimate that at school roughly more than 50 percent drop out.

AK: Really? Because you said the first wave did very well. You're talking now about the current situation?

SN: Yeah.

AK: About 50 percent are dropping out?

SN: The reason they are dropping out is that they are joining gangs, there's truancy, delinquency. The gangs are not always out to hurt anybody, some of them, it's just to have fun. They just don't want to go to school because they hate school.

AK: I've heard a lot of people say that kids are placed in grades that aren't appropriate for them and they get more and more discouraged at school and that's one reason they join the gangs.

SN: That's true, too, to a certain extent, but there is also racism, there are all kinds of things. One of the things I see is that the family is not able to support the kids. The parents, they are working. Some of them might be on public assistance but they still work on the side, and they leave the kids at home, and there's a lot of temptation. Young girls growing up, young boys growing up watching TV and the parents are not there. The parents need to support the children, take care of the children when they come back from school.

AK: The children need more supervision and guidance.

SN: Yeah. We don't have that, because people tend to, once they get here, encounter so many temptations. They want a new car, they want this, they want that. If you work hard, you get it, but in the process of getting what you want, you may have lost something more important.

AK: You alluded to the fact that there are some Cambodians on public assistance. What percentage would you say are on public assistance?

SN: I don't know. People tend to ask that. The percentage, I have no idea. Maybe 40 percent.

AK: You said many of those people are working on the side. What's the attitude toward public assistance? For example, is there a stigma or is there a feeling that the U.S. government owes them, that they deserve to get public assistance?

SN: They're not educated; they're in an environment that is not conducive to work. They have big families and they're not skilled enough to get the high-paying jobs with health benefits. They're smart; they're up for that. We discussed that a lot, why do they take the government's handout? It's a question of having no choice.

AK: There's no better alternative.

SN: Yeah. Public assistance is the best alternative. The government has to understand that when you don't speak the language, move to a new country, and you don't know anything, you don't have any skills, and there's public assistance, something more sure, more permanent, and there are only jobs that pay more or less . . .

AK: The minimum wage.

SN: Yeah. And you are likely to be laid off, there are no health benefits for the children, which choice do you make?

AK: Is it acceptable, then, in the Cambodian community, for people to get public assistance?

SN: There are always people who, Cambodian or Vietnamese, who work and who look down on people who receive public assistance. They don't earn any more than those people who are on public assistance. You see what I mean? People still have pride; there are still people who have pride. Even the parents who are on public assistance try to get their children to go to college.

AK: I heard someone say that for some parents they think because they don't have skills, can't speak English, they can stay on public assistance but there's the expectation that the kids will get jobs and move on. Do you see that? Or is it OK for the kids to continue on public assistance?

SN: It depends on the parents. It depends on the kids too, their level of education. Those who drop out of school early before they finish high school, get pregnant, have children, they'll probably remain on public assistance.

AK: They're perpetuating the cycle.

SN: But those kids who finish high school, go to community college or to a four-year college, those children can move on.

AK: Is there a big problem with teenage pregnancies?

SN: Yeah.

AK: What percentage of the kids are getting pregnant?

SN: Most of them, if they get pregnant, get married. Say, your daughter and my son, in high school, they like each other. Usually, the parents get them married. Since the kids like each other, that helps quite a bit, because the parents support them. But the main problem is that the kids don't finish school.

AK: So what happens to all those kids who don't graduate from high school?

SN: Most of them work, they work in the fields. Some of them become criminals.

AK: You've told me a little about the early group and the kinds of jobs they had. With the refugees who came in the '80s, the sense I am getting is that a large percent, maybe 40 percent, are on public assistance and then the rest are doing the same kind of work that the earlier group are doing, like plumbing or working in the fields. Is that correct? Do they pretty much have the same kinds of jobs as the earlier wave of Cambodians?

SN: The first group were more professional people. Although a lot of them don't speak English they have some skills; they switch jobs, move around for the better. It seems that all over the country, they have networks of friends. "Where is the best place to earn money?"

AK: So people move around a lot?

SN: People move around a lot.

AK: Where do they move to? Do people move here too?

SN: Yeah, people move here from California, also from here to California.

AK: Is that the big destination, California? Between California and Philadelphia, back and forth?

SN: I would say California, Boston, Rhode Island and that area. I think more people are moving in than out.

AK: More moving in than out? Is that because of the public assistance benefits here?

SN: No, I think because of the jobs, because of the job market. Under-the-table job market.

AK: Like picking fruits and vegetables?

SN: There are a lot of people coming to work just during the summer.

AK: How many Cambodians are there in this area?

SN: We estimate between seven thousand and twelve thousand.

AK: And how many were originally settled here? I'm trying to get a sense of how many people have come here through secondary migration and how many have moved out versus the ones who originally settled here.

SN: I have no idea, but my feeling is more are coming in than going out.

AK: So, for example, maybe eight thousand were settled here originally and then more came?

SN: Yes, something like that.

AK: In terms of the areas they live in, you mentioned that initially people were placed in lower-income areas where the housing was affordable. Have the Cambodians tended to stay in those areas or are they moving to better neighborhoods?

SN: Oh, they move; they move out.

AK: So people move around to different neighborhoods, to move up.

SN: Yes. They buy homes, usually where friends are.

AK: I know we're running short of time, but another question I wanted to ask you is, in other places, I've heard that another reason people aren't able to work, in addition to language problems, is the trauma these people experienced during Pol Pot's time. Do you see that as a big problem among the Cambodians that you work with?

SN: I heard a lot about people who lost their sight.

AK: Or just not being able to concentrate or focus.

SN: I don't know. I tend to suspect those.

AK: You mean maybe it's not really true?

SN: They might be real in some cases. People do a lot of things to stay on benefits, certain benefits. I haven't been through it [the Khmer Rouge regime] so I couldn't say.

AK: Can you tell me about how this agency was started and how you get your funding?

SN: We started in the early '80s. In 1984 this agency was born out of necessity, a coalition of five groups: Cambodian, Vietnamese, Laotian, Hmong, and ethnic Chinese. And the reason we became this organization was because of the funding problem. The federal government and the foundations, they want to give us money but they don't want to give it to the small MAAs.

AK: Oh really? Is the Pennsylvania state refugee coordinator saying they don't want to give money to the small MAAs?

SN: They don't say that but that's understood.

AK: In other states they do fund the small MAAs directly from the state.

SN: Different states have different funding programs. Pennsylvania is one of the worst. I was president of the Cambodian MAA. The presidents of the five MAAs are on the board [of SEAMAAC]. There are four non-MAA persons, so in all we have nine.

AK: There are nine people on the board?

SN: The reason is that we don't want the American-born or any single group to control SEAMAAC. The presidency of SEAMAAC is rotating: first year Vietnamese, second year Cambodian, that's the way it works.

AK: Is it a one-year term?

SN: It's a one-year term. And since it's that way, we have grown a lot. This year we have a budget pretty close to $1 million.

AK: How do the services you provide differ from the ones the Cambodian MAA provides?

SN: For example, the maternity program for pregnant women, the amount of money from each grant is almost $200,000. It's to serve the five groups. The funders don't like to give to five different groups. They want to give just to SEAMAAC to serve all five. The Cambodian association, in contrast, has different programs, but they serve only one group.

AK: Was the purpose of SEAMAAC to serve everybody or to give money to the different MAAs?

SN: To serve everybody, not to give away money.

AK: Do you get any money from the State Refugee Coordinator's Office?
SN: Yes.

AK: How about private foundations?

SN: Yeah, on and off. The last two or three years, we've gotten money from the federal, state, and city governments, and from foundations.

AK: Do you offer ESL (English as a second language)?

SN: Yeah, we do that but the MAAs also do that.

AK: How would a person decide whether to go here or to the Cambodian MAA?

SN: On the ESL thing, we are funded by the state. We provide teachers to the MAAs, not money. Teachers, so they can have classes. There is also a class here at SEAMAAC. At SEAMAAC you don't have to be Cambodian, you can be any nationality, including Korean, Japanese. The Cambodian MAA, they have services just for Cambodians. They get funding from foundations for programs that are more suitable for Cambodians.

AK: How many Cambodians do you serve on average?

SN: I think the number one clients are Cambodians. Cambodians are more needy.

AK: What kinds of services are they most involved in?

SN: It's mostly the health project.

AK: Like prenatal care, that kind of thing?

SN: Yes, immunization and AIDS education. We're working with the kids, the schools, that kind of thing.

AK: Do you do anything like cultural preservation?

SN: Very little. That is one component we don't want to do. We cannot do all five.

AK: You leave it to the MAAs.

SN: Yeah. We have little things, like one component of programs. But the big ones, the MAAs do their own.

AK: I went to the Indochinese Center in Washington and they said that since no new Southeast Asian refugees have come in recently, they're not serving very many Southeast Asians any more. But it sounds like rather than doing things like ESL, you're turning to ongoing projects like health.

SN: ESL is still going on. There are a lot of people who're not able to speak the language and we're trying to help them.

AK: You have a youth program too? Is that to curb the gang activity?

SN: Yeah, we do quite a bit of those things, but it's something that's very difficult. It's kind of like a flood. The organization doesn't have the resources to deal with that.

AK: I know you have another appointment, so we'll end now. Thank you so much for talking to me.

August 8, 1995

8. Sam-Ang Sam
The Cambodian Network Council

Dr. Sam-Ang Sam is currently a visiting scholar at the National Museum of Ethnology in Osaka, Japan. He was the executive director of the Cambodian Network Council (CNC) when Audrey Kim interviewed him on August 7, 1995, in his office in Washington, D.C. He left that post in 1996 to return to Cambodia to continue his efforts to revive Khmer classical dance and music. Regardless of where his home base is, Dr. Sam and his wife, the classical Khmer dancer Chan Moly Sam, constantly travel around the world to visit diasporic Cambodian communities in order to interest young people in the Khmer performing arts. In an effort to improve the quality of performances, the couple not only takes performers on tour but also teaches master classes. For most Cambodians, these performing arts, along with Theravada Buddhism and certain social norms, define Khmer national identity.

After receiving musical training at the Royal University of Fine Arts in Phnom Penh, Dr. Sam was sent by the Cambodian government to study at the Conservatory of Music in the Philippines. The Khmer Rouge came to power while he was there. Thus, he was one of the thousands of Cambodians who were outside their homeland and became stateless persons with the sudden change in government in Cambodia. Dr. Sam was admitted into the United States as a refugee, filling one of the five thousand slots set aside for Cambodians during the April 1975 evacuations from Phnom Penh and Saigon. Three days after he arrived in the United States he found a job in Philadelphia, where he and his brother helped to establish the first Cambodian community organization in that city. After working in Philadelphia for two years, he moved to Atlantic City, New Jersey, where he lived and worked for a year.

When he decided to continue his education, he enrolled at Wesleyan University in Connecticut, which awarded him a Ph.D. in ethnomusicology in 1988. The title of his dissertation is "The *Pin Peat* Ensemble: Its History, Music, and Context." The pin peat ensemble is a very old and versatile Khmer musical form. Dr. Sam's pioneering study explores how the pin peat ensemble emerged historically, its social and musical roles, the contexts in which it is played, and its musical characteristics and repertoire. The study ends with a discussion of how political developments, both in Cambodia and within Cambodian diasporic communities around the world, have affected Khmer music. Sam-Ang Sam has also published numerous articles about Khmer music.

After getting his Ph.D., Dr. Sam taught at a number of universities, including a three-year stint at the University of Washington in Seattle. He then moved to California and served as the folk arts coordinator at the Fresno Art Council. He moved once again, this time to Washington, D.C., when he was chosen as the executive director of the CNC. He was awarded a "genius grant" by the MacArthur Foundation in 1995 for his musical accomplishments as well as for his community leadership.

Despite the wonderful work the Cambodian Network Council was doing, it lost its funding in the late 1990s and no longer maintains an office in Washington, D.C. It now operates out of the offices of the Cambodian Mutual Assistance Association of Greater Philadelphia. Even more regrettably, the Cambodian-American National Development Organization (CANDO), which the CNC had helped establish, has folded. During CANDO's six-year existence, it enabled almost one hundred young people of Cambodian ancestry, eighty-seven of whom were Cambodian Americans, to spend one or more years in Cambodia as volunteers in much the same way that U.S. Peace Corps volunteers try to be of service in various countries around the world. The CNC itself still exists and is trying to maintain the network that had been built among Cambodian organizations in the United States.

*　　*　　*

AK: Can you start by telling me a little bit about this organization and how it was founded?

SS: This is a national organization called the Cambodian Network Council. It is perhaps the strongest or the largest in terms of membership among all the Cambodian organizations in the U.S. It was formed in 1988 by a group of Cambodians who, at that time, could be considered community leaders. They formed this organization with a need in mind—that Cambodians need to be coordinated and to work together, that we need some mechanism to enable us to coalesce with one another. This is an educational, social, cultural, and charitable organization; it's a nonpolitical group. Perhaps when you talk to politicians they would say that CNC is also a political organization because of the size of its membership and the fact that individuals on the board of directors represent a lot of political interests. For example, our former president was the president of a political party who ran in the election in 1993, and things like that. But, in fact, we try to be as neutral as possible, and the reason is once an organization has a tendency to support or to ally with a given party, you lose broad support. So the principle of this organization is to stay neutral. CNC mainly provides technical assistance and leadership to its members, which are MAAs [mutual assistance associations] across the nation. Also we have a skills bank, a database of Cambodian professionals and experts in America, the only Cambodian organization that has that. We are doing a lot of referrals as well. One of the mandates of this organization, with the agreement of, perhaps the imposition by, our members, is not to provide direct services. We are not, for example, providing translators for people going to court, taking people to the hospital, or providing ESL [English-as-a-second-language] classes. We do not do anything like that because when it comes to funding, we cannot compete against our own members. For that reason, we don't offer any direct service; direct service is the work that the local MAAs are doing.

AK: Direct service is not part of your mission.

SS: That's right. We also have another program, a cultural program to preserve and promote Cambodian culture. We arrange for performances. We have brought people from other parts of the country for residencies, conferences. We also have overseas programs. Right now we have four programs in Cambodia: one is our volunteer program similar to the Peace Corps called CANDO [Cambodian American National Development Organization]. The project is funded by the USAID [United States Agency for International Development] through PACT [Private Agencies Collaborating Together]. We are sending volunteers to work in Cambodia, placing them with departments or ministries of the Cambodian Royal Government or with NGOs [nongovernmental organizations]. In particular, we are interested in the development of, or the strengthening of, the foundation of indigenous NGOs in Cambodia. We have projects, mentorship-apprenticeship programs, with the Royal University of Fine Arts. We have a library development program with the university and we have the Khmer Artists Support Project with the Department of Arts and Performing Arts in Cambodia. So those are the things we are doing. Another significant path that CNC is following is serving as a bridge between the local MAAs—or serving as a representative of our local communities—and the mainstream service providers.

AK: You have so many different activities that you're involved in. Would you say that the bulk of your activities are domestically oriented or centered in Cambodia or is it about half and half?

SS: OK, I have to go through our history a little bit. The organization was developed to sustain, to help strengthen Cambodian refugees in the United States. So, it was local and domestic in nature. But if you're looking at today's operations in terms of our finances, we have about $1 million [of projects] in Cambodia. Over here, it's about a quarter of a million in operations under our domestic program. So, if you are looking at the size of the programs and the expenses of the programs, the emphasis is over there. Still, the main ideas and the goals and mission of the organization, I think, are domestic. I think we have, in a way, shifted to Cambodia because of our concern for the reconstruction and rehabilitation of Cambodia.

AK: You talked about trying to promote and preserve the arts and Cambodian heritage. Do you try to foster programs domestically or do you bring over artists from Cambodia to do performances?

SS: Both. There are three things. One is local residencies and local teaching programs. For example, I am involved with the organization here called Cambodian American Heritage. It is perhaps the most solid cultural organization here in terms of the qualification of the teachers and the number of students and also the frequency of activities which we're involved in. I coordinate artists, in fact, across the country. I have a database of artists who can serve as resources so we know what we have in this country: residencies, performances, video productions. This week I'm filming a documentary. That's one component. Another component is CNC's support for programs in Cambodia. There, we have the Mentorship-Apprenticeship Program and the Khmer Artists Support Project. The third component we have is the cultural exchange program. For the past five years, we have brought artists from Cambodia for residencies here. As we speak, CNC is bringing five administrators, musicians, and dancers for six weeks of study at the Jacob's Pillow Dance Festival. And then last year we did what we call a reverse flow. We sent master artists from here to Cambodia to provide master classes and also to work on collaborative projects, like creation of new choreographies and things like that.

AK: As I understand it, during the Pol Pot period many artists, dancers, were killed. So, has it been difficult to find people to even continue this sort of tradition?

SS: We have suffered in the quality of performance in terms of the skill of musicians and dancers but in terms of numbers we are recovering. Now we have more people practicing the arts than ever before. But it will take maybe five years, ten years from now for them to reach the quality level of teachers in the past.

AK: You mentioned that you don't provide any direct services to people in the metro D.C. area. Who is providing those services to Cambodians?

SS: The local organizations. We have, according to our list, more than twenty Cambodian MAAs, local organizations here, more than twenty. They provide those kinds of services. For example, the temple provides cultural classes, it also provides language classes. Then we have other organizations that provide translation at the court, at the hospital. The resettlement agencies are also providing that. On top of that, the refugees in the metro D.C. area are not the same as refugees in Long Beach, California. They are not the same as refugees in Lowell, Massachusetts. There are more professionals here. The more educated refugees are here.

AK: So they don't need as many services?

SS: Yeah, that's true. And if there are needs, sometimes we have an ad hoc meeting and we step in and help those in need.

AK: In addition to being a membership organization for MAAs, do you provide funding for the MAAs at all?

SS: We do not provide funding to them, but we provide technical assistance. For example, it's not like cash, real cash, but if, let's say, an organization has a problem with the board. There's a misunderstanding between the staff and the board. They call us and we'll send someone—if they have money, they pay for the cost, if they don't, we provide that. Because of the size of the membership we have, we can do that. Let's say we ask one member, an expert on a given area, like fundraising, from California and a member from Chicago. But we do not give direct cash. On top of that, we help them write proposals. We tell them where the funding sources are, where the foundations are and all that, what is available. And when we see announcements that they might not see because they are local, we tell them about it. We are national, we receive a lot of things, so we let them know. We also have contacts with other national organizations. When they send us things, we inform our member associations. So we help them that way.

AK: You really provide a lot of information and technical assistance. Do you have some sort of newsletter?

SS: We do, yes. We have a quarterly newsletter that we put out.

AK: Where do you get your funding from?

SS: For the domestic programs, we are funded by the ORR [Office of Refugee Resettlement].

AK: They fund you to be the umbrella organization?

SS: That's right, exactly. And the overseas program is funded by USAID through PACT.

AK: Do you get any contributions from other Cambodians or from the Cambodian community at all or is it all from ORR and the federal government?

SS: We have others. We have quite a few grants aside from that. For example, when we have projects like the cultural project, we get money from the Rockefeller Foundation, the United Board for Christian Higher Education in Asia, the Albert Kunstadter Family Foundation, NIPAD [the National Initiative to Preserve American Dance], from the Illinois Arts Council, from the NEA [National Endowment for the Arts].

AK: So, in addition to your main sources of funding, you have funding from other sources to provide monies for specific programs. Going back to the CANDO project, can you tell me a little bit more about that? How was it started and what has happened with the project?

SS: CANDO was developed with the idea that we should provide assistance to postwar reconstruction and development projects in Cambodia. As you know, the war and the Khmer Rouge destroyed the infrastructure—in fact, practically everything in Cambodia. CANDO was developed with the goal of providing services the way the Peace Corps does. At the initial stage we even called it Peace Corps for Cambodia or Cambodian Peace Corps. It was developed with the involvement of the Cambodian Students Association of America. They helped us collaborate with some of the community leaders working with USAID. That's how it started. We also wanted to provide outlets for Cambodian Americans, particularly the younger ones who just graduated from college, who want to help their people in Cambodia.

AK: How long has the program been in existence?

SS: Three years.

AK: Has there been much interest on the part of the young Cambodian community?

SS: Oh, yeah! We have a lot of applicants. We are sending another team in September.

AK: How many have you sent to date?

SS: Let me see, sixty, seventy volunteers so far.

AK: What sorts of projects are they involved in?

SS: All kinds, from health to education to economics. Art, archeology, agriculture, even English instruction, computer science. We place them. Some are teaching at the Faculty of Archeology, some are teaching at the Institute of Economics, or Institute of Technology. Some are working on immunization and other health programs, all kinds.

AK: That program is also funded by USAID?

SS: Yes.

AK: In addition to helping Cambodia rebuild through this program, is one purpose to help young Cambodian Americans get a better sense of their heritage and their cultural identity?

SS: Yes. These young volunteers go back to Cambodia because they want to be in touch with their own roots, their own people, their own community. A lot of them left Cambodia when they were young, and so, in a way, it's a renewal of their culture. And for them, I think they feel obligated to help their own people as they have had the opportunity to come to this country to live, to go to school, and since they have gained something, they want to give back, to help their old country. I think it's very, very significant.

AK: You alluded earlier to the fact that Cambodians in the metro D.C. area are different from Cambodians in other parts of the country. Can you tell me a bit more about that, starting from the resettlement pattern? First of all, have you been in this area long?

SS: I have been here for about three years now, but I have come to D.C. for the past fifteen years every year, every single year.

AK: So, you understand the development of the Cambodian community here.

SS: Yeah, because I'm also a performer by training, a musician, I travel across the country; I mean I travel everywhere. And I have worked with the community a long time, ever since I came to this country. In fact, my brother and I and other friends created the first Cambodian Association in Philadelphia and it still exists today. You know, over here, the Hill is here, the White House is here, the Pentagon is here; everything the American establishment controls is here. We have to understand that a lot of Cambodians are intimidated by the fact that it's a very urban area. Most of the Cambodian refugees are from rural areas. There were two waves of refugees coming to this country. One, coming during the mid-seventies included professionals, more educated people, officials, students, government officials and the like. Those who fled the first wave out of Cambodia . . .

AK: Was this before the Khmer Rouge took over? Or right around that time?

SS: Around that time, some before the takeover by the Khmer Rouge and some right after, immediately after. They were more sophisticated, I think, and figured out how to get out and had the vision that there was a need to get out. The third wave came around the early '80s. And that is because the Khmer Rouge were deposed in '79. So there began another influx to the refugee camps and those included a lot of rural farmer and peasants, I mean farmers and peasants in a good sense, I'm not saying this in a negative way. Because by 1980, a lot of educated people, city-dwellers, had been killed off. The Cambodians now in the U.S. who are, I guess, a little more sophisticated tend to stay away from the larger communities. They go to work there, go in to help, but don't want to live there. The reason is that a lot of times there is an image—we care about the image—of gang problems, something that we are not proud of, drugs, divorce, spousal abuse, child abuse, you name it, all of those things, gambling and all of that. I think the more educated people who have more responsibility do not like that.

AK: I want to make sure I understand. What I'm getting from what you're saying is that the more educated, sophisticated Cambodians tend to not live within the larger Cambodian communities but try to integrate into the American community, live among other Americans, and have more mainstream jobs.

SS: Yes, for several reasons. For example, in Long Beach, they would not live on Anaheim Street. They would go to live in Cerritos, go to live in Tustin, but they come and work for the agencies. They have organizations, they have workplaces within the community and they work for them. But they don't want to go and drink or spend time in the nightclubs, or fight in the gang. That is not a good image for us. At the same time, we feel a responsibility as Cambodians. When you do something, it's not only as an individual but as a Cambodian, so you want to do it well. For that reason, we cannot afford to be isolated from the mainstream. I mean, we are here to stay. Although we are recent immigrants or refugees, we are here to stay. You have to be competitive to be part of the mainstream.

AK: But also still wanting to give back to the Cambodian community?

SS: Exactly. They cannot be ignored because they are our people. If they do badly or if they do bad things, it also reflects on us. When I go anywhere I am still a Cambodian, although I am a U.S. citizen. Over here, what can an unsophisticated or uneducated Cambodian do here in D.C.? What can they do? We don't want to give a value judgment about jobs; every job is important. But you have to be able to survive, to handle yourself in situations.

AK: I have a question. It sounds like Washington, D.C. is a big magnet for these more sophisticated, educated Cambodians. Why is Washington such a big magnet?

SS: For us, for example, to have an office here, it was intentional. In order to do anything, you have to be in Washington because you have to have your profile there all the time. When you need to go to the White House for briefings, you can go, step on the Metro and go. And we do go to hearings, testimonies on the Hill. The big institutions and government offices are practically all here. The Cambodian embassy is here in Washington. So, it is very, very important that we be located here. A lot of people say, "Hey, while you live in America, you go to the heart of it." You go to where everything is if you want to stay active and involved. If you want to kind of sit back and retire, then you can go to Florida. Or you can go to Seattle, where it's peaceful, more peaceful.

AK: I can understand that from an organizational perspective, but for just an average Cambodian person who has a professional job, I'm still not sure I understand why Washington is a big draw.

SS: It's not really a big draw in that sense. For example, a lot of Cambodians get stuck. Cambodians, we usually, when we go somewhere, we stay there. Secondary migration happens only if we have friends, like in California. If you are not really independent, then you move. But if you are independent enough, even if you have relatives somewhere else, you don't want to move. Once you get settled, you want to stay there. You want to establish your roots. You don't want to sell a house and move. So, a lot of people here are those who have been here as students or as government officials. They have been here for thirty years. Lany Lang, for example, she has been here for over thirty years, a long time. And there are other people who've been here for twenty-five years. I moved here because of the job. I've lived in Connecticut, I've lived in Seattle, I've lived in California. But I'm an exception to the rule because I travel a lot. The reason I say it's not really an attractive place to many Cambodians, although I say a lot of the more educated and sophisticated Cambodians are here, is because in the metro D.C. area we have maybe five thousand Cambodians only. Not a whole lot, compared to thirty thousand in Lowell alone. I just came back yesterday from Lowell. After the conference we were taken to a restaurant and all you see are gangs, nightclubs, singing, drinking, all the things you don't find here.

AK: What are some areas of metro D.C. where you find the most Cambodians? Or are they scattered everywhere?

SS: Silver Spring is one. Arlington, Virginia; Fairfax, Virginia; Clarendon, the Reston area, around that area.

AK: Why are those areas popular?

SS: I don't really know why. I think, first of all, it's closer to the workplace and perhaps the housing is still cheap compared to D.C. For example, many people wouldn't be able to afford housing in D.C. And if you go to Frederick, for example, that's too far for them to find jobs.

AK: I see two distinct groups, the first wave and the later wave of refugees who came over later. Where did the later wave of Cambodians settle or did they settle in the same places you mentioned?

SS: You mean nationally?

AK: No, in this area.

SS: In this area, they are in Silver Spring, Arlington, Fairfax.

AK: Were those areas in which they were placed by the resettlement agencies?

SS: It started like that, something like that, yes.

AK: What I'm trying to understand is whether once they've been settled they tend to move around within the metro D.C. area or, as you mentioned, they pretty much stayed put in the locations where they were initially placed.

SS: They stay put. You know, sometimes people get affected by the environment, by the neighborhood. We have some gang problems, but compared to Lowell, compared to Fresno, compared to Long Beach, it's much less here. Runaways and the intergenerational gap, that affects even the educated families.

AK: It seems like a lot of those problems you'd find in any community in the U.S., but sometimes acculturation issues magnify problems like the intergenerational gap. Also it seems like you probably have less of a gang problem here just because you have fewer young Cambodians. So, is it a numbers issue, do you think? I'd like, if you don't mind, you to elaborate more about some of these problems that you see in this community, although, granted, they aren't as big problems as in other parts of the country.

SS: I think on the specific problems, Lany would be more qualified to discuss them because she's dealing directly with clients, and I don't deal directly with a given refugee who has a problem. For example, if certain refugees give me a call, we look into that. I could help them on a personal basis or I could refer them. If it's mental health, I refer them to Lany, if it's other cases, I refer them to different people. On specific cases, I don't think I can give you information.

AK: I understand that you're not working directly with clients, but I am interested in your perspective, a sort of macro perspective based on what you hear from the MAAs. You alluded to some of the problems that you've heard about like the gangs, intergenerational issues, that kind of thing. Can you tell me a little bit about that?

SS: In a way, I think it's just like any other ethnic group—the misunderstandings, for example, when the parents are coming here, particularly those who have a language barrier and cannot cope. When the children are learning a different culture and they are having problems communicating and there is a misunderstanding, for the traditional families who adhere to the traditional ways, practicing the customs and all that, they turn into conflicts with one another, with the young ones saying, "Hey, this is a free country; my friends are going out at night; they drink, they smoke, they drive at sixteen, they date." That creates a problem. The loss of traditional values for the old is a significant loss. It's very important that we give some respect to others. The young call people by their first names. They say "Hi" instead of bowing. So it is very difficult. Also I think when people come here, particularly the later-wave refugees, the fathers lose their traditional role as father. In Cambodia, fathers were breadwinners. The mothers were housewives, in a good sense, not in a bad sense; a lot of people think that the word *housewife* is bad. I used to say to my wife, "Please make me a househusband; I'll stay at home and cook, you go to work." It's the way a person conducts himself or herself, the way you behave, the way you do things, that makes you good or bad, high or low. It's not being a househusband or whatever, it makes no difference to me because I know who I am, I know what I can do. Over here, when they come here, the father is on welfare, the kids say, "Hey, he's not working. He needs support and when he needs to go to the hospital, I, the son, I'll have to translate for him." You see the reverse of everything and it becomes problematic. The fathers have no pride any more because they are not providing the things and services they used to, that traditional fathers used to. That becomes a problem. We had traumatic experiences back home, mistrust, so when you come here and you don't speak the language, that puts you back a few squares, a few squares back. The system over here is not like the system in our country. There, they do not treat you according to what you know but according to your age. In Cambodia when I was young I used to go out with friends who were twenty years older than I was, and it was OK. When you do things together, you know, you have the same interests, you can hang out together. Over here, no. A sixteen-year-old, even if that person does not speak English and did not go to school because during Pol Pot they did not go to school and at the refugee camps they did not go to school, coming here, they still have to play the sixteen-year-old. For example, sixteen would be tenth, eleventh grade. A lot of times, they are laughed at by their peers. They have a lot of pressure. When they come home, sometimes parents who do not have any education do not really support them. They do not get involved with the homework; they could not get involved with the homework even if they wanted to. So, a lot of pressure. Sometimes when you speak

English, people imitate you [to make fun of you], so, joining a gang is a solution. When they turn to someone, the someone who can provide support are gang members.

AK: It's a way to find a sense of belonging.

SS: Belonging and respect. And that's what the gangs are doing, these negative things that these gangs are doing could be out-of-control things. But I still think that the initial impetus—it's not that I'm encouraging gang activity—is that we have to understand why they did it or where they came from. They have no support. They think they are failures in school, so that's why we have gangs.

AK: So, what is happening to these young people? They're not, obviously, able to make it through the school system. Are they able to get jobs?

SS: We hope. We hope that they could still be helped by programs. That's why the local community agencies are creating programs to help them. For example, gang intervention and gang prevention programs, drawing gang members into activities instead of killing, coming to play basketball together, providing them with some form, some kind of training. Perhaps they can go out and look for jobs. We can give them some kind of love and care and support: "We are your big brothers, we still care for you; you are also Cambodians and we want you to be someone out there in the real world, we still have solutions for you." So we are still hoping, trying to do that.

AK: What percentage of the young people would you say are involved in gangs?

SS: Very small in fact. Very small percentage.

AK: For most of the young people, how are they doing in school? Are they making it through high school, going on to college?

SS: For Cambodians, I think, not as many as I would like to see. When I taught at the University of Washington, we had about thirty Cambodian students at the University of Washington. Looking at the total number of Cambodians, Seattle has about seven thousand; Tacoma about five thousand; the entire state about fifteen thousand. To me, thirty among fifteen thousand was a very low number. I'd like to see more than that, I'd like to see young people show more interest in getting higher education. But I did talk to those students a lot to ask them why they leave school. They said that they want to enjoy their life when they're young. That's number one. Number two, they said that they want to make some money and start a family first and then go back to school. A lot of times, if you don't have support from your family, you don't go to school unless you are super-conscious about education and have a very strong determination to have a very long, far vision of your future.

AK: You mentioned that the young people said, "I want to enjoy my life now." Do you think that relates to the suffering during the Pol Pot years—the realization you could be killed anytime? Does that relate to wanting to maybe enjoy life now rather than investing in the future?

SS: No. I think it's a matter of priorities. Again it has to do with what they see in their environment. People are so easily attracted and persuaded by things like new cars, nice houses, and nice dresses. Sometimes if you don't have anything and someone else drives a sports car, you ask, "What's wrong with me? Why do I drive an old Chevy, you know?"

AK: It's related to the materialism of this culture.

SS: Materialist culture and also what your friends are doing. And I guess enjoying yourself, this is the satisfaction, the priority. When I came here, I was a little older than those kids. My brother had a house and was driving a new car; he had money. I did not have money. I got a job three days after landing in America, after three days here I started working. I made, at that time, $24,000 or $25,000 a year. But I left my job. I asked myself, "Is this something I want to do the rest of my life?" And the answer to that was "No." So I gave up all that and I went to school. My priorities, my determination, and what gives me satisfaction, were different from these youngsters. I wanted to have a higher degree. My satisfaction was not a new car. If I can publish an article, publish a book, then I would be satisfied. I would be happy that way. So, people are different, but I did not go through Pol Pot. I left Cambodia before the fall of Cambodia. I have been a student all my life, so maybe I do not really see some things.

AK: I've heard that for Cambodians, for the young people, they have pressure from their families to support their families and not go to school. Do you see that a lot?

SS: That's true a lot. Particularly, women are told, "You don't want to get married at thirty or thirty-five, you want to get married at twenty, twenty-five, perhaps." And some people push their daughters to marry even earlier. I mentioned that having a family first and going to school is what some people say they'll do, but experience shows [once they're married] it's much less likely that they continue. Very, very less likely. When you are away from school for a while, you don't want to go back to school. You are caught up with the material world of making money. You have to make payments, your mortgage, you cannot go back to school. There are exceptions, but by and large . . .

AK: Even among mainstream American families, studies show that if your parents went to college, you're more likely to go to college. The phenomenon that you're describing among young Cambodians, are you finding that among children from more educated families, they tend to go to college in greater numbers?

SS: That is so true. Among my friends, all their kids go to college. It's almost automatic that after high school they go to college. After the B.A. maybe they work for a while but they have at least an undergraduate degree. The majority, if not all, of the gang members are from broken families, uneducated families. They don't have role models. They don't have anything to look up to. My children already have experienced pressure. They told me, "Dad, don't do too much, because when you do too much you give us pressure because then we are measured by your yardstick." Even though they jokingly told me that, [it's apparent] they already feel pressure to do this, do that.

AK: The media has made some comparisons: "Vietnamese children do so well in school; they do much better than other Southeast Asians." Do you think that that's really just a matter of class differences?

SS: We used to say that as well, but it's not always true. It's conditions; I talk a lot about that because I'm an advocate of education. When I talk to Cambodian students, I say, "Look at the Vietnamese community." At the University of Washington when I was there, there were only thirty Cambodians, but I was told there were six hundred Vietnamese at that school. And the Vietnamese population there, maybe there were ten thousand in Seattle, only three thousand more than the Cambodians, but the student populations are so different. And I ask, "How come?" The students say that the conditions are different. The Vietnamese didn't have the kind of experiences that we had. Their families were not killed by Pol Pot. They were not in the refugee camps like the Cambodians. I mean, some of them were in the refugee camps but, look at the media, they talk about the "boat people," so perhaps people pay more attention to them. I think by nature the Vietnamese perhaps are also more aggressive. So those are the different conditions. The Hmong used to be regarded as a tribal people and until recently you hardly saw any Hmong at all who were successful. But the Hmong now, the Hmong are becoming very successful. They've produced Ph.D.s, they've produced M.D.s, and their organizations are stronger than many other organizations. They want to get ahead, they want to erase the perception that Hmong are tribal and primitive. That's right. And some of them also, I think, came to this country with some money and gold.

AK: Along these lines, do you think maybe in a few generations there won't be any difference between Cambodians and Vietnamese in terms of the educational level?

SS: In terms of numbers, there will be a difference because they [the Vietnamese] have more people in this country. So, in terms of numbers, they have more kids in school, they have more Ph.D.s, they have more professionals than Cambodians.

AK: You mentioned earlier that there are some families on welfare. Can you estimate what percentage of Cambodians in this area are on some sort of public assistance?

SS: I have no idea.

AK: Do you have a sense of what percentage of households are headed by women? You said a lot of the men were killed leaving a lot of widows.

SS: Yeah, but I can't give you a number. Why, even the U.S. census is off, it is wrong.

AK: Can you tell me what kinds of jobs Cambodians have in this area? You mentioned there are professionals, educated people.

SS: We have Cambodians working at the Pentagon. We have people working for Sears Roebuck, for the county, driving cabs here, all kinds of jobs, and some people own stores.

AK: In terms of the people who have their own businesses, what kinds of businesses do they have?

SS: Jewelry stores, grocery stores, laundries, landscaping business, roofing, restaurants—but not a whole lot of restaurants.

AK: Where do they get the capital to start these businesses?

SS: A lot of times they pool capital from siblings, families. Some people, I think, save up.

AK: Do you know whether these businesses are owned by ethnic Chinese or are they owned by ethnic Khmer?

SS: What do you mean by ethnic Chinese?

AK: Cambodian Chinese.

SS: It's very difficult to say. I also have Chinese blood, you know. Grocery stores or jewelry stores here, if I talk about specific stores, they are owned by Chinese Cambodians. But it's very difficult to find a really pure Cambodian. Whether 50 percent, 30 percent, or 10 percent Chinese, many Cambodians have some Chinese blood.

AK: There's a lot of Chinese blood in the Cambodians?

SS: Yes.

AK: You mentioned that you haven't actually gone through the Khmer Rouge period, but for people who have, I know they are suffering from a lot of trauma and PTSD [posttraumatic stress disorder]. How are people dealing with the trauma? I know Asians don't tend to go to psychologists.

SS: That is true and we are very resistant, in fact. Resistant. The word *psychologist* or *mental health* is really bad if you want to translate that into Cambodian. We don't want to be associated with those terms. The term *mental health* is sometimes translated as "crazy." It would be a big deal for me to go see a psychiatrist. Respect in Cambodian society is very important. In the past, I used the word as a case manager and social worker with the Cambodian unaccompanied minors. When we placed the incoming minors with American parents, for example, and sometimes kids who cannot stay with their parents also came to us and we placed them with foster parents, whenever there were problems between the children and the parents, right away the agency recommended psychiatry. For the kids, you know, it's like punishment to them. Because when you go to school, when you go play ball with other Cambodian kids, they say, "He's crazy." So, a lot of times, people would refuse to go. In traditional society, people go to see the monks as counselors but usually it's not really a remedy. You go to the monk, you talk indirectly, sometimes there is an indirect process of healing, if you want to call it that, but it's not like going to see a psychiatrist. In Cambodia, there is no doctor specializing in psychiatry. Now Cambodians are getting M.S.W. [master's in social work] and degrees like that. A lot of the times, Lany Lang works with them. The cases are sometimes out of control. They don't really care. If a person joins a gang, do you think anyone really cares? They don't really care. That's why they join the gang.

AK: Are you saying that most people are dealing with this by going to the monks, through their Buddhist religion?

SS: Yes. When I worked as a case manager and also social worker, we would recommend that first. We would take a child to talk to the monk, not telling the child, "I am taking you to see a counselor or a psychiatrist," but, "Let's go visit the temple." We play and we discuss with the monk the child's problems, the monk would say something in a soothing way and sometimes the kid changes after the visit with the monk. My experience has been that taking the children to see a psychiatrist angers them even more.

AK: You mentioned at the beginning that your organization was nonpartisan, but do you find that Cambodians here are still involved in politics back home?

SS: A lot. Most of the members of my organization, the CNC, most of them have political interests. Not all of them have political interests but most of them have a political tie with a given party, formally or informally.

AK: Is that how the Cambodian community is broken up in the metro D.C. area?

SS: There are a lot of heads, political heads over here. Among the five thousand Cambodians, you have relatively more politicians here. Of course, Long Beach has a lot, too, but Long Beach has almost sixty thousand Cambodians. The thing is, percentagewise you have a lot more here.

AK: Are these politicians planning to go back to Cambodia?

SS: Some have returned. The current co-minister of defense is from here. The vice minister of finance is from here. A member of Parliament is from here too.

AK: Did you or anyone you know go back to vote in the 1993 elections?

SS: Very few. In the last election, among Cambodian Americans, only twenty-one of them voted.

AK: Oh, really?

SS: Only twenty-one.

AK: In the whole country?

SS: In the whole United States. Only twenty-one voted. Several hundred registered but only twenty-one voted. If you lived in California, you had to fly to the U.N., to New York. That, to me, is ridiculous. That was the only station where you could vote. Even people from here had difficulty. I went to vote, but I have my own reason. I wanted to vote whether it's counted or not. Another hurdle was that you had to go to Cambodia to register.

AK: Do you think there are many Cambodians here who plan to return to Cambodia at some point, who want to go back?

SS: A lot, a lot of Cambodians want to go back, particularly the old want to go back. Even some of the young want to go back, at least temporarily.

AK: What are they waiting for? Why aren't they going back now?

SS: There are several reasons. One, over there, you earn only twenty, fifty dollars a month. Two, the security, you don't have any security in Cambodia. Therefore, you are afraid to be there. And for those who have mortgages to pay, they cannot afford to be in Cambodia unless they are a member of Parliament. Members of Parliament are the only civil servants in Cambodia who earn over $1,000. They also have other benefits, so they can afford to be there; the rest cannot go unless they have funding from here. Then there are also those who can be in Cambodia because they are businessmen; they can do business with other Cambodians.

AK: That's assuming that they still want to maintain their houses here and what not, but I'm talking about people just going back to Cambodia permanently. No one wants to do that?

SS: No. You have to have some kind of guarantee. I mean everyone who wants to go back has been living here in security. You have to have some slot to go back to. I think when the country is really peaceful, prosperous, when laws are established, maybe people will want to go back to stay permanently. Even me, I'm thinking of going to stay there permanently; at the same time, I still want to have the option to come back here.

AK: I've asked you a lot of questions about the metro D.C. area but you obviously have a macro perspective on what's going on in the entire country in terms of the Cambodian associations. Can you comment briefly on what's going on in other places? I'm actually going to visit many of the MAAs along the eastern seaboard and we're going to be doing some interviewing in Long Beach as well, but from the headquarters perspective, can you comment on what's going on in these other areas?

SS: Well, I think in a way, I've touched upon those issues already. Although the situation in D.C. and in each local community is specific and unique, I think in general they are similar. For example, the problem of gangs, I mean, that's all over. The language barrier for the old, that's all over. And the intergenerational gap, each local MAA is trying to address those issues and to solve those problems. Perhaps there are more shops in Long Beach, you have television programs you don't have here because we don't have enough support to do that. Here, people are politically more active.

AK: Do you see, for example, similarities between Long Beach and Lowell?

SS: Yes. They are similar. Similar communities, similar problems. I think in terms of the welfare dependency, the gang problem, and gambling, they're very, very similar.

AK: What about Washington state, the Seattle area?

SS: Washington state, the gang problem, they have very little of that. And welfare dependency I would say is average. Organizationwise, in terms of activities, it is similar to any other state.

AK: Before we conclude, you've alluded to parts of your life, but I wanted to ask you if you could tell me a little bit about yourself, how you ended up as the executive director of the CNC.

SS: I was a student at the Royal University of Fine Arts and I was sent by the Cambodian government to study at the Conservatory of Music in the University of the Philippines. And then there was the war and the country fell. I came here first as a refugee and I began working, as I said, three days after I arrived.

AK: Did you come straight here?

SS: To Philadelphia. I worked in Philadelphia for two years and then in Atlantic City for one year. I went to Connecticut College and then Wesleyan. I received all my degrees, including a Ph.D. in ethnomusicology, from Wesleyan University. Right after my graduation I got a job at a college in Seattle and then the following year I got a job at the University of Washington. I taught there for three years and then I went to California to work as a folk arts coordinator for the Fresno Art Council for a while and then I got this job. But before that, communitywise, I worked with associations and I was very active. And, as I told you, I traveled a lot. I was the secretary of CNC before I took the directorship. As a performer, I perform and travel a lot. We are making movies now.

AK: Was the MacArthur Fellowship you were awarded (I learned about this award you got from the newspaper) related to your art work or to your community work?

SS: Both. For the preservation of Cambodian culture and for community development. As you know, for the MacArthur, after you are nominated through a secret process, you have to be recommended by a large number of people across the nation, so a nominee has to be very active. Getting the MacArthur alone shows that I have been active in community development and also in the arts.

AK: I know how busy you are, so I really appreciate the time you've spent answering my questions. Thank you very much indeed.

August 7, 1995

9. Sokhom Tauch
Cambodians in Portland, Oregon

MR. SOKHOM TAUCH, who uses "Philip" as his first name when talking to European Americans, is the executive director of the International Refugee Center of Oregon (IRCO) in Portland. IRCO is a multiservice agency serving multiethnic clients. As the number of new arrivals from Vietnam, Laos, and Cambodia dwindled in the early 1990s, IRCO began serving more and more refugees from such places as Ethiopia, Somalia, Afghanistan, the former Soviet Union, and the former constituent states of Yugoslavia. IRCO works very closely with Oregon's state agencies to maximize self-sufficiency and to minimize welfare dependency among the various refugee populations. As soon as refugees arrive, they have to register at IRCO, which then places them in English-as-a-second-language classes, vocational training programs, and classes that teach such job-hunting skills as how to fill out application forms and dress for interviews. When Audrey Kim interviewed Mr. Tauch in his office on September 9, 1996, he had already worked at IRCO for almost twenty years.

Mr. Tauch was sent to live in a Buddhist temple when he was ten because his widowed mother could not support him. As a novice monk, he learned the Buddhist scriptures and how to read and write from older monks at the temple. He left the monkhood in his late teens and went to Phnom Penh to attend college while supporting himself with two jobs. Before he could complete his college education, however, he joined the Cambodian navy in 1973 because he had trouble making ends meet as a civilian. When the Khmer Rouge captured Phnom Penh, he was stationed in Sihanoukville, Cambodia's only seaport. He and his fellow sailors and naval officers escaped in their boat and sailed southward to Malaysia. When the Malaysian shore patrol refused to let them land, they made their way to the U.S. naval base at Subic Bay in the Philippines. From there, he was flown to Fort Indiantown Gap in Pennsylvania—one of the four reception centers on the U.S. mainland processing refugees from Vietnam and Cambodia in 1975. Catholic Charities became Mr. Tauch's sponsor and sent him to Portland, Oregon.

After arriving in Portland, Mr. Tauch worked at several restaurants, busing and washing dishes, sweeping floors, and cleaning up the premises after closing. In 1977 he got a job as an interpreter and translator at IRCO. He attended school while working full time. He received a B.A. from City University (which is located in Seattle but has a branch campus in Portland) and an M.B.A. from Marylhurst College for Lifelong Learning (now Marylhurst University) in Portland. He rose through the ranks, serving as IRCO's accountant, then its fiscal manager, and finally its executive director.

When I talked to Sokhom Tauch by telephone on October 1, 2001, IRCO had just completed a move to new quarters in a large building on 1.7 acres of grounds ten miles from downtown Portland. The distance is not a problem because Portland has an excellent public transportation system. Mr. Tauch is particularly pleased that the building has a very large hall with a modern kitchen that can be used for community events. With funding from the federal, state, county, and city governments as well as from private foundations, IRCO now employs 116 staff members who represent thirty-three different ethnic groups and, collectively, can speak more than thirty languages. Its newest clients are refugees from Russia, Somalia, Cuba, Turkey, and Iraq. (Most of the refugees from Turkey and Iraq are Kurds, who are being persecuted there.) The only group of refugees still coming from Southeast Asia are Burmese. Since the 1980s, tens of thousands of Burmese political dissidents have escaped from Myanmar (the current name for Burma) to northwestern Thailand, where some of them have lived in tent cities for years. Some of these people are now finding their way into the United States as refugees.

The Cambodian-ancestry population in the Portland area has remained stable in number. As people leave, others come as secondary migrants, mainly from California, to replace them. The Californian Cambodians tend to be parents who do not want their children to grow up in areas of gang activity. The only Cambodians who are still being served by IRCO are mothers and children. The mothers are learning parenting skills that are appropriate for the American context. For example, the IRCO staff explains the importance of allowing children to receive immunization shots, feeding them a balanced diet, and becoming involved in their schooling. IRCO also has a program for high school students, some of whom are of Cambodian ancestry. The county government has established a "gang tracking" program in an effort to reach young teenagers before gang recruiters do. (Most gang recruiters who are Cambodian come from Long Beach, Sacramento, and Stockton). IRCO works closely with the Portland police department, which has community liaison officers who take part in the activities at the Asian Family Center at IRCO.

IRCO's main concern continues to be employment training and job placement to help maximize the self-sufficiency of Oregon's refugee population. Cambodians are still working at electronics assembly plants and in various kinds of factories. When the economy slows, Mr. Tauch advises the gainfully employed members of refugee families to find work in different industries so they will not suffer complete economic devastation should everyone in the same family be laid off at the same time. IRCO's other areas of emphasis include services to families, health education (focusing on health screening, immunization, breast cancer detection, tobacco addiction prevention, and drug abuse prevention), and citizenship education. An increasing number of refugees, including Cambodians, are becoming naturalized U.S. citizens in order to escape the negative consequences of welfare reform (which cut back services to noncitizens) and to ensure that youths who get into trouble cannot be deported. Mr. Tauch also notes that attempts to deport Cambodians are stymied by the fact that the Cambodian government has begun to refuse to accept such deportees.

Another factor that has caused some Cambodians who live in the United States to change their orientation is the realization that there "isn't much they can do to affect the political situation in Cambodia." Therefore, it is more useful to pay more attention to what is happening in the United States. IRCO offers citizenship classes, one of which is taught in Khmer. Mr. Tauch is pleased that a voter registration drive undertaken by IRCO has helped to increase the number of voters among the newly naturalized American citizens.

Although Sokhom Tauch has found it extremely satisfying to have worked at IRCO for twenty-five years, he would like to take time out to earn a Ph.D. He has not yet been able to realize that dream, however, because he has worked for a quarter of a century, day and night and often on weekends, to serve fellow refugees from around the world.

*   *   *

AK: Can you give me some general information about the Cambodian community in Portland? How many Cambodians are there in the Portland area right now?

ST: Just a wild guess, I think about three thousand. Most people moved from California; a lot of out-of-state people here. People like myself came

originally to Portland. A lot of Cambodians live in Washington County—
that's due to the electronics industry, Intel and companies like that. A number of people live in northeast Portland—not clustered but spread throughout the area. The concentration of Cambodians is mostly in the west side, in
Beaverton. In southeast Portland, there's a group of people living in an apartment complex but not as many as in Washington County. In Washington
County, most people are employed, own their own homes, raise their families. Most people who depend on public assistance usually live in this area of
the city where our office is located.

AK: And the ones in the outskirts, like Beaverton, are they the ones who
are working?

ST: Yes.

AK: Can you tell me when Cambodians first started coming to Portland?

ST: In 1975. Khat Neang and I were the first ones. [The two were in the
Cambodian navy together.] There were only five or six of us in Portland at
that time. Cambodians really started coming to Portland in 1979 and 1980.
There were only a few families in 1975, mainly the people from the Cambodian navy. We escaped together in a ship.

AK: Why did navy people end up coming to Portland?

ST: Well, actually, we were the first Cambodians who got out of the country because we had a boat. A group of us was sponsored by U.S. Catholic
Charities and that's how we came here.

AK: You mean, depending on where you had sponsors, that's where you
went? I've heard that many Cambodians from the military went to places like
Texas because of the military bases there. Is there such a connection in Portland?

ST: When we have one friend come over, that friend usually suggests to
his sponsor, "I have another friend, can you sponsor him, too?" That's how
I ended up in Portland; Khat was probably in the same situation.

AK: When Cambodians first started coming to Portland in large numbers
in 1979, where did they settle? Did they first settle in southeast Portland?

ST: Yes, in southeast Portland but once people get a job, they tend to move
to wherever the job is. At that time, Tektronix hired thousands and thousands
of Cambodians. I know a lot of people who work for Tektronix. Tektronix
was one of the first electronics companies in the west side. Then we got Intel
later on. People move to wherever the jobs are; they are not concentrated in
the southeast any more. But the southeast was the original site.

AK: What kinds of jobs do they have?

ST: A lot are in electronics. You probably see a couple of them in the body
shops and a few of them in welding, in metalwork. But most Cambodians

are in the electronics industry. That's why I said they're mainly concentrated in Beaverton. There are a few social workers like me. The children, however, are beginning to learn to adapt and to study computer science, accounting, and stuff like that.

AK: So they're diversifying into other occupations.

ST: Yeah. For the older generation like me or even older, probably whatever they can get, they try to keep it. There's not much chance for us to move.

AK: Are there many Cambodian-owned businesses in the Portland area?

ST: Not so many. There are a couple of grocery stores. There's one restaurant. Cambodians don't want to operate their own business; that is a given, back home, too. It was mostly Chinese and Vietnamese living in Cambodia who owned businesses. Cambodians usually become teachers, office workers, farmers [back in Cambodia]. Here, too, there are not so many Cambodian-owned businesses in Portland; probably five. We have a couple of laundromats, about two or three sandwich shops, and one grocery.

AK: Are those owned by ethnic Cambodians or ethnic Chinese?

ST: It's hard to say because even though their ancestors came from China, after generations the Chinese have become Cambodian. They never say that they are ethnic Chinese; they are Cambodian and they speak Khmer. I know two or three people who are not "real" Cambodians but they don't speak anything other than Khmer. Their grandparents are from China.

AK: Do you think most of these businesses are owned by ethnic Chinese?

ST: Ethnic Chinese or ethnic Vietnamese.

AK: Ethnic Vietnamese who were living in Cambodia and came over here?

ST: Yeah; it's very complicated. A Cambodian, like myself, nobody believes that I'm from Cambodia. They think I'm from India or somewhere like that. I like to work rather than own my own business. But to some others, wherever there can be more income, they go there. I have a sister who owns a doughnut shop [in Marina del Rey, California].

AK: It seems like Cambodians are doing pretty well here; in terms of work, they are actively employed.

ST: Yes, but there's also another side to it, you know, the older people. There are a lot of older people who cannot work and become SSI [Supplemental Security Income] recipients. But most of us are very active, gainfully employed. We have adapted and changed according to the environment rather than being the way we were back home. So, compared to Long Beach, in terms of public dependency, I think Portland is better off than places like Long Beach or Fresno.

AK: Do you have a sense of what percentage of people are on public assistance?

ST: I usually get a report from the state because we contract with the state. Probably only 5 to 10 percent.

AK: That's a very small percentage.

ST: Yeah, they're usually older people and sick people who cannot work. The rest of us try really hard to be employed. I work; I got a house. If you are just on welfare, there's no way you're going to buy a house. You can get more money by working. But families that have more children have a tendency to stay on public assistance because that's the way the system is: You have more children, you get more money. They go to work and get $700, but if they are on welfare they can get more than $1,000.

AK: Khat Neang was saying that in Oregon, it's very hard to be on public assistance if you are able-bodied.

ST: That's the system here. If a recipient is delivering a baby, she can stay at home only three weeks; used to be a year or so.

AK: The [public assistance] figures here are very different from anywhere else I've seen in the country, not just Long Beach, but the East Coast, too. What do you think is responsible for the difference?

ST: The system itself. Another thing is the people in the community. In Portland, most Cambodians are working. When they work, they save money, they buy a house. When others see that, that's where the encouragement comes from.

AK: What is the background of most of the Cambodians here?

ST: Yeah, another thing is the background. For us, who came before 1979, who were educated back home, we can take new classes here, no problem, learn new skills. But for those who came later on, you know, they have some problems. However, I think most of the people are willing to work wherever they can make $8 or $9 an hour, rather than be on public assistance. So they'll be able to own their own homes, their own cars. People survive in our community.

AK: What percentage of the Cambodians here came before 1979?

ST: The first wave is still probably 60 percent.

AK: You mean a majority are people who were in the military, the navy? This is very different from places like Lowell, where a majority of the people came out of the refugee camps.

ST: Exactly. Also, another distinction is the environment. People encourage each other to work here. If you work, you can still get some welfare; you're still taken care of by welfare.

AK: You can work and get welfare?

ST: If your pay is not enough.

AK: So, the system really encourages you to work.

ST: Very encouraging. And another thing is we have an organization like this, which is actively looking for jobs for people. See, when new arrivals come, they have to register here. We train them for English and preemployment skills. If they need skills, we train them, like power sewing or building maintenance. And we have people who go around and look for work. We've been in business since 1976 and we've done that since 1976. In addition, we have a volag [voluntary agency] that does case management. And if there's a problem they can call the state, the welfare office. The organizations work with each other. An organization like this, we've become a model nationwide because it is operated by a refugee like me. Our board members are all refugees; we have Ethiopians, we have Romanians, we have Russians, Cambodians, Laotians, Vietnamese. So a group of people came together to form this organization and we are able to help our own people to be self-sufficient. If you've been here eight months and you're still unemployed, the public assistance is stopped and you're going to be on your own. So, if we assign them a job, they have to take it.

AK: Are you still working with Cambodians since Cambodians aren't really coming as refugees any more?

ST: Cambodians have not been coming these last couple of years. We are dealing now with Russians and Somalians. But we did work with Cambodians when they first came. A lot of them, when they've saved so much money and are ready to own their own businesses, they've heard about Long Beach or Texas, they move there. The whole family moves there; in a few years, they become wealthy. That's the way it is in the Cambodian community.

AK: So, you have people moving out of Portland to go to other places? Have the numbers here shrunk? The three thousand, was it a larger number before?

ST: It used to be like five thousand around 1985. But again, people move in and out. Like people from California, when there's an earthquake, they all move up here. They sell their businesses, homes, and come to buy cheap homes up here. Both ways, moving in and out.

AK: Let me see if I have this right. It sounds like these high-tech jobs, they pay fairly well for low-skill work. So, people may earn some money here, save up, and then go to other places where they can start their own businesses?

ST: Mostly to California. A couple of families moved to Lowell. And some of them stay over here.

AK: Do you have people coming into Oregon from other places?

ST: Yes, mostly for family reunification. From California, it's mostly to avoid the earthquakes.

AK: Of the three thousand right now, do you have a sense of what percentage are people who've come from other areas versus those who were settled here originally?

ST: I think 40 percent are from what we call secondary migration. The original 60 percent are here and some have moved out. Some people have moved in, not just from California, but I see people moving from the East Coast, too. And, if people move from California, it's probably after years of doing business, or after years of living there and it's too crowded. They're moving here for the quiet, trying to raise children.

AK: That leads me to my next question. Can you tell me your impressions of what's going on with Cambodian youths?

ST: Yeah, every attention now is being paid to the youth in our community. We used to have problems, like parents have some conflicts with the children because the way we raise children back home is very different from here. The only sad thing I see now is not enough Cambodian kids are going to college.

AK: What percentage are making it to college?

ST: Probably less than 20 percent. I hope it increases because other ethnic groups, they have a lot of people going to college. Cambodians, they usually have other obligations, like family. They need to go to work right away. Or, in their personal desire for material things, they forget about the long-term, like education, that could help them fulfill that desire better. Comparing now to the early '80s, more Cambodian children are graduating from college. The numbers are moving up but not really fast enough compared to other ethnic groups.

AK: What's happening to the other 80 percent who aren't going to college?

ST: Well, they get a job. They enjoy life so much, they have to have a car, an expensive car, a sports car. Or, unfortunately, some of them join a gang and cause a lot of problems. We have to come up with a program that teaches both parents and children to work together. Each side has to give up their turf a little bit. I got a lot of problems from schools calling, from the Children's Service Division calling. So, it's not a happy scene.

AK: What are they calling you about?

ST: Well, misdemeanors. The children, what can we do? This is a continual education process because when you get old, it's hard to change. And, the younger people, with the peer pressure, come to act this way.

AK: Let me try to understand. Relatively speaking, there aren't that many Cambodians in this area. Are the Cambodian kids going to schools where there are lots of other Cambodian kids, or are they interspersed?

ST: There's only one school that has a lot of Cambodian kids; that's Cleveland High School right here. People from the southeast area, that's their school over there. But there are gangs from other ethnic groups. When they get one, they try to get two . . .

AK: You mean Cambodians aren't necessarily in Cambodian gangs, they're in multiethnic gangs?

ST: Yeah. There are also some gangs from California. They move up north to Portland and Seattle.

AK: How many Cambodian youths are involved in gangs? Do you have a sense?

ST: Not very many, but at least twenty or thirty. But once they get into gangs, they probably drop out of school. They probably isolate themselves, have problems with pregnancy and stuff like that. We got a couple of cases. And then they go back home and fight with their parents. The two of them are not getting along and the children run away. I've had to listen to all of that. Yes, the problem exists, but not as bad as in other states. Big states like Texas or Massachusetts or California.

AK: When you say there are only maybe twenty to thirty Cambodian youths in gangs, are there any gangs that are composed only of Cambodians, or are Cambodians just part of multiethnic gangs?

ST: They're parts of others, but when Californians move up north, they are the problem. The kids here tend to get along with other Asians. I've never seen a real Cambodian gang but there's a gang that calls itself by the name of CWA. I asked them, "What does that mean?" and they said, "Cambodians with attitude." I believe it's from Oakland or Fresno. Now, things are kind of quiet because the Portland police got firm with them. We have some problems in court, shootings . . .

AK: Shootings? Drive-by shootings?

ST: There's one case, it's sort of shootings among themselves. It's not as difficult as it used to be in the late '80s. But other ethnic groups still have their own gangs.

AK: So, there were Cambodian gangs before but they dispersed because of the crackdown, and now Cambodians are belonging to other ethnic gangs?

ST: Yeah. They probably don't call themselves ethnic, they are called something else.

AK: Why are Cambodians joining gangs? I think this area is unique in the high percentage of first-wave people. I'm assuming they are more educated, better able to deal with the American system. The sense that I got in other places, like Lowell and Long Beach, where you have parents who aren't educated, don't speak English, they're not able to control their kids who rebel and do their own thing. It seems that people from the first wave would have an easier time. You're saying that that's not really the case?

ST: Most of the gangs, most of the kids, are really spoiled. Where they get into trouble, the majority is not really from the families that came here in the first wave. Most of the children from those families are too old. Mostly, they go to college, they get professional jobs. But the new ones are around fourteen and younger. The freedom in this country, they try to take advantage of it. I have seen the gang members but they're not really anybody I know.

AK: I'm also surprised, for the same reason, that there aren't more Cambodians going to college. Because, in the first wave, you have people who are college graduates from Cambodia. Are they not pushing their kids to go to college in the U.S.?

ST: From 1975 to 1979, a number of us were struggling to survive. The number of kids at that time was so small. The successful cases probably are from those who came earlier. Still, the percentage is so small.

AK: Another thing I've seen in other places is that the Cambodians who came over when they were teenagers actually seem to do OK in the U.S. because they have a strong grounding in Cambodian values, they get along with their parents. It's the ones who are born here or who are raised in the U.S. who are caught between two cultures and don't know where they fit in; they're the ones who have problems, turn to gangs.

ST: That's very correct. That's my personal view on that issue. Because the kids are very confused. They say, "I have two countries to live in. One is at home and one is at school. What should I do?" This is the type of comment that I hear from them. What you said is very correct from what I can see. When a kid came from Cambodia as a teenager, he already knows the culture and already respects the parents. It's the kids who came at age two or three from Cambodia and then grew up here, or the ones born here, that's where the problem comes in. Both the parents and the kids have to come up with some middle ground.

AK: How is the Cambodian community in Portland working to preserve Cambodian culture and heritage? Are there classes in language, dance, that sort of thing?

ST: We used to have that. Sante Pheap was the organization that used to provide that. We also provide the same thing in the Cambodian Buddhist temple. But the problem comes when a parent has to take the kids, has to take time off from work and take the kids there. The association and the temple have no funds to provide transportation. Therefore, we cannot try to keep as much of our culture as we wish. We have holidays, Buddhist holidays, you see hundreds of people from Eugene to Longview come to this temple.

AK: Is this the only temple in all of Oregon?

ST: Yeah. Beyond Longview, they go to Tacoma or Seattle. So, everybody tries to keep their own tradition. The student association in Portland State, every year they have a celebration during Cambodian New Year and they do dancing, traditional dancing, just to keep up with it. We used to have a better organized community. We formed a group of associations. We met all the time, but people now are very busy. It's a balancing act between day-to-day living and doing whatever you want.

AK: Another thing that seems to be a trend is, in communities where Cambodians are doing OK, working, keeping busy, the organizations aren't very strong because people are so busy doing other things. And so there's a weakening of Cambodian culture in those communities.

ST: Yeah, that is the case. We used to, back in 1979 or the early '80s, there used to be an organization that celebrated every year the Cambodian New Year with dancing and cultural shows. But now there are only student groups that have time to do that. It's kind of a balancing act. I believe that we love to keep our own culture but there are also other obligations: You need to pay bills, you need to provide necessities for your children.

AK: Besides problems with the kids, what other things do you see as major challenges facing the Cambodian community in Portland?

ST: The challenge is again the way we raise our children. Back home, it's different. The way we do our job is different. It's completely different back home and here.

AK: Can you comment on that? What do you mean?

ST: In Cambodia, you may not work eight hours; you can take it easy, you work at your own pace. But here, you have to put in eight hours. In Cambodia, only one person working can support the whole family. But here, two persons are working and still not have enough for the children. And because of that, there tends to be problems at home between husband and wife. And another thing is the freedom of the women in this country. I see a lot of marriage problems because of that. The husband tends to still act the way he used to do back home. It involves authority, family violence.

AK: Is domestic violence a big problem in the Cambodian community?

ST: We don't know of very many cases because most women don't talk. If a woman talks, there's probably some problem, especially among the people who really don't have much education.

AK: You're not hearing about it a lot because people aren't talking, but you know it's out there?

ST: Yeah. The authorities encourage people to talk but Cambodian women are not really an outspoken group of people. They tend to compromise a lot. "If I do this, and my husband does this, that would be OK." That usually works out quite well. But deep down inside, there are problems. The way we raise children, for example. I know a family that I've been helping. You know, like hitting the kid. I know it exists, but it's never reported. Another problem that I see, besides the youth, are the old people. They don't have anywhere to go. They don't work and they are stuck at home. We have a Cambodian Buddhist temple and we encourage senior citizens to go there, but if they choose to go there it's because they are religious. If they don't like that religion, they're stuck. We couldn't come up with a common place where we can get all the older people together, share their concerns and talk, just be able to see each other. Problems also exist in that sector of the Cambodian population.

AK: Let me ask you some questions related to that. You said that it's a problem because maybe some of the older people don't want to go to the Buddhist temple. My perception is that a majority of Cambodians are Buddhist. Are there some who aren't?

ST: Back home, 99 percent of Cambodians are Buddhist. Here, Cambodians feel very obligated to their sponsors; they pay them back, they feel an obligation. If their sponsor happened to be a church, they have to . . . I mean, the church doesn't put any pressure on them but they feel that they have to pay back. That's important. I think about 25 percent of the people are not Buddhist in Portland. They even have a Cambodian pastor.

AK: What denominations are those 25 percent in?

ST: I don't know. Probably Seventh Day Adventists. I'm a Buddhist, so I don't really know. Probably also some Lutherans and some Mormons.

AK: Those were all groups that sponsored refugees?

ST: Yeah. There's a big church right here in downtown; I don't know what kind of church it is but they sponsor people. They help resettle them over here. And when one becomes well settled, the others follow. The church has money to do that but not the Buddhist temple. So, you see, of course we want the Buddhists to flourish, but in this country, it's people's choice.

AK: How long has the Buddhist temple been around?

ST: Since 1982.

AK: And how was it established?

ST: I am one of the original members that established it. In Washington, D.C., there's a temple there. We knew the head monk (who just passed away). He's considered to be an important monk in Cambodia and he came to visit us and said we can sponsor some other monk, a Cambodian monk. We did sponsor one and we found a house but we had only $80. But people kept donating money and later on we bought property and now the temple grounds and building are worth almost $1 million. So, we've been pretty successful. Every scheduled Buddhist holiday, hundreds of people show up.

AK: Does the temple have trouble maintaining its finances?

ST: People are very good about supporting it. Otherwise, we wouldn't be able to buy land.

AK: How many monks are there right now?

ST: I think there are four now.

AK: Are they from Thailand?

ST: Not from Thailand any more. The ones from Thailand have already gone some place else. These are from Cambodia. There are two new monks from Cambodia, one from Laos—but he was a Cambodian living in Laos—and the original one is from Cambodia.

AK: The ones from Cambodia, are they monks who stopped being monks during the Khmer Rouge and then became monks again?

ST: One of them. The rest, I don't really know. They seem very young to me. But there's one who gave up his monkhood and later became a monk again.

AK: I'm curious about how strong Buddhism is among the younger people. Are the kids going to continue the Buddhist tradition, do you think? Or is Buddhism going to die out among Cambodian Americans here?

ST: For us, in Portland, we always try to bring kids to the temple. That's our way of showing our children we want them to keep it up. But, you know, it's hard to predict how they're going to act in ten years or so. In my family, I have a five-year-old son who already goes to the temple with me. He is familiar with the monk and he keeps asking questions. A lot of families are doing exactly the same thing like me. We also used to have youth activities in the temple, like volleyball, or traditional dancing open to any Cambodian youth or any friends they want to bring along. And that's how we try to keep our Buddhist religion in the United States, in Portland. We also work with other Cambodians in the United States to get new ideas. The monk who recently passed away usually held an annual [national] meeting. But since he's gone, there has not been an annual meeting for monks. We used to send our monks to attend that meeting. Hopefully, we can keep on doing so for years to come. At one time, we taught the Cambodian language but parents are really too busy to bring their kids and we can't afford to buy a bus, a youth bus, to go around and transport kids.

AK: What I'm hearing you say is that a lot of families are trying to instill Buddhist values by taking their kids to the temple. But in the end, who knows what will happen?

ST: Yeah, in the end, who knows? All we can do is try our best to convey the religion to our children. And I've seen many families do that. Every time there's a Buddhist holiday, I've seen parents, the children, the whole family. Older kids, younger kids, babies. It's a lot of fun when you see everybody.

AK: Do you see any changes in doctrine or practice when Buddhism is practiced in the U.S.?

ST: Yes, it has changed already. Here [in Oregon], we're stricter than in other states because that's the way people here want it.

AK: You mean in your temple it's stricter?

ST: It's stricter because we don't let the monks drive. In other places, the monks drive. They have to go from place to place. We don't let that happen here.

AK: So, people here prefer the stricter way?

ST: Yes, to stick as much as possible to the way it is in Cambodia. We let the monks [here] go to regular school; in Cambodia, no, you cannot go to regular school. You have to go to Buddhist school. But since there's no Buddhist school here, we let the monks go to the community college.

AK: Does the strictness have anything to do with Thammayut or Mahanikay or is that something different?

ST: It has to do with that. Mahanikay is more lenient while Thammayut is stricter. Actually, there's one principle only, but Thammayut is the one that belongs to the king. The royal family created that just to distinguish themselves from regular people.

AK: Is your temple Thammayut or Mahanikay?

ST: We don't distinguish here. Back home, the reason for distinction is the royal family needs to be separate. They pray in a little different tone than the Mahanikay; they don't wear sandals when walking. But it's still the same Buddhist principle. Personally, I don't like the distinction. See, I was a monk back home. I was Mahanikay but I lived in a Thammayut temple. When I was a student I lived in a Thammayut temple but when I went back to my own village—my father was a monk there when he was alive—I had to become a monk [in a Mahanikay temple] for a year.

AK: That's typical for many Cambodian men, right?

ST: Yeah, before, but not now. Not even in Cambodia.

AK: Even in Cambodia, that practice is gone?

ST: Some people still practice it in their family, but it's not really common any more. Before, yes, the boy had to spend time in the temple—that's the only education they could get—before marriage.

AK: You were telling me a little bit about how Buddhism has changed in the U.S. You said that your temple is stricter than others in the U.S. Do you see any differences between how Buddhism is practiced in the U.S. versus in Cambodia?

ST: Yeah, in terms of practice, we can't do some things the way they are done in Cambodia. See, the monks actually have to go around asking for rice. But here, they cannot do that. So, that's one difference. In Cambodia, there's a big drum in the temple, you know, it sounds all over the village. In Cambodia, the monks cannot go to school. The monks cannot wear sandals, or wear shoes, but here the monks have to wear shoes because it's too cold. The monks in Cambodia can wear only what is wrapped around them, but here the monks probably have to wear some kind of long-sleeved shirt, the same color as their robe, just to be warm.

AK: So, there are slight modifications, to adapt . . .

ST: To adapt to the environment. In Long Beach, I see some monks driving cars, which I don't like, but they have to get to places. But people here, any change that can be avoided, we avoid it.

AK: There are these minor modifications, but in terms of the doctrine, has that pretty much stayed the same?

ST: The doctrine has very much stayed the same from what I can see. Doing good deeds, we still practice the ten commandments: do not kill, do not lie . . . the regular people have five, the nuns or people who shave their heads have eight, the monks have ten; we still practice them. We believe that when you do good things to others, others will, in the future, do good things to you. We still believe in that. In terms of the concept, the doctrine is still the same, but in practice, there are modifications.

AK: I heard someone say, and I'd like to hear your opinion on this, that in some ways, the practice has become different because people in the United States are more critical—they think and question Buddhism more. For example, rather than just going through the rote ceremonies or rituals, people really think about them and are more involved. Do you see that kind of change at all?

ST: Well, yes and no. But again, that is not a doctrinal change, it's a change in practice. We have to adapt, we have to adjust to the way it is wherever we are. In Oregon it may be too cold, but in California, where there is warm weather, it may be different, you see. To me, I've been very active in the temple and I feel as long as it [the modification] fits the purpose of the temple, which is to be honest, to not kill, that should be fine.

AK: Because of the environment and circumstances, you need to make these little modifications and ask whether they fit the doctrine?

ST: Yeah, yeah. The practice here, we try to minimize the modifications as much as possible. We really don't want to modify unless we have to. If the monk does something that is not appropriate, we yell at him, whereas in Cambodia, we cannot yell at a monk. What you heard is probably correct in some instances. You know, the monk is usually just like a king. We cannot challenge him. We not only challenge the monk here, our children challenge us too. The more you live here . . .

AK: It's the American influence?

ST: Yeah, yeah. There's no escape from it. And the monk knows that too.

AK: On a slightly different note, are there many Cambodians here who are involved in politics in Cambodia?

ST: Yes. There's a group of people who usually support Prince Sihanouk. But that has kind of faded a little bit now and now there's a new group forming to support somebody else. But there's a lot of political involvement with what's going on in Cambodia. Not all the people, but a lot of people.

AK: What percentage of people are involved in what's going on in Cambodia?

ST: I think about 70 percent or 80 percent, more or less, are involved in politics at some level.

AK: Involved in the politics or just sending money to relatives?

ST: Involved in politics.

AK: That's a large percentage.

ST: Yeah. You know, either they support the current government or they support a new person. There's only a handful who really don't care.

AK: Do you find factionalism within the Cambodian community here depending on who you support?

ST: Used to be, but after the [1993] election in Cambodia, things have calmed down and people forget about the past. But before, in the same room, people from different political parties, they don't even look at each other. And that's why the temple established a rule that it doesn't matter where you come from, you are at the temple. So, leave your politics behind. But it is still a problem with us in the temple because people tend to take their political beliefs and their feelings to the temple.

AK: Do you or anyone you know have any sort of explanation for what happened during Pol Pot's time in terms of the Buddhist framework? My understanding is that Cambodia is a country of Buddhists; Buddhists believe in peace and kindness. Yet there were horrible atrocities that occurred.

ST: Yeah, my personal feeling is, during the Khmer Rouge era, there were a couple of leaders who really didn't believe in anything. When those leaders got younger people, ten years old or even younger, to become their army, they could train them to do anything. They even trained them to hate their own fathers. That's where the problem started. Cambodians, in general, believe in peace, believe in their family; they're very family-oriented. But this group of people tried to influence their soldiers at a young age, as young as eight or nine years old. Any regime could do the same thing. The destruction of Buddhism was begun by that. I have had some discussions with other Cambodians; some people believe that because we are Buddhists, it was our karma. We believe so much in karma.

AK: I've heard lots of different, interesting explanations.

ST: Yeah. But I don't believe that [it was just karma]. I think the psychological warfare that the Khmer Rouge imposed on the Cambodian young people made their rule possible. If you put a kid in an English-speaking family, he's going to speak English at a young age, even if he's a Cambodian kid. And if you put an American in a Cambodian family who speak Khmer, he's going to definitely speak Khmer.

AK: So, it was the Khmer Rouge leaders being able to target young, impressionable kids to become their army?

ST: When I was young, I was so afraid when this group of people went out to catch children. We used to hide when I was young because those people would catch any unsupervised children. Communism started from that time when people, young children, were captured and sent to China or North Vietnam. And when they came back . . . I think you probably heard one name that was in the political arena a couple of years ago. He was definitely trained by North Vietnamese; you know, he married a Vietnamese lady. So, once you educate them from this young age, it doesn't matter whether they're Buddhist or Christian.

AK: I realize that I've taken up a lot of your time. Before we end, though, can you tell me a little bit about your own background? You mentioned that you were in the navy and that you came in 1975. Can you tell me more about your background?

ST: I was born in a village in 1952. My father was a government worker, a little government worker; he earned just enough to raise a family. Unfortunately, he passed away because of diabetes. My mother was not able to raise me and my sister, so I was put in a temple; I was raised by monks since I was ten years old. I lived with monks and I was going to school at the same time. And then in 1970, I became a monk for a year after I got my junior high school certificate. I wanted to work, so I came to the city looking for work, trying to become a soldier so I can earn a little money. I had left the monkhood already by that time. I went back to school to finish my baccalaureate and then got into this university of law, where I was taking business law courses. But I was so poor, I still lived in a temple but this time in a Thammayut temple because it was very close to the palace and my college. So, all the king's family, the royal family, came to my temple. I finished my first year of business law school, but in the second year, I finished about half only. I was too poor, so I got a job as a tutor at night for a rich young high school kid. I worked as a construction worker during the day. But even that was not enough because things were getting expensive. I got a scholarship to go to college, but they never gave us spending money; we just got the scholarship to pay the tuition. So, my financial situation was really down. I decided to take some tests to be a teacher, a French teacher at that time. Each teacher has a specialty and I took French because I was good at it. I failed the test, however, so I took a test to be a pilot but I failed that, too. Then I took a test to be a navy man and I passed it, so I took that job. I was in training for about a year.

AK: What year was it that you joined the navy?

ST: 1973. In 1974, they sent me to Kompong Som [Sihanoukville], a big port. I was there for about seven or eight months before the country fell. I was going to go back to Phnom Penh because my family was there; my father had died but my mother and my sister were in Phnom Penh. My mother had already engaged me to a lady to be married; it was only a couple more weeks before I was supposed to be married. But then the country fell and my friend kept pushing me into the ship. So we were on this warship and we navigated out to the open sea, thinking we were going to come back to the base in a few days. The communist soldier told us on the phone, "If you leave, don't come back. Otherwise, we're going to kill you." So we had to call around to see if there was any bigger ship around. We found three bigger ships around.

AK: You were in just a little ship?

ST: Yeah. Everybody who was on a small ship went to the bigger ships. We had about seven hundred people in three ships.

AK: These were just men or were there families too?

ST: Families and children, too. We called the naval headquarters in Phnom Penh and they said the communists were coming but we didn't believe them. Everybody put their families into the ships and what little belongings that they could take. We thought it would be for only one or two days.

AK: They thought the escape was temporary?

ST: Yeah. But some people put chicken and pigs and all their belongings, little motorcycles, on the ship. Finally, the commander, who is currently living in east Texas, said we couldn't go back. Otherwise, we were going to get killed. But we needed some fuel to go on to Malaysia, so what we did was to go to an island where the navy stored all its fuel. We went there and got out real fast, and went on to Malaysia. The Malaysian government wouldn't let us land; they sent some food to us but they wouldn't let us land. We had to anchor two miles away from the shore. They sent a boat out and threw us some bananas, just as though we're monkeys. Finally, they refueled our ship and sent us away. Our commander radioed the U.S. ambassador in Kuala Lumpur and they told us, "Why don't you go to the Philippines?" So we sailed to the Philippines, to Subic Naval Base. After we got to Subic, I stayed there for a month; then they took me to Pennsylvania. I stayed there for three months. The U.S. Catholic Conference sponsored me to come to Portland. I went to school for a while, and in 1977, I got this job.

AK: Working here?

ST: Yeah, as a translator. And then I went to school for accounting. When I got the bookkeeping certificate, they gave me the accounting job. Later on, I went to college to get my associate's degree, then a bachelor's degree, and finally I become the fiscal manager. And then I went on to get my master's degree in business. Four months ago, they give me the director's job. I've been here for twenty years.

AK: So, this is the only place you've worked at since you've been in the U.S.?

ST: The real job. I've been doing a lot of other things, like owning my own janitorial services as a second job while I was working here. Before I started working here, I was a dishwasher in a couple of restaurants; janitor, dishwasher, you know, all kinds of things. But this is the real job . . .

AK: Wow! Twenty years! I haven't spoken to another Cambodian who has worked in the same place for twenty years.

ST: I think they got tired of me [laughs], so they gave me this job, the director's position.

AK: That's great, a big step for you. Congratulations.

ST: It is, and a big responsibility, too. I, along with my colleagues, tried to move out to another area but I'm attached so much to people, especially to refugees. When I first came here, had there been this kind of organization, that would have reduced a lot of pressure on me. When I first came, there were only a couple of [Cambodian] families in Portland. And we were all dishwashers and worked in a kitchen. Every time we met each other, we usually talked about the situation back home and how we got here, how we got to this position. We have a lot of fond memories. Some of us cried because it was too difficult. Like the bus, for example. I usually take the bus. At first, a lot of times I got lost but I always carried my address in case I got lost. I'm dying for rice, my first bowl of rice. Back home, we have French bread but we eat it with all kinds of stuff. People laugh at me when I eat bread with ice cream. A lot of people get confused. They get confused about cat food and think it is human food.

AK: You have a lot of funny stories.

ST: Because all this was new to us. There was nobody better than anybody else at that time. We all made a lot of mistakes. I carried rice from Chinatown two or three miles because people told me you had to find Chinatown to buy rice. We looked for Chinatown, dying for a bottle of hot sauce and soy sauce and rice and stuff like that. But the bus driver wouldn't let me put the sack of rice in the bus. So, I ended up carrying it and walking on the freeway because that's the only way to get home. That's my memory of my first year in the United States.

AK: It's sort of bittersweet; sad, but happy, too.

ST: Happy ending, because we all probably settled down in a couple of years. We had problems ordering food in the restaurant because they didn't understand us. Walking in the store into a wall because there's a wall full of mirrors. It was a real wall but we saw another room in the mirror. We have a lot of funny memories. We just didn't know about such things. We didn't have an organization like this that provides orientation to newcomers. We provide people orientation, tell them what a check looks like, what you have to pay for this and that. We didn't have that kind of help when I first arrived. When I was looking for a job as a bookkeeper, I thought it was for people who work in the library; I also thought a busboy is someone who collects the fare on the bus. Those were the kinds of things that were really strange to me. Turned out a busboy works in the restaurant.

AK: You can personally relate to the difficulties of adjusting to life here, so you must be very sympathetic to newcomers.

ST: Yes. And that's how I can stick with this kind of job for twenty years. I usually take it so personally when a family comes here and they don't have a job or they say, "They just took my daughter away." These are the things you have to have been through to really feel it. That's the kind of thing that makes me love people, especially the new refugees who don't know where they're going. They take the wrong bus, they finally get home at 9 at night; their wives are crying at home thinking something is wrong with their husbands. I've been there. I was the first [Cambodian in Portland] to own a car. It's a bad Chevrolet car; I had a lot of problems with it; the car salesman took advantage of me. My friend who got lost called me and I asked him, "What street are you on?" He said "76." I went to 76th Street; I couldn't find him. He called again and it turned out that 76 is the gas station. That's the kind of thing we all, being the first wave of refugees, experienced. Every time we meet each other, we talk about our experiences. Sometimes we laugh, sometimes we cry. Being a newcomer at that time, it was nice that American citizens were really helpful to us at that time since there were not a lot of refugees. Now it's not so welcoming. I had plenty of people come to the airport to meet me when I came to the United States, but a few years later, they began to hate us. That is, the mainstream people.

AK: Do you see ethnic tension in Portland? Is there animosity among the different ethnic groups?

ST: Not much, but there are some instances.

AK: But in general, that's not a problem for the Cambodian community?

ST: No. That's why I stay here for twenty years in Portland. You know, I've been to many cities in the U.S., major cities like Dallas, Houston, L.A., San Francisco, Boston, but I still love this place. People here are very friendly. Where I live, I'm the only Cambodian there and nobody bothers me. They always come and say, "Hi, how are you?"

AK: Your stories are very poignant and inspiring. Thank you for sharing them with me.

September 9, 1996

10. Hay S. Meas
Cambodians in Tacoma, Washington

DR. HAY S. MEAS, M.D., F.I.C.S., is a surgeon and obstetrician who has a private practice in Tacoma, Washington. At the time that Audrey Kim interviewed him on September 12, 1996, he was the executive director of a mutual assistance association, the Khmer Community of Tacoma, Inc. (KCT). He remained in that post until 1999. At present, he is the secretary general of the Cambodian Network Council (chapter 8), which is undergoing what Doctor Meas calls a "transitional phase" after losing its funding.

Dr. Meas received his medical training in Phnom Penh and then went to France to do an internship. He came to the United States in 1973, hoping to find a residency in an American hospital, but that goal proved more difficult to realize than he had anticipated. When the Khmer Rouge came to power in 1975 he was working at the *Washington Post*, folding newspapers in order to support himself. Because he was already on American soil, the U.S. government granted his petition for political asylum; he was considered an asylee rather than a refugee.

It took a great deal of effort for Dr. Meas to acquire a license to practice medicine in the United States. He worked in an Amish community for some years and then moved to Houston, Texas, in 1981, where he practiced medicine for twelve years. So far as he knows, he is the only Cambodian medical doctor who is a Fellow of the International College of Surgeons. Meas moved to Tacoma in 1993 and was immediately asked to play a leadership role in the KCT. When I talked to him by telephone on September 25, 2001, he said that he and his family intend to remain in Tacoma because he has a thriving medical practice there. His children are doing well in school, and he likes the weather in the Pacific Northwest. He visited Cambodia in February 2001 but has no intention to return there to live.

Doctor Meas observes that the Cambodian-ancestry population in the Tacoma area has increased in recent years. In addition to births on American soil, there are many secondary migrants from California. There are now four Cambodian Buddhist temples in the area, one of which belongs to the Khmer Krom (chapter 12). When welfare reform was implemented in 1996, those Cambodians who were able to work received some vocational training through Washington state's WorkFirst program. Many have found jobs that require little knowledge of English. The most encouraging recent development, from Doctor Meas's point of view, is that young Cambodian Americans are showing more interest in Khmer culture. He was pleased that some students asked one of the temples to offer some classes so they can learn the Khmer language as well as something about their parents' ancestral land.

*   *   *

AK: Maybe we can start by having you tell about the Khmer Community of Tacoma, Inc.

HM: I will give you a brief summary about our organization. The Khmer Community of Tacoma, better known as KCT, is a nonprofit organization created in 1979 to provide leadership and support in addressing community issues of concern to the Cambodian community of Tacoma, Pierce County, Washington. Our mission is to support the adjustment of Cambodians to American society—strengthening families, preserving Khmer heritage, and providing economic and educational opportunities.

AK: Does the Cambodian American community in Tacoma consider itself separate from that in Seattle?

HM: Yes, we do because of the geographic distance between the two cities, but we still have a close relationship. Our organization is distinct for many reasons, including the struggle to survive. We have leaders who came in 1975, as well as later arrivals who were traumatized by the war. They established KCT as an organization to represent our people. KCT has developed into more than just an office. It is an organization filled with enthusiasm, talent, and a determination to serve the needy and to preserve the Khmer heritage.

AK: In 1979 how many Cambodians were in the Tacoma area?

HM: I have no idea. I am relatively new in the area myself. I moved here from Texas. I lived in Texas for over ten years. I came to the United States in 1973. I started my medical practice in Houston, Texas, in 1981. I came here in November 1993. In 1994, I was invited to join the organization as a member of the board of directors. At the first board meeting I attended in April 1994, I was told that KCT had never had a grant to help Cambodian people and had never even had an office to work out of. So, members of the board asked me to help—to do something to get those things. That was their goal; their dream was to have just a small office and get a grant to help our people. Why did they turn to me to address the issues? I knew I was being tested and challenged, so I just listened. Deep down, I believed I could do it because of my previous community involvement and experience on different committees in Texas. However, the demands of running the organization as president is quite a heavy duty.

AK: Because you're so busy with your own medical practice?

HM: Yes, I have a busy private practice.

AK: When you came on the scene in 1994, what was the association doing?

HM: Well, we did not have any grants. We used a post office address. We moved our meetings from house to house and from library to library within the community. On paper, we had by-laws and everything, but realistically speaking, except for our vibrant concept, we didn't exist. Well, we decided we had to work very hard. The first thing we did was to restructure the organization. That was the time when issues related to refugee fraud were coming out. The refugees were looking for a way to make a living. Now, imagine if you don't have any education, you don't have a job. How are you going to make a living? You've even lost your identity when you came here from overseas. However, wherever there is an opportunity to make money, people have a tendency to go there. But for personal gain, the middleman can use the situation to his own advantage. We had cases of welfare fraud. That was a bad situation. It did not give us, at least in my eyes, a good community image. I was embarrassed, not only as a Cambodian, but also as an Asian. Not only were Cambodians involved, but Vietnamese as well. If you read the newspaper, then you know the subject of welfare fraud was the talk of the town. Back then, the newspaper seemed to constantly dwell on the issue.

AK: Let me make sure I understand. In 1994, when you came on board, Cambodians had a bad image in town because of the welfare fraud situation?

HM: Not only that, there was a case of fraud involving a case manager as well as the middleman. During that time, there was a lot of unemployment, a lot of public assistance dependency, and, as you can imagine, crime developed from that. The community had other problems. Children were not respecting their parents. They had lost their culture. They went through a period of culture shock and they were floating between two cultures. It was as if they are not really Cambodians or Americans. You could not fit them in any category. Frustration and anger arose. It became more or less a racial identity issue.

AK: This is all happening at the same time—welfare fraud, crime, identity confusion?

HM: Everything at the same time. I came in the middle of that climate. I was overwhelmed by the situation. There were so many things to decide in addition to how to get a grant. From 1979 to 1994, KCT didn't get any grants during that entire fifteen-year period. Now, you wake up fifteen years later and you want to get one. How are we to compete with all the other agencies? That was the biggest challenge.

AK: The picture I'm getting is that for a fifteen-year period, the organization wasn't doing too much, but there were lots of problems. You came on board when all this was happening.

HM: I walked into a hornet's nest.

AK: Are you receiving some funding now?

HM: We do have some grants. We have a self-sufficiency program, employment services program, youth and family program, and a domestic violence prevention program currently in place. We are working on obtaining a grant for a mental health program.

AK: How many Cambodians are in the Tacoma area right now?

HM: That question I have been asking the State Refugee Department myself. I've been asking but nobody can tell me the answer. But, I can tell you roughly between five and six thousand. In Seattle, there are at least seven to eight thousand. I think some of the people are moving from Seattle to Tacoma because in a big city like Seattle, everything is set.

AK: Is there a part of town where Cambodians tend to live, or do they live all over?

HM: Well, there are a couple of areas. One is the East Side, the other is the Hilltop area.

AK: If you were to characterize the Cambodians in Tacoma versus those in Seattle, are there any differences?

HM: No. There's really not much difference.

AK: Why did people come to Tacoma, do you know?

HM: Because Tacoma has more job opportunities.

AK: What kind of jobs do Cambodians have here?

HM: It varies. A small portion works in government. The majority works in manufacturing, in the sewing business, and in the stores. Some open their own businesses.

AK: What kind of businesses do people have?

HM: It varies from mechanics to mushrooms.

AK: Mushrooms? Selling mushrooms?

HM: Yeah, they get them from the fields and they sell them at wholesale and then ship some of them to Japan and to other countries. We have to make it known to the mainstream that our people are concerned about the community. We have to tell them, crime is not only limited to the Asian community. Crime is all over. America, as we say, is like a salad bowl with carrots and everything in it. There are gifted people from Cambodia who have come to the United States. One of our professors in the music department at the University of Arizona, Dr. Chinary Ung [now at the University of California, San Diego], won the Grawmeyer Award for an orchestral composition. In 1986 a young Cambodian girl, Linn Yann, won the national spelling bee.

AK: What I'm hearing you say is that people are focusing too much on all the negative stuff about Cambodians.

HM: Negative, yeah. You can't be negative all the time; you must look at both sides. We have some good things to bring to America. We bring diversity, intelligence, and many other things here. Not just all bad. But let's look at the problems, not just as community problems, Asian ethnic community problems, but as problems of the whole society. That's the way I get their attention to try to resolve the problems. They cannot say this is this community's problem, so I don't need to care; it is *their* problem. No, it's *our* problem, a problem of the community that we live in.

AK: I think you're absolutely right. That's an important point. What we're trying to do in this book is to create an accurate and inclusive picture to show that there are some negatives, but there are also some positives. As for the negative things, there are explanations for why the situation is so. I'm trying to get a complete picture. People tend to either paint a very rosy picture or a very negative picture.

HM: You got to be fair, nonbiased. You cannot have a one-sided story. We have two newspapers. We now have a newspaper called the *New Image*. It took us a long time to get it started; we had never done a newspaper before. But, it shows the brighter side of what we are doing to turn our situation around.

AK: That's published by the association?

HM: Yeah, the association—the KCT. We spent over six hundred hours typing the English text into the computer and then had to translate it into Khmer text [and typesetting that]. So many hours. I was not trained to be a newspaperman!

AK: I think this is very impressive. I know there's a Cambodian Association in Seattle, but I don't think they do these kinds of things.

HM: No.

AK: It sounds like the organization is becoming very ambitious. You've gotten some funding. Where is the funding coming from?

HM: The source of the funding comes from the city, county, and state. Imagine, it takes a lot for officials to give us the money. We had to find a way to win their trust.

AK: What are the plans for the organization for the next five years or so?

HM: The first thing is to continue working to get our people off of welfare.

AK: How many are on welfare now?

HM: I cannot tell you the exact number; I don't have it.

AK: About half?

HM: I don't know. I don't want to tell you something for which I don't have the statistics.

AK: Are the numbers about the same as in Seattle do you think? More or less?

HM: I don't know. I have no idea; I never get a chance to compare. You look at my profession, what I do. I deliver babies day and night. I was just up delivering a baby until three o'clock this morning. I have my practice and everything. It's like a storm. I have a lifestyle that I don't think many people would like. I have a nice wife, she lives like a single parent. That has a sort of negative impact on my children. Sometimes, you know, my wife asks me, "Doctor, do you know the last time you ate with your children?" I say, "Sure, it was just the other day." She says, "No, it was two weeks ago." But, I have the full support of my family for what I'm doing.

AK: You know, this is something that I've heard from other leaders in the community, too. There are so few people who have the leadership skills that they're stretched really thin within the community. Is that something that you're experiencing?

HM: Yeah, it's kind of rare to find people who will devote their time. When you reach a certain level of comfort in life, what's going to make you get involved? This is not something where you go and play and get honor. This is something in which you're going to get burned, you're going to get hit, you're going to get criticized. You know, I'm a Fellow of the International College of Surgeons. As far as I know, I was the only Cambodian and one of only a small number of Asian physicians accepted to this prestigious organization. But my soul tells me I got to do something for the community. That's why I come back. I am not able to forget the community because when I sleep at night, I know that there are other people who are still struggling. I don't know how much I can do, but I will, I have to do something.

AK: I think you recognize that you're one of the more fortunate ones.

HM: Yeah, I do feel that way. Fortunate in one way, but unfortunate in another way.

AK: Because your wife is like a single parent?

HM: More than that, I am also a walking wounded person. I was interviewed by one of the Seattle newspaper reporters. She asked, "How do you feel being here? I think you are lucky." She meant that I was lucky to be here. I responded, "Not really, because we are so close in the family. Most of our brothers and sisters died in the war." I am here, but I am missing something. I should have been with them in happiness, or sadness, or in death, or whatever. It's just a sense of guilt. When one member of your family dies, you will cry. You feel sorry, you regret their loss. Imagine your whole family is wiped out; your friends are wiped out. You don't even have a tear to shed. This is a serious thing. It stays in your mind and in your heart. I'm not at all lucky. I just want to say that.

AK: Going back to what you were talking about earlier. You said that one of your missions is to get people off welfare. How do you plan to do that?

HM: With this welfare fraud, the SSI [Supplemental Security Income] fraud, back in March, April, and May, that was a hot time for Tacoma because the FBI got involved. Before I knew it, I got a call from a supervisor at the FBI. The fact that I was a concerned citizen, my name was already in their file. I'm not looking for that. I'm just looking to help the community. They handcuffed and took people away almost every night. There were people who defended themselves very well, but some of the people did not. It created a lot of fear in the community. I went to meet with the prosecutors. We went to see the different legal authorities. I tried to talk things over. What can we do with these people? They are already here in America. Is putting them in jail the solution to the problem? I do not think so. I feel that putting them in jail is going to create more problems. Their depression is going to get worse and crime will increase when they get out. The children who live with parents who are in jail are going to have more problems. Teenage pregnancy, crime, drugs, all of that. You name it. So, we talked and we had a good understanding and now it's kind of peaceful, at least for now.

Since that time we have opened up an orientation class. As you can see, the problems we face go way back. Why are the people doing this? Why are the children doing this? I've talked to officials, I've talked to the state legislators, the U.S. senator. We talk to the mayor of the city, we talk to the city manager, to get them to understand what we are trying to do. To get our people off of welfare, you got to understand their culture. You got to understand the challenges; you got to understand the shock. It's not a simple situation. Just putting them to work, that will not work. You put them to work today, tomorrow they leave. Because they don't understand many concepts, sometimes they fight with the employers. We have to give them some orientation. We say, "Look, you've come here, you represent our people. You should do no wrong because it not only hurts you, it hurts other people. Because you create a bad impression, nobody can use that channel again to get a job."

So, we have a lot of work like that to do. We go to the church, we go to the temple, to try to make people understand. Finally, we got a grant from the city. Going back to how we did that, they gave us $20,000. That is a lot of money; it's a huge sum of money for an organization that never had a dollar. We're so proud. During that time rent [for our office] was $250 a month. One of the Cambodian guys offered us his whole house; rent was supposed to be $750 to $800 a month but they gave it to us for $250. That's what we are doing; saving and stretching the money we have to reduce welfare dependency. When you look at the full picture of what needs to be done and what we have actually accomplished, then you can see the importance of our organization. We have done a lot in so little time, but we've only scratched the surface of our problems.

AK: It sounds like you're trying to put together a holistic program to get people oriented to the work style here.

HM: We're doing that. We ask for $20,000, they asked us to place sixteen people at work. In a very short period, we were able to place forty. Forty! At the very beginning, our organization, the Khmer Community of Tacoma, was not able to get going because it was so pressed by the competition. Cambodian clients represent 45 to 48 percent of all clients served in Tacoma, in terms of public assistance. There are four or five agencies here that had been here before 1979. KCT was the one that was just getting started, so you can imagine the challenge we had. Now, we are able to place people in jobs. Placing people to work is not only bringing them to work and talking to an employer. It takes more than that. It takes orientation. It takes cultural understanding. It takes talking, it takes understanding, so the people will stay there on the job.

AK: Who's doing all of this?

HM: Our organization. All the staff members volunteer their time. We only could afford to pay one person part time. Twenty thousand dollars doesn't go that far. Now, we are very successful and we are very proud. The city is very proud of our efforts and we hope to get more money.

AK: What kinds of jobs did you place people in?

HM: Different kinds of jobs. From cleaning chickens to computer work; all kind of jobs.

AK: I'm starting to get the picture of what's happening with the adults: You're trying to get them oriented toward working. What about the children? You alluded to a lot of issues that they're facing.

HM: We have a Youth and Family Program that focuses on children. We want to give them some identity, a sense of where they belong, so they will not fall between the cracks of the two cultures.

AK: That's something you're implementing?

HM: Right. We've brought some school teachers, some leaders, to come in and give a push to see what we can do.

AK: Do you know what the dropout rate is among the kids?

HM: I don't have an exact number but it's not very high. We're proud of that. But it's still a problem. I don't have an exact number to quote you.

AK: I know one thing you're concerned about is not painting an overly bleak picture of the community. What are some success stories that you can share?

HM: You see stories in the newspaper. We have the man at the university who won the award, the composer. We have a teenager who won the Teenager of the Year Award for Washington state. We have some success stories in the schools.

AK: Do you see the majority of young people going to college, getting professional jobs?

HM: More and more. In the last three years, we've seen some growth.

AK: One thing that people keep telling me is that they're disappointed there are not more young people pursuing higher education.

HM: Not in the Tacoma area. There are some graduates. Two years ago, in Tacoma at least, we rarely saw bachelor degree graduates. But now, we have more.

AK: Is there a Buddhist temple in Tacoma?

HM: Yeah, there are two temples.

AK: Two temples in Tacoma? There are two in Seattle, too.

HM: Well, that is a dilemma actually. I do not want to say two temples, I want to say one temple. Well, we have to change a lot in the way we believe, in the way we practice religion. There was a fire, a big fire. One of the temples now is barely open.

AK: It sounds like you've been very busy.

HM: We meet, our board members meet. Although they are all working for the government or in private business, we meet on the average seventy times a year.

AK: Seventy times a year! That's a lot.

HM: A lot. And each time for a minimum of three hours. We have to go through a lot of things, through orientation, through leadership, through commitment, whatever you want to call it.

AK: How many members are there who meet seventy times a year?

HM: About fifteen. We have more members than that. We have about twenty-five members. At least fifteen are very involved.

AK: So, it sounds like the major focus of the organization right now is on getting people to work. You mentioned the Youth and Family Program.

HM: That's what we are doing: family self-sufficiency. We promote small business. We encourage students to push for more education. That's the image we want to create. We have to show that we are not criminals here.

AK: You mentioned earlier that there's some ethnic tension in Tacoma. Can you tell me more about that?

HM: Well, it's really not ethnic. I don't think it's really doing any harm. Maybe I didn't make myself clear. We have four or five agencies here. There's a Laotian one, there's a Vietnamese one, there are other groups, Korean, and so forth. Meanwhile, KCT is trying to emerge. Earlier, we could not emerge. So, they look at us and give us no credit. We had no track record. We couldn't apply for any grant. So, when we started to emerge, there were a lot of challenges. If you want to call it tension, it could be that. But with all the competition, emerging was not easy.

AK: It seems like you've overcome a lot of obstacles just to get to where you are today.

HM: The challenges are not only coming from the mainstream, not only from the other agencies, not only from the difficulty of communicating with our people. Because you are dealing with a traumatized people, a mentally traumatized people, you have to find ways to communicate with them. They've lost [the ability to] trust. People have been treating them so badly for so many years, so many times, with the holocaust and all that, now when we go and talk with them . . .

AK: There's a lot of distrust?

HM: Distrust, a tremendous, tremendous amount. Now, we try to build trust. We are starting to come together. We have a place. The organization didn't have a good name, people talked bad about it. We had to change that image. It's not something we could do overnight.

AK: What are some other effects you see in Cambodians here from having survived the cruelties of Pol Pot? You talked about distrust.

HM: Lack of trust is the main thing. With the lack of trust, people are not together.

AK: Do you think that their suffering stops them from being able to work?

HM: Well, they are handicapped in many ways. Handicapped from the war, handicapped because their children try to imitate the mainstream. They are in culture shock themselves. They are here in America and they don't have higher education, they don't have work, they get more depressed, they get sick, they don't have any respect from their children. Unlike their home in Cambodia, even if they're poor there, they still had trust in the culture. The concept of village was there; children could not run around and do whatever they wanted. There would be an uncle, or a teacher, or a mom, or somebody watching. Everybody watched and the children's behavior was reported to their parents. So, the whole village knew what was going on because everyone knew everyone else. Here, you know, we're at the mercy of whatever is happening. Children have more contact with the new society. They see the freedom and they take advantage of the freedom the wrong way. And nobody is able to tell them anything because the parents are not as educated as the children are. The children look down on their parents; their parents get more depressed. All those barriers separate them.

AK: It's a big vicious cycle that is hard to break.

HM: Right. We're trying to put this shattered situation back together.

AK: We've covered a lot of the topics I wanted to cover, and you've told me a little about your background. But I'm curious as to how you ended up here in Tacoma.

HM: Well, first of all, I left Cambodia in 1973. I went to France to study but I wanted to go to Canada since some Canadians speak French.

AK: Did you go to medical school in Cambodia?

HM: Yes, I graduated from medical school in Cambodia in 1971. I did my internship in France. Then I came to do my residency in the States. When I first got here, after three months, I had already spent all the money I had saved. I could not go back to Cambodia, I could not go to Canada, I could not go anywhere. I had to survive.

AK: So, you were in the U.S. when the Khmer Rouge took over?

HM: Yeah. I was folding newspapers at the time. Working at the *Washington Post* folding newspapers and sorting newspapers. I could not go anywhere; the country had fallen to the communists and there was nowhere to move to. You don't have a choice, you got to make a living. I had to study for my residency here in the States. When you are studying medicine [and you have to prepare] for a test without any assistance from teachers, it is very difficult. There are some diseases that exist here that we never learned of in France or in Cambodia. You see, I studied medicine in Cambodia in a school where the curriculum was set by the Faculty of Medicine in Paris, France. The medical knowledge was based on diseases in Europe. So, even though I had already attended and completed my formal schooling and training, I had to study on my own to prepare for the residency test here in the States.

AK: It's very unusual, isn't it, for someone who studied medicine in another country to be able to get a medical license here?

HM: Yeah, they make it very hard. Medical practice in Western countries is better than in the Asian countries because it is more modernized. The Western countries have more access to books and things like that. It's very hard for people from our country because it is a very small country. There is a high failure rate; a lot of people don't make it, even if you may have graduated. Now, when you've been a medical director, like I was in Cambodia, and then you have to sort newspapers, your identity is not very stable. "Wow, where, who am I?" But, when you don't have a choice, you do whatever is necessary to survive. I think that's the ground for success.

AK: But eventually you were able to practice medicine in Texas, you said, for several years?

HM: Yeah, ten years.

AK: At the school that your children attend, are there lots of other Cambodian kids?

HM: No. They don't have any Cambodian kids there.

AK: Do you live in Tacoma?

HM: No, I live in Federal Way, Washington.

AK: Do you know of many families here with no father, single-parent families?

HM: Someone from the Welfare Department can tell you about that better than I can.

AK: Do you or other people you know keep abreast of what's going on in Cambodia?

HM: Yeah, as a personal interest.

AK: In the Tacoma area, do you find that there's any kind of factionalism that results from people taking sides?

HM: No, no. Well, in the past, maybe, but not at this time, because what I tried to bring to their attention is that you cannot get together on the issues of politics or religion or anything like that. We have to concentrate on one goal and that is helping the community. That's all. Leave the rest to other interested people; they can join any faction; that's their choice, and we have no control over that. But as an organization, we have to concentrate on progress in the community.

AK: Do a lot of people send money back to Cambodia?

HM: Oh, I don't know a lot about that, but I hear they do. Myself, I send some to our poor relatives.

AK: Do you hear people talking about going back to Cambodia to live?

HM: Yes, I've heard. People who don't do well here, I think it's best for them to go back to their home.

AK: Do you think Buddhism provides unity for the Cambodian people?

HM: Yes, but the Buddhist religion needs to change with the times, with the location, with their frame of thinking. You cannot take Buddhism purely and put it in Tacoma, in a new adopted land. You have to make some modifications.

AK: Have modifications been made?

HM: There are probably some, but they're not very obvious to me. What are the modifications that I'd like to see? I want religion to serve the community as well as God. What does that mean? We see two lives: the life here, and the life after death when the spirit leaves. I tell the people, "You've got to live in this life too." You think about the other life when you're not comfortable with this life. The temple was built by the people. The temple needs to return the favor and help the community members at a time when they have no money, when they have death in the family, when they have problems or no jobs. The temple should help them. Compare that with the church. I am not on the side of the church but I'm not against the church, either. I have friends who are pastors; I have friends who are heads of the temple. I see both sides. The church helps the people. The people make contributions but they also get something in return. It should be a two-way street. It's not only one way, like a well. You should not have to bring the water to the temple all the time. If the well is collapsing, there will be no more water for the temple. That's what I've told the people and the community. Of course, we got a lot of resistance at the beginning but now people are beginning to understand a little better. You got to drink the water to survive, so you can contribute to the temple. If you are unhealthy, if you are too thirsty, you cannot work.

AK: What sorts of things do you think the temple should do for the people?

HM: For the people? Take care of them. Look after the people of the community, the welfare of the community. Don't just expect people to bring things to you, to bring food, to bring money.

AK: Do all the Cambodians in Tacoma go to one of the temples?

HM: No. Some practice Christianity. I don't know what the ratio is. But I think the majority still goes to the temple.

AK: Do you know what denominations of Christianity are popular among Cambodians?

HM: We have a pastor upstairs. He's the head of the Cambodian church. He probably can answer that question.

AK: There's even a Cambodian church here?

HM: Cambodian church, yeah. Sure, we have a Cambodian church.

AK: Do the temples try to do anything to attract the young people?

HM: I haven't seen that. If they try, I am not aware of their efforts.

AK: Are young people drifting away from Buddhism?

HM: In a way, yes, because they don't understand what the monk says. It is not a laymen's language that they speak. They lecture and chant in Pali. Some people don't understand what the monks say. The monk will say something in that language and then translate it into laymen's language, but some of the children, the new generation, do not even understand the laymen's language. So, they don't appear to have much interest. In a very well-oriented family, Buddhism can be maintained. There are young children who are very attracted to the religion. They always want to go to the temple ceremonies. I don't know how many there are but I think a large majority of the people is still going to the temple.

AK: How many monks are there at the two temples?

HM: Roughly four or five.

AK: In each?

HM: Yeah.

AK: Do you know where they came from?

HM: Some of them came from Cambodia. Some of them just became monks here.

AK: My understanding is that most of the monks in Cambodia either were forced to stop being monks or were killed.

HM: There are more now.

AK: Can you tell me more about your program?

HM: In this program, the participants who are able to go to work will go to counseling, job training, and ESL [English as a second language] at the same time. For those who are not able to work, the program will help them gain access to social services such as food stamps, transportation, and housing. Our argument for trying to get funds from the government for our program is that having people remain on welfare indefinitely is more expensive than providing services to help them become self-sufficient. A large part of the program is focused on orienting Cambodians to the American system and to the culture here. For example, because Cambodians are not used to the idea of preventive medicine, they will wait until they are really sick and

then have to take an ambulance to the emergency room. If they are on public assistance, the government pays for this expensive treatment. Another part
of our program helps Cambodians learn the bus system so that they can get
around town by themselves.

AK: It's really inspiring to hear about the efforts you and your organization are making. Good luck in your work and thank you for taking the time
to talk to me.

September 12, 1996

11. Dharamuni Phala Svy Chea
A Holistic Approach to Mental Health

Ms. PHALA CHEA is a clinical case manager and cross-cultural training specialist at the Asian Counseling and Referral Services (ACRS), a multiservice agency in Seattle. ACRS has a behavioral health department that offers counseling for mental health problems, chemical dependency, and domestic violence. It also has a medical clinic, a job-training program, an assisted living program, a day-care center, a preschool program, a children's afterschool program, an adult program, a program for the elderly who come for day activities in order to reduce their social isolation, English-as-a-secondlanguage classes, a food bank, and an immigration and naturalization counseling service. In addition, the agency manages two houses for its mental health clients who are able to function more or less independently but who benefit from a group-living situation. There is an expresso coffee shop and a bakery in the building where ACRS is located run by "lower-functioning clients" who are learning rudimentary job skills. These individuals also operate a recycling program. Although most of ACRS's clients are of Asian ancestry, the agency also serves members of other ethnic groups who need help.

Phala Chea's family escaped from Cambodia when the Khmer Rouge came to power in 1975. They spent a year in a refugee camp in Thailand and in 1976 were resettled in York, Pennsylvania. The nearest large city to York is Baltimore, more than thirty miles to the south. Chea recalls that she and her brother were the only students of Asian ancestry in the public elementary school they attended in York. The family moved to Seattle in 1980. Because she is bilingual in Khmer and English, she was asked by a refugee resettlement agency to be a volunteer interpreter when she was only in her early teens. At that time, large numbers of Cambodian refugees who did not speak English were arriving in the greater Seattle area.

Ms. Chea received a B.A. in psychology from the University of Washington in 1990 and began working for ACRS right out of college. While working, she took evening classes and obtained her M.S.W. degree in 1996, also from the University of Washington.

When I talked to her by telephone on September 26, 2001, Phala Chea told me that ACRS has grown since the mid-nineties and moved into new quarters, occupying two floors of a building at Village Square in Seattle's International District. ACRS is one of the largest Asian community service agencies in the United States. It has a staff of 150 persons who have competence in twenty-two Asian languages and dialects. They serve clients who speak various dialects of Chinese, Japanese, Korean, Tagalog, Ilocano, Hmong, Lao, Mien, Khmer, Vietnamese, Thai, and several other Asian languages. Ms. Chea observes that it is quite difficult to find staff members with both the required language skills and the professional training. Given its commitment to meeting the needs of underserved Asian immigrant and refugee communities, ACRS often has to hire people who can speak a particular language and have experience working in their own ethnic communities but who do not have the professional degrees desired. The agency gives these people on-the-job training after they are hired.

The number of clients that ACRS serves has increased substantially since the mid-nineties. Clients are also presenting different symptoms. In the past, most suffered from posttraumatic stress disorder and major depression, but today more and more individuals who seek help at ACRS are suffering from schizophrenia and bipolar disorder. Their condition is often quite severe. Some of Ms. Chea's new clients are relatively young—people in their early thirties who were traumatized as children under the Khmer Rouge regime, during their escape, and in the years when they were confined in refugee camps in Thailand. Most of these individuals had not sought help before but are doing so now because their mental health problems are interfering with their daily living.

*   *   *

AK: Can you start by telling me about the kind of work you do at this organization with Cambodians?

PC: I'm a clinical case manager as well as a trainer. The majority of the people I work with are Cambodian clients. I'm three-quarters case manager and one-quarter trainer. As a case manager, I have anywhere between thirty-five to forty-five clients at a given time. My caseload with mental illness are of different severities and different diagnoses—anywhere from mood disorder, depression, to people who have psychosis, schizophrenia.

AK: How do they come to you?

PC: Depending on the severity—we're close to Harborview Medical Center here—we get a lot of our referrals, the ones that are acute, because they went into crisis and are hospitalized. Some of them come to us through the social system, like DSHS [Department of Social and Health Services], or the school system, even from colleges, and some just from community referrals.

AK: What is your relationship to the Refugee Clinic [at Harborview]?

PC: The Refugee Clinic? Well, we don't have a formal relationship. Sometimes we see the same client for different things: They see the medical and we see the mental health aspects.

AK: Do you do the counseling here?

PC: Right. They have some mental health staff but their specialty is more physical health.

AK: Do people pay for your services here, or are you working off a grant?

PC: This agency is a private nonprofit agency, so we have different sources of funding. Most of our clients use coupons because a lot of them are chronically mentally ill, because they have long-term illnesses. So, they're on SSI [Supplemental Security Income] or on some sort of grant. There are some on insurance which is privately paid.

AK: Are you working mainly with a low-income population?

PC: Yes, we are.

AK: Are people coming to you specifically with disorders related to surviving through the Pol Pot period, or is it more things you would see in any population?

PC: A lot more of the ones I see are diagnosed as posttraumatic stress disorder, which is related to what they've gone through during the Pol Pot regime. The majority of them have illnesses that can be traced back to those years, like a lot of their families have been killed, they're separated, things like that. There are other people who have been here before the country fell, but that's just a small number.

AK: My understanding of Asians in general, and Cambodians specifically, is that they're not usually going to seek out mental health services. Do you find a reluctance on their part to come to you? Can you tell me what it's like to work with Cambodians?

PC: There are different degrees. The term a lot of Cambodians use for mental illness is they "go crazy." So, if they look at it that way, of course, they're reluctant, like when the doctor refers them to us. To give an example, a client who has never heard of us but has an anxiety attack, he thought he was dying, everything was physical. He ends up in the emergency room saying he's dying. The doctor says, "Well, go to the Mental Health Agency." And he says, "Why are you sending me to a crazy place when I have physical problems?" But then, when you dig into their history, you find out that they have a lot of trauma and things involved that antianxiety drugs and counseling can help. A lot of times, we do have to educate a lot of our clients.

AK: People are usually being referred to you. They're not just coming out of their own volition, is that correct?

PC: Usually they're referred by other people. There are very few who come because they heard about us through the words of friends. If they haven't heard through somebody, they just don't come, because it's a mental health agency.

AK: Are you doing talk therapy with them?

PC: It's a combination. You do everything and anything. It depends on whether it fits. That's where clinical case management comes into play, because you do anything from if they need food, you take them to the food bank, if they need housing, you work on housing. If they need counseling, then you do therapy. It depends on what you mean by therapy, if you're talking about the American traditional therapy where you're sitting there on the couch. I think what we do is therapeutic as well; it's just not the old traditional Freudian kind of thing. But everything we do, in my mind, is therapy. Like if they're starving, sitting there talking to them isn't going to help, but if you get food for them, it helps. If they're out of clothes, you go and get clothes.

AK: You're providing for all their needs.

PC: Right. Exactly. It's a holistic view. We're not just doing the mainstream thing. A lot of our clients practice the old tradition, whether it be Buddhism or other means, but a lot of what we do can be called spiritual healing, with herbal medicine, with the old healer from the old country. The thing that's unique about us is we incorporate all that.

AK: How many Cambodians are there right now who work here?

PC: There are three in the mental health program and there are two in the elderly program.

AK: About how many Cambodians do you see at this agency?

PC: I don't know offhand the total number at the agency, but I know we have about two hundred mental health clients, or maybe 150 right now.

AK: They're all Cambodians?

PC: Yeah. I think it's about 150. I'm not sure about the elderly program.

AK: You mentioned things like posttraumatic stress disorder, anxiety attacks. What other kinds of things are you seeing?

PC: Besides those, major depression. Usually it overlaps with posttraumatic stress disorder. And then we see people with diagnoses such as schizophrenia, whether it be paranoid or other types. There's all kinds, you know, of diagnoses.

AK: Do they try to talk to you about the trauma they experienced from living through the Pol Pot regime, or do they try to repress those memories?

PC: It's hard to generalize because everyone is different. We have groups.

AK: You have group therapy here?

PC: Yes. We call it "support and medication group." A lot of women participate—I see more women than men.

AK: Women tend to be more receptive to therapy?

PC: Either that or there's a lot more women who are by themselves. And so, they're here and we have a group. Today, for example, this morning, I had a group, a two-hour group, about seven women and a male, who get together. This group is pretty old, so they've gotten to the point where they're helping each other with the current issues rather than going back and digging up everything. But when we first started the group, a long time ago, maybe ten years ago, that's what the main theme was, what was happening then and how that affected them and how it carried through. But that particular group now has moved over to what are they doing to survive, how are they dealing with the kids, and so forth. So the groups evolve, depending on how long ago we started the group. We have a new group, people who have never talked about the past. They were doing fine with their lives, and then something happens, like a car accident, or somebody died in their family, then the trauma somehow gets triggered. So then those people now are starting to talk about their trauma. This car accident somehow makes them remember the trauma that happened during Pol Pot. To them, it's really fresh and new. So, you have different levels for different people. Even though they got out of the country about the same time, some people are delayed in their reaction to the trauma.

AK: From being in these groups, you've probably heard a lot of stories. Can you give me some case examples?

PC: I'll just take the woman who has two kids, who has two children now with a second husband. But when she was in Cambodia, she was married and had two other children. Between 1975 and 1979, her two kids and she were forced to work; the parents and kids were separated—her husband was in the army, and he was killed right off the bat. He was murdered. She witnessed one of her sisters being pushed off a second floor to her death. She worked in the rice fields, and then she remembered some of the people who had said something wrong or weren't working the way they were supposed to work were taken away. A lot of the soldiers in charge were young children; they were twelve or thirteen years old. They would take a plastic bag and wrap it around a person's neck and kill him. She survived and in 1979 she fled to Thailand. During the escape, you see a lot of corpses; you become sort of desensitized. Her journey from Cambodia to Thailand took several days on foot and there were bandits along the way, robbers. Before she got to the refugee camp, she ran into robbers. Sometimes the Thai soldiers took advantage of the women. The people she came with—they traveled in groups—some women got raped, some ran away. Some people stepped on land mines before they even got to a camp. The horror stories in camp: especially at night, it was not safe. If you're single, whether you used to be married or not, if you're by yourself, you could be raped and abused in different ways. She met her present husband in camp and got married and moved here. Hers is not an isolated story.

AK: I've heard a lot of horror stories, but from a mental health perspective what do you see as the result of those kinds of experiences?

PC: Well, it depends. Sometimes, it makes them feel like they've worked very hard, done a lot of things, but all of a sudden, at the drop of a hat, their lives can get turned upside down. So, some people always sort of feel hopeless, like, what's the point? You made all the effort, you've done everything, and then everything is gone, everything is so vulnerable. They feel vulnerable when they get to this point. But some people, they say they've gone through all that, now they have another chance, and they're working hard at it.

AK: What about working? Are people able to work, the ones you're seeing?

PC: Some people can. The ones I see are such extreme cases. The people in the community that I know are different from the ones I see in my work.

AK: I'd like to hear about both, so let's talk first about your limited perspective here and then go to the more general.

PC: Some of the people who have severe schizophrenia, they work at places like espresso stands. They need something they can focus and concentrate on because a lot of these people have poor concentration, they have limited English ability, and they have limited skills. So, if they do work, it's at really low-paying jobs. They work part time at a labor-intensive kind of job. And then we try to wean them. That's another part of what we do. We have a job counselor. Whichever clients are ready to work, we push them in that direction. They'll either do a janitorial job a couple of times a week, a couple of hours a day. Some people can do housekeeping, so we push them toward that direction. We refer them, the ones who are stable enough, who're not extremely psychotic or too depressed where they're always wanting to kill themselves, they do work, but it takes a long time for someone we're seeing to get a good job. Some of the people we're seeing, they decompensate, they get really sick, and they're back where we started. So, we're seeing the extreme population. It's hard to paint a glamorous picture, but they do have jobs or we have activities where we get these clients who are really chronic, really, really have a lot of illness, we have them practice different life skills. Some of these people live in half-way houses, where it's not independent, but it's not restricted, either.

AK: Half-way houses where there are just Cambodians?

PC: No, there are different kinds of people. There aren't houses that are just Cambodian; the population just isn't big enough. But the people that are there, they come to this activity center, which we also have, where they practice life skills, so they can go out in the community and do cooking, cleaning, speak English, just real basics. And once that's done, if they can handle that, they can look into whichever jobs they can get.

AK: In your estimate, what percentage of the Cambodian population here is suffering from problems like this?

PC: The trauma?

AK: Trauma-related illnesses.

PC: Oh, that's hard for me to say. I would probably say the severity of how they are affected is different, but I would think that 80 percent, one way or another, are affected. Just because they're affected doesn't mean they're not working or going through their daily lives. A lot of friends my age are affected by the trauma, but they still go on with their lives. So, in terms of how many are affected, probably 80 percent, but not all 80 percent are disabled. The disabled part is very small, maybe 10 or 15 percent, but a lot of people are affected one way or another.

AK: What are some of the other things you hear from your clients or in the groups, problems they're having—not just related to trauma—adaptation to this culture, family stresses, that kind of thing?

PC: I think that right now, at this point, for the people who've been here a lot, the major problem is dealing with their children, with the generation gap, with the communication gap. It's harder for the parents because the kids and the parents are both first generation; the kids pick up English more quickly, they know the system better. The parents don't have English-speaking abilities; they can't really deal with the schools. So, there are control issues between the parents and the children, where the kids somehow have more power than the parents because they know the language and they know the system. A lot of the times, the parents have to depend on the kids: reading letters, taking them places, interpreting for the parents. So, we're running into a lot of situations where the kids are undermining the parents, if the parents are uneducated in this country or in our old country. That seems to be the main problem that's coming up now. Some kids are going into gangs because when they go to school it's hard for them to turn to the parents. Even when the parents are supportive, it's difficult for them to help their kids out in a system which they can't understand. And when they go to school, they face discrimination from the mainstream, so the kids turn to each other. They turn to each other and they form gangs. There are different levels of gangs. There are some gangs which are harmless; they're just hanging out. And other gangs where they do delinquent activities, like stealing cars, whatever.

AK: Are there certain schools in the Seattle area where there are lots of Cambodians, or are Cambodian kids sort of spread out all over?

PC: At Chief Seattle School, there are a lot of Cambodian kids there. I don't know the names of all the schools, but there's the White Center area, there's a lot of Cambodian children there. Down here, the Rainier Beach area, there's a lot of Cambodian kids.

AK: Do you have any sense in those areas where there are lots of Cambodians, what is the dropout rate?

PC: I have no idea; I can't speak to that.

AK: What about the percentage involved in gangs?

PC: I don't have that either. I don't have the statistics.

AK: Do you see people who talk to you about violence in the family, domestic violence, child abuse?

PC: I think that's something they don't talk about much. There are very few we get who are referred from CPS [Children's Protective Services]; the children's department, they deal with that. Right now, it's a very small percentage. Doesn't mean it's not there, but a lot of my clients aren't really talking so much. There's an agency that works with domestic violence and they do have Cambodian workers there do outreach. With my women's group, what I'm doing is setting them up to do outreach and talk about domestic violence.

AK: Do you have any kids whom you're counseling?

PC: I work with the adults, but we do have a children's program that's separate. It's kind of a family thing, too, because it's not like you only work with the adults or the kids. If something's wrong with the kids, you don't just leave them there. If you go on a home visit, and there's a family issue, you work with that too. But mainly the children's program works with the children and if I have a client who has children who have problems, then I refer them to the children's program and we work together.

AK: So, you have the elderly program, the adult program, and the children's program. Are there Cambodians who specialize in each of the three areas?

PC: Yes.

AK: Do you have a sense of how many Cambodians there are in the greater Seattle area?

PC: All I know is that it's the third-largest in the United States. Long Beach is first; Lowell, Massachusetts, is second; Seattle's the third-largest. So, I think there are about thirty thousand or twenty-nine thousand; I'm not sure.

AK: Earlier, you were saying that there's a difference between the clients whom you work with and other Cambodians you know. Can you paint a picture for me of the Cambodians you know in terms of the kids and the parents.

PC: Yeah, because when you hear or when you read, you always hear things related to Pol Pot, but nobody ever writes about what are Cambodians like growing up here as children, going to school, going to college, with parents who are working, struggling. There's the one case that I just talked about, but then there are others, whether they lived through the communists or not, who for some reason, are able to adjust and they go to school like anybody else. Say, children, for example, I came at the age of ten, and a lot of them came at about the same age. We came earlier and went through the school system. We came here as young children, and our parents raised us to be Cambodian, but you go to school and the society you're raised in is mainstream American, so there's a lot of conflicts, identity conflicts, there are a lot of issues you go through. You, as an Asian American, perhaps you can understand that. The other Cambodians are a lot like other Asian Americans who didn't go through the trauma or for some reason are able to make it. The parents tell us to work very hard; they have to put in ten, twelve, sixteen hours, at one or two jobs, so their kids can go to school, or they can buy a house outside of the bad neighborhood, so their kids don't get affected by all the crime. People work hard. We form associations, like at the University of Washington when I was going to school here. We have presidents; I was one year and other people were the other years. We would try to get other kids to go to college, trying to influence other children. We had things like cultural preservation, on a small scale, we tried to start programs, whether it be dancing groups or singing or language classes for kids who are going through this and maybe forgetting the language or not appreciating the culture. Because when you go to school day in and day out, you're not speaking Khmer. What you had before is just strange or queer or weird. Kids are so into being accepted, they reject what they have and misunderstand and feel bad about themselves and their culture; they start to look down on their culture and their families. And then you don't have an identity. You don't really fit in with the mainstream and you don't totally fit in with the Cambodian, so you're kind of like a lost generation, going through a lot of struggle. That whole generation, it probably took them the whole way through college to try to find themselves and where they fit in. What does it mean to be bilingual and bicultural? You have to get to a point where you do accept that you are bilingual, bicultural; you're not nei-ther/nor, you're both. That population goes to college and they go to work.

AK: You said that you came to the U.S. when you were ten. When you went to school, were there lots of other Cambodians at your school?

PC: No. I went to Pennsylvania when I first came here. I came in '76 and me and my brother were the only Asians in school; it was mostly Black and White. It was this tiny little town called York, Pennsylvania. We were the only ones; we didn't speak English; we didn't have anything. We went to that school and just picked things up.

AK: Did your family leave before the Khmer Rouge came to power?

PC: We left at the same time they came to power. The same day the com-munists came into the capital—we lived at the border of Thailand—when we heard they were coming, we just took off. We went to Thailand and then we came to the United States in '76. We were in camp one year, but we never stayed with the communists.

AK: So, growing up, it sounds like you weren't really around other Cam-bodians.

PC: No, I wasn't. When I was in York, it was mainly Black, White, or Puer-to Rican. Barely any Asians; we had to go to Virginia for [Asian] groceries, food, things like that. And then when I moved here, that's when I started to run into more Asians.

AK: When did you come to this area?

PC: In 1980, when I was in the middle of my eighth grade. In 1980, a big group of refugees came because the Vietnamese invaded Cambodia in 1979 and people came out. There were a lot of people and since I was among the few who had come earlier, the community leaders recruited us to help out, to take people to different places, to interpret. So, I started interpreting and volunteering when I was thirteen and that's how I got involved in the com-munity. We just happened to know one of the leaders and it's like, "Can you help out with the cultural dancing?" So, we connected with the new group of refugees and then I got involved with volunteering and started different associations. That's when I started wanting to know more about who I was.

AK: When you came here, were you in school with other Cambodian kids?

PC: There were other Cambodian kids, but they were different. A lot them had just gotten here and they didn't speak English. They have kind of a dif-ferent culture, while I was already in the middle of everything. There were Cambodians coming, they had ESL, and I was going to help them at ESL. So, it wasn't like other kids I could relate to. It wasn't until college that I met other kids from my generation, other kids who had become bilingual in high school and we could understand each other.

AK: In college, the other Cambodians you knew, were they people who came in that third wave in 1980? Or were they people like you who came in '75, '76?

PC: It was a combination, but a lot of them were from the third wave who came in the 1980s, but they'd gotten to the point where they were acculturated in some sense and they were working hard. A lot of my friends are from the third wave.

AK: Can you paint a picture for me of what people your age are doing?

PC: Well, there aren't many social workers. When I was going to college, in the '80s and '90s, a lot of them went into science. A lot of my friends are either in computer systems, managing computer systems, or they went into pharmacy, or they went into engineering. A lot of my close friends, like one of my best friends, he's an engineer. My brother, their generation, they all went into engineering. They're in some kind of science field because they felt that in order to survive, they need to get a job that's more practical, which is in science. Some people are into math and different things like that. At the time I was going to college, there were about thirty-five of us at the University of Washington in our group, we called it the Cambodian Students Association. I was the only social worker; the rest of them went into medical school, pharmacy, computer science, or engineering. They all have graduated. Every single one of us has graduated and we are all doing what we are supposed to be doing.

AK: Would you say that the majority of Cambodians your age went to high school and college, or are you folks the exception?

PC: I don't think we're the exception. I think we're the ones who had the opportunity, the ones who came young enough to understand; we could tackle the language. But the ones who came a lot later—if you come here at the end of high school and you're starting college, it's a little harder to grasp the language. The concepts here are totally different. For the ones who come here in their twenties, it's a lot harder. But if they come in their teens, like my generation, then it's easier. And there are new generations who were born here who are now going through college, so I don't think we're the exception. I think that those who do have the same opportunities are going through the process. We don't hear a lot about that because I think people in gangs capture more attention, but I think people should also be paying attention to those that are making it.

AK: That's one thing we're really concerned about—trying to paint a complete picture.

PC: Nobody really writes about what life is like for Cambodian women here; there's more to it than just the illness, the trauma. There's a whole community of people who live here. What are their lives like? Even though they're sick, they go to the temple and they do other things. The same with us. We came here when we were young, we grew up here, but we do things with the older people as well. I think it's easier for people who are able to go in and out of the two different worlds; we do live in two different worlds. I think you probably know what that means. It's harder if you are more Cambodian or more Americanized. I think it's a lot harder for those people than for someone who can balance the two worlds. I keep speaking a lot about my generation because that's what I know. I noticed that if one goes either one way or the other, it's harder. When you're in school, you have to deal with the system and you have to deal with the people, like how do Americans think? You have to compete with them, and you have to present yourself in a way that they can understand. But then when you come home to your parents, how can you present yourself so your parents can understand you while you don't offend your parents? And how can you bridge the two so they can understand both of your worlds? It's a major task. A lot of people think that some of these kids are just bad in nature. But it's really because they have a hard time balancing the act. They don't know where to go. A lot of kids don't know that they have the ability. And who's there to talk to? A lot of the parents are on this side and society is on that side. It's like one's pulling the other. The kids who don't have other means of support, who don't have any guides or any model, they're going to get lost. And that's when they get into trouble. It doesn't matter how old you are, but if you're caught in that in-between . . .

AK: I don't know if you have an opinion on this. Some people have told me that it's actually harder for kids born here, because they grow up totally rootless. The ones born in Cambodia who were raised in that culture have a sense of who they are.

PC: I think that's very true. Same thing with people who were born in camp. Because we were at least exposed to the values that were Cambodian values, we have that to hang on to, we have that identity. But the kids born here, they're told that they're Cambodian but they don't really know what that means. So, it is a lot harder for the newer generation. Their parents expect them to know all that. But how are they supposed to know when they're stuck with the babysitter or they're on the other side all the time? So, I think it's harder for the kids who were born here unless they have a big extended family who lives with them and kind of guides them and teaches them and takes them by the hand, which I've seen happen in some families. Those kids have an easier time—their families have to be supportive of them and the way they live their lives, because they're mainstream-American in some ways. Just because they look Cambodian doesn't mean they are only that, you know. Educating them about the Cambodian values and how they are supposed to live, and, at the same time, to support them when they go out into the world—those are the kids who can succeed more than some of the kids who were born here and whose parents don't have that sense, you know; yet they expect them to be Cambodian.

AK: In your opinion, the kids who are successful are the ones whose parents recognize that they're trying to do this balancing act and support their efforts rather than insisting that they be 100 percent Cambodian.

PC: I think for the most part that's true. A lot of parents don't recognize that, but it's not their fault.

AK: Of the people in your generation, do you have a sense of whether they're interested in maintaining Cambodian culture and values, or do they just want to be American?

PC: I think we go through a phase. That was one of the things that really connected us in college because we were going through a phase. At one time in our lives, like high school age, it's important to fit in—peer pressure and so forth. I think at that point in our lives, many of us, we often have group meetings and discuss what it means, what we are going through. When we were in high school, it was like, Cambodians are so strict. The mainstream is more dominant, they have more power, we want what they have. So, you want to reject your own culture and you want to be just all American and that's it. But when you get to a certain age, like by the time when we are in college, we start saying, "No, we don't want to be just American. We like who we are. We love our values. We'll take the best of the two worlds." There are some things about Cambodians maybe we don't like, so we don't take that. Not everything about American culture is great; so we don't take everything that's American, either. We get to a certain point at a certain age where we learn to take the best of the two worlds and combine them. We start to value our culture, like a lot of us who don't know how to read Khmer are going back to school. They have classes at the temple; we study on our own or with each other. There are people in my generation who went through the war. A lot of them are starting to talk about what happened. They were so busy with their lives they never thought about it before. They had nightmares but they would push those aside, and they do get to a point where they say, "OK, we got a job now, we're pretty stable. What happened?" A lot of them are starting to do that. And it's not affecting them to such a degree that they're losing their jobs. Now they can sit down and relax a little bit and think about what happened, who they really are, how that [experience] has helped them or not helped them. The University of Washington and the University of California did a study where they studied Cambodian social networks. I was involved in that study. They interviewed people who've lived through Pol Pot at least six months and were of different ages, between the ages of thirty and sixty. They just got done with that process and they're doing the transcription.

AK: Do you see a difference in backgrounds among your peers in terms of the ones who were able to make it through college versus the ones who didn't?

PC: In some senses, yes, in some senses, no. A lot of the people who came, even though they went through the communists, came from a background where their parents had more education, they're making it better than people whose parents are illiterate. It's harder for the latter's kids because the parents themselves didn't understand the school system even back then. So, in some senses, yes; we do notice that. In other senses, the kids are doing fine now in school. But I do think it has a lot to do with how much the parents already know and how hard they push the children. If you never knew what education was before, how can you do so now? Kids have to be really, really strong. That's true of my generation. But the later children are in a different boat altogether.

AK: In what sense?

PC: Well, I guess they are, in some ways, the same, because the ones who are born here, their parents' background does have something to do with how they do. If their parents are able to support their kids and know what the system is like, it makes it easier for them. Even if their parents didn't have education over there but they understand English and they know the system here a little bit, by picking it up, then their kids are OK.

AK: You mean there's a general pattern, but it's not a solid rule?

PC: Yeah. It never is. If anything, there are always general and individualistic conditions.

AK: Another question I have concerns your commentary on what it's like to be a young Cambodian American woman. My sense is that a woman's life in Cambodia is very different from the options that are available here. What's it like for someone of your generation versus someone of your mother's generation?

PC: Well, because I haven't lived in Cambodia that long, I couldn't speak to everything.

AK: For example, your parents might have certain expectations about how you should be.

PC: Oh, yeah! OK, I see what you mean. It's very different, because, for my mom's generation—when she got married, it was arranged. And whatever their parents wanted them to study, they studied. Whatever their parents told them to do, they did it because their parents have the words of wisdom. But when you come here, like my generation, it's hard just to take that: "You do that," and that's it. You want to respect your parents, but at the same time, you have your own interests and you're also influenced by Western thinking that says you should be yourself. In Cambodia, you are your family. Whatever you do affects your family. Whether you're a bad apple or a good apple, you stand for your family. So it's hard. There's a pull, especially as a woman. My parents didn't believe I should be dating. Throughout high school, I wasn't allowed to date when I wanted to. They wanted me to be an engineer; I wanted to go into psychology. So, that was hard. I had to find ways to cope, asking why am I disappointing my parents? When is it OK and when is it not? When am I hurting them because I'm doing something vicious? When am I hurting them because this is just a different concept for them? As a young child, when they said no, I said "OK." But later, I did date because I didn't think I was doing anything harmful. But why tell our parents when doing so just hurts them because they don't think it's very nice?

AK: Do you think that's common?

PC: Oh, yeah, it's very common, where the parents think, oh, the kids are not dating, but the kids, we share our secrets with each other. We know who's going with whom but the parents don't know. It's like there's almost a conspiracy where we keep certain things secret. I think that's just one prime example for women, because even if you're born here, some parents don't think you should date. But you do; you just don't tell your parents about it.

AK: What about the older generation? Are there conflicts that you see between husbands and wives, especially when the wives work just like the husbands and have more freedom?

PC: I haven't seen that so much. There are some situations my group talks about, but it seems that everybody is trying to survive, so it's good that both the wife and husband work. There are very few instances where the wife gets to stay home. It's accepted: You're in this country and you both work. That's the bottom line. I'm talking now about the group in their thirties, forties, where there's not that much conflict because you know you have to survive. They know they have to work in this country, so both of the parents work. And in some ways, the women do still come home and do a lot of the same things. The men, they help out in their own way on the outside and in the house, things like that. The roles are still somewhat defined but they know that their wives have to work. The husbands know that they can't survive with just one income.

AK: What kinds of jobs do people have? You said that in your generation, a lot went into scientific fields.

PC: It depends on what they know from the old country. A lot go into manual labor. A lot of people work in assembly lines. Some people go into cosmetology, janitorial work, teacher's aide, depending on their skills. A lot of them, whatever they know, they go into it. Like those who were more educated when they came, they can go to school a couple of years and pick up a skill, like being counselors. If they know computers or engineering, they can go get a degree in that area. But if they had low skills, then most of them get jobs like assembly-line, just blue-collar kinds of jobs.

AK: Do you have a sense of what percentage of people are on public assistance?

PC: I really don't know because all I know is my clients and my clientele is very small. I don't think it's as big as the media makes it out to be. I think the people who are working get hidden.

AK: You mean they just kind of blend in?

PC: Yeah, they just kind of blend in. I don't have the statistics for any given time because people get on and get off welfare; at one time or another, they were on it. In my mind, it's probably 20 percent. But then again, I don't know for sure. I can't call myself an expert on these statistics.

AK: You alluded earlier to some of the activities at the temple. Are people of your generation invested in continuing the Buddhist traditions?

PC: Not a lot of people. I think they go for cultural reasons more than as a Buddhist. Some people do know the religion but they're not as devoted as the older generation. But as they get older, they seem to pay more attention to it.

AK: Will Buddhism die out in the Cambodian community in America?

PC: I don't think so. I don't think it'll die out because even in the Cambodian community back home, when you're young you just go [to the temple] for cultural reasons. It's when you get older that you pay attention more closely. The new generation now, they're all going to the temple. They're going all the time. We don't have weekly sessions like the church, but you see different ages if you go to the temple. Thousands of people; we have to rent a hall when we have certain ceremonies during the year. People of different ages come. Teenagers go and play games. Take the Cambodian New Year, for example, they'll rent a big hall with lots of space. Teenagers meet each other and they play games. They'll go through the ceremony with their parents or whatever. I don't think it will die out but I think they'll understand it differently.

AK: It seems the religion is very tied to the culture, so if you're interested in preserving the culture, the religion is part of it.

PC: Right, right.

AK: It seems like you're concerned, and I am, too, about the media portraying things in a skewed way. Is there anything else that you want to clarify, that you want to make sure that we cover in this book?

PC: It always gets to me: If someone kills someone, it always gets blown up. If somebody is doing good things, like if little kids are going to dancing classes or are learning to read Khmer, it never gets shown. The kids who are in gangs get blown out of proportion. If one person has a fraud in the welfare system, somehow the whole Cambodian community is clouded. That's one person out of thousands and thousands of people. I want people to know that there are Cambodians who are hard-working, who are struggling, and they're making it. They're balancing their jobs and the cultures and going through life. There are many sides to people. There's more to life than just either you're in a gang or you're not. People are going about carrying on their daily lives. They're going overseas to help others. There are so many different varieties, one should not just focus on illness. That's not what all the Cambodian community is about: It's not just about sickness, it's just not about trauma. There are people who were affected but there are people who are doing something about it. And it's not just about the welfare system. I really want to make it clear that there are people who are working hard and making it. We're going through a phase where a lot of people are worried about surviving. The first generation, they're focusing more on the practicalities. Maybe they are on welfare this year, but—that was one of the issues, that there are a lot of people who've been on welfare for several years—they've also worked hard. They work very hard till they get out of low-income housing. Even my family had to go on welfare because when you first get here, what could you do? You don't know the language; you don't know anything. For a couple of years, yes, but then you have to get out; do something for yourself. It's nice to get free money. But that's about $339 a month.

AK: It's not going to buy you a fancy car.

PC: No, it's not. You think that people are lazy. It's not because of that. Some people are in that spot for a reason; there's something wrong and that's why they're there. Sometimes, it's also the system. You make that much money, but if you go to work, you make less and all the benefits get cut off. So, there's not much incentive for people to work. They have to survive; basic survival is the bottom line. You think that when people are smart they're crooks, but no, they just learned how to beat the system. They know how to survive. I give them credit for doing things so they could live. Anyone would do the same.

AK: I think we'll end on that positive note. Thank you very much.

September 11, 1996

12. Bunroeun Thach
The Khmer Krom

Dr. Bunroeun Thach was born in Vietnam in an area that Cambodians call Kampuchea Krom, where millions of Khmer Krom live. (Khmer Krom are people of Cambodian ancestry who live in their ancestral land in the Mekong Delta of Vietnam, which used to belong to Cambodia.) When he was a young boy, his parents sent him to Cambodia to be educated. He was a sophomore in college in Phnom Penh when the Khmer Rouge captured that city on April 17, 1975. Three days later, while evacuating the city along with everyone else, he decided to escape to Thailand. It took him two and a half months to reach Aranyaprathet, a town on the Thai-Cambodian border. With the assistance of people he knew at the Voice of America, he was admitted into the United States as a refugee in late 1975.

He found a job washing dishes at a small Catholic college in Syracuse, New York, but he felt discriminated against and soon left. He enrolled in a community college in upstate New York, where he met and married an American woman from whom he was later divorced. During these years, the second Cambodian civil war was being fought along the Thai-Cambodian border between the Phnom Penh government headed by Heng Samrin and Hun Sen—a regime the Vietnamese had installed when they invaded Cambodia at the end of 1978 and ousted the Khmer Rouge—and the three resistance factions headed by Prince Sihanouk, former prime minister Son Sann, and the remnants of the Khmer Rouge. Dr. Thach felt he had to go to Washington, D.C., in order to talk to members of Congress, and anyone else who would listen, and inform them about what was going on. He attended George Washington University but soon transferred to the State University of New York at Cortland, where he completed his B.A. in 1983. He received an M.A.

in international relations from Syracuse University in 1984 and a Ph.D. in political science from the University of Hawaii in 1993.

In his Ph.D. dissertation "Santiphum Khmer: A Buddhist Way to Peace," he argued that "the centuries-old absolute and corrupting power of the Khmer state," as well as the Buddhist concept of karma, subdued the Khmer people and forced them to accept suffering as "the essence of their lives." The autocratic nature of the Khmer state "produced soul-rending self-doubt among the Khmer people" and enabled Cambodia's twentieth-century rulers to "embrace the realist 'balance-of-power' theory, which led to force and counter-force strategies being employed by the many Khmer factions." Thach coined the term *santiphum* (*santi* means peace, and *phum* means village or zone) to suggest that the best way to break the seemingly endless cycle of suffering in Cambodia is to abandon a statecraft based on balance of power and replace it with cooperative strategies based on Buddhist principles. He yearned for a Cambodia where the common people can enjoy a peaceful life.

Throughout the years Dr. Thach was in college and graduate school he was deeply involved in the politics of Cambodia. A strong supporter of Prince Sihanouk, he returned to Cambodia to establish a think tank after receiving his Ph.D. but ran into some trouble there. He returned to the United States in 1996 and became the manager of a project funded by the U.S. Department of Housing and Urban Development. Audrey Kim interviewed him in his home in Des Moines, Washington in 1996. In the last communication I had from him, a letter dated November 25, 1997, he told me that Prince Norodom Ranariddh (son of King Sihanouk) had appointed him as his personal representative in Washington, D.C. He was to leave for Bangkok the following day, on his way to Phnom Penh as a member of a United Nations advanced technical team that would plan and monitor the Cambodian elections scheduled originally for May 1998 but postponed until July of that year. A letter I sent to him in September 2001 was returned by the post office stamped "Addressee Unknown."

*   *   *

AK: Maybe you can start by telling me a little about your background and how you got to the Seattle area.

BT: Thach, actually, is not a Khmer name; it's a Vietnamese name. When the Vietnamese conquered Kampuchea Krom, which is currently the southern part of Vietnam, they made sure that they would have policies to control us. Therefore, they gave us that last name in order to identify who we are, what group we are. "Thach" means "black stone" in Vietnamese. It's almost like "nigger" in American terminology. It's a derogatory term because we have darker skin than the Vietnamese.

AK: Did all Khmer Krom have to take on Vietnamese names?

BT: Yes. Every Cambodian [in Kampuchea Krom], every Khmer Krom, had to take a Vietnamese last name. Therefore my last name is "Thach." My first name, Bunroeun, is a very popular name from Thailand, especially in the '40s and '50s. I was born in 1955. During that time, we received a lot of influence from Thailand. Cambodia, even though it has two thousand years of history, was very much divided and suppressed for a long time. The Khmer empire fell in the 1500s and Cambodia was conquered by both the Vietnamese and the Thai. Part of the territory belonging to Thailand today was at one time a part of the Khmer empire. The same is true of Laos and the southern part of Vietnam. These two peoples conquered our land. And so Kampuchea Krom became gradually part of southern Vietnam, but it was not until 1949 that the French illegally ceded our region to Vietnam in support of the Bao Dai regime—the Vietnamese royal family—in order to counter the communist movement controlled by Ho Chi Minh, which, in 1945, proclaimed its independence. But legally Cambodia still has a claim over that territory. That's why my name, Thach, is Vietnamese while my first name is Thai. I'm a Khmer, but I don't have a Khmer name.

AK: It seems like your name symbolizes the condition of the Khmer Krom.

BT: Exactly. So, we, Khmer Krom, we have been discriminated against by the invaders, the conquerors. Although I was born in Vietnam, I grew up in Cambodia because my parents sent me there to live during the war in the early 1960s when I was just a little boy.

AK: What kinds of occupations did your parents have?

BT: My parents were farmers. We indigenous people, we owned the land; that's the only economic means we had. We are not commercially oriented people. The Vietnamese have more traders and petty bourgeoisie. But the Khmer Krom live in [villages and] small towns with small plots of land. There has been no recent census figures, but a census conducted in the mid-sixties showed that the Khmer Krom numbered four million. So, if you multiply that by a 2 percent annual growth, right now possibly there are between eight to ten million Khmer Krom. In Vietnam they were not massacred in great numbers like what happened in Cambodia [during the Khmer Rouge regime].

AK: So, there may be as many as ten million Khmer Krom in Kampuchea Krom. What about in the rest of the world?

BT: In the United States there are only three hundred Khmer Krom families here in Washington state. The largest group is five hundred families in the state of Pennsylvania, around Philadelphia. There are also some in New Jersey. Scattered around the U.S. as well as throughout the world, in Canada, in Australia, I think the number of Khmer Krom comes to more than a quarter-million people outside of Vietnam and Cambodia. I think in Cambodia we have possibly one million Khmer Krom. That's because they migrated there.

Let's talk about the Khmer Krom here in the United States. Right now, there's a problem. And the problem exists all over, not just here, where there are Khmer Krom. Here, one of the Buddhist temples, the Khmer Krom Buddhist temple in Tacoma, is involved in a court case, a recision case. The issue is who this temple belongs to—the Khmer Krom or the Khmer from Cambodia. The abbot of the temple is Khmer Krom and he is the one who built it and it is supported by the Khmer Krom Association. He also founded the Khmer Krom Buddhist Association, but because the Khmer Krom don't have that many people, we got outnumbered when a lot of Cambodians from Cambodia arrived. Many of these people are ethnic Chinese born in Cambodia—when they come here, they continue to count themselves as Cambodian—and they participate actively as members of this temple. Now, after this temple has grown big, the first thing they want to do is get rid of the abbot. The second thing they want to do is to drop the name *Khmer Krom Temple.* They just want to call it the Khmer Temple. They say, "Why don't we just use the term *Khmer Temple?* Why do we continue to have Khmer Krom? If we have Khmer Krom, we have some kind of division between the Khmer from Cambodia and the Khmer from Kampuchea Krom." So, their argument is valid in the sense that they prefer unity. We, Khmer Krom, respond that we love Khmer—that's our dream, to have only one Khmer people. But geographically we have been divided. The Khmer Krom have no voice; we are the Palestinians of Southeast Asia. The indigenous people have no claim to their own identity, their nationhood, their religious rights. So, we continue to demand that legally we, the Khmer Krom who started the temple, we beg them to allow us to continue to call it the Khmer Krom Temple. Secondly, we argue that the Khmer Krom, since we do not have a voice as Khmer in Cambodia, whether to vote or not, why can't we have just a temple on one or two acres of land in the entire universe that we can call a Khmer Krom temple?

AK: Let me get this straight. It was Khmer Krom who set up the temple, but now other Khmer want to make it a generic Khmer temple. But you're saying this is the one thing that you can call Khmer Krom, so you want to keep that name.

BT: Right. At least, let the world know the Khmer Krom exist. So, we take the matter to court. I think the court will come to a decision some time this month. We brought many of the Khmer Krom Buddhists from California, from other parts of the world, to testify in this case, to argue why this should remain a Khmer Krom temple. But it's going to be difficult because they are using American law to say that the church belongs to the members of the church and not to the abbot. But in the Buddhist tradition, in Kampuchea Krom, when the abbot establishes a temple, the members of the temple cannot just come and kick him out as they wish. He has been recognized by the Kanak Sangha—the Buddhist Monks Organization. And if he does anything wrong, the Kanak Sangha will decide, but if he has not done anything wrong, why kick him out? So, it's very sad. We, in Kampuchea Krom, even though we are the indigenous people, we do not have the right to our own land, to our own dignity, to our own way of life, the way as human beings we should have. We have been discriminated against by the Vietnamese in Kampuchea Krom. When we come to Cambodia, even though we speak the same language, exactly the same Khmer language as the Khmer in Cambodia speak, unfortunately, because we have a different intonation, in Cambodia they're accusing us of being Vietnamese.

AK: Is that in recent years or in the past?

BT: Has been going on for many years. During the Khmer Rouge occupation from 1975 to 1978, they hunted down the Khmer Krom. The Khmer Krom were persecuted in Cambodia even more than in Vietnam. In Vietnam, the main reason the Vietnamese did not persecute us en masse like they did in 1945 or in the 1700s and 1800s was because the Khmer Krom were very strong and very united. We have six hundred temples, one in every single village. Here, the Americans, the Whites, have dominated, have persecuted all the indigenous people, the American Indians, until they became very small in numbers. The Vietnamese cannot do that to us because our numbers are so large and we occupy almost the entire territory in Kampuchea Krom. One day, the Khmer Krom will rise up. Anyway, let's get back to the life of the Khmer Krom here.

AK: Actually, I'm interested in the history, too. One question I have is, What educational opportunities were available for Khmer Krom in Kampuchea Krom? One hypothesis I've heard is that because the French thought more highly of the Vietnamese, all the people in Vietnam, including the Khmer Krom, had access to better education than the Khmer in Cambodia did.

BT: Yes, that's true. It was very fortunate in the sense that the French tried to make certain that Kampuchea Krom was a French colony, so the French could claim to have a larger territory. But when they gave that land to Vietnam, Cambodia was the one that lost the most. Economically, in the southern part of Vietnam, in Kampuchea Krom, the land is very rich because the Mekong Delta is an alluvial plain like [the Nile Delta in] Egypt. The economic power of Egypt allowed it to build pyramids. Economically, if you go back a thousand years, [one of] the trading center[s] of Southeast Asia [Oc Eo] was in Kampuchea Krom. It was the Singapore of those early years. It was a trade center [on the trade route] between Rome and Japan; that's where traders met in Southeast Asia.

When the French arrived, the irrigation system that was built by the Khmer Krom six hundred years earlier was still intact and we became the granary of French Indochina, where the French exported rice throughout the world. I think Vietnam today is still the third-largest rice exporter in the world because of the economic know-how, the water system, and the wet rice culture that the Khmer developed.

When the French arrived, they wanted to educate these people so they could be better servants. So, the Khmer Krom had better access to education than the people in Cambodia itself, thanks to a French lady by the name of Suzanne Karpeles who was sent by the French Overseas Ministry to carry out Le Mission Civilisatrice—that is, to go civilize the people. They sent her out there and told her to go to every single temple to try to change each one into a Catholic church. Unfortunately for the French but fortunately for the Khmer Krom, Suzanne Karpeles came to every single temple and built schools in all six hundred temples in Kampuchea Krom for the Khmer Krom. When the Khmer Krom got educated, she brought a lot of them to Cambodia to continue their education in Cambodia. She was the first one to establish the Buddhist Institute in Cambodia.

AK: About what time period was this?

BT: 1930 to 1940. She was the one who educated the Khmer Krom. Not just that, she also took Khmer Krom to be educated in France. And thus the Khmer Krom became the most nationalistic and most educated [group of Khmer], better educated than the Khmer in Cambodia. During the Sihanouk years, during the '60s, many Khmer Krom became ministers and high officials. Even right now, we still have a lot of Khmer Krom in every single political group or faction. But our people as a whole are still being discriminated against by the Khmer in Cambodia.

We turn now to the Khmer Krom here in United States. The Khmer Krom who came here, who are they? There are two groups: the Khmer Krom who lived in Cambodia, like myself . . .

AK: Did a lot of the Khmer Krom go to Cambodia to study?

BT: To study and to escape from persecution during the wars in Vietnam, during the '40s, '50s, '60s, and '70s. Even now, whenever Khmer Krom escape from Vietnamese oppression, they escape to Cambodia. Back to the two groups of Khmer Krom who reside in the United States: First, there are the Khmer Krom who came from Cambodia, who had been there a long time and came along with other Cambodians to escape the Khmer Rouge and [later] the Vietnamese occupation. Then, there is another group who had worked with the American Special Forces. These people came directly from Vietnam, though some of them also came from Cambodia because they had been sent over there in early 1970 to help Lon Nol overthrow King Sihanouk. They were fierce fighters, very militaristic; they are very conservative in one way or another, and very nationalistic as well. The first and second groups came at the same time because when Vietnam fell to the communists as did Cambodia, those who had been sent from Vietnam to help Lon Nol, we came here directly. A third group, the latest group, is the Khmer Krom who came as Vietnamese together with the Vietnamese refugees. Some of them come as Amerasians.

AK: The first two groups came in 1975?

BT: Yes, '75. Some came in '75, some came in the '80s because some of them returned from Cambodia to Vietnam and were put in prison, in reeducation camps. Some of them later escaped from the reeducation camps, or were let go, something like that. So, this latter batch came in the early '80s—'84, '85. Then, the latest group, they are coming in the '90s, along with the Amerasian children and their relatives.

AK: Did groups one and two come through the Thai refugee camps, or did they come by boat like some of the Vietnamese?

BT: Both ways. We have the older generation, who are in their fifties and older, they're the ones who formed Khmer Krom associations around the world in order to keep in contact with one another and to preserve our identity.

AK: I'm very curious, why are there so many Khmer Krom in Washington state and in Pennsylvania?

BT: I think it depends on who sponsored them, as well as on who got there first. Just like here—there are many Khmer Krom here—let's say four or five Khmer Krom sponsor four or five more, so it spreads. The same thing in Pennsylvania.

AK: How did you come to the U.S.?

BT: I came to the U.S. as a Cambodian from Cambodia. When the Khmer Rouge walked into Phnom Penh on April 17, 1975, I witnessed everything that was going on in the city. When the Khmer Rouge emptied the city, on the third day, when the city was nearly completely empty, I decided to leave. The main reason I waited so long was because we were hoping that the Khmer

Krom forces, those who were part of the American Special Forces, would come and liberate us from the Khmer Rouge. We waited and waited but nobody showed up. It took me two months and two weeks to get to Thailand. I arrived in Aranyaprathet in June or July 1975. By October, I had arrived here [the United States]. So I didn't stay long in a refugee camp. I was able to come here because I happened to know a few friends who worked at the Voice of America.

AK: Were you working for the Voice of America in Cambodia?

BT: Not exactly, not officially. I was a string reporter, they just hired me, paid me to do something, sometimes translation, pick up some news, something like that during the '70s. So, with that affiliation, I was able to come here.

AK: To the state of Washington?

BT: No, I first arrived in Harrisburg, Pennsylvania. From there, they dispersed us throughout the country, whoever wanted to pick up these poor refugees. I was sponsored by one of the Episcopalian priests in a small town called Oswego in the southern part of New York state bordering Pennsylvania. Unfortunately, I discovered later that he wanted to abuse me sexually, so I escaped. Americans are weird.

AK: I've heard other people talk about their sponsors taking advantage of them. Is that a common thing, sexually or financially?

BT: Yeah, I think that happened a lot; that's the reality. When I left [the home of the priest], I moved in with a Cambodian Christian family. Unfortunately, the head of that family, too, forced me to go to church and become a Christian. So, again, I was kicked out from the house.

AK: Was he a Khmer Krom?

BT: He was a Vietnamese born in Cambodia. He's a born-again Christian.

AK: I have another question. My understanding is that there are a lot of churches and Christian families that sponsored Cambodians. I'm wondering was there pressure to convert to Christianity?

BT: Yes, yes. A lot of pressure. Fortunately for you, you're not a refugee. If you're a refugee or homeless, you become very oppressed and feel degraded. You'd feel unwanted and lonely and unnoticed. And so you try to reach out, you feel like you're in the middle of the river, you try to grab anything that you can hold onto. This is is where the Christian groups come in.

AK: When you're the most susceptible?

BT: Exactly, as their prey. When I escaped from Cambodia to Thailand, as soon as I arrived there, the first thing they handed me was a Bible, not food. Fortunately, when I was in Cambodia I was educated already, I had gone to the university already. In the refugee camp in Thailand, I felt like these people treated me and my people like monkeys. Look at us, we have over two thousand years of history, two thousand years of civilization. Who are these Christians who came here giving us the Bible? Don't they know that we have our own literature, our own great authors, great civilization? You mistreat us. Our survival was at stake. You came and put pressure on us in the refugee camps. When we got to the U.S., we were also under a lot of pressure.

AK: In those earlier years in the camp [in Thailand] and after you came to Pennsylvania, did you find other Khmer Krom?

BT: No. I associated with other Cambodians.

AK: Were you accepted?

BT: I've been very accepted by other Cambodians, especially educated Cambodians. Educated Cambodians, they accept the Khmer Krom more because they see the Khmer Krom are very nationalistic, very Khmer.

AK: They understand the history?

BT: That's right; understand the history. So, they're aware, they respect the Khmer Krom greatly.

AK: So, it sounds like maybe it's the more uneducated Cambodians who hear the accent and . . .

BT: Exactly; you got it. Anyway, I arrived in the U.S. in October or November 1975. By January, February, I had already found a job as a dishwasher at a small private Catholic college called Le Moyne College in Syracuse, New York. And there I was washing dishes. The American students were very arrogant. They looked at me, just as though I were a yellow rat or something like that. I was very discriminated against. They'd do anything to make me suffer. For example, if you do dishes, you'll see what American students have for breakfast. They have cornflakes, they have peanut butter, they drink juice. So, what do they do? They put peanut butter into the glass and stick another glass into it, one on top of the other and you have to wash them. You wash six hundred plates or five hundred glasses.

AK: They did that on purpose?

BT: They did that on purpose. Tears came to my eyes, and I said, "I'm not going to be their slave."

AK: Were there other Cambodians working there?

BT: No, just me. It was very rare to see an Asian in a small town in the U.S. at that time, other than in a Chinese restaurant. So, finally, I found a way to go to school through financial aid at a community college.

AK: Did you have a degree from Cambodia as well?

BT: No, I did not. I was in my second year at the university in Cambodia majoring in philosophy when I left. I started at a community college in upstate New York called Onondaga Community College. It's named after an American Indian tribe. There, I was very lonely and I wanted to get accepted by American society. I ended up getting to know an American girl and we married at the end of my second year. But my mind was always in Cambodia.

AK: Where was your family at this time?

BT: My family was still in Vietnam; even right now, they're in Kampuchea Krom. Even though I wanted to be accepted by Americans and wanted to have a life here, my mind was always in Cambodia because in 1978 that's all we heard about: torture, killing, and all that. To us, the Khmer, we thought the end of the Khmer race had come because people were dying every single day. Nobody cared, nobody talked about it. The leftists in the United States, they were accusing us of being the bourgeoisie or [lackeys of] the CIA. The American leftists, the [former] antiwar activists, they called us the bourgeoisie. They do not see us as victims. [They think] we are the bad people, tools of American foreign policy. So I tried to talk to antiwar activists like Father [Daniel] Berrigan and all those people. Some of them finally accepted us. A lot of the leftists and the Democrats refused to do anything to help us. In order for America to hear about Cambodia, I had to go to the source, to the heart of America, which is Washington, D.C. So I applied to Georgetown University for studies in foreign affairs. I was able to convince one of the persons who was a peace activist, Father Berrigan—everybody in the United States knows how strong he was; he was very anti-U.S. policy in Vietnam—to write me a recommendation letter when I applied to Georgetown University. I was not admitted but George Washington University accepted me, so I went there for my studies.

I tried to lobby the U.S. Congress, the White House, the Pentagon, the State Department, anybody I could get my hands on to let them know about Cambodia. In December 1978, the Vietnamese invaded Cambodia and overthrew the Khmer Rouge. Prince Sihanouk was released from his house arrest and came to the United Nations to defend, not the Khmer Rouge, but Cambodia, because the Vietnamese had invaded Cambodia. I was the first person to write to the prince, while the whole world condemned him. They said because of him, because of his tightrope foreign policy, that's what made Cambodia what it was. But I wrote to him from Washington, D.C., and told him that he's the only person who can make Cambodia once again into a nation. He wrote back to me and said that no, he's no longer the head of state and he wanted to just live in a small house, a home that he owns in the south of France and get out of political life. But as a Cambodian, he must continue to fight against the foreign occupation of Cambodia.

It was impossible to give my letter directly to the prince, so I sent it to Andrew Young, who was the American ambassador to the United Nations at the time, and he delivered my letter personally to Prince Sihanouk. When he saw my letter, I think the prince came to tears. Since then, the king [Sihanouk was recrowned king in 1993] and I have become like father and son. In 1979, as I continued my studies, I had my first child. I felt a lot of pressure. I wanted to help my country but at that time I just had my A.A. degree. If I wanted to move to the top to help the country successfully, I had to get a better education. Meanwhile, I continued to work for Cambodia by lobbying Congress. One of my friends was Senator Mark Hatfield of Oregon. Then, in 1981, a friend offered to help me move to New York and continue my schooling there. He helped me by letting me pay only half-rent for my apartment. So, I went to SUNY [State University of New York] in Cortland. There, in 1983, I got my bachelor's degree. During that time, I was always active in helping Cambodia.

AK: Were you in touch with other Cambodians?

BT: Every Cambodian I could find, especially the leaders. I served as secretary to the group. After I got a bachelor's degree, I continued with my master's degree at Syracuse University. By '84, I had received a master's degree in international relations at Syracuse University. Then, the king appointed me as his political advisor at the United Nations. I had not seen my mother since I left Vietnam, since I left Kampuchea Krom as a little boy. The same day that I received the fax from Beijing [where Sihanouk lived] telling me that the king had nominated me, I also received two letters: one from my family in Vietnam and the other one from the king. I said, "Which one should I open first?" Well, I gave priority to the king. So, I opened the letter and I said, "Wow, that's a great honor." I was very happy. Then, I opened the letter from my family in Vietnam. The letter said that my mother had passed away. And so my mood was all the way up and all the way down. I was so upset about my mother. She had given me no chance at all to make her happy. All this time, I had wanted to bring honor to the family, so she could be proud of me.

From '84 on, I got even more involved in Cambodian politics. To make the story short, when you devote so much of your time to your country, my wife—she's a born-again Christian—said I had to choose either her or Cambodia. She said that politics is world affairs, and world affairs are in the hand of God. Only God can solve the whole world's problems. You cannot do it alone. I said, "Yeah, but I have to do it in some way, somehow, because I cannot close my eyes on my people." She made me choose, and so in 1985, we separated and I devoted my time to Cambodia. We divorced a few years later. We have two children, Nathaniel and Christina.

I am still involved with the country. When I was at the United Nations, I saw that Cambodia had lost a lot of human capital, many intellectuals. Especially when you speak with the high-ranking officials in the U.N. or any place like that, you lack respect and people do not talk directly to you. Therefore, I said to myself, the only way I shall have these people listen to me is if I get a Ph.D. And so I searched for a way to go to school. I did not want to continue at Syracuse University even though they offered to let me to do my Ph.D. program there. A professor at Cornell University offered to help me, but I could not accept his offer because in the '70s he and his colleagues said the Khmer Krom were CIA agents or something like that. So, I refused to go to Cornell. In 1987–88, I received a grant from the East-West Center in Hawaii to do my Ph.D. there. I enjoyed myself in Hawaii. I refused to go home to Cambodia until we have a government that does not belong to any group, until we have an elected government.

In 1993, I finished my Ph.D. and then I went to Cambodia and established a think tank, a foreign policy studies institute. And His Majesty blessed me with his name. The institute became known as the Preah Sihanouk Raj Academy. King Sihanouk has never been a good friend of the United States. He supported the Vietnamese communists during the Vietnam War because he saw that the Vietnamese communists were nationalists. They wanted to rid their country of American imperialism, French colonialism, foreign invaders. So, Washington did not like Sihanouk that much. But in Cambodia, people still see Sihanouk as their king, as their leader. To me, I could care less what Americans think. I care for what is good for Cambodia. At the beginning, I received some funds for the academy from the Asia Foundation. But little by little, people in Washington put the pressure on me to change the name of the organization. I refused. They finally said OK. I was the acting president of the institute because I refused to be the president since I was still young; I had just got out of school. I brought an American in to become the president of the institute. But when he got there—Americans, they are not that stupid—he saw that I was using him to get American support [as] nobody [in the U.S.] was giving us any funds but I was able to find funding from other embassies. Then the royal government suggested, Why don't you make this a national institution so that you can get funds from the national budget? When the prime minister agreed to do that and wrote a letter to me, I said OK. So, the institute became a national academy. The day that the prime minister wrote to me, I went to the American whom I had brought there and said, "Since the institute is now a national academy, I must take it back. Thank you for your help." He was furious; he went to the press to create a lot of trouble. The king did not want to have his name tarnished by this bickering, so he withdrew his name and said, "Please don't allow my name to be associated with that institute." I felt disgraced when the king did that to me. So, I decided to close down the academy. I closed it on March 19. I purposely did not choose March 18 as the closing date because that was the day Lon Nol had overthrown Sihanouk [in 1970 allegedly] with American support. I received a lot of death threats, so I left Cambodia on March 22 and arrived here on March 28, 1996.

AK: So, you've been in this area only a few months.

BT: A few months. Since April. OK, that's the end of my personal story. For the Khmer Krom, the question remains, Do the Khmer Krom want to have their country back? I think as human beings, we all want our own identity. The Khmer Krom people, just like any other people, want recognition, we want human dignity. Therefore, the question of nationhood is always in the back of the mind of every single Khmer Krom. The number of Khmer Krom is now around ten million. As we watch Chechnya and all the small states in the former Soviet Union claim their independence, the Khmer Krom always hope that one day we will also claim our independence. But I think it will be unrealistic and troublesome if the Khmer Krom have an uprising with regard to this issue. A lot will depend on the leadership. The Khmer Krom, even though we have ten million people, we do not have many intellectual leaders. Therefore, the struggle by these people to get their independence might take quite some time.

AK: Why is there a lack of leaders? Earlier on, we were talking about how the Khmer Krom were educated by the Frenchwoman.

BT: The thing is, they were executed in Vietnam as well as in Cambodia. Educated Khmer Krom were executed in Cambodia [by the Khmer Rouge].

AK: You mean the ones who worked for the U.S. were killed? The Khmer Rouge killed the ones who worked for the Special Forces?

BT: Yes. Not just the Special Forces, but also the Khmer Krom intellectuals in Cambodia. I think we have to wait ten or twenty years before we'll be able to revive. The main concern right now is how the Khmer Krom can live, can survive economically in Vietnam. One thing that the Khmer Krom have, I think, that's very fortunate, is that Khmer Krom have their temples. They have six hundred temples. Each village has a temple. So education over there will continue. But the sad part is that they will not be able to get any higher education because all the public education is always for the Vietnamese.

AK: What about the Khmer Krom in the United States, how are they doing compared to other Cambodians or compared to the Vietnamese?

BT: It depends on which group you're talking about. I think the first group, the people who had worked for the Special Forces, they pretty much were educated already in Vietnam as well as in Cambodia. And so when they came here, I think you'll find almost none of them is on welfare. They've bought their own homes, have their own careers.

AK: Do these people mostly associate with one another or with Cambodians in general?

BT: I think they pretty much cling to one another.

AK: To other Khmer Krom?

BT: Yes, to other Khmer Krom, and not so much to Cambodians from Cambodia. But the Khmer Krom who came here with the Vietnamese, some of them associate closely with the Vietnamese. And the Khmer Krom who grew up in Cambodia, like myself, I associate with all kinds.

AK: Even among the Khmer Krom, there are different groups.

BT: Right.

AK: I don't know if you can make any generalization, but are the Khmer Krom trying to keep a distinct identity as Khmer Krom, or would they like to be considered just Cambodians?

BT: They really would like to be considered as Cambodians, as Khmer in general. But politically, we want to have our own say as Khmer Krom. But not culturally, not religiously, not ethnically. We are Khmer people. Khmer Krom and Cambodians from Cambodia, we're the same, we're not different at all. But politically, due to history and geography, we want to claim we are distinct.

AK: So, as a people, you consider yourself to be like any other Cambodian. But politically, you want to make a distinction, because there's the hope of regaining the land.

BT: Exactly.

AK: I'm trying to get a better sense of where Khmer Krom fit in the United States within the Southeast Asian population. Are they accepted for the most part by other Cambodians?

BT: Khmer Krom can go anywhere, including to the Vietnamese community. People treat you differently, I think, when you don't talk about politics. The Khmer Krom are very well accepted by the Vietnamese community and by the Cambodians from Cambodia.

AK: Really? Weren't you discriminated against in Vietnam?

BT: Yes, but here, we're in the same boat. Just like Japanese and Koreans, you know, back home it's very difficult for them to get along.

AK: You mean, actually, relations here with Vietnamese Americans are pretty good?

BT: Yeah, pretty good. We very much support one another. Especially here, the Vietnamese who do not like the communists in Hanoi, they're really in our favor.

AK: What kind of jobs do Khmer Krom have here?

BT: It depends on their education. For example, we have a lot of Khmer Krom here who are working in the city school district as tutors, as teaching assistants. Other Khmer Krom, they fit very well into manufacturing because they are very astute and a lot of Americans here really like them.

AK: Those are the types of jobs that I hear that other Cambodians have. In terms of jobs, there are no differences really between Khmer Krom and other Cambodians?

BT: I think Khmer Krom are more well off than many of the Cambodians. Forgive me for saying that, because if you go to Vietnam or Cambodia, you see differences. Those who are not well educated, when they come here, they join gangs. The Khmer people from Cambodia, the majority of the refugees here, came from farms because the Khmer Rouge had executed all the intellectuals. When they came here, they tried to get decent jobs. But they could not, so a lot of them stay on welfare and live in public housing. Khmer Krom are different, because most of us were educated and [one group among us] worked with the American Special Forces. Almost none of us here are living in public housing.

AK: So, even though Khmer Krom are coming from farming areas and rural backgrounds, they were educated and have been able to get jobs. Do you know of any who are on public assistance?

BT: I think there are a few, especially the elderly.

AK: What about the children? I hear that in the Cambodian community, in general, the kids' dropout rates, their joining gangs, their relationships with parents, those are big problems.

BT: In [both Vietnam and] Cambodia, the Khmer Krom are Buddhists. You know Buddhists, we have two groups: Theravada Buddhists and Mahayana Buddhists. Mahayana Buddhism is very much tied to Chinese Confucianism and is very much family-oriented, with strong family values. The Khmer Krom, because of our encounter with the Vietnamese, we observe the Vietnamese tradition of being family-oriented, we're very family-tied. Cambodians in Cambodia are Theravada Buddhists. The Theravada Buddhists, they think mostly about going to heaven. The Khmer Krom are also Theravada Buddhists, but we have been influenced by the Vietnamese in terms of being family-oriented. A lot of people would not understand this subtle difference. The Khmer Krom, we are very, very family-oriented. Therefore, our children finish school and a lot of them are outstanding students.

AK: High dropout rates, gangs, those are not problems in the Khmer Krom community?

BT: I've never heard that they are.

AK: What about cultural and generational gaps between parents and children? That's something that I hear about a lot.

BT: The Khmer Krom here are trying to help the students to learn about their own history, learn about their identity, to make them feel stronger when they face other races, other cultures.

AK: Do the Khmer Krom young people have a sense of their Khmer Krom identity, versus being just Cambodian?

BT: It depends on the level of their education. For the young, Michael Jackson is their god; they're into rap music and all that. It's very difficult for them to know what being Khmer Krom means, but when some of them go to the university or college, they always reflect on who they are. So, those would like to learn more about the history of the Khmer Krom; they want to have their identity and be proud of who they are.

AK: You've told me more about the Khmer Krom than can be found in any books, so I really appreciate your granting me this interview. Thank you for your time.

September 13, 1996

Selected Bibliography

This bibliography has three parts. Because the existing literature on Cambodia is substantial, almost all the items listed in Part 1 are books, and only a handful of the journal articles, book chapters, and Ph.D. dissertations that are explicitly cited in the Introduction are included. In contrast, writings on Cambodians in the United States are sparser and deal mainly with the refugees' problems and needs as well as certain aspects of their adaptation to American society. Only four scholarly books on Cambodians in the United States have been published so far, with two more forthcoming. Out of necessity, therefore, almost all the items included in Part 2 are journal articles. (The autobiographies written by Cambodian refugees are listed in Part 1 rather than Part 2, because they focus mainly on the narrators' lives under the Khmer Rouge regime.) Almost a hundred unpublished doctoral dissertations and master's theses have been written on Cambodian refugees in the United States but are not listed due to the limitations of space. Part 3 provides the references cited in the Methodology section.

Part 1: Cambodia

Ablin, David A., and Marlowe Hood, eds. 1990. *The Cambodian Agony.* Armonk: M. E. Sharpe.

Ashe, Var Hong. 1988. *From Phnom Penh to Paradise: Escape from Cambodia.* London: Hodder and Stoughton.

Ayres, David M. 2000. *Anatomy of a Crisis: Education, Development, and the State in Cambodia, 1953–1998.* Honolulu: University of Hawaii Press.

Becker, Elizabeth. 1986. *When the War Was Over: The Voices of Cambodia's Revolution and Its People.* New York: Simon and Schuster.

Bit, Seanglim. 1991. *The Warrior Heritage: A Psychological Perspective of Cambodian Trauma.* El Cerrito, Calif.: Seanglim Bit.

Brady, Christopher. 1999. *United States Foreign Policy towards Cambodia, 1977–1992: A Question of Realities.* New York: St. Martin's Press.

Brown, MacAlister, and Joseph J. Zasloff. 1998. *Cambodia Confounds the Peacemakers, 1979–1998.* Ithaca: Cornell University Press.

Burchet, Wilfred. 1981. *The China Cambodia Vietnam Triangle.* Chicago: Vanguard Books.

Burgler, R. A. 1990. *The Eyes of the Pineapple: Revolutionary Intellectuals and Terror in Democratic Kampuchea.* Saarbrucken, Germany: Verlag Breitenbach.

Cady, John F. 1964. *Southeast Asia: Its Historical Development.* New York: McGraw-Hill.

———. 1974 (1980). *The History of Post-War Southeast Asia: Independence Problems.* Athens: Ohio University Press.

Carney, Timothy. "The Unexpected Victory." 1989a. In *Cambodia, 1975–1978: Rendevous with Death.* Ed. Karl D. Jackson, 13–36. Princeton: Princeton University Press.

———. 1989b. "The Organization of Power." In *Cambodia, 1975–1978: Rendevous with Death.* Ed. Karl D. Jackson, 79–108. Princeton: Princeton University Press.

Chanda, Nayan. 1986. *Brother Enemy: The War after the War.* San Diego: Harcourt Brace Jovanovich.

Chandler, David P. 1983. "Seeing Red: Perceptions of Cambodian History in Democratic Kampuchea." In *Revolution and Its Aftermath in Kampuchea: Eight Essays.* Ed. David P. Chandler and Ben Kiernan, 34–56. Monograph series no. 25. New Haven: Yale University Southeast Asia Studies, 1983.

———. 1991a. *The Land and People of Cambodia.* New York: HarperCollins Children's Books, 1991.

———. 1991b. *The Tragedy of Cambodian History: Politics, War, and Revolution since 1945.* New Haven: Yale University Press.

———. 1992a. *Brother Number One: A Political Biography of Pol Pot.* Boulder: Westview Press.

———.1992b. *A History of Cambodia.* 2d ed. Boulder: Westview Press.

———. 1999. *Voices from S-21: Terror and History in Pol Pot's Secret Prison.* Berkeley: University of California Press.

Chang, Pao-min. 1985. *Kampuchea between China and Vietnam.* Singapore: Singapore University Press.

Coedès, George. 1968. *The Indianized States of Southeast Asia.* Trans. Susan Brown Cowing; ed. Walter F. Vella. Honolulu: East-West Center Press.

Criddle, Joan D. 1992. *Bamboo and Butterflies: From Refugee to Citizen.* Davis: East/West Bridge.

———, and Teeda Butt Mam. 1987. *To Destroy You Is No Loss: The Odyssey of a Cambodian Family.* New York: Atlantic Monthly Press.

Curtis, Grant. 1998. *Cambodia Reborn? The Transition to Democracy and Development.* Washington, D.C.: Brookings.

Dith Pran, comp. 1997. *Children of Cambodia's Killing Fields: Memoirs by Survivors.* Ed. Kim DePaul; introduction by Ben Kiernan. New Haven: Yale University Press.

Doyle, Michael W., Ian Johnstone, and Robert C. Orr, eds. 1997. *Keeping the Peace: Multinational United Nations Operations in Cambodia and El Salvador.* New York: Cambridge University Press.

Ebihara, May M., Carol A. Mortland, and Judy Ledgerwood, eds. 1994. *Cambodian Culture since 1975: Homeland and Exile.* Ithaca: Cornell University Press.

Elliott, David W. P., ed. 1981. *The Third Indochina Conflict.* Boulder: Westview Press.

Etcheson, Craig. 1984. *The Rise and Demise of Democratic Kampuchea.* Boulder: Westview Press.

Evans, Grant, and Kelvin Rowley. 1984, rev. ed. 1990. *Red Brotherhood at War: Vietnam, Cambodia, and Laos since 1975.* London: Verso.

Fiffer, Sharon Sloan. 1991. *Imagining America: Paul Thai's Journey from the Killing Fields of Cambodia to Freedom in the U.S.A.* New York: Paragon House.

Findlay, Trevor. 1995. *Cambodia: The Legacy and Lessons of UNTAC.* New York: Oxford University Press.

Frieson, Kate G. 1981. "The Impact of Revolution on Cambodian Peasants: 1970–1975." Ph.D. diss., Monash University.

Getlin, Josh, and Kari René Hall. 1992. *Beyond the Killing Fields.* Photographs by Kari René Hall. New York: Aperture Foundation.

Groslier, Bernard Philippe, and Jacques Arthaud. 1966. *Angkor: Art and Civilization.* New York: Praeger.

Hall, D. G. E. 1968. *A History of South-East Asia.* 3d ed., 94–139, 436–43, 644–55, 758–66, 786–90, 845–50, and 873–83. New York: St. Martin's Press.

Haas, Michael.1991a. *Cambodia, Pol Pot, and the United States: The Faustian Pact.* New York: Praeger.

———. 1991b. *Genocide by Proxy: Cambodian Pawn on a Superpower Chessboard.* New York: Praeger.

Heder, Stephen, and Judy Ledgerwood, eds. 1996. *Propaganda, Politics, and Violence in Cambodia: Democratic Transition under United Nations Peace-keeping.* Armonk: M. E. Sharpe.

Heng, Samrin. 1979. "The Overthrow of the Reactionary Regime Kampuchea: Towards Rebirth and Renewal." In *Kampuchea: From Tragedy to Rebirth.* Comp. E. V. Kobelev, 114–26. Moscow: Progress.

Higham, Charles. 2002. *The Civilization of Angkor.* Berkeley: University of California Press.

Him, Chanrithy. 2000. *When Broken Glass Floats: Growing Up Under the Khmer Rouge.* New York: W. W. Norton.

Hinton, Alexander L. 1996. "Agents of Death: Examining the Cambodian Genocide in Terms of Psychological Dissonance." *American Anthropologist* 98: 818–31

———. 1998a. "A Head for an Eye: Revenge in the Cambodian Genocide." *American Ethnologist* 25: 352–77.

———. 1998b. "Why Did You Kill? The Cambodian Genocide and the Dark Side of Face and Honor." *Journal of Asian Studies* 57: 93–122.

Isaacs, Arnold R. 1983. *Without Honor: Defeat in Vietnam and Cambodia.* Baltimore: Johns Hopkins University Press.

Jackson, Karl D. 1989a. "The Ideology of Total Revolution." In *Cambodia, 1975–1978: Rendevous with Death.* Ed. Karl D. Jackson, 37–78. Princeton: Princeton University Press.

———. 1989b. "Intellectual Origins of the Khmer Rouge." In *Cambodia, 1975–1978: Rendevous with Death.* Ed. Karl D. Jackson, 241–50. Princeton: Princeton University Press.

———. 1989c. "Introduction: The Khmer Rouge in Context." In *Cambodia, 1975–1978: Rendevous with Death.* Ed. Karl D. Jackson, 3–12. Princeton: Princeton University Press.

Jessup, Helen Ibbitson, and Thierry Zephir, eds. 1997. *Sculpture of Angkor and Ancient Cambodia: A Millenium of Glory.* Washington, D.C.: National Gallery of Art.

Kamm, Henry. 1998. *Cambodia: Report from a Stricken Land.* New York: Arcade.

Kiernan, Ben. 1982. "The Samlaut Rebellion, 1967–68." In *Peasants and Politics in Kampuchea, 1942–1981.* Ed. Ben Kiernan and Chanthou Boua, 166–205. London: Zed Press.

———. 1985. *How Pol Pot Came to Power: A History of Communism in Kampuchea.* London: Verso.

———. 1989. "The American Bombardment of Kampuchea, 1969–1973." *Vietnam Generation* 1(1): 4–41.

———. 1996. *The Pol Pot Regime: Race, Power, and Genocide in Cambodia under the Khmer Rouge, 1975–79.* New Haven: Yale University Press.

———, and Chanthou Boua, eds. 1982. *Peasants and Politics in Kampuchea, 1942–1981.* London: Zed Press.

Klintworth, Gary. 1989. *Vietnam's Intervention in Cambodia in International Law.* Canberra: Australian Government Publishing Service.

Kobelev, E. V., comp. 1979. *Kampuchea: From Tragedy to Rebirth.* Moscow: Progress.

Krasa, Miloslav. 1963. *The Temples of Angkor: Monuments to a Vanished Empire.* Photographs by Jan Cifra. London: Allan Wingate.

Krepinevich, Andrew F., Jr. 1986. *The Army and Vietnam.* Baltimore: Johns Hopkins University Press.

Lafreniere, Bree. 2000. *Music through the Dark: A Tale of Survival in Cambodia.* Honolulu: University of Hawaii Press.

Lawyers Committee for Human Rights. 1987. *Seeking Refuge: Cambodians in Thailand.* New York: Lawyers Committee for Human Rights.

———. 1989. *Refuge Denied: Problems in the Protection of Vietnamese and Cambodians in Thailand and the Admission of Indochinese Refugees into the United States.* New York: Lawyers Committee for Human Rights.

Le Bonheur, Albert. 1995. *Of Gods, Kings, and Men: Bas Reliefs of Angkor Wat and Bayon.* Photographs by Jaroslav Poncar. London: Serindia.

Ledgerwood, Judy L. 1990. "Changing Khmer Conceptions of Gender: Women, Stories, and the Social Order." Ph.D. diss., Cornell University.

———. 1994. "Gender Symbolism and Culture Change: Viewing the Virtuous Woman in the Khmer Story 'Mea Yoeng.'" In *Cambodian Culture since 1975: Homeland and Exile.* Ed. May M. Ebihara, Carol A. Mortland, and Judy Ledgerwood, 119–28. Ithaca: Cornell University Press.

Leifer, Michael. 1967. *Cambodia: The Search for Security.* New York: Praeger.

Levy, Barry S., and Daniel C. Susott, eds. 1986. *Years of Horror, Days of Hope: Responding to the Cambodian Refugee Crisis.* Millwood: Associated Faculty Press.

MacDonald, Malcolm. 1987. *Angkor and the Khmer.* Photographs by Loke Wan Tho. Singapore: Oxford University Press.

Mam, Teeda Butt. 1997. "Worms from Our Skin." In *Children of Cambodia's Killing Fields: Memoirs by Survivors.* Comp. Dith Pran; ed. Kim DePaul; introduction by Ben Kiernan, 11–17. New Haven: Yale University Press.

Mannikka, Eleanor. 1996. *Angkor Wat: Time, Space, and Kingship.* Honolulu: University of Hawaii Press.

Martin, Marie Alexandrine. 1994. *Cambodia: A Shattered Society.* Trans. Mark W. McLeod. Berkeley: University of California Press.

Mason, Linda, and Roger Brown. 1983. *Rice, Rivalry, and Politics: Managing Cambodian Relief.* Notre Dame: Notre Dame University Press.

May, Someth. 1986. *Cambodian Witness: The Autobiography of Someth May.* Ed. with an introduction by James Fenton. New York: Random House.

Morris, Stephen J. 1999. *Why Vietnam Invaded Cambodia: Political Culture and the Causes of War.* Stanford: Stanford University Press.

Ngor, Haing, with Roger Warner. 1987. *Haing Ngor: A Cambodian Odyssey.* New York: Macmillan.

Nguyen-vo, Thu-huong. 1992. *Khmer-Viet Relations and the Third Indochina Conflict.* Jefferson: McFarland.

Norodom, Sihanouk. 1973. *My War with the CIA: The Memoirs of Prince Norodom Sihanouk as Related to Wilfred Burchett.* Harmondsworth, Eng.: Penguin.

———. 1980. *War and Hope: The Case for Cambodia.* Trans. Mary Feeney. New York: Pantheon.

Osborne, Milton. 1969. *The French Presence in Cochinchina and Cambodia: Rule and Response (1859–1905).* Ithaca: Cornell University Press.

———. 1973. *Politics and Power in Cambodia: The Sihanouk Years.* Camberwell, Australia: Longman Australia.

———. 1979. *Before Kampuchea: Preludes to Tragedy.* London: George Allen and Unwin.

———. 1994. *Sihanouk: Prince of Light, Prince of Darkness.* Honolulu: University of Hawaii Press.

Ouk, Vibol, and Charles Martin Simon. 1996. *Goodnight Cambodia: Forbidden History.* Soquel, Calif.: Charles Martin Simon.

Picq, Laurence. 1989. *Beyond the Horizon: Five Years with the Khmer Rouge.* Trans. Patricia Norland. New York: St. Martin's Press.

Pin, Yathay, with John Man. 1987. *Stay Alive, My Son.* New York: Free Press.

Ponchaud, Francois. 1978. *Cambodia: Year Zero.* Trans. Nancy Amphoux. New York: Holt, Rinehart and Winston.

———. 1989. "Social Change in the Vortex of Revolution." In *Cambodia, 1975–1978: Rendevous with Death.* Ed. Karl D. Jackson, 151–77. Princeton: Princeton University Press.

Porter, Gareth. 1983. "Vietnamese Communist Policy towards Kampuchea, 1930–1970." In *Revolution and Its Aftermath in Kampuchea: Eight Essays.* Ed. David P. Chandler and Ben Kiernan, 57–98. Monograph series no. 25. New Haven: Yale University Southeast Asia Studies.

Quinn, Kenneth M. 1989a. "Explaining the Terror." In *Cambodia, 1975–78: Rendevous with Death.* Ed. Karl D. Jackson, 215–40. Princeton: Princeton University Press.

———. 1989b. "The Pattern and Scope of Violence." In *Cambodia, 1975–78: Rendevous with Death.* Ed. Karl D. Jackson, 179–208. Princeton: Princeton University Press.

Reynell, Josephine. 1989. *Political Pawns: Refugees on the Thai-Kampuchean Border.* Oxford, Eng.: Refugee Studies Programme.

Shawcross, William. 1979. *Sideshow: Kissinger, Nixon and the Destruction of Cambodia.* New York: Simon and Schuster.

———. 1984. *The Quality of Mercy: Cambodia, Holocaust and Modern Conscience.* New York: Simon and Schuster.

Smith, Roger M. 1964. "Cambodia." In *Government and Politics of Southeast Asia*. 2d ed. Ed. George M. Kahin, 594–675. Ithaca: Cornell University Press.

———. 1965. *Cambodia's Foreign Policy*. Ithaca: Cornell University Press.

Strand, Paul J., and Woodrow Jones, Jr. 1985. *Indochinese Refugees in America: Problems of Adaptation and Assimilation*. Durham: Duke University Press.

Stuart-Fox, Martin. 1985. *The Murderous Revolution: Life and Death in Pol Pot's Kampuchea Based on the Personal Experiences of Bunheang Ung*. Drawings by Bunheang Ung. Chippendale, New South Wales, Australia: Alternative Publishing Cooperative.

Sutter, Robert G. 1992. *The Cambodian Crisis and U.S. Policy Dilemmas*. Boulder: Westview Press.

Szymusiak, Molyda. 1986. *The Stones Cry Out: A Cambodian Childhood, 1975–1980*. Trans. Linda Coverdale. New York: Hill and Wang.

Um, Khatharya. 1990. "Brotherhood of the Pure: Nationalism and Communism in Cambodia." Ph.D. diss., University of California, Berkeley.

Ung, Luong. 2000. *First They Killed My Father: A Daughter of Cambodia Remembers*. New York: HarperCollins.

Vek Huong Taing. 1980. *Ordeal in Cambodia: One Family's Miraculous Survival—Escape from the Khmer Rouge*. As told to Sharon Fischer. San Bernardino: Here's Life.

Vickery, Michael. 1984. *Cambodia, 1975–1982*. Boston: South End Press.

———. 1990. "Refugee Politics: The Khmer Camp System in Thailand." In *The Cambodian Agony*. Ed. David A. Ablin and Marlowe Hood, 293–331. Armonk: M. E. Sharpe.

Welaratna, Usha. 1993. *Beyond the Killing Fields: Voices of Nine Cambodian Survivors in America*. Stanford: Stanford University Press.

Part 2: Cambodians in the United States

Aronson, Louise. 1987. "Health Care for Cambodian Refugees: The Role of Refugee Intermediaries." *Practicing Anthropology* 9: 10–11, 17.

Baughan, David M. et al. 1990. "Primary Care Needs of Cambodian Refugees." *Journal of Family Practices* 30: 565–68.

Boehnlein, James K. 1987a. "Clinical Relevance of Grief and Mourning among Cambodian Refugees." *Social Science and Medicine* 25: 765–72.

———. 1987b. "Culture and Society in Posttraumatic Stress Disorder: Implications for Psychotherapy." *American Journal of Psychotherapy* 41: 519–30.

Boehnlein, James K. et al. 1985. "One-Year-Follow-Up Study of Posttraumatic Stress Disorder among Survivors of Cambodian Concentration Camps." *American Journal of Psychiatry* 142: 956–59.

Burton, Eve. 1983. "Khmer Refugees in Western Massachusetts: Their Impact on Local Communities." *Migration Today* 11: 29–34.

Canniff, Julie G. 2001. *Cambodian Refugees' Pathways to Success: Developing a Bi-Cultural Identity*. New York: LFB Scholarly Publishing.

Carlson, Eve B., and Rhonda Rosser-Hogan. 1991. "Trauma Experiences, Posttraumatic Stress, Dissociation, and Depression in Cambodian Refugees." *American Journal of Psychiatry* 148: 1548–51.

———. 1993. "Mental Health Status of Cambodian Refugees Ten Years after Leaving Their Homes." *American Journal of Orthopsychiatry* 63: 223–31.

Chan, Sucheng. Forthcoming. *Survivors: Cambodian Refugees in the United States.*

Chow, Robert T. P., and Seba Krumholtz. 1989. "Health Screening of a Rhode Island Cambodian Refugee Population." *Rhode Island Medical Journal* 72: 273–77.

Chow, Robert T. P. et al. 1989. "Psychological Screening of Cambodian Refugees in a Rhode Island Primary Care Clinic." *Rhode Island Medical Journal* 72: 178–81.

Clarke, Gregory N., William H. Sack, and Brian Goff. 1993. "Three Forms of Stress in Cambodian Adolescent Refugees." *Journal of Abnormal Child Psychology* 21: 65–77.

Coleman, Cynthia M. 1990. "Cambodians in the United States." In *The Cambodian Agony.* Ed. David A. Ablin and Marlowe Hood, 354–74. Armonk: M. E. Sharpe.

D'Avanzo, Carolyn E., Barbara Frye, and Robin Froman. 1994a. "Culture, Stress and Substance Use in Cambodian Refugee Women." *Journal of Studies on Alcohol* 55: 420–26.

———. 1994b. "Stress in Cambodian Refugee Families." *Image: The Journal of Nursing Scholarship* 26: 101–5.

Ebihara, May M. 1985. "Khmer." In *Refugees in the United States: A Reference Handbook.* Ed. David W. Haines, 127–47. Westport: Greenwood Press.

Eisenbruch, Maurice, and Lauren Handelman. 1989. "Development of an Explanatory Model of Illness Schedule for Cambodian Refugee Patients." *Journal of Refugee Studies* 2: 243–56.

Frye, Barbara A. 1991. "Cultural Themes in Health-Care Decision Making among Cambodian Refugee Women." *Journal of Community Health Nursing* 8: 33–44.

Frye, Barbara A., and Carolyn D'Avanzo. 1994. "Themes in Managing Culturally Defined Illness in the Cambodian Refugee Family." *Journal of Community Health Nursing* 11: 89–98.

Gann, Peter, Luan Nghiem, and Stanley Warner. 1989. "Pregnancy Characteristics and Outcomes of Cambodian Refugees." *American Journal of Public Health* 79: 1251–57.

Glynn, Ted, and Vin Glynn. 1986. "Shared Reading by Cambodian Mothers and Children Learning English as a Second Language: Reciprocal Gains." *Exceptional Child* 33: 159–72.

Haines, David W., ed. 1985. *Refugees in the United States: A Reference Handbook*, 3–55. Westport: Greenwood Press.

Hein, Jeremy. 1995. *From Vietnam, Laos, and Cambodia: A Refugee Experience in the United States.* New York: Twayne.

Herbst, Patricia K. R. 1992. "From Helpless Victim to Empowered Survivor: Oral History as a Treatment for Survivors of Torture." *Women and Therapy* 13: 141–52.

Holgate, Susan L. 1994. "Early Marriages of Khmer High School Students: Influences and Consequences of Culture, Education and Intergenerational Conflict." M.A. thesis, California State University, Stanlislaus.

Hopkins, Marycarol. 1996. *Braving a New World: Cambodian (Khmer) Refugees in an American City.* Westport: Bergin and Garvey.

Hubbard, Jon J. et al. 1995. "Comorbidity of Psychiatric Diagnoses with Posttraumatic Stress Disorder in Survivors of Childhood Trauma." *Journal of the American Academy of Child and Adolescent Psychiatry* 43: 1167–73.

Jorgensen, Karen K. 1989. "The Role of the U.S. Congress and Courts in the Application of the Refugee Act of 1980." In *Refugee Law and Policy: International and U.S. Responses.* Ed. Ved P. Nanda, 129–50. Westport: Greenwood Press.

Kemp, Charles. 1985. "Cambodian Refugee Health Care Beliefs and Practices." *Journal of Community Health Nursing* 2: 41–52.

Kiang, Peter N. 1994. "When Know-Nothings Speak English Only: Analyzing Irish and Cambodian Struggles for Community Development and Educational Equity." In *The State of Asian America*. Ed. Karen Aguilar-San Juan, 125–45. Boston: South End Press.

Kinzie, J. David. 1989. "Therapeutic Approaches to Traumatized Cambodian Refugees." *Journal of Traumatic Stress* 2: 75–91.

———. 1990. "The 'Concentration Camp Syndrome' among Cambodian Refugees." In *The Cambodian Agony*. Ed. David A. Ablin and Marlowe Hood, 332–53. Armonk: M. E. Sharpe.

Kinzie, J. David, and James K. Boehnlein. 1989. "Post-traumatic Psychosis among Cambodian Refugees." *Journal of Traumatic Stress* 2: 185–98.

Kinzie, J. David et al. 1984. "Posttraumatic Stress Disorder among Survivors of Cambodian Concentration Camps." *American Journal of Psychiatry* 141: 645–50.

———. 1989. "A Three-Year Follow-Up of Cambodian Young People Traumatized as Children." *Journal of the American Academy of Child and Adolescent Psychiatry* 28: 501–04.

Koehn, Peter. 1989. "Persistent Problems and Policy Issues in U.S. Immigration Law and Policy." In *Refugee Law and Policy: International and U.S. Responses*. Ed. Ved P. Nanda, 67–87. Westport: Greenwood.

Kulig, Judith. 1988. "Conception and Birth Control Use: Cambodian Refugee Women's Beliefs and Practices." *Journal of Community Health Nursing* 5: 235–46.

———. 1989. "Childbearing Beliefs among Cambodian Refugee Women." *Western Journal of Nursing Research* 12: 108–18.

———. 1994a. "Old Traditions in a New World: Changing Gender Relations among Cambodian Refugees." In *Reconstructing Lives, Recapturing Meaning: Refugee Identity, Gender, and Culture Change*. Ed. Linda A. Camino and Ruth M. Krulfeld, 129–46. Basel, Switzerland: Gordon and Breach.

———. 1994b. "Sexuality Beliefs among Cambodians: Implications for Health Care Professionals." *Health Care for Women International* 15: 69–76.

Kuoch, Theanvy, Richard A. Miller, and Mary F. Scully. 1992. "Healing the Wounds of the *Mahantdori* [Cambodian Holocaust]." *Women and Therapy* 13: 191–207.

Law, Chi Kwong. 1988. "Economic Assimilation of Refugees: Human Capital, Job Information and Ethnic Enclave." D.S.W. diss., University of California, Los Angeles.

Ledgerwood, Judy L. 1990. "Portrait of a Conflict: Exploring Changing Khmer-American Social and Political Relations." *Journal of Refugee Studies* 3: 135–54.

Lenart, Janet C., Patricia A. St. Clair, and Michelle A. Bell. 1991. "Childrearing Knowledge, Beliefs, and Practices of Cambodian Refugees." *Journal of Pediatric Health Care* 5: 299–305.

Lew, Lillian S. 1991. "Elderly Cambodians in Long Beach: Creating Cultural Access to Health Care." *Journal of Cross-Cultural Gerontology* 6: 199–203.

Lind, Louise. 1989. *The Southeast Asians in Rhode Island: The New Americans*. Providence: Rhode Island Heritage Commission and the Rhode Island Publication Committee.

Lipsky, Sherry, and Ky Nimol. 1993. "Khmer Women Healers in Transition: Cultural and

Bureaucratic Barriers in Training and Employment." *Journal of Refugee Studies* 6: 372–88.

Loescher, Gil, and John A. Scanlan. 1986. *Calculated Kindness: Refugees and America's Half-Open Door, 1945–Present.* New York: Free Press.

McKenzie-Pollock, Lorna. 1996. "Cambodian Families." In *Ethnicity and Family Therapy.* Ed. Monica McGoldrick, Joe Giordan, and John K. Pearce, 307–15. New York: Guilford Press.

McNamara, Dennis. 1989. "The Origins and Effects of 'Humane Deterrence' Policies in South-east Asia." In *Refugees and International Relations.* Ed. Gil Loescher and Laila Monahan, 123–33. New York: Oxford University Press.

Melnick, Leah. 1990. "Cambodians in Western Massachusetts and Bronx, New York." *Migration World* [formerly *Migration Today*] 18: 4–9.

Mortland, Carol A. 1994a. "Cambodian Refugees and Identity in the United States." In *Reconstructing Lives, Recapturing Meaning: Refugee Identity, Gender, and Culture Change.* Ed. Linda A. Camino and Ruth M. Krulfeld, 5–27. Basel, Switzerland: Gordon and Breach.

———. 1994b. "Khmer Buddhism in the United States: Ultimate Questions." In *Cambodian Culture since 1975: Homeland and Exile.* Ed. May M. Ebihara, Carol A. Mortland, and Judy Ledgerwood, 72–90. Ithaca: Cornell University Press.

———, and Judy Ledgerwood. 1987. "Refugee Resource Acquisition: The Invisible Communication System." In *Cross-Cultural Adaptation: Current Approaches.* Ed. Young Yun Kim and W. B. Gudykunst, 286–306. Newbury Park, Calif.: Sage.

Muecke, Marjorie A. 1995. "Trust, Abuse of Trust, and Mistrust among Cambodian Refugee Women: A Cultural Interpretation." In *Mistrusting Refugees.* Ed. E. Valentine Daniel and John Chr. Knudsen, 36–55. Berkeley: University of California Press.

Muntarbhorn, Vitit. 1992. *The Status of Refugees in Asia.* Ch. 12, "Thailand," 113–20. New York: Oxford University Press.

Ong, Aihwa. 1995. "Making the Biopolitical Subject: Cambodian Immigrants, Refugee Medicine, and Cultural Citizenship in California." *Social Science and Medicine* 40: 1243–57.

Palinkas, Lawrence A., and Sheila M. Pickwell. 1995. "Acculturation as a Risk Factor for Chronic Disease among Cambodian Refugees in the United States." *Social Science and Medicine* 40: 1643–53.

Pho, Hai B. 1991. "The Politics of Refugee Resettlement in Massachusetts." *Migration World* 19: 2–10.

Ratliff, Sharon K. 1997. *Caring for Cambodian Americans: A Multidisciplinary Resource for the Helping Professions.* New York: Garland.

Realmuto, George M. et al. 1992. "Adolescent Survivors of Massive Childhood Trauma in Cambodia: Life Events and Current Symptoms." *Journal of Traumatic Stress* 5: 589–99.

Robinson, W. Courtland. 1998. *Terms of Refuge: The Indochinese Exodus and the International Response.* London: Zed Books.

Rosenberg, J. A. 1986. "Health Care for Cambodian Children: Integrating Treatment Plans." *Pediatric Nursing* 12: 118–25.

Rozee, Patricia D., and Gretchen Van Boemel. 1989. "The Psychological Effects of War

Trauma and Abuse on Older Cambodian Refugee Women." *Women and Therapy* 8: 23–50.

Sack, William, Gregory H. Clarke, and John Seeley. 1995. "Posttraumatic Stress Disorder across Two Generations of Cambodian Refugees." *Journal of the American Academy of Child and Adolescent Psychiatry* 34: 1160–66.

———. 1996. "Multiple Forms of Stress in Cambodian Adolescent Refugees." *Child Development* 67: 107–16.

Sack, William et al. 1986. "The Psychiatric Effects of Massive Trauma on Cambodian Children: The Family, the Home, and the School." *Journal of the American Academy of Child Psychiatry* 25: 377–83.

———. 1993. "A Six-Year-Follow-Up Study of Cambodian Refugee Adolescents Traumatized as Children." *Journal of the American Academy of Child and Adolescent Psychiatry* 32: 431–37.

Sargent, Carolyn, and John L. Marcucci. 1984. "Aspects of Khmer Medicine among Refugees in Urban America," *Medical Anthropology Quarterly* 16: 7–9.

———. 1988. "Khmer Prenatal Health Practices and the American Clinical Experience." In *Childbirth in America*. Ed. Karen Michaelson, 79–89. Westport: Bergin and Garvey.

———, and Ellen Elliston. 1983. "Tiger Bones, Fire, and Wine: Maternity Care in a Kampuchean Refugee Community." *Medical Anthropology* 7: 67–79.

Shaw, Scott. 1989. *Cambodian Refugees in Long Beach, California: The Definitive Study.* Hermosa Beach: Buddha Rose.

Sheehy, Gail. 1984. "A Home for Cambodia's Children." *New York Times Magazine,* Sept. 23, 44–47, 50–54, 60, 66–68.

Smith, Frank. 1989. *Interpretive Accounts of the Khmer Rouge Years: Personal Experience in Cambodian Peasant World View.* Wisconsin Papers on Southeast Asia, occasional paper no. 18. Madison: University of Wisconsin–Madison, Center for Southeast Asian Studies.

———. 1994. "Cultural Consumption: Cambodian Peasant Refugees and Television in the First World." In *Cambodian Culture since 1975: Homeland and Exile.* Ed. May M. Ebihara, Carol A. Mortland, and Judy Ledgerwood, 141–60. Ithaca: Cornell University Press.

Smith-Hefner, Nancy J. 1990. "Language and Identity in the Education of Boston-Area Khmer." *Anthropology and Education Quarterly* 21: 250–68.

———. 1993. "Education, Gender, and Generational Conflict among Khmer Refugees." *Anthropology and Education Quarterly* 24: 135–58.

———. 1994. "Ethnicity and the Force of Faith: Christian Conversion among Khmer Refugees." *Anthropology Quarterly* 67: 24–37.

———. 1995. "The Culture of Entrepreneurship among Khmer Refugees." In *Migrants in the Marketplace: Boston's Ethnic Entrepreneurs.* Ed. Marilyn Halter, 141–60. Amherst: University of Massachusetts Press.

———. 1999. *Khmer American: Identity and Moral Education in a Diasporic Community.* Berkeley: University of California Press.

Strober, Susan B. 1994. "Social Work Interventions to Alleviate Cambodian Refugee Psychological Distress." *International Social Work* 37: 23–35.

Sutter, Valerie O'Connor. 1990. *The Indochinese Refugee Dilemma.* Baton Rouge: Lousiana State University Press.

Tan, Terpsichore N. K. 1999. "Cambodian Youth in Long Beach, California: Parenting and Other Sociocultural Influences on Educational Achievement." Ph.D. diss., University of Hawaii.

Thompson, Janice L. 1991. "Exploring Gender and Culture with Khmer Refugee Women: Reflections on Participatory Feminist Research." *Advances in Nursing Science* 13: 30–48.

Uba, Laura, and Rita Chi-Ying Chung. 1991. "The Relationship between Trauma and Financial and Physical Well-Being." *Journal of General Psychology* 118: 215–25.

Ui, Shiori. 1991. "'Unlikely Heroes': The Evolution of Female Leadership in a Cambodian Ethnic Enclave." In *Ethnography Unbound: Power and Resistance in the Modern Metropolis.* Ed. Michael Burawoy et al., 161–77. Berkeley: University of California Press.

Um, Khatharya. In press. *Born of the Ashes: World Revolution and Exile—the Cambodian Experience.* Berkeley: University of California Press.

van Boemel, Gretchen B., and Patricia D. Rozee. 1992. "Treatment for Psychosomatic Blindness among Cambodian Refugee Women." *Women and Therapy* 13: 239–66.

Welaratna, Usha. 1998. "The Presence of the Past in Conflicts and Coalition among Cambodians, African Americans, and Hispanics in Central Long Beach, California." Ph.D. diss., University of California, Berkeley.

Wilkinson, Alec. 1994. "A Changed Vision of God." *The New Yorker,* Jan. 4, 52–68.

Zucker, Norman L., and Naomi Flink Zucker. 1992. "From Immigration to Refugee Redefinition: A History of Refugee and Asylum Policy in the United States." In *Refugees and the Asylum Dilemma in the West.* Ed. Gil Loescher, 54–70. University Park: Pennsylvania State University Press.

Part 3: Oral History Methodology

Agar, Michael. 1987. "Transcript Handling: An Ethnographic Strategy." *Oral History Review* 16: 209–19.

Allen, Susan E. 1982. "Resisting the Editorial Ego: Editing Oral History." *Oral History Review* 10: 33–45.

Anderson, Kathryn et al. 1987. "Beginning Where We Are: Feminist Methology in Oral History." *Oral History Review* 15: 103–27.

Bennett, James. 1983. "Human Values in Oral History." *Oral History Review* 11: 1–15.

Blee, Kathleen. 1993. "Evidence, Empathy and Ethics: Lessons from Oral Histories of the Klan." *Journal of American History* 10: 596–606.

Bornat, Joanna. 1989. "Oral History as a Social Movement: Reminiscence and Older People." *Oral History* 17: 16–20.

Chase, Susan E., and Colleen S. Bell. 1994. "Interpreting the Complexity of Women's Subjectivity." In *Interactive Oral History Interviewing.* Ed. Eva M. McMahan and Kim Lacy Rogers, 63–81. Hillsdale: Lawrence Erlbaum.

Clifford, James. 1986. "Introduction: Partial Truths." In *Writing Culture: The Poetics and Politics of Ethnography.* Ed. James Clifford and George E. Marcus, 1–26. Berkeley: University of California Press.

Danielson, Larry. 1980. "The Folklorist, the Oral Historian, and Local History." *Oral History Review* 8: 62–72.

Di Leonardo, Micaela. 1987. "Oral History as Ethographic Encounter." *Oral History Review* 15: 1–20.

Dorson, Richard. 1972. "The Oral Historian and the Folklorist." In *Selections of the Fifth and Sixth National Colloquia on Oral History,* repr. in *Oral History: An Interdisciplinary Anthology.* 2d ed. Ed. David K. Dunaway and Willa K. Baum, 283–91. Walnut Creek: Alta Mira Press.

Friedlander, Peter. 1975. *The Emergence of a UAW Local, 1936–39: A Study of Class and Culture.* Pittsburgh: University of Pittsburgh Press.

Frisch, Michael. 1990. *A Shared Authority: Essays on the Craft and Meaning of Oral and Public History.* Albany: State University of New York Press.

Fry, Amelia. 1975. "Reflections on Ethics." *Oral History Review* 3: 17–28.

Futrell, Allan W., and Charles A. Willard. 1994. "Intersubjectivity and Interviewing." In *Interactive Oral History Interviewing.* Ed. Eva M. McMahan and Kim Lacy Rogers, 83–105. Hillsdale: Lawrence Erlbaum.

Gluck, Sherna. 1977. "What's So Special about Women? Women's Oral History." *Frontiers: A Journal of Women's Studies* 2: 3–13.

Grele, Ronald J. 1978. "Can Anyone over Thirty Be Trusted? A Friendly Critique of Oral History." *Oral History Review* n.v., n.n., 36–44.

———. 1985. "Movement without Aim: Methodological and Theoretical Problems in Oral History." In *Envelopes of Sound: The Art of Oral History,* 127–54. Chicago: Precedent Publishers.

Hansen, Arthur A. 1994. "A Riot of Voices: Racial and Ethnic Variables in Interactive Oral History Interviewing." In *Interactive Oral History Interviewing.* Ed. Eva M. McMahan and Kim Lacy Rogers, 107–39. Hillsdale: Lawrence Erlbaum.

Hareven, Tamara. 1978. "The Search for Generational Memory." *Daedalus* 106: 137–49.

Henige, David. 1982. *Oral Historiography.* London: Longman.

Ingersoll, Fern, and Jasper Ingersoll. 1987. "Both a Borrower and a Lender Be: Ethnography, Oral History, and Grounded Theory." *Oral History Review* 15: 81–102.

Klempner, Mark. 2000. "Navigating Life Review Interviews with Survivors of Trauma." *Oral History Review* 27: 67–83.

Lummis, Trevor. 1983. "Structure and Validity in Oral Evidence." *International Journal of Oral History* 2: 109–20.

———. 1988. *Listening to History: The Authenticity of Oral Evidence.* London: Hutchinson.

McMahan, Eva M. 1987. "Speech and Counterspeech: Language-in-Use in Oral History Fieldwork." *Oral History Review* 15: 185–207.

———. 1989. *Elite Oral History Discourse: A Study of Cooperation and Coherence.* Tuscaloosa: University of Alabama Press.

Mintz, Sidney. 1979. "The Anthropological Interview and the Life History." *Oral History Review* 7: 18–26.

Morrissey, Charles T. 1987. "The Two-Sentence Format as an Interviewing Technique in Oral History Fieldwork." *Oral History Review* 15: 43–53.

Neuenschwander, John A. 1978. "Remembrance of Things Past: Oral Historians and Long-Term Memory." *Oral History Review* [no volume number]: 45–53.

Okihiro, Gary Y. 1981. "Oral History and the Writing of Ethnic History." *Oral History Review* 9: 27–46.

Portelli, Alessandro. 1991. *The Death of Luigi Trastulli and Other Stories: Form and Meaning in Oral History.* Albany: State University of New York Press, 1991.

———. 1997. *The Battle of Valle Giulia: Oral History and the Art of Dialogue.* Madison: University of Wisconsin Press, 1997.

Rabinow, Paul. 1986. "Representations Are Social Facts: Modernity and Post-Modernity in Anthropology." In *Writing Culture: The Poetics and Politics of Ethnography.* Ed. James Clifford and Geroge E. Marcus, 234–61. Berkeley: University of California Press.

Ritchie, Donald A. 1995. *Doing Oral History.* New York: Twayne.

Rogers, Kim Lacy. 1987. "Memory, Struggle, and Power: On Interviewing Political Activists." *Oral History Review* 15: 165–84.

———. 1994. "Trauma Redeemed: The Narrative Construction of Social Violence." In *Interactive Oral History Interviewing.* Ed. Eva M. McMahan and Kim Lacy Rogers, 31–46. Hillsdale: Lawrence Erlbaum.

Rosaldo, Renato. 1986. "From the Door of His Tent: The Fieldworker and the Inquisitor." In *Writing Culture: The Poetics and Politics of Ethnography.* Ed. James Clifford and George E. Marcus, 77–97. Berkeley: University of California Press.

Sangster, Joan. 1994. "Telling Our Stories: Feminist Debates and the Use of Oral History." *Women's History Review* 3: 5–28.

Serikaku, Laurie R. 1989. "Oral History in Ethnic Communities: Widening the Focus." *Oral History Review* 17: 71–87.

Sypher, Howard E., Mary Lee Hummert, and Sheryl L. Williams. 1994. "Social Pscyhological Aspects of the Oral History Interview." In *Interactive Oral History Interviewing.* Ed. Eva M. McMahan and Kim Lacy Rogers, 47–61. Hillsdale: Lawrence Erlbaum.

Thompson, Paul. 1988. *The Voice of the Past.* 2d ed. New York: Oxford University Press.

Tuchman, Barbara. 1972. "Distinguishing the Significant from the Insignificant." *Radcliffe Quarterly* 56: 9–10.

Tyler, Stephen A. 1986. "Post-Modern Ethnography: From Document of the Occult to Occult Document." In *Writing Culture: The Poetics and Politics of Ethnography.* Ed. James Clifford and George E. Marcus, 122–40. Berkeley: University of California Press.

White, Naomi Rosh. 1994. "Marking Absences: Holocaust Testimony and History." *Oral History Association of Australia Journal* 16: 12–18.

Wilmsen, Carl. 2001. "For the Record: Editing and the Production of Meaning in Oral History." *Oral History Review* 28: 65–85.

Wyatt, Victoria. 1987. "Oral History in the Study of Discrimination and Cultural Repression." *Oral History Review* 15: 129–41.

Yow, Valerie. 1995. "Ethics and Interpersonal Relationships in Oral History Research." *Oral History Review* 22: 51–66.

Index

SUCHENG CHAN is professor emerita of Asian American studies at the University of California, Santa Barbara. She is the recipient of two distinguished teaching awards (in 1978 and 1998) and the author or editor of a dozen books, including the award-winning *This Bittersweet Soil: The Chinese in California Agriculture, 1860–1910* (1986) and the widely used college text *Asian Americans: An Interpretive History* (1991).

AUDREY U. KIM is a counseling psychologist at the University of California, Santa Cruz. She received her Ph.D. from the University of California, Santa Barbara, after completing a dissertation entitled "Feminist Therapy: A Culturally Responsive Treatment for Asian Americans and Collectivist Women?" She has published articles in *Professional Psychology: Research and Practice, Journal of Mental Health Counseling,* and *Counseling Diverse Populations,* edited by D. R. Atkinson and G. Hackett (1998).

The Asian American Experience

The University of Illinois Press
is a founding member of the
Association of American University Presses.

Composed in 10.5/13 Adobe Minion
with Adobe Minion display
at the University of Illinois Press
Manufactured by Thomson-Shore, Inc.

University of Illinois Press
1325 South Oak Street
Champaign, IL 61820-6903
www.press.uillinois.edu